Republican passions

Manchester University Press

Studies in
Modern French and
Francophone History

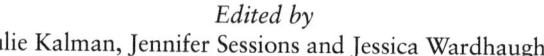

Edited by
Julie Kalman, Jennifer Sessions and Jessica Wardhaugh

This series is published in collaboration with the Society for the Study of French History (UK) and the French Colonial Historical Society. It aims to showcase innovative monographs and edited collections on the history of France, its colonies and imperial undertakings, and the francophone world more generally since *c.* 1750. Authors demonstrate how sources and interpretations are being opened to historical investigation in new and interesting ways, and how unfamiliar subjects have the capacity to tell us more about France and the French colonial empire, their relationships in the world, and their legacies in the present. The series is particularly receptive to studies that break down traditional boundaries and conventional disciplinary divisions.

To buy or to find out more about the books currently available in this series, please go to:
https://manchesteruniversitypress.co.uk/series/studies-in-modern-french-and-francophone-history/

Republican passions

Family, friendship and politics in nineteenth-century France

Susan K. Foley

MANCHESTER UNIVERSITY PRESS

Copyright © Susan K. Foley 2023

The right of Susan K. Foley to be identified as the author of this work has been asserted by them in accordance with the Copyright, Designs and Patents Act 1988.

Published by Manchester University Press
Oxford Road, Manchester M13 9PL

www.manchesteruniversitypress.co.uk

British Library Cataloguing-in-Publication Data
A catalogue record for this book is available from the British Library

ISBN 978 1 5261 6153 6 hardback
ISBN 978 1 5261 9081 9 paperback

First published 2023
Paperback published 2025

The publisher has no responsibility for the persistence or accuracy of URLs for any external or third-party internet websites referred to in this book, and does not guarantee that any content on such websites is, or will remain, accurate or appropriate.

EU authorised representative for GPSR:
Easy Access System Europe – Mustamäe tee 50,
10621 Tallinn, Estonia
gpsr.requests@easproject.com

Typeset by Newgen Publishing UK

For Chips

Contents

List of figures	*page* viii
Acknowledgements	ix
Abbreviations	xi
Léon Laurent-Pichat and his family networks	xii
Introduction	1
1 'Born alone and sad': family passions, 1823–51	17
2 'My brothers in poetry': passionate friendship and political upheaval, 1841–52	40
3 'Placing our pen at the service of liberty': friendship networks and the republican press, 1851–65	65
4 'Pure happiness': shaping a bourgeois family for the Republic, 1851–75	90
5 'Bound together forever': friendship, family bonds and republican solidarity, 1861–70	119
6 'The revolution was so beautiful and pure': family, friendship and trauma, 1868–71	146
7 'Steadfast and enduring fidelity': friendship and honour in the fledgling Republic, 1871–76	171
8 'Such hope is in the air': bourgeois marriage and republican politics, 1851–80	197
9 'The task is magnificent and enormous': family politics in the 'Republic of republicans', 1877–85	225
Conclusion	256
Appendix: The social and political network of Léon Laurent-Pichat	269
Bibliography	288
Index	310

Figures

3.1 Léon Laurent-Pichat, c. 1860. (Source: Photograph by Sergei Levitsky. Archives privées de la famille [APF], courtesy of Mme Caroline Lesieur Flury.)   76

4.1 Mme Geneviève Deslandes, mother of Léon Laurent-Pichat, c. 1960. (Source: Unknown photographer. APF, courtesy of Mme Caroline Lesieur Flury.)   91

4.2 La Princesse de Beauvau-Craon. (Source: Unknown photographer. APF, courtesy of Mme Caroline Lesieur Flury.)   95

5.1 Léon Laurent-Pichat in prison attire, 1866. (Source: Unknown photographer. APF, courtesy of Mme Caroline Lesieur Flury.)   134

7.1 Portrait of Léon Laurent-Pichat, by Ernest Hébert [1865]. (Source: Public domain via Wikimedia Commons.)   172

8.1 Geneviève Laurent-Pichat, c. 1876? Photograph by Jean Geiser. APF, courtesy of Mme Caroline Lesieur Flury.)   206

9.1 Léon Laurent-Pichat, c. 1880. (Source: Unknown photographer, APF, courtesy of Mme Caroline Lesieur Flury.)   226

9.2 Ginette and Charlotte Risler, granddaughters of Léon Laurent-Pichat. (Source: Unknown photographer. APF, courtesy of Mme Caroline Lesieur Flury.)   243

Acknowledgements

This project has taken some years to complete and would have been impossible without the assistance of others. The staff at a number of repositories greatly facilitated my research. Those at the Bibliothèque historique de la ville de Paris (BHVP), in particular Mme Laurence Gambier and Mme Marie-Françoise Garion-Roche, were always generous with their assistance, ensuring my access to research materials even during renovations to the reading room. Those at the Médiathèque de Saint-Dié-des-Vosges, notably M. Alexandre Jury and Mme Marie-Christine Aubry, went out of their way to assist me. I am most grateful, too, for the generosity of Mickaël Bouffard, who shared both his knowledge about Laurent-Pichat's house at 39, rue de l'Université, and the relevant notarial records. I also thank Brian McKay, who undertook vital research for me when I was unable to visit Paris. Sharon Harrup designed the family tree, solving problems and making my many amendments rapidly and with good humour. I am indebted to Kelly Walker, whose scrupulous copyediting greatly improved the clarity and precision of the text.

A number of colleagues and friends responded generously to my queries. Jean-Yves Mollier shared his expertise on the intricate politics of the Third Republic, as did Jean-Claude Yon on cultural matters. I benefited, too, from Robert Nye's expertise on the culture of masculinity. I am greatly indebted to them all, both for their generosity and for their friendship. The members of my Melbourne writing group have been invaluable, reading the entire book as it evolved and offering both encouragement and salient criticism. Their support, sustained by Zoom when necessary, has ensured that the project continued to move forward, despite COVID waves and lengthy lockdowns. David Garrioch saw the potential in the project from its beginnings and provided valuable advice on several occasions, while Patricia Grimshaw has constantly challenged me to think more deeply, and to complete the project. Manchester University Press has also been most supportive of this book, and I thank Alun Richards, in particular, for his assistance.

I am especially indebted to Mme Caroline Lesieur Flury, a descendant of the family at the centre of this study, whose mother, Mme Catherine Lesieur, gifted a major collection of family papers to the BHVP in 1987. Other materials remain in the family's possession. Mme Lesieur Flury kindly made available to me a number of documents and photographs, and responded graciously to my many queries. Thanks to her, important details about the family have been clarified and key characters in this book have been brought to life in photographs. The study is much richer for her generous assistance.

Finally, I owe an enormous debt to Charles Sowerwine. He has read numerous drafts of this work and readily shared his insights into the period. Our many discussions of the ideas in this book have always been enjoyable and illuminating, and his keen attention to detail has been invaluable as I have shaped the text. I treasure his unfailing support.

Abbreviations

AD	Archives départementales
AGAL	Association Générale d'Alsace-Lorraine
AN	Archives nationales
AP	Archives de Paris
APF	Archives privées de la famille, détenues par Mme Caroline Lesieur Flury
BAN	Bibliothèque de l'Assemblée nationale
BHVP	Bibliothèque historique de la ville de Paris
GC	Eugénie (Ginette) Claretie (née Risler), granddaughter of Léon Laurent-Pichat
GLP	Geneviève Laurent-Pichat
GR	Geneviève Risler (née Laurent-Pichat)
LLP	Léon Laurent-Pichat
MSDV	Médiathèque de Saint-Dié-des-Vosges

Léon Laurent-Pichat and his family networks

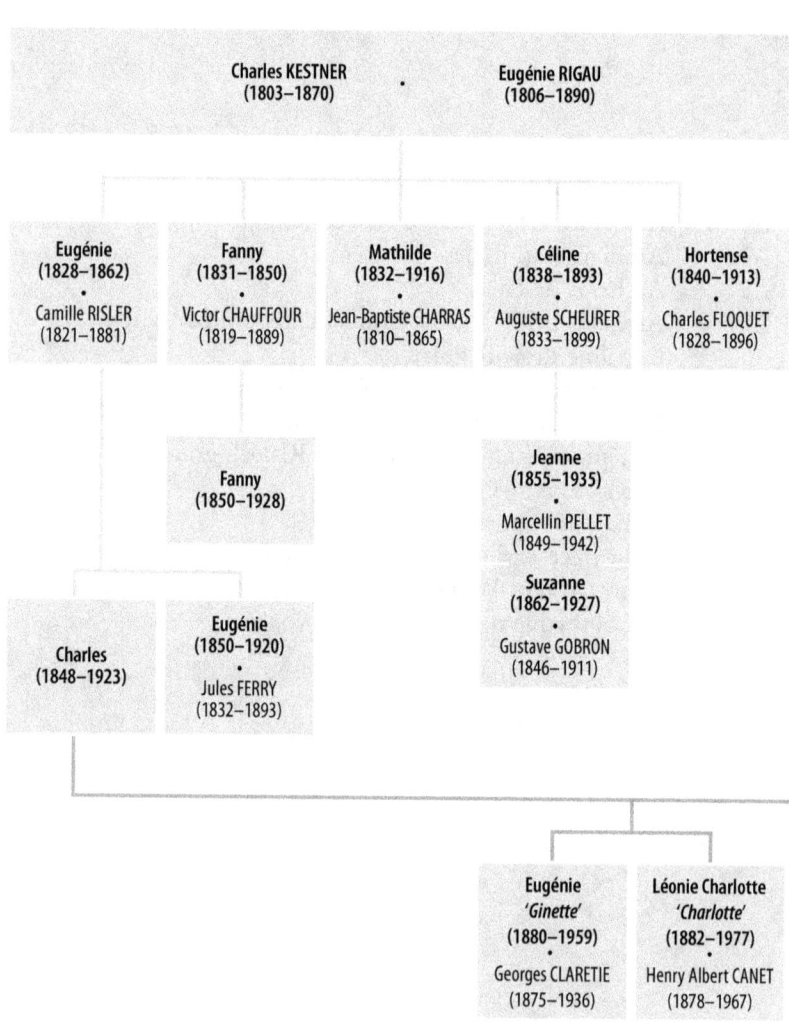

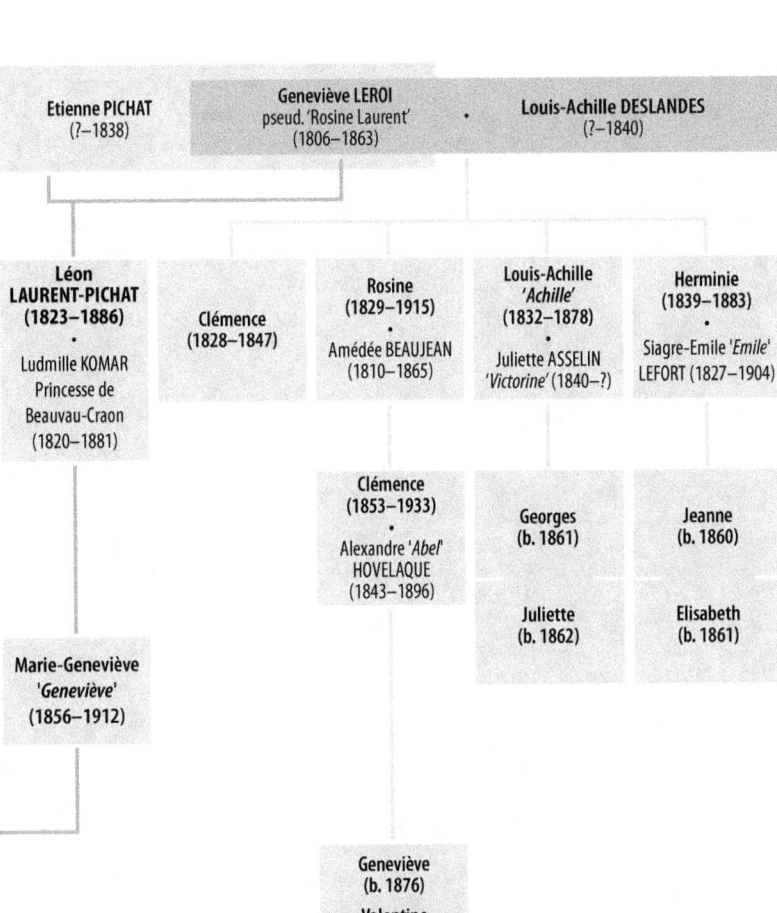

Introduction

This book began with a letter that I came across by chance while undertaking research on republican leader Léon Gambetta. Four pages long, the letter was adorned with a series of sketches. Two showed the writer at table; others showed a chateau, some Breton dancers and a horse-drawn carriage with its passengers. 'I can draw too', the writer noted.[1] That writer was Léon Laurent-Pichat and the letter was written to a little girl named, I soon learned, Geneviève Laurent-Pichat.[2] The warmth and humour of the letter captivated me. There were more such letters, and the letters from Geneviève to Laurent-Pichat were also in the collection. So, too, were other family papers and Laurent-Pichat's daily journal covering twenty-four years. A web of connections emerged, as journal entries led me to other individuals and other sources, extending beyond the family circle to a network of friends. Thus, from a small seed – an illustrated letter to a child – this book gradually evolved. The story of this family and their social network is a unique one, reflecting their particular experience. But at the same time, it casts light on the history of bourgeois republican society in France during the Second Empire and early Third Republic. That is the subject of this book. As it demonstrates in rich detail, family and friends, through their networks of sociability, sustained republicanism and kept the movement alive when political activities in the public domain were prohibited.

The lynchpin of the story is Léon Laurent-Pichat (1823–1886). Largely unknown today, he played a central role in nineteenth-century French political and cultural life.[3] Laurent-Pichat was a self-described *homme de lettres*, a prolific author, poet and journalist; a financial backer and editor of major literary periodicals and of Parisian and provincial newspapers. He was also an ardent republican, contributing substantial amounts of both money and time to the cause. He would become a Deputy and Life Senator in the early Third Republic. His individual history highlights that many bourgeois activists, not only the handful of most prominent leaders, played vital roles in implanting republicanism in the community.

Laurent-Pichat's personal life was not that of a typical bourgeois. Born outside wedlock, he was later officially adopted by his father who left him his fortune. Laurent-Pichat found his mother in adulthood, establishing close bonds with her and her four children, his half-siblings. He never married, but Geneviève Laurent-Pichat, with whom he exchanged the letters discussed above, was his daughter. In a repeat of his own childhood experience, Laurent-Pichat took responsibility for her care and legitimised her when she was five years old. Her mother's identity was never revealed publicly. Laurent-Pichat and his daughter formed a joint household with his half-sister Rosine, her husband Amédée Beaujean and their daughter, Clémence. Over time, with the marriages of Laurent-Pichat's younger siblings, and then of Clémence and Geneviève, Laurent-Pichat's family circle expanded further to incorporate their spouses' extended families, which included many of the republican elite.

Members of this family network constantly cross the pages of this study, living their lives from childhood to adulthood, from monarchy to republic to empire and again to republic, through revolution and war. We pick up their story in 1823 with the birth of 'Léon Laurent' (he only became Laurent-Pichat on his adoption in 1837), under the Bourbon monarchy. When a revolution in Paris overthrew the Bourbons in 1830, seven-year-old Léon witnessed its aftermath off-stage in the Luxembourg Gardens. The July Monarchy, to which that revolution gave rise, was itself overturned by revolution in February 1848. Twenty-five-year-old Léon and his friends were enraptured by the Second Republic that resulted. But they were horrified by the massacre of insurgents in June and frustrated by the slow death of the Republic over the following years.

The coup d'état of December 1851 put paid to their republican aspirations. The reactionary backlash was confirmed by the establishment of the Second Empire (1852–70) under Napoleon III. During the Empire it was illegal to promote republican views under threat of imprisonment or exile. Cat and mouse politics and journalistic guerrilla warfare were republicans' main recourses in these years. Laurent-Pichat and his friends were in the thick of things. The Empire would come to an end only with its defeat in the Franco-Prussian War of 1870. Republicans in Paris proclaimed the Third Republic, and Laurent-Pichat and several of his friends were elected representatives in 1871. But nearly ten more years of struggle would be needed before the Third Republic was securely in the hands of republicans. That struggle would continue to preoccupy the family and friends of Léon Laurent-Pichat. This study follows their paths into the mid-1880s as they set the Republic in place.

Republican families

Laurent-Pichat's family life illustrates the intimacy and affection that has been richly demonstrated in bourgeois families from at least the late eighteenth century.[4] Indeed, his family shows that even those who remained unmarried aspired to replicate the intimate family model, so pervasive had it become. Raised without knowing his family, Laurent-Pichat's passionate struggle to find that family and then to create a family of his own throws into relief the enormous cultural impact of the intimate family ideal. By considering a highly atypical case, this book thus deepens our understanding of the history of the bourgeois family. In doing so, it also casts light on the taboo subject of bourgeois children born out of wedlock. Few studies of those children have been possible to date owing to a lack of sources. This family included two such children in successive generations, however, and recorded their lives in rich detail. It thus provides a unique insight into how extramarital births were handled in bourgeois families and how the boundaries of acceptance for extra-nuptial children were delineated.[5]

This study of Laurent-Pichat and his network goes well beyond a concern with family structure and relationships. At its heart is an analysis of the vital role played by the family in the making of the Third Republic. The disastrous experience of the Second Republic (1848–52) had convinced many that a republic could not be successfully installed unless republicanism was first implanted in hearts and minds. Republicans looked to the family to achieve this goal. During the Second Empire, republican theorists such as Jules Michelet and Eugène Pelletan criticised the authoritarian family model and portrayed idealised images of a revitalised family.[6] Some republican women aspired to go even further than male theorists, not only creating a more egalitarian family, but also allowing the more equal participation of men and women in republican political life.[7]

The family established by Laurent-Pichat went some way towards achieving that goal. Founded on friendship – the friendship between Laurent-Pichat and his sister Rosine, and that between Laurent-Pichat and Amédée Beaujean – it departed from the patriarchal nuclear family model based on marriage enshrined in the Civil Code. The family around Laurent-Pichat came together and stayed together through choice, not through legal injunction. In doing so it replicated the 'chosen-ness' that made friendship superior to family ties in post-Revolutionary thinking.[8]

Furthermore, this family's foundation in friendship undermined – though it did not eliminate – the hierarchical assumptions about male and female roles, and about public and domestic space, that flowed from the divisions enshrined in the Civil Code. This study traces, over several decades, the fluid boundaries between domestic and political life in the extended family circle, and the coming together of men and women in the cause of the Republic. Laurent-Pichat's family life suggests that the vision of a 'sweet and gentle republic' in the home was, to some degree, borne out in practice.[9] Republicanism was not just 'men's business' but also the business of women, who hosted salons and political dinners, and actively engaged in political discussion and alliance building.[10] Politics was conducted not just in the halls of power but in the home.

By identifying the family as an important site of republican activism, this study casts fresh light on republican masculinity. As Anne-Marie Sohn has demonstrated, young men's recognition that they were destined for citizenship, unlike young women, was an important component in their emerging adolescent sense of masculinity. They expressed their feeling of political entitlement in the public protests and demonstrations that have left a significant mark in government reports and court records.[11] Laurent-Pichat encountered such young men, full of republican enthusiasm and bravado, during his imprisonment. Their youthful political actions, however, are not those of the adult males with financial and social responsibilities who are the subject of this book. In this study, republican men emerge not as comrades in student politics or as isolated protagonists in the political struggle but as family men surrounded by other such men and by women and children. Men's lives, like women's, were marked by family events as well as political events; they attended dolls' tea parties as well as political meetings; their emotional lives reflected personal joys and sorrows as well as political ones, and those personal emotions affected their political actions.

Indeed, this study demonstrates that men's political relationships were heavily freighted with personal emotion. Republican men's political activities across varied forums expressed their identities as gendered beings whose political personae were inseparable from their personae as fathers, sons, husbands and friends, as Matthew McCormack has argued was also the case in Britain.[12] In republican circles, all those expressions of masculinity were valued.

Republican friendship

More than a family history, this book is an interwoven history of family and friendship. It reveals how closely the two were interconnected and, further, how integral both were to the making of the Third Republic. The circles around Laurent-Pichat provide a particularly rich case study of that connection because friendship was central not only to Laurent-Pichat's social bonds but also to his construction of a family. By cultivating friendship with his sister Rosine, for instance, Laurent-Pichat gradually inserted himself into his maternal family: friendship provided access to a family denied him in childhood. Similarly, republican sentiment and the bonds of friendship that united Laurent-Pichat with the Kestner/Risler family combined to overcome the obstacles presented by his own and his daughter's irregular birth, enabling him to find a suitable husband for his daughter from within that family.

Friendship among republicans played a vital role in maintaining the republican vision during the Empire. The friendship circles of Laurent-Pichat and his family were wide and diverse, spanning the cultural and intellectual elites of the day. They included writers like Victor Hugo; historians like Jules Michelet; publishers like Jean Georges Hachette; artists like Jules Dupré; philologist Emile Littré (whose multi-volume *Dictionary of the French Language* was abridged by Laurent-Pichat's brother-in-law, Amédée Beaujean). Family friends in the scientific world included society doctor Samuel Pozzi, Dr Achille Proust (father of the novelist) and Dr Paul Broca, the renowned anatomist and anthropologist. But in many cases these friendships were shaped by shared republicanism as much as by shared intellectual interests. The closest friends of Laurent-Pichat and his extended family were dedicated republicans like themselves.

Deep personal bonds of friendship linked republican political activists in the mid-nineteenth century as they had also linked some politicians in earlier decades.[13] During the post-Revolutionary years, however, temporary strategic alliances in factional contests were sometimes metaphorically designated 'friendship'.[14] By contrast, embattled republicans sought not metaphorical but real friendship in the hostile environment of the Second Empire and during the Moral Order regime, which endeavoured to restore the monarchy in the early 1870s. They sought personal attachments that provided them with the emotional support they needed to persevere in the struggle. With the Republic secure in the late 1870s, factionalism could undermine friendship at times, although, as Laurent-Pichat demonstrates, friendship could also endure despite political differences.

A number of valuable studies have demonstrated the crucial role played by institutions of republican sociability in the formation of the Third Republic.[15] This study focuses attention on the dynamics of republican friendship rather than on its institutional forms. It argues that friendship was not merely a personal relationship but a 'radical practice' that provides insights into republican mobilisation, motivation and political connection.[16] Just as friendship played crucial roles in the unfolding of the French Revolution and the founding of the American Republic, it was also central to the process of making the Third Republic.[17] Friendship also provided the foundations for a shift in political personnel and the embedding of new political practices as the Third Republic was established.[18]

This analysis offers a new perspective on friendships between men. Studies of male friendship frequently focus on homosocial spaces, the clubs, circles and masonic lodges where male friendship reigned. Such studies have shown how friendship, as an idealised relationship between men that echoed brotherly love, was deemed foreign to women – or women to it – given its civic purpose of creating social cohesion in the nation.[19] Studies of family, on the other hand, focus on relationships between couples and generations in a heterosocial space. Male friendship thus appears to be exclusive to the homosocial world. This study shows, rather, that male friendships spanned both the homosocial world and the family: men encountered their friends in the drawing room with their families as well as among other men in the republican *cercle*. Friendships among men in these republican networks, even those men who were unmarried, were embedded in family contexts.

At the same time, this study attests to the eloquence and deep emotion with which men in these republican networks proclaimed their attachment to each other. Their correspondence speaks of 'love', not merely of 'friendship'. As young men, they expressed the desire for intimacy and wept when friendships were strained by political conflict; in later life they admitted being overtaken by waves of affection for old friends. References to friendship and to the heart (the key bodily symbol of desire at the time) might sometimes provide a coded language for sexual desire.[20] Friendship and passionate love are difficult to disentangle with historical distance, given that friends and lovers described their emotions with equal 'exaltation' in the nineteenth century.[21] While passionate declarations are typically read today through a sexual lens, however, that was not necessarily the case in a period when the linguistic boundary between love and friendship remained to be rigidly defined.[22] 'Friendship' could refer to a wide variety of relationships, as Michael Lucey has demonstrated by examining use of the term in Balzac and Proust.[23]

In examining male friendship and the depth of men's attachment to each other, this book demonstrates the emotional bonds that united them and argues that those bonds provided a vital resource to republicanism. Republican men unabashedly exhibited what has been described as 'emotive fraternalism'; for them, tenderness was a masculine trait, not the exclusive domain of women. Unlike some politicians of earlier generations, therefore, they had no need for female intermediaries in order to emote.[24] They expressed their tenderness openly to each other and to all those who mattered in their lives, both men and women, adults and children.

Women were not absent from the culture of friendship that underpinned the emerging representative polity of nineteenth-century France, as this study demonstrates. Unfortunately, many of the letters that might have illustrated the friendships between the women in these circles, letters to which they sometimes refer, have not survived. Their friendships must often be reconstructed, therefore, from the women's activities, both social and philanthropic. Moreover, friendship between women and men played a vital role in republican politics in the mid-nineteenth century just as it had in the politics of post-Revolutionary France.[25] Deep friendships between the men and women of these circles were possible because these women were devoted, like men, to the Republic.

This study thus challenges the standard picture of devout women whose religiosity presented a barrier to mutual understanding and sympathy with anticlerical republican men.[26] It shows, rather, that both men and women in republican circles observed religious rites when this was seen as necessary or appropriate, although women perhaps did so more often than men. But women shared the same world view and political outlook as the men – religious weddings, masses for the dead and children's catechism notwithstanding. Women repeatedly displayed their knowledge of and interest in republican politics, which men acknowledged. Women and men co-operated on republican endeavours like secular education, therefore, and regarded their complementary roles as simultaneously advancing the republican cause. Still, women in these circles accepted that electoral politics were the preserve of men. They demonstrated little interest in the emerging feminist movement, despite the feminists' republican sentiments.[27]

Intimacy, emotion and politics

This study argues that republican political networks cannot be understood in isolation from the family links and friendship circles that underpinned and sustained them. More than that, it demonstrates that the boundary between the political and the domestic was highly permeable and constantly negotiated. It takes a broad definition of political action that includes participation in a wide variety of practices on a variety of sites.[28] As historians have argued of Britain, 'politics took place in both the public and the private, and commonly in heterosocial environments such as *salons*, dinners and civic ceremonials.'[29] Politics imbued the activities of the republican families in this study in diverse ways. Their intimate practices, interpersonal relationships, patterns of sociability and child-raising methods existed on a continuum with their more overtly political activities. To study those intimate practices, therefore, is not to abandon the investigation of republican politics but to explore them more deeply.[30] Within republican homes, as this study suggests, political bonds were personalised and thus reinforced and renewed. Both women and men were pivotal to those processes.[31]

In exploring the interconnections between family, friendship and politics, this study draws on insights and approaches developed by historians of emotion. It considers the gestures and practices by which individuals announced their devotion to each other, to their families and to the Republic.[32] It examines the role of emotion in creating family unity, republican solidarity and enduring friendships. In doing so, it casts light on the processes by which a steadfast republican community was built; a community, united by emotion, that gave republicans solace and respite under the authoritarian Second Empire and then fortified their efforts to build the new Republic.

Through its interest in republican intimacy, this book also contributes to the debate on the history of emotions in nineteenth-century politics. William Reddy has argued that, after the French Revolution, emotion was relegated to a 'secondary role … or a safe haven in the feminine space of the home', that is, outside politics.[33] If that was so in the early nineteenth century, it was no longer the case by mid-century, as studies of emotion in revolutionary moments and nationalist movements have shown.[34] As my study suggests, emotion could not easily be 'relegated' at mid-century, given that the intimate and the political were deeply enmeshed.[35] The possibility that France might become an enduring Republic on the third attempt was another moment when political change was at stake. Emotion contributed to the mobilisation of participants for and against that change. Republicans had to strike a balance between self-control, which was a guarantee of stability, and the emotion that would mobilise a republican constituency. The passionate speeches of republican leader Léon Gambetta, for instance, enraged conservatives but won him an enormous popular following in the 1870s. Contemporaries likened his oratory to that of Mirabeau during the French Revolution.[36] If post-Revolutionary politics had seen a dramatic shift in emotional regimes, then, that new emotional regime, like the new political regime, was not an enduring one.

Intimate sources

This examination of the porous relationship between the 'political' and the 'intimate' is possible thanks only to the abundance of intimate sources that have seen the nineteenth century described as the 'century of intimacy'.[37] Along with letters and diaries, a large collection of Laurent-Pichat's verse, much of it unpublished, has survived. It was often written for family members and served much the same purpose as letters.

It is mainly through such sources, which are rich in descriptions of emotion, that I (like other historians) attempt to 'read felt emotion' in words.[38] Yet as Michelle Perrot observes, 'nothing is less spontaneous than a letter'.[39] A letter, by definition, is written for another to read and the writer is ever mindful of the intended recipient. As this study demonstrates, rather than being simply outpourings of natural feelings or transparent accounts of events, letters between family members and friends were intended to convey, and to reinforce, ideas about their relationship. They were at once instruments of connectedness, and performances of that connectedness. The extended family around Laurent-Pichat actively embraced the letter's ability to create, not merely reflect, family unity. Their letters work to draw the family together and reinscribe the bonds of affection.[40] Similarly, letters between friends, by expressing the bonds that joined them, asserted and strengthened those bonds. In these circles, the bonds being reinscribed through the letter were also republican bonds. Laurent-Pichat's letters to his daughter Geneviève in adulthood, for instance, switch constantly between the political and the intimate registers, demonstrating the artificiality of attempting to conceive the two as entirely separate.

The journal of Léon Laurent-Pichat, spanning the years 1861 to 1885, is also an invaluable source for this study. Journal-keeping was not unusual in this age of growing self-observation and interiority. However, Laurent-Pichat's journal focuses on events and activities, documenting his social contacts, financial transactions, political meetings, dinner guests and the activities of family members.[41] Far from a complete record, it reveals lapses of memory and self-censorship.[42] The journal was a site for managing and shaping his emotions, and for practising emotional self-control. For instance, references to family in the journal are almost entirely positive: anger, conflict and criticism are almost invisible. The family presented is, in this sense, a 'fictional' family, a paradise of harmony and happiness, confirming Laurent-Pichat's intense investment in the domestic ideal. How Laurent-Pichat sought to present his family in the journal is as significant for this study as the information he records about it.

Laurent-Pichat's journal entries are often enigmatic as far as political events are concerned. They were intended for their writer's purposes rather than for an imagined reader, highlighting the journal's role as a personal *aide-mémoire*. While Laurent-Pichat had little to say about political proceedings – they were more likely to be reported in his letters – he assiduously recorded his personal contacts and social gatherings. In the process, he paints an extraordinarily rich picture of his political alliances, social connections and friendships. A panoply of names represents a web of affiliations, one that enmeshes Laurent-Pichat in a world of like-minded people whose recurring presence in his journal testifies both to their place in his political and social life, and to his place in theirs. The journal, reassuringly for its writer, secures his place, not only in the intimate world of family and friends who are ever-present in the diary, but also in the broad social network that was the republican family.

This book offers fresh insights into the history of republicanism by delving deeply into the realm of feelings and the inner life, and into modes of social enculturation. By reaching beyond sociability to the intimate spheres of family and friendship, to the realms of personal attachment and emotion, it seeks to provide an innovative perspective on political activism and to illuminate the cultural mode of being – the habitus – of mid-nineteenth-century bourgeois republicans. While the book informs our understanding of the implantation of the Republic in the 1870s, its broader significance lies in enriching our understanding of nineteenth-century French political culture, in the period before the institutions of electoral democracy were fully established.

Notes

1 BHVP, MS-FS-07-0007, vol. 6 (hereafter BHVP, 6), no. 2: Léon Laurent-Pichat [LLP] to Geneviève Laurent-Pichat [GLP], 'Wednesday 28' [1866?].
2 I use Geneviève's legal name throughout, but her stationery bore the monogram GP and in 1875 she signed her cousin's marriage contract 'Geneviève Pichat'.
3 Jacqueline Lalouette, 'Laurent-Pichat, Léon', in Jean-Marie Mayeur and Alain Corbin (eds), *Les Immortels du Sénat 1875–1918: Les Cent seize inamovibles de la Troisième République* (Paris: Publications de la Sorbonne, 1995), pp. 380–82; Arlette Schweitz, *Les Parlementaires de la Seine sous la Troisième République. II: Dictionnaire biographique* (Paris: Publications de la Sorbonne, 2001), pp. 355–6; Jérôme Grévy, *La République des Opportunistes, 1870–1885* (Paris: Perrin, 1998). No biography of Laurent-Pichat exists.
4 David Garrioch, *The Formation of the Parisian Bourgeoisie, 1690–1830* (Cambridge, MA: Harvard University Press, 1996); Catherine Pellissier, *La Vie privée des notables lyonnais au XIXe siècle* (Lyon: Editions lyonnaises d'art et d'histoire, 1996); Christopher H. Johnson, *Becoming Bourgeois: Love, kinship, and power in provincial France, 1670–1880* (Ithaca, NY: Cornell University Press, 2015); Leonore Davidoff and Catherine Hall, *Family Fortunes: Men and women of the English middle class, 1780–1850*, rev. edn (London: Routledge, 2002).
5 Rachel G. Fuchs, *Poor and Pregnant in Paris: Strategies for survival in the nineteenth century* (New Brunswick, NJ: Rutgers University Press, 1992); Michelle Perrot and Anne Martin-Fugier, 'The family triumphant', in Michelle Perrot (ed.) *A History of Private Life. IV: From the fires of revolution to the Great War*, trans. Arthur Goldhammer (Cambridge, MA: Harvard University Press, 1990), pp. 143–7; Alain Corbin, 'Intimate relations', *ibid.*, pp. 565–6, 602–7. For an aristocratic example, see *Marthe: A Woman and Her Family: A nineteenth-century correspondence* (Harmondsworth: Viking, 1985).
6 Judith F. Stone, *Sons of the Revolution: Radical democrats in France, 1862–1914* (Baton Rouge, LA: Louisiana State University Press, 1996); Susan Foley, 'The republican family and republican politics: Léon Laurent-Pichat and his kin (1861–1883)', *French History and Civilisation*, 6 (2014), 159–71.
7 Whitney Walton, 'Republican women and republican families in the personal narratives of George Sand, Marie d'Agoult and Hortense Allart', in Jo Burr Margadant (ed.), *The New Biography: Performing*

femininity in nineteenth century France (Berkeley, CA: University of California Press, 2006), pp. 99–136.
8 Andrew J. Counter and Nicholas White, 'Introduction: The soul's sentiment: Friendship in nineteenth century France', *Romantic Review*, 110:1–4 (2019), 1–13.
9 Marie d'Agoult, quoted in Walton, 'Republican women', p. 126.
10 Anne Martin-Fugier, *Les Salons de la Troisième République: Art, littérature, politique* (Paris: Perrin, 2003).
11 Anne-Marie Sohn, *'Sois un homme!' La construction de la masculinité au XIXe siècle* (Paris: Editions du Seuil, 2009).
12 Matthew McCormack, 'Introduction,' in Matthew McCormack (ed.), *Public Men: Masculinity and politics in modern Britain* (Houndmills: Palgrave Macmillan, 2007), pp. 1–12.
13 Sarah Horowitz, *Friendship and Politics in Post-Revolutionary France* (University Park, PA: Pennsylvania State University Press, 2018).
14 Ibid., pp. 10–11.
15 Katherine Auspitz, *The Radical Bourgeoisie: The ligue de l'enseignement and the origins of the Third Republic, 1866–1885* (Cambridge: Cambridge University Press, 1972); Maurice Agulhon, *Le Cercle dans la France bourgeoise, 1810–1848* (Paris: Armand Colin, 1977); Sylvie Aprile, 'La République au salon: Vie et mort d'une forme de sociabilité politique (1865–1885)', *Revue d'histoire moderne et contemporaine*, 38 (1991), 473–87; Philip Nord, *The Republican Moment: Struggles for democracy in nineteenth-century France* (Cambridge, MA: Harvard University Press, 1995); Grévy, *La République des Opportunistes*; Carol E. Harrison, *The Bourgeois Citizen in Nineteenth Century France: Gender, sociability, and the uses of emulation* (Oxford: Oxford University Press, 1999).
16 General studies of friendship include Anne Vincent-Buffault, *L'Exercice de l'amitié: pour une histoire des pratiques amicales aux XVIIIe et XIXe siècles* (Paris: Seuil, 1995); Barbara Caine (ed.), *Friendship: A history* (London: Equinox, 2008). See Laura C. Forster, 'Radical Friendship', available at https://www.historyworkshop.org.uk/radical-friendship/. Accessed 14 September 2020.
17 Marisa Linton, *Choosing Terror: Virtue, friendship and authenticity in the French Revolution* (Oxford: Oxford University Press, 2013); Richard Godbeer, *The Overflowing of Friendship: Love between men and the creation of the American Republic* (Baltimore, MD: Johns Hopkins University Press, 2009); Claire White, '*Patrie, peuple, amitié*: Sand and Michelet on the politics of friendship', *Romantic Review*, 110:1–4 (2019), 149–67.

18 Horowitz, *Friendship and Politics*; Counter and White, 'Introduction: The soul's sentiment', 5.
19 Victor Manuel Macías-González, 'Masculine friendships, sentiment, and homoerotics in nineteenth-century Mexico: The correspondence of José María Calderón y Tapia, 1820s–1850s', *Journal of the History of Sexuality*, 16:3 (2007), 416–35; Stefan-Ludwig Hoffmann, 'Civility, male friendship and Masonic sociability in nineteenth century Germany', *Gender and History*, 13:2 (2001), 224–48; White, '*Patrie, peuple, amitié*', 160–62; Kenneth Loiselle, *Brotherly Love: Freemasonry and male friendship in Enlightenment France* (Ithaca, NY: Cornell University Press, 2014).
20 Counter and White, 'Introduction: The soul's sentiment', 5–6; Macías-González, 'Masculine friendships', 418, 433; Donald Yacavone, '"Surpassing the love of women": Victorian manhood and the language of fraternal love', in Laura McCall and Donald Yacavone (eds), *A Shared Experience: Men, women, and the history of gender* (New York: New York University Press, 1998), pp. 195–221.
21 Vincent-Buffault, *L'Exercice de l'amitié*, p. 121.
22 Yacavone, '"Surpassing the love of women"'; Gabrielle Houbre, *La Discipline de l'amour: L'éducation des filles et des garçons à l'âge du Romantisme* (Paris: Plon, 1997), pp. 139–40; Hoffmann, 'Civility, male friendship', 232.
23 Michael Lucey, '*Ami ou protégé?* Balzac, Proust, and the variability of friendship', *Romantic Review*, 110:1–4 (2019), 187–202.
24 On 'emotive fraternalism': Macías-González, 'Masculine friendships', 420. Hoffmann likewise identifies an 'emotional cult of brotherhood' in 'Civility, male friendship', 225. Sarah Horowitz found that women played an important role in emotional management for men: 'The Bonds of concord and the guardians of trust: Women, emotion, and political life, 1815–1848', *French Historical Studies*, 35:3 (2012), 577–603.
25 Horowitz, *Friendship and Politics*.
26 Studies of bourgeois women frequently emphasise their ideological estrangement from men, often due to women's religiosity: Bonnie G. Smith, *Ladies of the Leisure Class: The bourgeoises of northern France in the nineteenth century* (Princeton, NJ: Princeton University Press, 1981); Caroline Ford, *Divided Houses: Religion and gender in modern France* (Ithaca, NY: Cornell University Press, 2005).
27 Claire Goldberg Moses, *French Feminism in the Nineteenth Century* (Albany, NY: State University of New York Press, 1984); Steven C. Hause with Anne R. Kenney, *Women's Suffrage and Social Politics in the French Third Republic* (Princeton, NJ: Princeton University Press, 1984); Laurence Klejman and Florence Rochefort, *L'Egalité*

en marche: Le féminisme sous la Troisième République (Paris: Des femmes/Antoinette Fouque, 1989).

28 On varied forms of political participation: Anne Verjus, *Le Cens de la famille: Les femmes et le vote, 1789–1848* (Paris: Belin, 2002); Jennifer Ngaire Heuer, *The Family and the Nation: Gender and citizenship in revolutionary France, 1789–1830* (Ithaca, NY: Cornell University Press, 2005); Denise Z. Davidson, *France After Revolution: Urban life, gender, and the new social order* (Cambridge, MA: Harvard University Press, 2007).

29 Matthew McCormack, 'Men, "the public" and political history', in McCormack (ed.), *Public Men*, p. 22. See also Elaine Chalus, 'Elite women, social politics and the political world of late eighteenth-century England', *The Historical Journal*, 43:3 (2000), 669–97.

30 On the significance of the intimate for the political in other historical contexts, see Ann Laura Stoler, 'Intimidations of Empire: Predicaments of the tactile and the unseen', in Ann Laura Stoler (ed.), *Haunted by Empire: Geographies of intimacy in North American history* (Durham, NC: Duke University Press, 2006), pp. 1–22; Ara Wilson, 'The Infrastructure of intimacy', *Signs: Journal of women in culture and society*, 41:2 (2016), 247–80; Margot Finn, 'The Female world of love and empire: Women, family and East India Company politics at the end of the eighteenth century', *Gender and History*, 31:1 (2019), 7–24.

31 On women's role in 'personalising' political bonds, see ChaeRan Y. Freeze, *A Jewish Woman of Distinction: The life and diaries of Zinaida Poliakova* (Waltham, MA: Brandeis University Press, 2019).

32 See especially William M. Reddy, *The Navigation of Feeling: A framework for the history of emotions* (Cambridge: Cambridge University Press, 2001); Monique Scheer, 'Are emotions a kind of practice (and is that what makes them have a history)? A Bourdieuian approach to understanding emotion', *History and Theory*, 51 (2012), 193–220; Benno Gammerl, 'Emotional styles – Concepts and challenges', *Rethinking History*, 16:2 (2012), 161–75.

33 Reddy, *The Navigation of Feeling*, p. 205.

34 Nicole Eustace, 'Emotion and political change,' in Susan J. Matt and Peter N. Stearns (eds), *Doing Emotions History* (Urbana, IL: University of Illinois Press, 2014), pp. 136–83.

35 James Smith Allen makes a similar point in 'Navigating the social sciences: A framework for the history of emotions', *History and Theory*, 42 (2003), 82–93 (90).

36 Charles Sowerwine, 'Democratising oratory: Léon Gambetta and the construction of male democracy in France, 1868–1882,' in Véronique Duché (ed.), *Franco-Australian Connections: Essays in honour*

of Professor Colin Nettelbeck (Paris: Classiques Garnier, forthcoming 2023).

37 Brigitte Diaz and José-Luis Diaz, 'Le Siècle de l'intime', *Itinéraires: Littérature, textes, cultures*, 4 (2009), 117–46. See also Philippa Lewis, *Intimacy and Distance: Conflicting cultures in nineteenth-century France*. NED-New edition. Modern Humanities Research Association, 2017. https://doi.org/10.2307/j.ctv16kkxgs.

38 Susan Broomhall, 'Emotions in the household', in Susan Broomhall (ed.), *Emotions in the Household 1200–1900* (Houndmills: Palgrave Macmillan, 2008), p. 11.

39 Perrot, 'Introduction', in Perrot (ed.), *A History of Private Life*, IV, p. 4.

40 Cécile Dauphin, Pierrette Lebrun-Pézerat and Danièle Poublan, *Ces bonnes lettres: Une correspondance familiale au XIXe siècle* (Paris: Albin Michel, 1995), introduction; Susan Foley, 'Becoming a woman: Self-fashioning and emotion in a nineteenth-century family correspondence', *Women's History Review*, 24:2 (2015), 215–33; Cécile Dauphin, 'Pour une histoire de la correspondance familiale', *Romantisme*, 90 (1995): 89–99; Willemijn Ruberg, *Conventional Correspondence: Epistolary culture of the Dutch elite, 1770–1850* (Boston, MA: Brill, 2011).

41 Diaz and Diaz, 'Le Siècle de l'intime'; Alain Corbin, 'The secret of the individual', in Perrot (ed.), *A History of Private Life*, IV, pp. 498–502. On 'external' diaries like this one, see Rebecca Steinitz, *Time, Space and Gender in the Nineteenth Century British Diary* (New York: Palgrave Macmillan, 2011), pp. 50–51.

42 In 1876, for instance, LLP transposed the entries for 7 and 8 February, noting that he had confused them.

1

'Born alone and sad': family passions, 1823–51

'I was born alone and sad',[1] Léon Laurent-Pichat declared in the life story he wrote for his half-sister, Rosine, in May 1850. Taken literally, this statement cannot be true, but in an autobiographical narrative it reveals a great deal, not only about how he understood his own family background, but also about how he imagined the ideal family into which he might have been born: a family in which, surrounded by those who loved him, he would have been happy.

This chapter examines the early years of Léon Laurent (he did not become Laurent-Pichat until 1837), considering both the documentary evidence and his retrospective account of his childhood. It uncovers the origins of his passion for family, an enduring passion that would shape both his personal and political life. Further, it argues that his individual story exemplifies the triumph of the sentimental bourgeois family – based on domestic affection and imagined as the foundation for individual happiness – over the patriarchal family enshrined in law, in which affection had little priority.

Historians have documented a gradual shift towards intimacy and affection in bourgeois family life during the eighteenth century.[2] However, despite this cultural shift, the Napoleonic Civil Code of 1804 institutionalised paternal power. Paternal rights in law diminished only slowly. This meant that different models of fatherhood and thus different patterns of family life coexisted in the culture.[3] Léon Laurent's childhood, and his narrative re-imagining of that childhood, illustrate the potential conflict between these two conceptions of family. The comparison he drew between them, which emphasised the merits of the affectionate family model, served his personal claim to inclusion in his maternal family. It also heralded his determination to create a family united by bonds of tenderness and shared sympathy. That same family model, as we shall see, would underpin republican intimacy, and provide vital support to the republicans' political project in the 1860s and 1870s.

A child without a family

Léon Laurent's entry into the world in the early hours of 11 July 1823 had much in common with the arrivals of other children born outside wedlock in this period. No celebration marked his birth. He was presented for obligatory registration at the town hall, not by male family members (as was customary), but by the attending doctor and two neighbours.[4] Neither parent claimed him as their own. Legally, he had no father since, according to the framers of the Civil Code, 'only marriage makes a father'.[5] His seventeen-year-old mother, Geneviève Leroi, distanced herself from him by using the name 'Rosine Laurent', hence his birth name, 'Léon Laurent'. If most children born outside wedlock carried at least their mother's name, this false name placed him outside the family entirely, unmoored from any genealogy or network of social ties.

Geneviève Leroi had much in common with other unmarried women who gave birth in Paris each year. Like many of those women, she came from the hinterlands of the capital.[6] She was born in 1806 at Mandres-les-Roses, some twenty-two kilometres southeast of Paris, where her father, François Leroi, was a landowner.[7] But the family are not listed there in the 1817 census.[8] Perhaps the entire family had migrated. Geneviève did not tell her own story for posterity, however, and no information survives on her childhood years.

Geneviève Leroi also fits the standard profile of the unwed mother in Paris in that she was poor. At Léon's birth, her address was registered as 90, rue Saint-Denis: an area of Paris synonymous with poverty and prostitution. She was unlikely to have lived there except from financial necessity. Laurent-Pichat's granddaughter later recorded that Geneviève Leroi had worked as a *lingère*, someone who made or sold linen.[9] The garment trades, known for their precarious work and seasonal layoffs, placed many women in financial straits. They also produced many single mothers because a liaison with a man might well be an economic choice, if not an act of desperation, for such young women.[10] Perhaps that financial imperative explains Geneviève's relationship with a man more than thirty years older than her: Geneviève became pregnant at sixteen; Léon's father, Etienne Pichat, was about fifty-one.[11]

In other respects, however, Geneviève Leroi's situation differed dramatically from that of most single mothers. Geneviève was not alone as she faced motherhood and Léon's birth was not left to chance. She delivered her child not in one of the free maternity hospitals where many single mothers had their babies, nor in her room on the rue Saint-Denis. Rather, her son was born some two kilometres from there at 17, rue du Chemin-Vert, the address also given by a neighbour who witnessed the baby's registration. Perhaps this building housed the consulting rooms of the doctor who attended the birth. The presence of a doctor is quite surprising: while middle-class women were beginning to have doctors deliver their babies, a single mother from the rue Saint-Denis could not have afforded a doctor's services.[12] Someone else was anxious, it seems, to ensure that this child survived. The evidence suggests that Etienne Pichat, the baby's father, was that person and that, while Pichat retained his anonymity, he welcomed this child's arrival and assumed responsibility for him at birth. Whether he did so from paternal affection is less certain.

A quest for family

The only detailed source on Laurent-Pichat's early years is a personal account he wrote in instalments between 20 May 1850 and 29 June 1851. It was addressed to his half-sister, Rosine, the eldest surviving child of his mother's marriage. The account began: 'I am going to tell you the story of my childhood'.[13] When he began his story, Léon was twenty-seven years old; Rosine was six years younger. A budding poet, Léon wrote his account in verse. It tells his life story, based partly on his own memory and partly on information probably provided by his mother, with whom he had established a relationship by 1850. The writer explicitly addresses his intended reader, Rosine, insisting that his account is truthful, and endeavouring to cultivate her sympathy and affection.[14] This aim surely influenced his account. Like other autobiographical narratives, too, it is by no means a transparent and unmediated presentation of facts.

Literary scholars note that 'how a personal story is remembered is always in dialogue with emergent cultural formations'.[15] As a product of nineteenth-century culture, Léon Laurent-Pichat's autobiography has elements of the *Bildungsroman*, the novel of development: by declaring his childhood attraction to 'melodious words' and his early dedication to poetry, for instance, his account foreshadows his adult vocation.[16] But the autobiography has more in common with the Romantic quest narrative in which the subject is driven by pursuit of an ideal: in Léon Laurent-Pichat's story, the ideal that drives him and shapes his life is his search for a loving family.[17] Love, or the denial of love, is the frame for his narrative; the ideal of the affectionate family is its foundation.

That the ideal of the affectionate family could evoke such a sense of need in Laurent-Pichat and prompt a personal quest to fill that need illustrates the cultural power of the affectionate family model at the time he was writing. In the nineteenth century, the affectionate and sentimental family was increasingly idealised as essential to 'the bourgeois experience'.[18] Contemporaries reported love and tenderness between spouses, and between parents and children. The affectionate 'papa' increasingly replaced the stern and remote 'father' in novels.[19] Painters portrayed domestic warmth and intimacy. Nineteenth-century families lived in close proximity, celebrated birthdays and festivities, took holidays together, and studiously developed their close bonds through correspondence.[20]

Laurent-Pichat could assume that Rosine would understand and respond to his narrative of longing for family, therefore, since the ideal of the affectionate family was common currency. The very concept of the 'affectionate' family, the ways it was described and imagined, was linked to a range of positive emotions: the 'tenderness' that described family relations, for instance, assigned to family members feelings of warmth and sympathy for each other. People had learned to associate those feelings with family relationships, shaping their emotions to cultural expectations.[21] This 'self-shaping' is evoked in Laurent-Pichat's autobiography. He was clearly familiar by adulthood with the idealised 'affectionate' family even if he experienced it only in other people's families during childhood. He had also learned that, by not having an 'affectionate family' of his own, he lacked an element of life essential for happiness. His autobiographical account is highly 'emotional', therefore, reporting not only the events of the past (however he knew about them) but also his current feelings, the imagined or remembered feelings of his childhood, and the feelings he attributed to others about those events.

Moreover, as an epistolary document addressed to his sister, the autobiography is driven by the logic of the letter-writing relationship, by 'the bond between the correspondents, the state of their relationship, and their hopes for its future'.[22] The document is written in twenty-eight instalments, sometimes on successive days, sometimes with gaps of more than a month between entries. It is thus an extended conversation (albeit a one-sided one), a way of maintaining contact with Rosine. While no response by Rosine has survived, Laurent-Pichat's focus is on the reader, seeking to make a favourable impression and to elicit a sympathetic response.[23] The account, therefore, does a great deal of 'emotion work'. By describing emotion, it evokes that emotion in the narrator and seeks to evoke reciprocal emotion in Rosine, the intended reader.[24]

The opening pages of this document tell the story of a child encountering a series of adults and considering whether they loved him and whether he was part of their family. This focus illustrates Laurent-Pichat's assumptions about the primacy of family life. The first adult he considered was the nurse at Deuil-la-Barre, in the Val d'Oise, fourteen kilometres north of Paris: like many Parisian infants, he was sent to a nurse shortly after birth.[25] While he cannot have remembered his life with her, he reports that she left him alone in bed in an empty house all day. She did not love him, he concludes, since she was 'ignorant and cruel'.[26]

He was then sent to live with Mme Cointet, in the rue Cassini in Paris.[27] Unlike the nurse, she 'put her heart into' caring for him. 'She raised me. I loved her.'[28] The language of feeling permeates Laurent-Pichat's account as he recalls the affection shown him by Mme Cointet, her sister and Mme Cointet's adult son. How long he lived there is unclear, but Léon believed he belonged in this household: 'In this humble home which I believed was mine, / ... my affections ... had already taken root'.[29]

The narrative then introduces the adults who visited Léon at Mme Cointet's place. These, we learn, were his parents, though they did not reveal their identities. In describing his encounters with them, he again explores questions of love, affection and belonging. Again, too, he names his own feelings and attributes feelings to others, simultaneously seeking to evoke feelings in Rosine, his reader, and constructing his own emotional history.[30]

Laurent-Pichat first describes the visits of two young women who came swathed in veils so as not to be identified. They were terrified of every sound, fearful of being discovered visiting him. He hints that one woman was his mother, but his portrait of her is sketchy, perhaps because his mother was still alive when he was writing and he did not wish to jeopardise his developing relationship with her and her daughter. Visiting him in secret at Mme Cointet's place, '[She] would raise my forehead to a tender mouth / Saying words I could not hear!'[31] These were words of love, he implies, although unable to hear them he could not be sure. With hindsight, the adult Léon recognises that her visits under such duress were signs of affection, but he notes that as a child he was not equipped to make that evaluation: 'When I was small I did not understand / the value of a kiss that cost so many steps!'[32] If the child was left uncertain of this woman's place in his life, however, the narrative is open to the possibility of a loving relationship between them, which was perhaps the main point of this scene. Laurent-Pichat presents his memory of those visits as proof that his mother loved him despite having surrendered him. He reports them to his sister in his narrative to awaken her sympathy, to demonstrate their mother's apparent plight and show that he deserved a place within the family circle.

Laurent-Pichat's narrative also reports that he was visited at Mme Cointet's place by two men who generally came together. One was a 'friend'. 'The other was my father!' But Léon did not know this at the time: 'It was only after his death that I learned / That my father was dead and that he was my father!'[33] Laurent-Pichat provided clues to the identity of this man: he was elderly and lived at La Rotonde du Temple, a six-hectare complex in the centre of Paris, which fronted onto four streets; its forty-three shops with accommodation above housed hundreds of people.[34] La Rotonde would be demolished during Baron Haussmann's renovation of the city at mid-century, but its owner in the 1820s was Etienne Pichat, a wealthy businessman. Pichat, he tells Rosine obliquely, was his father. This man, too, made clumsy gestures of affection, pulling the little boy close and giving him a coin on each visit. But Laurent-Pichat writes that he did not recognise them as signs of love. Rather, he was terrified of this austere and serious stranger: 'he made me tremble'; 'I was afraid'.[35]

In Laurent-Pichat's narrative, Léon learned that he did not belong in Mme Cointet's family when this man, his father, suddenly removed him from her care: 'I cried at leaving my humble abode! / I sobbed and rebelled! / With my little hands I tried to hold on / To the skirts of the old woman; she was my rock / And I clung instinctively to her [...].' Pichat took Léon to live at La Rotonde, instructing the boy to call him 'Godfather'.[36] But Mme Cointet's family was the only family Léon Laurent knew, and he presents that transition not as a homecoming, but as a bereavement. His manuscript stops abruptly and without explanation at that point. But Léon's quest to find a family where he belonged and was loved continued.

The bourgeois family and the Civil Code

While Léon Laurent-Pichat's autobiography is personal, it is also a moral tale with broader social ramifications, promoting love and affection as the ideal basis for family life. However, the tenderness associated with the affectionate family was irrelevant to the Civil Code that governed family formation and regulated family relations. The situation into which Léon Laurent had been born, under the terms of that Code, allowed little room for him to be acknowledged by his parents, let alone welcomed with love. If his autobiographical narrative is set alongside the legal records, therefore, we gain insight, not only into these mute parents, unable as individuals to express their relationship to this child, but also into the structures of family life that hampered the operations of affection: structures that directed love towards some children and not others; structures that motivated Léon Laurent-Pichat's critique of his childhood and sent him on his quest for a loving family.

The story of the terrified mother in Laurent-Pichat's autobiographical account might reflect his desire to paint her in a positive light, but insofar as it has a basis in real events it represents her as a young unwed mother fearful of exposure and public shaming. Barely three months after the birth of Léon Laurent, however, Geneviève Leroi had married Louis-Achille Deslandes, a hatter, in the church of Sainte Elisabeth de Hongrie on the rue du Temple.[37] If his fearful mother did visit Léon at Mme Cointet's place, then, her anxiety was probably that of a married woman afraid that her husband might discover her visits to this child.

How did this speedy marriage come about? Etienne Pichat is the common thread linking Leroi with her husband. In 1823, Louis-Achille Deslandes was apparently living at no. 8 La Rotonde: he was a tenant of Pichat, therefore, or employed by one of Pichat's tenants.[38] Did Pichat play a role, then, in arranging this marriage? A speedy marriage might have suited an unwed mother with few prospects who was trying to rebuild her life. It might also have suited Pichat, alleviating his sense of moral responsibility, even though he had no legal obligations to Geneviève Leroi or their child. Did Louis-Achille Deslandes know that Geneviève Leroi had borne a child and choose to marry her despite that fact, or was this a marriage of convenience, arranged quickly between virtual strangers for some inducement? In either case, Laurent-Pichat's account of Geneviève's fear of discovery suggests either that the baby's existence, or her visits to the child, remained a secret from Deslandes. As a married woman, Geneviève Leroi was reliant on her husband's support and was required by law to obey him. Love for a child who was not his, and to whom he had no obligations, would undermine her subordinate position as a wife and threaten the inheritance of the children born to the marriage. If Léon's existence were made public, moreover, this child would dishonour her husband.

What of Etienne Pichat, Léon's father? The Civil Code was designed to protect the interests of the legal family. Born out of wedlock, Léon had no right to paternal support or to the family name and inheritance. Nor could Pichat 'recognise' Léon – that is, formally acknowledge him as his natural son, giving him the rights of a son – because the Civil Code explicitly forbade the recognition of children born of adultery. Pichat was a widower when Léon was conceived, but the fact that he then married a woman other than Geneviève Leroi made Geneviève's child 'illegitimate'. This measure was designed to protect legally sanctioned inheritance lines and penalise behaviour 'contrary to good morals'.[39] The adoption of minors was illegal also. However, the Civil Code allowed a man aged over fifty with no legitimate descendants to become the 'unofficial guardian' (*tuteur officieux*) of a child under fifteen and, after five years, to adopt the child in his will.[40] Beginning in 1832, Pichat took steps to adopt Léon Laurent under this provision.

By early 1832, Léon Laurent was in boarding school in Saint-Mandé, on the eastern outskirts of Paris. On 28 January, the nine-year-old was belatedly baptised there in the parish church, with Etienne Pichat as his godfather and Marie Delannoise, an employee of Pichat, as his godmother.[41] In September that year, Etienne Pichat made a will naming Léon Laurent his sole heir.[42] After the requisite five-year delay for testamentary adoption, in 1837, Léon became Pichat's adopted son. Pichat's name was added to Léon's birth name, as the law required, and he then became Léon Laurent-Pichat. Etienne Pichat died the following year, leaving fifteen-year-old Léon with an inheritance worth more than 535,000 francs in capital, producing annual revenues of 27,000 francs. This income placed him not in the ranks of the *haute bourgeoisie* with bankers and industrialists but among the very solid bourgeoisie, able to live a life of luxury.[43]

Children, inheritance and affection

Etienne Pichat was determined to make Léon Laurent his son and heir. But the evidence suggests that his determination was not necessarily born of paternal affection. Rather, the move was part of a family feud over wealth: Léon was the lynchpin of Pichat's strategy to prevent his nephews from inheriting. The feud demonstrated that two elements of the Civil Code were potentially at odds: its stated intention was to preserve family wealth by confining inheritance to children born of marriage, but its patriarchal assumptions gave fathers enormous power to control their inheritance.

Etienne Pichat's nephews challenged his will on the basis of family interest. They submitted that Léon was an *enfant étranger*, an 'outsider' whose successful claim to the estate would not only 'despoil' the family but undermine 'family honour'.[44] In the process, they demonstrated a long history of family conflict over money: this was a family in which 'interest' had driven out affection. The nephews claimed that Pichat had defrauded his brothers and thus seized their inheritance, which he was now passing to an 'outsider'. Although Pichat had supported Léon from infancy, as they acknowledged, the nephews claimed that he had taken little interest in Léon until Valérie – the only child born of his three marriages – died in 1830. He then made Léon Laurent his legal heir to prevent them from inheriting. Pichat's decision, they claimed, was based not on a 'deep and well-founded affection' for Léon, therefore, but on hatred for his family.[45] The nephews lost the case, and the judgement was confirmed in the court of appeal.[46] Etienne Pichat had followed the requirements of the adoption laws exactly, so the courts upheld his right to install his adopted son as his heir, even though that son was born outside wedlock in what was defined as an adulterous union.

This saga of family conflict shows that Pichat had a definite interest in Léon Laurent's birth and survival. Léon, born five months before Valérie, provided an insurance policy for the ageing Pichat, desperate for an heir, in case his attempt to secure a legitimate heir through marriage failed.[47] That desperation in turn suggests an explanation for several curious aspects of Léon Laurent's birth. Keen to ensure the baby's survival, Pichat most likely paid for the services of the doctor who attended the birth. Further, Pichat's fear of a family conspiracy against him (detailed at length in the court case) may explain why Geneviève Leroi's child was born at the address of a third party, and under a false name, making mother and baby more difficult for an ill-intentioned person to trace. This was the interpretation that Laurent-Pichat later offered for his secluded life with Mme Cointet: 'When he [Pichat] visited me / He feared for my life, / He had taken care to hide me away, as one hides a treasure; / He had terrors that have long since disappeared: / He feared that people were following him in the streets, / He saw a storm gathering over our heads.'[48] Pichat's concealment of Léon Laurent was consistent with other strategies he deployed in what he regarded as a battle of wits with his avaricious relatives – hiring a bodyguard, having his food tasted in case of poisoning, taking our advertisements in the papers to warn against forgeries of his signature – all of which were recounted at length in the 1825 legal document.[49] Pichat's nephews dismissed his claims as paranoia.

Whether Pichat felt affection for Léon remains uncertain. On Pichat's death in 1838, fifteen-year-old Léon learned that Etienne Pichat was his father. He realised simultaneously that, while his father had expended money on his education and left him a fortune in his will, he had chosen not to acknowledge their relationship face to face. For Léon to learn the identity of his father, then, was to experience once again a painful sense of rejection by him.

Laurent-Pichat wrote in his autobiography: 'I was everything for this man; he found in me / Both his accuser and his saviour!'[50] He saw in his father's behaviour the expression of guilt and the desire for forgiveness, taking the burden of their relationship upon himself: 'If I had loved him[,] if I had / Looked him in the eye, instead of trembling before him, / It would have been a pardon; if he had said to himself: he loves me! / He would have died content.'[51] But Pichat never told his son directly that he was his father; and if indeed he loved Léon, it seems he never said so. Léon presents himself as emotionally bereft. He described the well-appointed apartment at La Rotonde as a 'gilded cage' where he was often alone.[52]

Léon's escape from that 'gilded cage' came via boarding school in Saint-Mandé, where he spent nine years in the establishment run by Jean-Henri Chevreau and his wife, Eulalie Collas. Perhaps there was a family connection to Saint-Mandé: Pichat's second wife, Clotilde, who was also his niece, died there in 1826.[53] Léon was one of a number of boys who boarded with the Chevreau family.[54] He became a close friend of Henri Chevreau, the eldest son of the household. Just as Laurent-Pichat later recalled being loved by Mme Cointet, so too he recalled the Chevreau household as a warm and loving environment in which he was treated like a family member. Many years later he would attend the funerals of both Monsieur and Madame Chevreau, suggesting that he retained happy memories of his years there.[55]

Whereas the small boy living on the rue Cassini had believed mistakenly that he was part of the Cointet family, the adolescent in Saint-Mandé was well aware that he was not part of the Chevreau family. As Léon observed in a poem addressed to Henri in 1842: 'in this hostile world, you have lent me your family so as to more readily love me like a brother!'[56] But having been 'lent' a family, he could not share that family's sense of togetherness: 'All this happiness that I love and that I envy, / reveals to me the gloomy isolation of my life! / I feel, alas! in seeing you all happy, / with all this good fortune, my own empty and hollow past!'[57]

Laurent-Pichat's unpublished writings suggest that his sense of deprivation remained vivid into adulthood. That was why he was so anxious to secure a place in his maternal family once he discovered their whereabouts. That was why his autobiography emphasised the theme of loneliness. He had opened his life narrative to Rosine: 'I was born alone and sad.' His story continued: 'I came into the world [...] useless and cursed – like an alien star / born in the heavens to disrupt everything!'[58] It is perhaps significant that Laurent-Pichat's fiction also explores loss and abandonment in childhood. *Le Secret de Polichinelle,* one of Laurent-Pichat's earliest short stories (1855), portrays a harsh and unaffectionate father and a tragic absent mother. Jean Delayen, the father character, is described as a man who 'thought about his son only as his heir'. Unwilling to have his son live with him, he placed him in boarding school and then in an apartment, instructing him to come for dinner 'two or three times per week'. Delayen says to his son, Maurice, in the novel: ' "Those are my conditions; if you find them too harsh, if I am too demanding a father, say so. – You are excellent, father!" replied Maurice calmly and with reserve, as he might have said "You do not love me!" '[59]

The mother in this story had died at Maurice's birth. Many years later, as his father is interred in the family vault, Maurice reads on the wall the epitaph for the mother he had never known: 'Poor mother! he thought, God [...] confided to you a creature to bring into this world; you placed him in his cradle, and you fled without saying goodbye to him.' The narrator comments: 'Certain tears that one hasn't shed collect in the heart, and nothing can dry them, neither time, nor happiness. Maurice had never cried for his mother.'[60] The fictional Maurice grieved, not simply for the death of his mother, but also for the relationship they had never shared. Similarly, by writing his living mother's death in fiction, Léon mourned her absence from his childhood.

Nevertheless, to grow up motherless or separated from one's biological parents was not unusual in the early nineteenth century. Bourgeois children were cared for by nurses and governesses; boys were often sent off to boarding school at a young age, as

Laurent-Pichat was.[61] Moreover, many children experienced the death of a parent before they reached adulthood. The nuclear family of two parents and their children was only a 'stage' in family life for many.[62] Blended families generally resulted from death and remarriage rather than the presence of natural children, but Laurent-Pichat's motherless childhood differed little from that of many of his peers.[63]

Even within Laurent-Pichat's own extended kin group, children often grew up without their mothers. Charles Risler, future son-in-law of Laurent-Pichat, lost his mother to measles when he was fourteen and his sister, Eugénie, was twelve. Eugénie would marry Jules Ferry, who was four years old when he lost his mother. Jules and his younger brother, another Charles, were raised by a governess. Jules Ferry and his wife, Eugénie Risler, would later raise Abel, the son of Charles Ferry, whose wife died from tuberculosis when Abel was eighteen months old.[64]

Laurent-Pichat's experience in growing up outside the biological family and away from his mother was far from unique, therefore, although the shame of his origins cast his childhood in a different light. Moreover, while Jules and Charles Ferry, and Charles and Eugénie Risler, were all separated from their mothers while young, all had fathers, grandparents and other relatives engaged in their lives; all knew the warmth of the affectionate family. Their maternal grandmother and aunts played an important role in raising Charles and Eugénie Risler, offering a warm extended family with which they retained strong affective ties. Their grandmother wrote eloquently of the love with which she and their 'grandpapa' had taken them in on the death of their mother.[65] Laurent-Pichat's early years, on the other hand, were not spent in the extended family and he was forced to look farther afield for the affect that was missing from his childhood. For him, the task of weaving the 'emotional fabric of the self' began among strangers.[66]

Léon Laurent-Pichat's quest complete

Laurent-Pichat most likely learned the identity of his mother when he attained the age of civil majority in mid-1844. He soon learned as well that he had four half-siblings: Clémence, then aged sixteen,

Rosine fifteen, brother Louis-Achille (always called simply Achille), aged twelve, and Herminie, aged five. Léon's writings suggest that he established contact with the family towards the end of 1844. A poem Léon wrote to Rosine, dated 23 September 1848, begins: 'It was four years ago that one day, without knowing who I was, / ... / You saw me arrive bearing a mystery'. 'I ... threw myself into your life out of the blue', he noted.[67] That he entered their lives unexpectedly in late 1844 is also suggested by another poem written in early 1845, which describes his introduction to the family as a recent event: 'Perhaps you have often asked yourselves / Who is this young man who came from Saint-Mandé, / Who is this unknown stranger, this young man / Who remains silent about who he is and about his name!' The poem urged them to restrain their curiosity and accept him as a friend. 'What does it matter / Who I am?' he asked somewhat disingenuously, since he was anxious to establish a family relationship with them.[68] He was soon in correspondence with his sisters. 'Heartfelt thanks, my dearly-loved children, / For your letters!' he wrote to them in mid-1845. 'Your words, strewn with joy and regret, / Have poured sweetness and perfume on my heart.'[69] If he was also in correspondence with his mother or his brother, no trace of those letters has survived.

These poems, along with the narrative of his life written for Rosine, were part of a series of works composed between 1845 and 1851 as Laurent-Pichat sought acceptance by his maternal family. Some early poems were addressed to his two sisters Clémence and Rosine.[70] After Clémence's death, aged nineteen, in 1847, his poems were addressed primarily to Rosine. Like the autobiography addressed to her, these poems also performed like letters, reaching out to seek affirmation of their relationship, striving to make a favourable impression on her. The poems provided a form and a forum in which to express his deep emotion to Rosine and perhaps, through her, to others, including his mother. But in expressing his own emotion he was also hoping to evoke reciprocal emotion: it was sentiment, not rational argument, that would gain him acceptance into the family. By asserting his feelings of 'love' and 'friendship' for his siblings, the poems endeavour to evoke those sentiments in his readers.

Moreover, Laurent-Pichat also invoked the emotions embedded in contemporary notions of women's moral role in the family and society: he expressed his vulnerability, seeking compassion from his readers. As part of the family, Laurent-Pichat declared, he would come under the care of the female 'guardian angels' that all men needed. Significantly, those beings were 'sweet creatures, sisters and mothers': 'This ever-vigilant eye always watching over us / Causes us to do good! It is our safeguard!'[71]

It is far from certain, however, that Laurent-Pichat's encounter with his mother's family proceeded smoothly. This is hardly surprising. Geneviève Leroi and her family were taken by surprise when Laurent-Pichat appeared. Placing his faith in the model of the affectionate family, Laurent-Pichat hoped that sentiment would trump hostility or indifference, and that his place in that family would be recognised. But the family more likely saw him as the 'outsider', the disruptive figure from outside the marriage that Etienne Pichat's nephews had challenged earlier in the courts. The family's financial fears would have been allayed when they learned of his wealth: Laurent-Pichat would not compete for the inheritance of the children of the marriage.

The disruption centred not on money but on the reputation of Geneviève Leroi. As Laurent-Pichat realised, his mother now faced the shame associated with premarital pregnancy that she had apparently avoided at the time of his birth. While he expressed regret at being responsible for his mother's suffering, there was no way to gain entry to the family without exposing her past. He was thus his mother's 'misfortune', a 'vampire-child' whose wellbeing came at her expense. Even as his verses drew attention to his mother's pain, Laurent-Pichat pulled out all the emotional stops by emphasising his own guilt and torment, working to evoke, again, the reader's compassion for his situation. That alone would secure his place in the family:

> Our mother has kept her sorrowful secret!
> And she has tried to stay silent about the cause of her suffering!
> And because no one sees her sad and closely-guarded heart,
> I, who am her misfortune, I will reveal her secret!
> Because her first tear was for my life – and fell
> On my cradle; why did it not fall on my tomb?
> Very often, like Job, the wretched one,
> I have repeated: God! Why was I born?[72]

The happiness of children like him 'is not worth all the harm they do!' he declared. 'They [have] no place in the world – and fortune /

Does an injustice to someone if it gives them one,' he wrote.⁷³ Yet it was precisely this place for which he was pleading.

Laurent-Pichat felt compelled to convince his family that, despite his apparently fortunate life, he was deeply unhappy and needed their sympathy: 'My life appears to everyone / To be happy ... / Fortune smiles on me! ... To a superficial glance / I seem blessed by heaven.' But he declared to his sister that he would only acquire 'true happiness [...] when my happiness could one day be called ours!', that is, when his happiness was shared by the entire family.⁷⁴

Addressing the family situation directly, Laurent-Pichat urged a new and united beginning, for their mother's sake: 'Let's leave the past there – with no reproaches!' he wrote, 'So that in seeing our harmony our mother might smile!'⁷⁵ Had he himself expressed 'reproaches' to the mother who had surrendered him? Did his siblings level 'reproaches' at their mother, or at the intruder who had suddenly appeared in their life? Significantly, perhaps, while Léon's poems specifically address his unnamed sister or sisters, they never mention his brother, Achille (who turned seventeen in 1849). Perhaps Achille had more difficulty than his sisters in welcoming this interloper. Perhaps he was less readily won over by poetry. Léon may have struggled with jealousy, too, as he sought an accommodation with the son born of marriage, who had replaced him in his mother's affections. In the light of this poem in particular, Laurent-Pichat's encounter with his mother and her family appears to have been painful for all concerned, at least at first.

It is remarkable, however, that Geneviève Leroi did not turn away her son when he reappeared. Rather than choosing her own personal wellbeing and security over his, she accepted and acknowledged him. According to Laurent-Pichat: 'wishing to give birth to me a second time, / It was she who made my existence known at that moment!'⁷⁶ How long it took for her to reach that acceptance is unclear; how much of Laurent-Pichat's persuasive verse was aimed at touching her heart is uncertain. Not only did the ties of the affectionate family triumph over the legalistic family of rights and entitlements, however, but in this case the two forms of family were reconciled by the legitimation of this natural child. Léon's reappearance in late 1844 set in train a series of events that culminated on 5 September 1851. On that day Geneviève Leroi accompanied Léon Laurent-Pichat to the offices of notary Pierre

Planchat, where she signed a legal document in which she 'voluntarily and freely recognised as her natural son M. Léon Laurent', rescinding the false name she had used twenty-eight years before which had effectively disowned him. 'Léon Laurent' now became, at his mother's request, 'Léon Leroi Laurent-Pichat'.[77]

The document by which Geneviève Leroi and Léon Laurent-Pichat became legally mother and son provides no window onto the emotion that suffused this moment. We can assume, however, that, after a gruelling emotional quest, Léon was overjoyed to be reconciled with his mother and to have a recognised legal place in her family. The cultural myth of the affectionate family had assured him that he would find happiness there. In his autobiographical poem to Rosine, he likened this momentous development in his life to discovering America, the country greatly admired in France at this time as the land of liberty.[78] In invoking America, Laurent-Pichat also evoked the mystery and possibility of the 'New World', transposing them onto the family that he was joining. Being accepted into the family, he wrote, was like entering the Promised Land:

> Everyone has their America to find; an instinct
> Drives you until the day the goal is reached!
> The America to be found, the unknown, the chimera,
> For me – was two sisters, my family and my mother!
> Now that I have arrived, I bless
> All my resting places, child – all my sparrow's nests![79]

His quest for family was complete.

Léon Laurent-Pichat's life was affected significantly by the legal strictures governing marriage and reproduction under the Civil Code. His case supports the argument that people found ways around the provisions of the Code, creating family forms that allowed them to pursue their own personal and familial goals.[80] As a woman, and one without wealth, Geneviève Leroi was less readily able to do so than Etienne Pichat, but she took the opportunity, when it arose, to reconnect with the son she had surrendered and to recognise him in law. Etienne Pichat set aspects of the Code against each other, utilising its provisions in order to adopt Léon Laurent and make him his heir, despite his extramarital birth. Moreover, he left Léon his fortune. Few children born outside wedlock were so lucky.

However lucky he was, the powerful and ongoing resonance of the quest for love dominates Laurent-Pichat's writings about his early life. He imagined that acceptance into his maternal family would provide the love he sought. This illustrates how the cultural narrative of the affectionate bourgeois family, envisaged not only as the natural and ideal family form but also as the prerequisite for personal happiness, impacted on the way individuals interpreted their lives. That Laurent-Pichat was eventually accepted by his extended maternal family of aunts and cousins, that he formed a household (as we shall see) with his mother's family and later with his sister Rosine, marked the triumph in this case of the affectionate family model, a model which proved open to a range of family forms and relationships. It is true that Laurent-Pichat's wealth aided his quest for acceptance, but time would demonstrate the depth of affection and the solidity of the bonds that united this family.

At the same time as Laurent-Pichat was building family relationships, he was also becoming a republican activist. Interspersed with poems that document his emotional engagement with his family, then, are others recording his developing sympathy for the Republic, a sympathy that many others were nurturing at the same time. For Laurent-Pichat and his kin, the emotional turmoil of creating family bonds coincided with the political turmoil of mid-century that saw revolution, civil war and a coup d'état. Living in central Paris, this family was caught up in these momentous events and certainly discussed them.[81] It was as a newly legitimised family member, recognised by his mother in September 1851, that Laurent-Pichat watched, with them, the destruction of the Second Republic in December.

Forging a family thus coincided with forging political loyalties, so that the family in which Laurent-Pichat was now embedded became a republican family, connected by friendship to other such families. As the following chapters will show, the affectionate bonds uniting families would be vital to republicanism during the bleak years of the Second Empire and would become a critical emotional foundation for establishing a solid Republic thereafter. So, too, would the bonds of friendship, and it is to the forging of those bonds that we now turn.

Notes

1 BHVP, MS-FS-07-0014, vol. 16 (2) [hereafter BHVP, 16 (2)]: LLP, 'Poésie de jeunesse (suite)', fo 336.
2 Anne Verjus and Denise Davidson, *Le Roman conjugal: Chroniques de la vie familiale à l'époque de la Révolution et de l'Empire* (Paris: Champ Vallon, 2011); Maurice Daumas, *Le Mariage amoureux: Histoire du lien conjugal sous l'Ancien Régime* (Paris: Colin, 2004); Garrioch, *Formation of the Parisian Bourgeoisie*; Johnson, *Becoming Bourgeois*.
3 Alain Cabantous, 'La fin des patriarches', in Jean Delumeau and Daniel Roche (eds), *Histoire des pères et de la paternité* (Paris: Larousse, 2000), pp. 333–58; Olivier Faron, 'Father-child relations in France: Changes in paternal authority in the nineteenth and twentieth centuries', *History of the Family*, 6 (2001), 365–75; Colin Heywood, *Growing Up in France from the Ancien Regime to the Third Republic* (Cambridge: Cambridge University Press, 2007), pp. 145–7.
4 A reconstituted summary of the birth certificate is available at Archives de Paris [AP]: Naissances, V3E/N1322. For the original, see Archives nationales [AN] MC/ET/XXXIII/1204: 'Reconnaissance d'enfant naturel par Mme Deslandes', 5 Sept. 1851.
5 Quoted in Rachel G. Fuchs, *Contested Paternity: Constructing families in modern France* (Baltimore, MD: Johns Hopkins University Press, 2008), p. 12. See also Yvonne Knibiehler, *Les Pères aussi ont une histoire* (Paris: Hachette, 1987), pp. 182–9.
6 Fuchs, *Poor and Pregnant*, pp. 27–31.
7 Archives départementales [AD] des Yvelines, naissances, Mandres-les-Roses (Val-de-Marne), 5M179BIS, 9: 62/214: Geneviève Elisabeth Rose Leroi, 9 April 1806.
8 AD du Val-de-Marne, 6M5: census of 1817, Mandres-les-Roses.
9 Archives privées de la famille [APF], Mme Ginette Claretie (GC) née Risler, notebook, unpaginated.
10 Fuchs, *Poor and Pregnant*, pp. 11–34; David Harvey, *Paris, Capital of Modernity* (New York: Routledge, 2003), pp. 177, 180–89.
11 Geneviève Leroi must have become pregnant about October 1822. Etienne Pichat's birth certificate is lost but he was sixty when he made his will: AN MC/ET/LXXXIV/892: 'Testament de Mr. Pichat', 5 September 1832.
12 Fuchs, *Poor and Pregnant*, pp. 31–4.
13 BHVP, 16 (2), fos 336–72: LLP, 'Poésie de jeunesse (suite)'. See Susan Foley, '"My God! Why was I born?" Illegitimacy, emotion, and

family in nineteenth-century France', *Journal of Family History*, 43:4 (2018), 357–73.
14 BHVP, 16 (2): LLP, 'Poésie de jeunesse (suite)', fos 343, 344. On the 'autobiographical pact' by which writers assure readers of their truthfulness, see Philippe Lejeune, *On Autobiography*, ed. Paul John Eakin, trans. Katherine Leary (Minneapolis, MN: University of Minnesota Press, 1989).
15 Sidonie Smith and Julia Watson, *Reading Autobiography: A guide to interpreting life narratives*, 2nd edn (Minneapolis, MN: University of Minnesota Press, 2010), p. 103.
16 BHVP, 16 (2): LLP, 'Poésie de jeunesse (suite)', fo 340.
17 Smith and Watson, *Reading Autobiography*, pp. 117–21.
18 Peter Gay, *The Bourgeois Experience: Victoria to Freud. V: Pleasure Wars* (New York: Norton, 1998), pp. 18–19.
19 Heywood, *Growing Up in France*, pp. 145–9; Claudine Giachetti, 'Figures du père dans les romans de la Comtesse de Ségur', *Nineteenth Century French Studies*, 38:1–2 (2009–10), 24–38.
20 Anne Martin-Fugier, 'Bourgeois rituals', in Perrot (ed.), *A History of Private Life*, IV, pp. 261–307. For case studies, see Johnson, *Becoming Bourgeois*; Pellissier, *Vie privée*; Helen M. Davies, *Emile and Isaac Pereire: Bankers, socialists and Sephardic Jews in nineteenth-century France* (Manchester: Manchester University Press, 2015).
21 'AHR conversation: The historical study of emotions', *American Historical Review*, 117:5 (2012), 1487–1531, contributions by William Reddy and Eugenia Lean (1497–8); Scheer, 'Are emotions a kind of practice?'
22 Susan K. Foley and Charles Sowerwine, *A Political Romance: Léon Gambetta, Léonie Léon and the making of the French Republic, 1872–1882* (Houndmills: Palgrave Macmillan, 2012), p. 4.
23 See Mireille Bossis, 'Methodological journeys through correspondences', in 'Men / women of letters', Charles A. Porter (ed.), special issue, *Yale French Studies*, 71 (1986), 63–75.
24 On 'emotion work', see Arlie Russell Hochschild, *The Managed Heart: Commercialisation of human feeling*, rev. edn (Berkeley, CA: University of California Press, 2012), Introduction; Martha Tomhave Blauvelt, 'The work of the heart: Emotion in the 1805–35 diary of Sarah Connell Ayer', *Journal of Social History*, 35:3 (2002), 577–92.
25 BHVP, 16 (2): LLP, 'Poésie de jeunesse (suite)', fo 346. See Fuchs, *Poor and Pregnant*, pp. 152–5.
26 BHVP, 16 (2): LLP, 'Poésie de jeunesse (suite)', fo 346.
27 Only hinted at in his narrative, that address is confirmed in Laurent-Pichat's journal, 22 February 1864. See BHVP, MS-FS-07-0007,

vol. 8–9 (1861–79) and MS-FS-07-0008, vol. 10 (1879–85) (hereafter LLP, journal, date).
28 BHVP, 16 (2): LLP, 'Poésie de jeunesse (suite)', fo 337.
29 *Ibid.*, fo 342.
30 On the way emotions are evoked by naming, see Scheer, 'Are emotions a kind of practice', 210.
31 BHVP, 16 (2): LLP, 'Poésie de jeunesse (suite)', fo 342.
32 *Ibid.*, fo 344.
33 *Ibid.*, fos 351–2.
34 *Rotonde du Temple, M. Laurent-Pichat propriétaire* (Paris: Imp. N. Chaix, [1863]). See also www.carreaudutemple.eu/historique.
35 BHVP, 16 (2): LLP, 'Poésie de jeunesse (suite)', fos 353, 354.
36 *Ibid.*, fos 354–5. He gives no date for these events.
37 Eglise de Sainte-Elisabeth-de-Hongrie, registre paroissial: Leroi, Geneviève Elisabeth Rose et Deslandes, Louis-Achille, 29 October 1823. The marriage is listed in the *table* conserved at the AP, but the register for 1823–6 has disappeared from the parish archives (personal communication with the parish Secretariat, 12 March 2016). The record of the civil marriage is lost.
38 http://gw.geneanet.org/bourelly: Deslandes, Louis-Achille. Accessed 29 October 2021.
39 See Narcisse-Epaminondas Carré, *Premier examen sur le code civil, contenant le premier livre du code, présenté par demandes et réponses, avec des définitions, notes et explications tirées des meilleurs auteurs et commentateurs, par un avocat à la Cour royale de Paris* (Paris: N.-É. Carré, 1823), pp. 126–8, 131, n. 1. See Fuchs, *Contested Paternity*, esp. chapter 1.
40 *Code civil des Français: édition originale et seule officielle* (Paris: Imp. de la République, An XII 1804), clauses 361, 364, 366; Carré, *Premier examen*, pp. 132–5, 142–3.
41 AD du Val-de-Marne, 28J 947: baptême, Léon Laurent, 28 January 1832. For the connection between Pichat and Delannoise, see *Mémoire pour les héritiers Pichat* (below, note 44), pp. 47, 55.
42 AN MC/ET/LXXXIV/892: 'Testament de Mr. Pichat', 5 September 1832.
43 *Ibid.*; AP, décès, V3E/D1189: Pichat, Etienne, 20 April 1838. Cf. Lalouette, 'Laurent-Pichat, Léon', pp. 380–82. On wealth, Christophe Charle, *A Social History of France in the Nineteenth Century*, trans. Miriam Kochan (Oxford: Berg, 1994), p. 265.
44 *Mémoire pour les héritiers Pichat, appelans, contre le Sieur Thibault, ancien notaire, tant en sa qualité de tuteur du mineur Léon Laurent, se disant légataire universel d'Etienne Pichat, qu'en son nom*

personnel, se disant légataire particulier dudit Pichat (Batignolles-Monceaux: Impr. A. Desrez, undated), p. 19.
45 *Ibid.*, pp. 3–4, 29–31, 33.
46 AN MC/ET/XXXIII/1204: 'Reconnaissance d'enfant naturel par Mme Deslandes'.
47 AP, naissances, V3E/N1803: Clotilde Valérie Pichat, 3 December 1823.
48 BHVP, 16 (2): LLP, 'Poésie de jeunesse (suite)', fo 354.
49 *Mémoire pour les héritiers Pichat*, pp. 15, 17–18, 20–21.
50 BHVP, 16 (2): LLP, 'Poésie de jeunesse (suite)', fo 352.
51 *Ibid.*
52 *Ibid.*, fo 357.
53 *Mémoire pour les héritiers Pichat*, p. 30.
54 The census of 1836 lists ten students in the household. The census of 1831 lists teachers but makes no mention of students: AD du Val-de-Marne, Commune de Saint-Mandé, 1NUM067 2: census of 1831; 1NUM067 3: census of 1836.
55 On Chevreau: LLP to Théophile Gautier, 11 (?) Jan. 1854, in Théophile Gautier, *Correspondance générale. VI: 1854–57*. Claudine Lacoste-Veysseye, ed. (Geneva and Paris: Librairie Droz, 1991), no. 1979. On Mme Chevreau: LLP, Journal, 3 Aug. 1882.
56 'A H. CH.', in Henri Chevreau and Léon Laurent-Pichat, *Les Voyageuses* (Paris: Dauvin et Fontaine, 1844), p. 102.
57 *Ibid.*, p. 103.
58 BHVP, 16 (2): LLP, 'Poésie de jeunesse (suite)', fo 336.
59 Léon Laurent-Pichat, 'Le Secret de Polichinelle', in his *Cartes sur la table: Nouvelles* (Paris: Michel Lévy Frères, 1855), pp. 4–5.
60 *Ibid.*, pp. 21–2.
61 Heywood, *Growing Up in France*, pp. 123–32.
62 Sylvie Perrier, 'The blended family in Ancien Régime France: A dynamic family form', *The History of the Family*, 3:4 (1998), 459–71 (459).
63 On the frequency of blended families, see also Johnson, *Becoming Bourgeois*; Pellissier, *Vie privée*.
64 Jean-Michel Gaillard, *Jules Ferry* (Paris: Fayard, 1989), pp. 23–5, 80, 82.
65 BHVP, MS-FS-07-0001, vol. 1 [hereafter BHVP, 1], fos 243–4: 'E. K' [Eugénie Kestner] to Eugénie Risler, undated.
66 Daniela Saxer, 'Forum: History of emotions', *German History*, 28:1 (2010), 67–80 (73).
67 BHVP, MS-FS-07-0013, vol. 16 (1) [hereafter BHVP, 16 (1)]: LLP: Literary works: 'I: Loyse, 23 Sept. 1848', fos 199–201 (199).
68 *Ibid.*, untitled: 'March? 1845', fos 1–3.

69 *Ibid.*, IV, 'Lettre', 9 June 1845, fos 8–9.
70 APF, GC, notebook, unpaginated.
71 BHVP, 16 (1) LLP, Literary works: VI, March 1846, fos 19–20.
72 *Ibid.*, IX: part 1, 14 April 1849, fo 227; IX part 3, 27 April 1849, fo 230.
73 *Ibid.*, part 1, 14 April 1849, fo 227.
74 *Ibid.*, part 3, 27 April 1849, fos 230, 231.
75 *Ibid.*, part 4, 29 April 1849, fo 232.
76 *Ibid.*
77 AN MC/ET/XXXIII/1204: 'Reconnaissance d'enfant naturel', 5 Sept. 1851.
78 Tom Sancton, *Sweet Land of Liberty: America in the mind of the French Left, 1848–1871* (Baton Rouge, LA: Louisiana State University Press, 2020), pp. 5–12.
79 LLP, BHVP, 16 (2): LLP, 'Poésie de jeunesse (suite)', fo 340.
80 Fuchs, *Contested Paternity*, introduction. See also Verjus and Davidson, *Le Roman conjugal*, pp. 135–6.
81 BHVP, 16 (1): LLP: Literary works: 14 March 1848, fos 132–4.

2

'My brothers in poetry': passionate friendship and political upheaval, 1841–52

Friendship offered the youthful Léon Laurent-Pichat an emotional lifeline that compensated for his lack of family ties. It also proved vital to him and his comrades as they set out on their adult paths in the 1840s. As this chapter shows, the political and cultural dynamics of that decade shaped their relationships in enduring ways. Their friendships were profoundly influenced, first of all, by the Romantic sensibility of the day, which revered inwardness and reflection, viewed feelings as a source of truth, and admired deep passion and suffering heroes.[1] The young men's relationships, and their nascent republicanism, were imbued with the optimism of youth and the exuberance of the Romantic age.

Theirs was also the 'generation of 1848'. Like the 'generation of 1820', which grew to adulthood during the French Revolution and was marked indelibly by this momentous event, Laurent-Pichat's generation was marked indelibly by the political turmoil of mid-century and the traumatic events to which they were witness.[2] Widespread joy greeted the Revolution of February 1848 that installed the Second Republic. But Léon Laurent-Pichat was distraught when a second uprising in June 1848 was brutally repressed and a coup d'état in 1851 overthrew the Republic.

These events confirmed Laurent-Pichat's identity as a republican. But his close friend Henri Chevreau became a Bonapartist, shattering their friendship. The years 1848 to 1852 were decisive for these friends and for many others, therefore, in both personal and political terms. Laurent-Pichat never fully recovered from the disintegration of his friendship with Henri. But other friendships, like that between Laurent-Pichat and Louis Ulbach, were reinforced by a shared dedication to the Republic. Forged in the crucible of revolution, such friendships were deeply held, providing the personal resilience and comradeship that would sustain the republican faith during the repressive years of the Second Empire.

Young Romantics in the 1840s

Léon Laurent-Pichat remained at the boarding school run by Jean-Henri Chevreau in Saint-Mandé until he had completed his secondary education: a privilege reserved for about 1 percent of French boys in this period.[3] He formed intense friendships with Henri Chevreau, son of the schoolmaster, and with Louis Ulbach. All three were day students at the prestigious lycée Charlemagne in Paris.[4] Their friendships resonated long after their school days had passed. While Laurent-Pichat drew closer to Ulbach in adulthood, his growing estrangement from Henri Chevreau distressed him deeply.

Having finished school in the summer of 1841, Léon and Henri embarked on a 'grand tour' to Italy, Greece and the Middle East, as young men of means and education frequently did. On their return to France in early 1842, Laurent-Pichat resumed life with the Chevreau family.[5] This highlights his social isolation as a nineteen-year-old: his father was dead and he himself was not yet financially independent, so he probably had nowhere else to go. Ulbach had left school, too, so the group pursued their friendship by mail. The trio had developed a love of poetry at school and had already tried their hand at writing verse.[6] Poetry became the vehicle through which they now communicated.

The friends' enthusiasm for writing verse was not unusual at the time. Anne Martin-Fugier might well have had Laurent-Pichat and his companions in mind when she described 'a generation of young men imbued with romanticism, who were turned head over heels by the young school [of Romantic poets], recognised themselves in its values, adored Hugo, placed poetry above all else, [and] saw themselves as poets.'[7] This trio certainly revered Victor Hugo and other prominent Romantics like Alphonse de Lamartine and Lord Byron. They clearly thought of themselves as poets. In 1844, Ulbach would capture the friends' optimism and zest for living, as well as the quasi-familial bonds between them: 'Is it not sweet, my brothers in poetry, / To love, to be twenty years old, and to be starting out in life.'[8]

Poetry became the means by which these young men cemented their friendship. Writing verse was a 'sweet battle', a competitive sport requiring agility and inventiveness, as when they wove their names into their verses while observing the strict requirements of French verse forms.[9] But if they made a game of poetry, it also offered a vehicle for expressing their emergent political ideas. They had imbibed the Romantic view that the poet was a prophetic figure whose mission was to articulate the suffering of the needy, speak 'Truth' to contemporary society and educate 'the People'.[10] For Louis Ulbach, the poet was 'placed on earth, between man and the grave, / To explain life ... / ... to complement the priest'.[11] Similarly, Léon and Henri declared in a jointly written poem in 1843: 'Poetry enlightens or guides, like a star or a lighthouse! / The poet, advancing with no regrets, / Must set the pace in the vanguard of progress!'[12] The poet, they assumed, had superior knowledge of the direction society should take.

The year 1844 was momentous for these friends. Léon and Henri both turned twenty-one, the age of legal adulthood. Ulbach was a year older. Laurent-Pichat gained access to his inheritance and became financially independent. In 1844, the trio also published their first books of verse: Louis Ulbach produced *Gloriana* while Henri and Léon produced a joint collection, *Les Voyageuses*, a work largely inspired by their travels in 1841–42.

The verses in *Les Voyageuses* are unsigned and only those the writers addressed to each other can be attributed individually. While the young poets embraced the Romantic urge to focus on their own emotions, their encounter with foreign places and peoples had also heightened their sense of national identity and provoked a political response. In visiting the Mediterranean, they declared, 'we wanted to see the Greece of Homer and of Chateaubriand!'[13] They had read Homer at school. Had they perhaps read Chateaubriand's *Itinerary from Paris to Jerusalem* (1811) in preparation for their trip?[14] Revising this work in 1826, Chateaubriand had included a 'Note on Greece', which made the geopolitical case for Greek independence from the Ottoman Empire, an independence for which the Greeks fought during the 1820s.[15] While the 'poet-travellers' (as the friends called themselves) enjoyed experiencing Homer's Greece, then, they also presented an emotional tribute to Greek valour and heroism across the centuries. 'A new Iliad will one day be written, the sacred poem of your rebellion,' they declared. Unlike Homer's epic, it would end in victory: the seizure of the new Helen, 'today called liberty!'[16] Their defence of 'liberty' indicated that, as they entered adulthood, Chevreau and Laurent-Pichat were already attuned to the political issues of the day in France itself. 'Liberty', proclaimed in the Revolution of 1830, had continuing resonance there as political discontent increased in the 1840s.

Passionate friendship

The playful verses exchanged between Laurent-Pichat and Louis Ulbach in their youth reflected a warm and light-hearted relationship that would prove enduring. But the friendship between Laurent-Pichat and Henri Chevreau was more intense. Léon had spent most of his childhood with Henri's family, where he had felt at home again after having been wrenched away from Mme Cointet. Léon and Henri had grown up together, more like brothers than friends, perhaps even like twins since they were the same age. While Léon and Henri described their bond with Louis Ulbach as metaphorical 'brotherhood', denoting their shared aspirations and experiences as they faced the world together, the relationship between Léon and Henri was described in more intimate terms.[17] In a sonnet written for Henri Chevreau in January 1842, Laurent-Pichat styled himself 'your beloved poet … your sweet Lamartine'.[18] He aspired to produce verse that evoked the poignant emotions for which Lamartine was renowned. While Laurent-Pichat's relationship with Henri was intense, however, it was fated by political differences. Forced to choose in 1851, Laurent-Pichat would opt for loyalty to the Republic over loyalty to his Bonapartist friend. He would never fully recover from this painful split.

The exchange of verses, like the exchange of letters between friends, played a key role in fostering the emotional bonds between Léon and Henri. If the letter was open to the expression of feeling, poetry invited a greater intensity of emotion than other genres; it thrived on and even relied on emotion. Besides, Léon and Henri produced jointly written verse, suggesting that they shared together the intense emotion they evoked on the page. Their poetry thus testified to their passionate friendship. Moreover, it illustrates the heightened emotion that friendship acquired under the influence of Romanticism, an emotion that would mark Léon (and others) for life.[19] As Léon wrote to Henri in 1844:

> My hope is that we stay together,
> It is that our future, whatever it may be, draws us to each other;
> It is to seek as my goal the gaze of your eyes;
> It is your voice amidst my hubbub; it is my brow in your heavens!
> My hope is to take my rest beside you,
> Under shared canvas, beneath the same stars.[20]

This verse was published in 1844: clearly Laurent-Pichat did not regard its sentiments as private or as infringing norms of acceptable conduct. Such passionate friendships between young men were common at the time and often enduring. Adult men continued to reminisce warmly about intimate friendships formed at boarding school when, starved of affection, they sought solace with an alter ego or confidant.[21]

Nor were the terms in which Henri and Léon expressed their friendship unusual for the day. If Léon and Henri were 'pressed one to the other'[22]; if they sought to lie 'under shared canvas', other friends also shared beds and wept on each other's bosoms. They addressed one another as *chéri*, or as 'friend of my heart'. The image of being made whole in the other's presence, becoming but one soul or one 'self', was common: 'The day before yesterday I guessed what your heart was feeling ... Were we no longer but a single close friend?' asked Léon Cornudet of Charles de Montalembert.[23] Even the writings of Maurice de Guérin (a devout Catholic) to his intimate male friends contained what Carol Harrison has described as an 'erotic frisson', illustrating the cultural reach of such modes of thought in the early nineteenth century.[24] This phenomenon was not uniquely French. In England and in Germany, men praised the 'sweet secret' of friendship between 'brothers': 'I feel your heart beat upon my breast, / and mine beats back upon yours. / I love you!'[25]

Such vibrant and intimate language is now reserved for lovers. The linguistic boundary between the erotic and the platonic was not rigidly defined at the time, however, and nor was the boundary between friendship and sexual attraction.[26] If sexual intimacy provided a language for the expression of friendship in the nineteenth century, therefore, the language of friendship could act as a cover for deeper passion and provide a subtle language for homosexual desire.[27] But understandings of male friendship, and of intimacy within friendship, are historically variable. Michael Lucey cautions, therefore, that 'modern Western ways of being preoccupied with sexuality might distort the view one takes on historical materials'.[28] Whether same-sex desire existed between these young men as part of their friendship we shall never know, although it is striking that Laurent-Pichat would later liken the breakdown of his friendship with Henri to the end of a love affair. Regardless of whether the intense and highly expressive friendships between these young men were sexual or platonic, however, those friendships began their 'sentimental education', an education in the ways of the heart and the expression of emotion.[29]

The effusive emotion that marked Léon's attachment to Henri also marked his relationship with his half-sister, Rosine Deslandes, further illustrating that the language of intimacy in the mid-nineteenth century was open to a range of meanings. Léon first encountered Rosine late in 1844 when she was fifteen and he was twenty-one. Like other siblings whose upbringing and education separated them until the verge of adulthood, they met as strangers, and this opened their relationship to an erotic charge.[30] That Laurent-Pichat was turned head over heels is evident in a number of his poems from the late 1840s. Rosine left no record of her reactions to him, but they may have been comparable. Léon's status as her brother allowed him to share her company in a way that was inconceivable for other young men. The fact that Léon continued to write to her suggests that she was happy to receive his verses. Indeed, she may well have been the one who transcribed and preserved them.

Léon's earliest surviving poems to his family are addressed to his sisters. But Clémence died in 1847. Herminie was a small child: even if she could read, his poems were not written in terms she might understand.[31] While Laurent-Pichat may have felt real affection for his little sister, therefore, it seems certain that Rosine was his imagined reader. It was Rosine's letters, 'sweet and perfumed', that offered him 'a secure friendship' and reassured him of his acceptance by the family.[32] It was Rosine he imagined in verse as the pure and angelic figure of contemporary gender stereotypes; the sister whose guidance would sustain his virtue: 'I look questioningly into your eyes! I listen to your voice! / And observing your smiling or worried face / My soul, like a confident pilgrim, sets its course!³³

When Laurent-Pichat published his first sole-authored collection of verse, *Libres Paroles*, in 1847, it was dedicated to Henri.³⁴ But he turned to Rosine for consolation when it drew no critical acclaim. Laurent-Pichat imagined the distant future – 'we shall be old then, my dearly beloved' – when they would re-read the collection together and his sister would crown his efforts.³⁵ Comparing Laurent-Pichat favourably to Shakespeare and Dante and smothering his brow with kisses, she would declare: 'You are the first and the only one in my heart!' The disdain of the critics would no longer matter; nor would exclusion from the Pantheon, the shrine housing the remains of revered citizens: 'I have been baptized by a sister's kiss! / ... / I have made my Pantheon in the heart of a woman!'³⁶

Laurent-Pichat's declarations of passionate attachment to Rosine came hot on the heels of his equally passionate declarations to Henri. That he dedicated *Libres Paroles* to Henri while penning heartfelt verses to Rosine reminds us that the two 'passions' overlapped. Indeed, while some of Laurent-Pichat's writings might suggest homosexual desire, others apparently express heterosexual desire. In a brief personal note dated 16 April 1842, Léon Laurent-Pichat, not yet nineteen, observed:

> There are three things that stir my soul to the supreme degree, three things that make a strange and sweet impression on my being, that cause a delightful trembling [*frémissement*], and that create in my veins an indescribable thrill of happiness and desire: An orchestra in harmony; an emotional performance at the theatre; a regimental parade, musicians in the lead; and a fourth which for me is more stirring and more powerful than the other three: The sight of a woman.³⁷

This note linked overwhelming feelings with physical arousal: the mere 'sight of a woman', regardless of her specific identity, stirred Léon's soul (and no doubt his body). Perhaps Léon felt free to express sexual desire in a heterosexual context, particularly since his note was not intended to be seen by anyone else. However, his intertwining of attachment to men and to women was not unique.³⁸ Again, it reflects the fluid boundaries between friendship and sexual attraction, and the shared language in which such attachments were described. But the knowledge that Rosine was his sister also placed his feelings for her, strong though they may have been, in a separate category.

Laurent-Pichat's relationship with Rosine, brought to life in his poetry, vividly illustrates the extraordinary cultural weight that sibling relationships – especially brother–sister relationships – carried in European culture in the first half of the nineteenth century. Fictional siblings pervaded literature, and a 'cult' of siblinghood in real life produced a host of devoted brother–sister couples, many well-known still: William and Dorothy Wordsworth, Honoré and Laure de Balzac, Edgar and Blanche Quinet, Felix and Fanny Mendelssohn. The intensity of such sibling relations has generally been attributed to the transformation of the bourgeois family, which had become inward-looking and expressive, its members bound by deep affection rather than by 'interest'.[39] This family affection hardly explains the depth of attachment between Léon and Rosine, who were raised separately and met as complete strangers. Nevertheless, the shock of discovery when they met was similar to that experienced by adolescent siblings who were reunited after lengthy separation for their education.[40] Intense passion between siblings was not unusual, although families would intervene to separate them if they overstepped the mark. While the language of sibling exchanges sometimes hinted at incest – a theme well developed in the Romantic literature of the day – the taboo against incest remained deeply entrenched. A passionate language of sibling affection coexisted, therefore, with an emphasis on female innocence, sweetness and purity. This was the case for Léon and Rosine.

The sibling relationship was envisaged as the perfect form of complementarity, uniting male and female as mirror images, the 'like unlike'.[41] This understanding inspired many sibling-couples to embark on shared artistic pursuits. In 1847, Laurent-Pichat envisaged a literary partnership in which Rosine would provide the illustrations for a book of his verse. The project never eventuated, to his great disappointment: 'This would have been our album', he wrote. 'It would have been charming, I assure you!'[42] But perhaps the partnership took a different form. In mid-1848, the handwriting in the archive of his poetry suddenly changes: it becomes neater, finer and more rounded; sometimes it has corrections in Laurent-Pichat's hand. This new handwriting is consistent with the elegant style expected of young women at a time when more utilitarian standards were set for men.[43] While it is impossible to be sure whose hand it is, Rosine was the person most likely to have made the fair copy of Léon's verses, and the script is compatible with the few examples of her handwriting that have survived.[44] Perhaps theirs was a literary partnership after all, but one in which Rosine occupied a modest 'feminine' role behind the scenes.

Throughout 1848, Laurent-Pichat continued to express his deep attachment to Rosine. In April, he asked: 'What more can I say to you? Your heart is my nest! / It's the refuge where each of my dreams comes to rest!'[45] She was also a 'refuge' from his own angst as he grappled with issues of faith and doubt. In several poems he imagined Rosine interceding with God on his behalf. In one poem, he painted a series of scenarios in which Rosine, as an angelic figure, saved him from perishing. He imagined, 'if God sent me to purgatory for a thousand years':

> For a thousand years and more, if I had to endure them,
> You would be there I am sure, standing by the door,
> Like a sculpted angel praying on a tomb,
> And when I had finished my long penance,
> On the path to heaven, sweet and dear support,
> You would go before me carrying the torch![46]

Reflecting in September 1848 on the four years since he had encountered his family, Léon singled out Rosine as the one who had transformed his life: 'Indeed, I had not lived before that moment! / I was like a flower … / That needs the vital ray of sunlight in order to open! / … / My soul blossomed beside you – and my life / Was awakened and enraptured beneath your gaze.' 'The dream that my soul had long pursued / Took bodily form,' he added, 'and it came to life on that day!'[47] Laurent-Pichat's relationship with Rosine would remain a lifelong attachment, evolving from the intense sibling passion of youth into an enduring friendship and companionship.

Awakening to republicanism, 1840–48

Laurent-Pichat's verses to his beloved sister in the 1840s were interspersed with others that record his political awakening. Their relationship reached a crescendo just as a major revolutionary crisis unfolded in France. Paris was the epicentre of political and social radicalism in a decade marked by economic crises and unrest. The extremely narrow property franchise excluded even many bourgeois.[48] The 'social question' – the question of the condition of the working classes under incipient industrialisation – was the subject of constant debate. A bevy of socialist thinkers promoted imaginative ideas for social change, from the experimental communities espoused by Charles Fourier or Etienne Cabet, to the 'workers' union' advocated by Flora Tristan and the 'organization of labour' promoted by Louis Blanc.

Laurent-Pichat's writings suggest that he was well aware of such debates. He fitted the profile of the emerging republican bourgeois of the day. Despite his wealth, he remained an outsider to the social elite; he lacked the social connections required in a nepotistic system, and so had nothing to gain from supporting the old establishment. Further, he was young, well educated and anxious to succeed as a writer in an increasingly crowded and competitive literary marketplace. Frustrated young men like him – struggling writers, journalists and legal hacks – were a fertile breeding ground for republicanism.[49]

Republicanism was not a uniform set of ideas in the 1840s. Laurent-Pichat's republicanism resembled that of Alphonse de Lamartine, his poetic hero and alter ego, who would be elected head of the Provisional Government following the February Revolution in 1848. Both men embraced politics as 'a matter of sentiment'.[50] Lamartine's republicanism combined sympathy for the poor with a desire for social unity: themes common in progressive literary and political circles in the 1840s.[51] Lamartine's idealistic and generous version of republicanism appealed, in Theodore Zeldin's words, to 'poets, orators and dreamers'.[52] Laurent-Pichat was one such figure. As he would write in 1849: 'I am a dreamer in the strongest sense of the word.'[53]

Laurent-Pichat wrote sympathetically about 'the people' in his earliest political poems. They were 'the eternal slave', always cheated out of gains when a new division of the political spoils occurred. Addressing those 'people', he wrote: 'I love you, because I believe / That your cause is essentially just!'[54] His understanding of that cause was vague, although in a later poem he again likened 'the people' to those who were enslaved, seeing them as similarly oppressed and despised. Using the terminology of the day, he wrote:

> Tell the negro [and the] beasts of burden
> That they are free – will they understand?
> No ...
> I am one of a still small number
> Who cherish the chimera of equality,
> Dream of a sublime accord for the world!

He dreamed of a day when everyone's heart was inscribed with the words: 'All men are equal – and all peoples are free!'[55]

Despite the poet's desire for social harmony, poetry was unsuited to analysing the causes of oppression or of racism. Laurent-Pichat had little familiarity with workers and none with enslaved peoples. He never addressed the question of slavery in any depth although, like most French republicans, he admired Abraham Lincoln for his role in ending slavery, and he was friendly in later years with the leading French abolitionist Victor Schœlcher.[56] If workers resembled enslaved peoples, to his way of thinking, he perhaps nursed the hope that both groups of oppressed peoples could be 'freed' by decree.

Laurent-Pichat's well-meaning if patronising attitude towards workers reflected the enormous social and educational gulf between the classes. 'When thinkers speak to poor folk, / They should be kind, patient, indulgent', the twenty-one-year-old declared. 'Teach them how to use their time and their labour; / show them the wise purpose of revolutions.' Like many of his fellow-republicans, and like most socialists of the day, he envisaged social reform as a co-operative venture between workers and bourgeoisie, between 'those who do the deed and those who inspire it, / the arm of the people and the head of the thinker.' Laurent-Pichat was critical, therefore, of those who (he believed) misled the people with false hopes. Directing a barb at so-called 'utopian' socialists, he criticised the 'inventors of systems' with their 'absurd means' of solving the social question: 'Don't make workers believe ... that they are kings; – first make them citizens.'[57]

Laurent-Pichat insisted in 1847 that he belonged to no party and was beholden to no cause.[58] But by 1847 he certainly rejected monarchy, even if it promised democratic reforms. He was scathing of the search for a 'better king': 'The hands of kings always carry the same sceptre; / The same tree bears the same fruit; / Conquerors have always carried the same two-edged sword; / Despotism – quietly – or with a fanfare!'[59] Moreover, when many of the people's so-called defenders were traitors to their cause, he argued, republicans were their true friends. Identifying himself with this group, he concluded: 'I have taken up the pen – and here I am!'[60]

Laurent-Pichat confirmed that claim the following year. Between 22 and 24 February 1848, revolution engulfed Paris, part of a wave of revolutionary uprisings that swept across Europe as oppressed peoples sought to win freedom from autocrats. In France, the Second Republic was proclaimed. Laurent-Pichat's poetry of March and April, most of which remains unpublished, was ecstatic, capturing the optimism and joy of a year that became known as the 'springtime of peoples'.[61] A verse dated 1 March, opened: 'Long live liberty! Long live the Republic'. It celebrated the departure of the monarchy that he despised: 'Take with you ... your sceptres and thrones, your cloaks in tatters, your shattered crowns.'[62] A few days later, he hailed the dawn of liberty and fraternity and welcomed the prospect of universal peace: 'the first step has been taken in the promised land and Utopia has triumphed!'[63] Once a critic of utopianism, he now seemed to embrace it.

Such optimism was widespread in progressive circles in the wake of February's events, as the joy that greeted recitations of the Marseillaise by 'Mademoiselle Rachel', star of the Comédie Française, testifies. The Marseillaise, closely associated with republicanism and banned for much of the nineteenth century, was sung spontaneously by revolutionary crowds in February. On 6 March 1848, at the conclusion of a performance of Corneille's *Horace*, the audience called on Rachel to sing this anthem. She did so on her knees, wrapped in the tricolour flag, and her performance brought the house down. According to the poet Théophile Gautier: 'this truly sublime pose saw the room burst into transports of enthusiasm; bravos, applause, foot-stamping echoed like thunder from every side.' Rachel performed the anthem forty times over the following weeks before departing on a tour of the provinces, where audiences also demanded to hear the Marseillaise.[64]

Laurent-Pichat was present at one of those performances and was thunderstruck. On 9 April, he penned verses annotated

'To Rachel, after having heard her sing the Marseillaise'. For Laurent-Pichat and the rest of the audience she became the embodiment of France:

> Sacred angel of the people and the nation,
> It's more than art, it's an incarnation!
> /.../
> In a strange harmony, your beauty combines
> Jeanne d'Arc, the soul, with Minerva, the body!

Rachel's voice was unforgettable: 'When your voice captivates us, empty hands / Call for muskets and look for their swords!' He added: 'For the time has come and men are ready! "To arms, citizens" – even if that means death!'[65]

In invoking the Marseillaise, Laurent-Pichat invoked the First Republic of 1792, a republic that had given no quarter to enemies without or within. But his verses also alluded to the divisions that would soon shatter the dream of peace and progress in the Second Republic. While celebrating the 'good people' who had made the revolution, he also sought to reassure the many bourgeois who feared them. He emphasised the 'order' and 'courage' of the worker-revolutionaries who, covered in grime and perhaps in gunpowder, intimidated their social betters. 'Come down! Come and see!' he invited, hinting at the gulf of familiarity that separated the classes:

> And those black faces over there, those sinister faces? –
> Salute them, – they are heroes!
>   They are the victors who are guarding their conquest!
>   Men of the February days!
> You ask their names! Your quest is over!
>   These people are called the worker!

As their self-appointed representative, and clearly familiar with their demands, Laurent-Pichat explained what the workers sought of the Republic: 'That work be provided, that wages be regulated / That labour be rewarded with bread!' But like other bourgeois who shared Lamartine's visionary and idealistic republicanism, his stance was paternalistic. He sought the 'fusion' of classes and insisted that workers, too, were committed to class unity: they sought to 'unite workers and master, / Like father and children.'[66]

Faith in class harmony was shared by many republicans and socialists at the time. The elections of April, however, destroyed that vision. Urban workers had placed their faith in 'universal suffrage' (actually manhood suffrage), believing that the democratic process would deliver social and economic justice. But while some rural communities were passionate about the 'democratic and social republic', many others took their lead from local elites in casting their ballots.[67] The result was a strongly conservative Assembly dominated by rural notables. In June, the Assembly closed down the National Workshops that had been established in February to provide work for the many unemployed in Paris. This ignited a second revolution, which was crushed with enormous bloodshed during the June Days.

If Laurent-Pichat re-read in June a poem he had written on 28 March, it must have been with bitter irony. That poem addressed the Republic, the 'virgin of the people', the 'Jeanne d'Arc of the crowd'. It contrasted the Republic of 1792 with the Republic of 1848. The former had arrived amid violence and war; the latter, Laurent-Pichat proclaimed, had arrived amid peace and harmony. 'You will no longer climb the reddened staircase / Of our scaffolds of the Revolutionary Terror!' You will 'no longer feel the blood fall drop by drop on your white shoulders!'; 'No more decapitated heads around you!' This Second Republic would clothe herself anew, discarding the revolutionary garb associated with the First Republic of 1792:

> Don't go searching in your old wardrobe
> For your jacket [*carmagnole*] and your [Phyrigian] bonnet!
> Leave your past full of anger and upheaval behind you!
> /.../
> Be serene today! Let your alabaster forehead
>   Be crowned with majesty![68]

But now, in the name of the Republic, the conservative Assembly had slaughtered its own citizens.

Whether Laurent-Pichat witnessed the June Days or only read about them from afar is uncertain. He had foreshadowed his departure from the capital in a joyful poem dated 14 March, apparently written to Rosine. It anticipated a holiday in the countryside where they would amble in the fields, laughing and chatting:

'We won't talk any more about our civil conflicts'. He added presciently, however, that they would 'say a holy prayer for France! / May God protect her from all danger', whether from 'the despot or the foreigner!'[69] In September and October 1848 he signed his poems from Loyse, south-east of Paris, but exactly when he left Paris remains unknown.

A poem entitled 'Idylls of May', published in 1856, responds directly to the events of June 1848. It was probably written at the time, since there are echoes of his personal struggle for family acceptance as well as of political issues. A section headed '1849' reflects on 'the storm that battered us last year', its verdict on June resembling Victor Hugo's later assessment in *Les Misérables*: the uprising was a tragic conflict between those who should have been united.[70] Domestic violence provided Laurent-Pichat with an analogy for the violent suppression of the June insurrection, which he likened to a husband's attack on the wife he should cherish. 'Like a loving and faithful son', the poet declares, he has kept watch beside his mother, whose 'name is the Republic':

> The beautiful bride
> Was wed in February;
> Her children were legitimated.
> But her husband, like a scoundrel,
> Wants to get rid of her, the poor woman,
> And I, her son, am defending her!
> /.../
> Since my mother is the *patrie*,
> I cry aloud in my song.

But Laurent-Pichat's was a helpless watch, like that of the imagined child.[71]

Although shocked by the June events, Laurent-Pichat retained his faith in the vision of the Republic encapsulated by the February Revolution. The draft introduction to an unidentified book of verse, dated December 1849, opens: 'People claim that the revolution of February was too evil [*sinistre*] in character to be celebrated by the poets and they have concluded that it was not legitimate'. But he sought to defend its principles, even if his voice would not carry the weight of Hugo or Lamartine: 'I am well aware that it is not me that people are waiting for! But others will sing and I will be amongst their number.' Addressing 'unknown and scattered friends, honest hearts that love France and the Republic', Laurent-Pichat proclaimed his faith in the eventual triumph of the Republic:

> The old monarchical edifice is shaking and is no longer stable. It rested on solid columns and Samson has already given it three shoves [in 1789, 1830 and 1848] ... Perhaps God is labouring in silence and preparing a new world for a fortunate generation to enter ... It is our duty not to give up.[72]

The unpublished verses he wrote in March and April 1848 may well have been envisaged as part of this volume, given Laurent-Pichat's description of its contents:

> The verses that I am publishing were inspired by past emotions. They are songs of hope, cries of joy – aspiration and even doubts; all the feelings experienced by a heart that proclaims its honesty; it is the dossier of a good citizen. I believed and still believe in goodness; I am a dreamer in the strongest sense of the word.[73]

His idealistic and 'Lamartinian' vision of the Republic remained intact.

In December 1851, President Louis-Napoleon Bonaparte overturned the Second Republic in a coup d'état. The coup was brutal for republicans. Thousands were arrested; hundreds of republican newspapers were shut down; thirty-two departments – a third of the total –were placed under military control.[74] A period of repression and persecution began. Many republicans fled into exile or were proscribed. Despite an amnesty in 1859, many chose to remain in exile until the regime fell in 1870.

Laurent-Pichat's response to the coup was summed up in a poem entitled 'The Whitened Sepulchre', written in 1852 and published in 1856. It condemned Louis-Napoleon, the author of the coup, who had immediately moved into the Tuileries palace and begun its restoration. But his sumptuous court, the poet declared, was contaminated by the odour of 'badly-interred flesh'. Buried under the palace was a corpse: 'to construct his happiness, / He had to kill his conscience, murder his honour.'[75] This poem, hidden in the book of an unknown poet, slipped through the censor's net in 1856, despite its savage criticism of the man who was by then Emperor Napoleon III. However, with the coup d'état, Laurent-Pichat's optimistic embrace of 'Truth' and 'Liberty', his aspiration to 'think as you live, or otherwise be silent', had passed from a youthful ideal to an existential challenge.[76]

Friendships on trial, June 1848 – December 1852

In a poem to Rosine, written during a voyage down the Rhône in September 1849, Laurent-Pichat reflected nostalgically on the passage of time and the role of destiny: 'One day time brings to an end all the joys of childhood; / There is no way of struggling, no defence against it. / We have to separate; each one leaves when their turn comes.'[77] The mid-century crisis coincided with the assumption of adult roles and responsibilities by Laurent-Pichat and his friends. That transition to adulthood brought changes in their personal lives, which, along with political differences, took them their separate ways, reshaping or even destroying their friendships.

Louis Ulbach's marriage in 1846 had been the first moment of separation for the friends. The responsibilities of marriage necessarily altered Ulbach's relationships with his male comrades. But physical separation came only when he left Paris for Troyes in 1848, either to escape the conflict or unable to survive in the capital as the economy unravelled. A committed republican like Laurent-Pichat, Ulbach had already launched a career as a writer and republican journalist. In Troyes, he became editor of *Le Propagateur de l'Aube*, to which Laurent-Pichat would contribute a number of pieces. Following the 1851 coup d'état, however, *Le Propagateur de l'Aube* was shut down and Ulbach, whose radical republican views had already seen him prosecuted, returned to Paris in search of work.[78] His friendship with Laurent-Pichat resumed its earlier patterns, though shorn of the exuberant poetic exchanges of their youth. They would remain friends for life.

Laurent-Pichat's relationship with Rosine was also transformed by the demands of adulthood. For Rosine, these brought not the need to choose political sides as for the young men, but the expectation of marriage. Laurent-Pichat had written to her in September 1849: 'What is my destiny! It's you! ... You are the real happiness placed on my path!'[79] But the 'joys of childhood' had passed for them, too, and this meant the transformation of their close sibling bond. Rosine's 'destiny' was to be the wife of another. On 27

November 1851, Rosine, now aged twenty-two, married Amédée Beaujean, professor at the lycée St-Louis in Paris.[80] Marriage would inevitably place her relationship with Léon on a less intense footing, but the siblings would remain close throughout their lives. Indeed, Laurent-Pichat's deep attachment to Rosine, his sense that she was the most singular of women, may help to explain why he never married.

Laurent-Pichat's friendship with Henri Chevreau did not survive the political differences that emerged between them in the political turmoil of mid-century. During his voyage down the Rhône in September 1849, Laurent-Pichat had a chance encounter with Henri at Privas. It was this encounter that sparked his wistful reflection on change and destiny in his poem to Rosine. Henri's star was rising at the time. Having stood unsuccessfully in the elections for the Constituent Assembly of 1848, Henri had made the choice to support Louis-Napoleon Bonaparte, who defeated the republican candidate in the presidential elections of December 1848. In January 1849, aged only twenty-six, Chevreau was appointed Prefect of the Ardêche. Chevreau's father, too, chose Bonaparte and would soon win a seat in the Legislative Body (*Corps Législatif*). The Chevreau family became a Bonapartist family, part of Louis-Napoleon's system of government. Henri's political views were the antithesis of Laurent-Pichat's ideals.[81]

Laurent-Pichat's pain at the emerging gulf between himself and Henri was expressed in a poem entitled 'Alibée'. Written in November 1851, it drew on fables by La Fontaine and Fénelon to create a new fable about a shepherd who became king.[82] The shepherd acquired the trappings of power but at a high price, and he retained in some secret place 'a few old fading garments from his youth'. 'One still finds on this earth / shepherds who become kings ... / Such happiness is a burden, I believe'. Laurent-Pichat's poem continued:

> I know more than one person who is envied,
> Who appears proud and happy,
> Whose soul appears to be content.
> Recount the life of the shepherd to him
> And tears will come to his eyes.

The poem, dedicated to Henri but unpublished at the time, was a lament for the lost friend of his youth, for 'the poet who [was] dead'.[83]

After the coup d'état the following month, Henri Chevreau remained loyal to Bonaparte, who was soon to become Emperor Napoleon III. Henri was rewarded with further high office, rising to become Minister of the Interior in January 1870. His friendship with Laurent-Pichat died painfully. In 1856 Laurent-Pichat published 'Alibée', with its dedication to Henri Chevreau. In the public domain, the poem was both an accusation against Henri and a statement of Léon's grief.

A second poem, written in April 1852 but initially unpublished, might also be a coded allusion to the breakdown of Laurent-Pichat's relationship with Henri Chevreau, likening the break to the end of a love affair. Titled 'To an unfaithful woman', the poem describes a man's pain on catching sight of the lover who has left him to become 'sultana of the harem'. Seeing her pass by 'brought sorrow to my thoughts / And tears to my eyes', the poet declares. He recalls their happy days together, their youth, their travels. Now she has thrown herself into the arms of a new lover:

> Ah! Cruel one, I loved you
> And purely – I swear to God!
> I loved you like my *patrie*.
> You have betrayed me; you have dishonoured yourself;
> You have prostituted yourself, farewell![84]

The image of the harem was frequently deployed by republicans to condemn the Empire as a promiscuous haven for those on the make. If the poem was written with Henri in mind, its use of the image of the 'unfaithful woman' to describe a political turncoat and a fractured relationship between men illustrates yet again the ambiguities between friendship and sexual passion, and between heterosexual and homosexual desire. Léon's deep feelings for Henri tapped into the same reservoir of passion as sexual love, even if their relationship remained platonic. Despite its dismissal of the unfaithful one, the poem concludes: 'Remember that I loved you!'

While he condemned Chevreau's political choice, Laurent-Pichat could not easily disavow their friendship. He continued to describe Henri to others as his friend, despite the gulf between them.[85] In 1867, more than twenty years after his first youthful expression of affection for Henri, an encounter with Henri still reduced Léon to tears. He wrote to another friend, Camille Risler:

> My friend Henri Chevreau lost a child. I went to St-Sulpice and I saw him walk past me, with his brother, before and after the ceremony. They saw me and made no effort to approach me. I believe I did the right thing in not taking a step! But it's hard! I don't know if they felt any emotion – but I cried about it – that was my right, don't you think? [86]

For years to come he made a note in his diary whenever he encountered Henri.[87]

Léon's break with Henri Chevreau was more than the breakdown of a friendship; it was the loss of an intimate relationship that had shaped his childhood and adolescence. The importance he placed on this quasi-familial bond explains his attendance, years later, at the funerals of both Monsieur and Madame Chevreau, and at that of Henri's child. Friendship with Henri had filled an emotional vacuum in Léon's adolescence, offering him the support he needed as he entered adult life. After the forced separation from Mme Cointet, separation from Henri was the loss of family for a second time. In an age of dramatic political upheavals and bitter political conflict, however, politics became a decisive proving ground for male friendships. Politics helped to cement the relationship between Ulbach and Laurent-Pichat, who shared republican aspirations. But Henri Chevreau's support for the Empire was a step too far for Léon. The division proved irreparable.

The three friends' relationships reflected the passion and idealism of the Romantic age in which they emerged to adulthood. A Romantic sensibility inflected not only their literary efforts, but also their politics and their friendships; it made for exuberant hopes, extravagant gestures and full-blooded commitments. That sensibility helps to explain the fact that, for Laurent-Pichat, the choice of republic or empire was a moral choice. As a wealthy man, Laurent-Pichat had the luxury of being 'a man without reproach',[88] acting out his idealistic principles. Both Chevreau and Ulbach had to look to their futures. Both gave up poetry; Chevreau, in addition, chose a new political direction. Hopes and ideals were no match, therefore, for the realities of adult life. Faced with its demands, the friends made choices or accepted necessities that separated and divided them physically, and even ideologically. The passions of adolescence were abandoned, but friendship remained an essential bond, a source of personal sustenance in daily life and a source of political support in the republican struggle against the hostile Empire.

Notes

1. Ceri Crossley, 'Romanticism', in Peter France (ed.), *The New Oxford Companion to Literature in French* (Oxford: Clarendon Press, 1995), pp. 714–16.
2. See Berndt Weisbrodt's contribution to Alex Lichtenstein (ed.), 'AHR conversation: Every generation writes its own history of generations', *American Historical Review*, 123:5 (2018), 1505–46; Alan B. Spitzer, *The French Generation of 1820* (Princeton, NJ: Princeton University Press, 1987).
3. Theodore Zeldin, *France 1848–1945. II: Intellect, taste and anxiety* (Oxford: Clarendon Press, 1977), p. 292.
4. AP 704/73/2: Collège royal de Charlemagne. Entrées et sorties, 1838–1841; Zeldin, *France*, II, pp. 243–6, 264, 278.
5. AD du Val-de-Marne, Commune de Saint-Mandé, 1NUM067 4: census of 1841.
6. BHVP, MS-FS-07-0015, vol. 17 (hereafter BHVP, 17): LLP, fo 14, untitled, 1838.
7. Anne Martin-Fugier, *Les Romantiques 1820–1848* (Paris: Hachette Littérature, 1998), pp. 13–15, 22; Stone, *Sons of the Revolution*, chapter 1.
8. L. Ulbach, 'A mes amis H. Chevreau et L. Pichat [*sic*] (April 1844)', in Louis Ulbach, *Gloriana* (Paris: W. Coquebert, 1844), pp. 271–81 (271).
9. BHVP, 17 fos 30–31, 32–3: LLP, 'A L. Ulbach', 11, 19 March 1842; L. Ulbach, 'A mon ami Laurent Pichat', Troyes, Oct. 1843, in Ulbach, *Gloriana*, pp. 323–32.
10. Martin-Fugier, *Les Romantiques,* pp. 23, 69–70; Crossley, 'Romanticism', pp. 714–16.
11. Ulbach, 'A mes amis H. Chevreau et L. Pichat', in Ulbach, *Gloriana*, p. 276.
12. H. Chevreau and L. Laurent-Pichat, 'A notre ami L. Ulback (*sic*)' [Dec. 1843], in H. Chevreau and L. Laurent-Pichat, *Les Voyageuses*, pp. 341, 345.
13. H. Chevreau and L. Laurent-Pichat, 'Les Deux Grèces', *ibid.*, p. 176.
14. François-René de Chateaubriand, *Œuvres complètes de Chateaubriand*. V: *Itinéraire de Paris à Jérusalem et de Jérusalem à Paris, en allant par la Grèce et revenant par l'Egypte, la Barbarie et l'Espagne*, nouv. édn (Liechtenstein: Nevdeln, 1828; Kraus reprint, 1975).
15. Sophie Basch, 'François-René de Chateaubriand (1768–1848)', Bibliothèque nationale de France. Available at https://heritage.bnf.fr>francois–rene–de–chateaubriand. Accessed 1 July 2021.

16 H. Chevreau and L. Laurent-Pichat, 'Les Deux Grèces', in *Les Voyageuses*, pp. 175–81.
17 'A notre ami L. Ulback (sic)', *ibid.*, p. 333.
18 BHVP, 17 fo 46: LLP, 'Sonnet: A Henri Chevreau, en lui offrant un Lamartine'.
19 Counter and White, 'Introduction: The soul's sentiment', 2.
20 'A H. CH.', in *Les Voyageuses*, p. 104.
21 Houbre, *La Discipline de l'amour*, pp. 89, 95–100; Marc Brodie and Barbara Caine, 'Class, sex and friendship: The long nineteenth century', in Caine (ed.), *Friendship*, pp. 244–5; Peter Gay, *The Bourgeois Experience: Victoria to Freud. III: The Tender Passion* (New York: Oxford University Press, 1986), p. 217.
22 H. Chevreau and L. Laurent-Pichat, 'A notre ami L. Ulback (sic)' [Dec. 1843], in *Les Voyageuses*, pp. 331–46 (332).
23 Quoted in Houbre, *La Discipline de l'amour*, p. 106.
24 Carol E. Harrison, *Romantic Catholics: France's postrevolutionary generation in search of a modern faith* (Ithaca, NY: Cornell University Press, 2014), p. 97.
25 Quoted in Hoffmann, 'Civility, male friendship', 232; see Gay, *The Bourgeois Experience*, III, p. 208.
26 See Carol Smith-Rosenberg, 'The Female world of love and ritual', *Signs: Journal of women in culture and society*, 1:1 (1975), 1–30; Yacovone, ' "Surpassing the love of women" ', pp. 195–221; Houbre, *La Discipline de l'amour*, pp. 139–40; Horowitz, *Friendship and Politics*, pp. 9–10, 65–80.
27 Gay, *The Bourgeois Experience*, III, p. 217.
28 Lucey, *'Ami ou protégé?'*, 189.
29 Houbre, *La Discipline de l'amour*, pp. 102, 108.
30 *Ibid.*, p. 142.
31 BHVP, 16 (1), fo 16: LLP, 'Sonnet', 25 Aug. 1845.
32 *Ibid.*, fos 8–11: LLP, 'Lettre', 9 June 1845.
33 *Ibid.*, fos 19–21: LLP, untitled, March 1846. On the moral role of sisters, see Marie-Françoise Lévy, *De mères en filles: L'Education des françaises 1850–1880* (Paris: Calmann-Lévy, 1984), p. 127; Leonore Davidoff, *Thicker Than Water: Siblings and their relations, 1780–1920* (Oxford: Oxford University Press, 2011), p. 202.
34 Léon Laurent-Pichat, *Libres Paroles* (Paris: Comptoir des imprimeurs-unis, 1847).
35 BHVP, 16 (1), fos 129–31: LLP, no. XLVIII, 17 Feb. 1848.
36 *Ibid.*
37 BHVP, 17, fo 56v: LLP, 'Quelques idées (prose)', 16 April 1842.
38 Gay, *The Bourgeois Experience*, III, pp. 206–16.

39 Davidoff, *Thicker Than Water*; Gabrielle Houbre, 'Amours fraternelles, amours romantiques', *Adolescence*, 11:2 (1993), 295–314; Christopher H. Johnson, 'Siblinghood and the emotional dimensions of the new kinship system, 1800–1850', in Christopher H. Johnson and David Warren Sabean (eds), *Sibling Relations and the Transformation of European Kinship, 1300–1900* (New York: Berghahn, 2011), pp. 189–220; David Warren Sabean, 'Kinship and issues of the self in Europe around 1800', *ibid.*, pp. 221–38; Johnson, *Becoming Bourgeois*, pp. 125–70; Gay, *The Bourgeois Experience*, III, pp. 178–97.

40 Houbre, 'Amours fraternelles', 302.

41 Davidoff, *Thicker Than Water*, pp. 201–5.

42 BHVP, 16 (1), fos 119–20: LLP, no. XLIII, 20 Dec. 1847.

43 *Ibid.*, fo 189: LLP, no. XLIX, 31 July 1848. On female handwriting, see Dena Goodman, *Becoming a Woman in the Age of Letters* (Ithaca, NY: Cornell University Press, 2009), pp. 100–14; Stacey Sloboda, 'Between the mind and the hand: Gender, art and skill in eighteenth century copybooks', *Women's Writing*, 21:3 (2014), 337–56; Caroline Franklin, 'Introduction: The material culture of eighteenth-century women's writing', *Women's Writing*, 21:3 (2014), 285–9.

44 See, e.g., BHVP, 6, no. 47: Rosine Beaujean's addendum to the letter from LLP to GLP, 6 Sept. [1877].

45 BHVP, 16 (1), fos 135–8: LLP, untitled, 15 April 1848.

46 *Ibid.*, fos 189–91: LLP, untitled, 31 July 1848.

47 *Ibid.*, fos 199–201: LLP, untitled, 23 Sept. 1848.

48 Pamela Pilbeam, *Republicanism in Nineteenth Century France, 1814–1871* (Houndmills: Macmillan, 1995), pp. 143–6; H. A. C. Collingham, *The July Monarchy: A political history of France 1830–1848* (London: Longman, 1988).

49 Zeldin, *France 1848–1945*. I: *Ambition, love and politics* (Oxford: Clarendon Press, 1973), pp. 477–82; Stone, *Sons of the Revolution*, pp. 17–20.

50 Zeldin, *France*, I, pp. 484–503.

51 David Owen Evans, *Social Romanticism in France 1830–1848* (New York: Octagon Books, 1969); Crossley, 'Romanticism', pp. 715–16; Martin-Fugier, *Les Romantiques*, pp. 267–70.

52 Zeldin, *France*, I, p. 487.

53 BHVP, MS-FS-07-0017, vol. 18 (2) [hereafter BHVP, 18 (2)], fo 138: LLP, 'Xbre 1849'.

54 BHVP, 18 (2), fos 71–6: LLP, '1847'.

55 *Ibid.*, fos 108–15 (August).

56 See chapter 5 on Lincoln, chapter 9 on Schœlcher.

57 LLP, 'La Vie est de nos jours' [Jan. 1845], in *Libres Paroles*, pp. 51–61.

58　BHVP, 18 (2), fos 71–6: LLP, '1847'.
59　*Ibid.*, fos 77–83 [79].
60　*Ibid.*, fos 71–6 (76).
61　Eric Hobsbawm, *The Age of Capital, 1848–1875* [1975] (London: The Folio Society, 2005), pp. 9–28.
62　BHVP, 18 (2), fos 121–6: LLP, untitled, 1 March 1848.
63　*Ibid.*, fos 127–30: LLP, untitled, 9 March 1848.
64　Théophile Gautier, quoted in Sylvie Chevalley, 'Rachel et la Marseillaise', *1848: Révolutions et mutations au XIXe siècle*, 4 (1988), 109–111 (109).
65　BHVP, 17, fos 84–7: LLP, untitled, 9 April 1848. The annotation is in a different, perhaps feminine, hand.
66　BHVP, 18 (2), fos 121–6: LLP, untitled, 1 March 1848. See Zeldin, *France*, I, p. 485.
67　See Maurice Agulhon, *The Republic in the Village: The people of the Var from the French Revolution to the Second Republic*, trans. Janet Lloyd (Cambridge: Cambridge University Press; Paris: Editions de la maison des sciences de l'homme, 1982); Peter McPhee, *The Politics of Rural Life: Political mobilisation in the countryside, 1845–1852* (Oxford: Clarendon Press, 1992).
68　BHVP, 18 (2), fo 131: LLP, untitled, 28 March 1848. The *carmagnole* and the Phyrigian bonnet were strongly associated with the popular revolutionaries of the First Republic.
69　BHVP, 16 (1), fos 132–4: LLP, XLVIII, 14 March 1848.
70　Stone, *Sons of the Revolution*, pp. 30–31.
71　Léon Laurent-Pichat, 'Idylles de mai', in his *Chroniques rimées* (Paris: A la librairie nouvelle, 1856), pp. 244–54 (253–4). The verses in this collection were dated between 1847 and 1856.
72　BHVP, 18 (2), fos 137–42 (141): LLP, 'Xbre 1849'.
73　*Ibid.*, fo 138.
74　On the impact of the coup d'état on the republican community, see Roger Price, *The French Second Empire: An anatomy of political power* (Cambridge: Cambridge University Press, 2001), chapter 11.
75　LLP, 'Le sépulcre blanchi', in *Chroniques rimées*, pp. 283–7 (287).
76　LLP, 'L'Homme a besoin de croire [Feb. 1847],' in *Libres Paroles*, pp. 46–7.
77　BHVP, 18 (2), fos 261–2: LLP, untitled, Privas, 6 Sept. 1849.
78　Claude Bellanger et al., *Histoire générale de la presse française*. II: *De 1815 à 1871* (Paris: Presses universitaires de France, 1969), p. 357.
79　BHVP, 18 (2), fos 261–2: LLP, untitled, Privas, 6 Sept. 1849.
80　AP, Mariages, V3E/M302: Rosine Deslandes /Amédée Beaujean, 27 Nov. 1851. On Beaujean's career, see his professional file: AN F^{17}: 20117. On this marriage, see chapter 8.

81 'Jean-Henri Chevreau' and 'Julien-Théophile-Henri Chevreau', in Adolphe Robert, Edgar Bourloton et Gaston Cougny (eds), *Dictionnaire des parlementaires français depuis le 1ᵉʳ mai 1789 jusqu'au 1ᵉʳ mai 1889* (Paris: 1889–1891), II, p. 96.
82 See François Salignac de la Mothe Fénelon, 'Histoire d'Alibée, Persan', in his *Fables et opuscules divers composés pour l'éducation du Duc de Bourgogne* ... (Paris: Hachette, 1875), XXV, pp. 82–88; Jean La Fontaine, 'The shepherd and the king', in *The Complete Fables of Jean La Fontaine* (Proquest eBook central, University of Illinois Press, 2006), Book X, pp. 277–81.
83 LLP, 'Alibée', in *Chroniques rimées*, pp. 273–81 (276, 279).
84 LLP, 'A une infidèle', [April 1852], *ibid.*, pp. 265–71.
85 LLP to Théophile Gautier, 11[?] Jan. 1854, in Gautier, *Correspondance générale*, VI, no. 1979.
86 BHVP, MS-FS-07-0006, vol. 7 (hereafter BHVP, 7), fos 1–2: LLP to Camille Risler, 16 Dec. 1867.
87 LLP, Journal, 10 June, 9 July 1873; 21 Oct. 1880.
88 LLP, 'L'Homme a besoin de croire', in *Libres Paroles*, pp. 46–7.

3

'Placing our pen at the service of liberty': friendship networks and the republican press, 1851–65

In August 1853, *Le Messager des théâtres et des arts* invited subscriptions to a collection of lithographs of notable people by the prominent photographer Gaspard-Félix Tournachon (known as Nadar). The first issue, featuring literary figures, would include Léon Laurent-Pichat, his friend, Louis Ulbach, and the hero of his youth, Alphonse de Lamartine.[1] As his inclusion indicates, Laurent-Pichat's reputation in literary circles was already well established. Throughout the 1850s and 1860s, he published prolifically across many genres: poetry, novels, short fiction and criticism. His works were widely reviewed and serialised in the press. He was also active as a journalist, contributing to a variety of Parisian, provincial and foreign publications, and serving on a number of editorial boards. Moreover, he was a major financial supporter of authors and of the periodical press.

Laurent-Pichat's literary activities at this time illustrate the crucial role of the print media, and particularly republican newspapers, in opposing the Empire.[2] He and his network of activists and intellectuals were deeply engaged in the struggle for press freedom, fighting the strict censorship laws imposed by a regime determined to suppress opposition. Laurent-Pichat himself was prosecuted several times, most famously for publishing Gustave Flaubert's scandalous novel *Madame Bovary* in the pages of *La Revue de Paris*. He was twice fined and imprisoned for press offences; at other times he suffered financially when publications he had underwritten were suppressed. Given that most forms of political activity were prohibited, however, publishing remained a leading form of political action for republicans. For radicals like Laurent-Pichat, the role of the print media – like the arts more broadly – was to 'shift ideas',[3] not to indulge in 'art for art's sake'.

Exploring Laurent-Pichat's publishing activities in the 1850s and 1860s enriches our picture of opposition activity in a period when political action was heavily repressed. Moreover, it deepens our understanding of the role of friendship in ensuring the durability of opposition to the Empire. Laurent-Pichat's friendship circles in the 1860s illustrate his pivotal role, as interlocking networks of republican journalists moved from one ephemeral paper to another in a form of literary guerrilla warfare against the regime.[4] The republicans' self-appointed mission was to defend 'liberty' against 'autocracy' in all its guises. In the process, as Laurent-Pichat himself illustrates, they tentatively explored a question that preoccupied many in the wake of 1848: whether and how urban workers, whose radicalism and volatility many bourgeois republicans feared, could participate in the movement towards democracy.

The press in the shadow of 1848

France remained technically a Republic from February 1848 until the proclamation of the Second Empire in December 1852, but it was a Republic governed by monarchists with a would-be emperor as president. While press censorship had been lifted briefly after the Revolution of February 1848, it was reimposed following the June uprising and reinforced by a series of draconian decrees between the coup d'état of December 1851 and March 1852. A rigorous system involving warnings, suspensions and the closure of newspapers was instituted. Those founding or editing newspapers required official authorisation. Punitive security bonds for the political press threatened bankruptcy if the laws were infringed. Publishing political material in a 'non-political' journal was a criminal act and trial by jury was abolished for such offences. In this difficult climate, many papers self-censored in order to survive, but many others, especially political newspapers, went under. Subscriptions to opposition newspapers plummeted.[5] The fate of *La Politique nouvelle* is indicative of this trend. Founded in early March 1851, this weekly survived only eight months. When it folded in November, Laurent-Pichat was offered a replacement subscription to the less provocative weekly *L'Illustration*, modelled on the *Illustrated London News*.[6]

The main outlet for Laurent-Pichat's published writings in 1849–51 was *Le Propagateur de l'Aube* at Troyes, edited by his friend Louis Ulbach.[7] Despite the hostile environment, Laurent-Pichat found ways to express his republican principles in its pages. Like many other journalists, he reported on foreign news or set his stories in foreign places which readers might see as similar to France.[8] Between May and mid-June 1849, for instance, his short story 'Les Deux Momies' was serialised in *Le Propagateur de l'Aube*. It carried a sub-plot about student revolutionaries from Bohemia and Poland plotting a revolution, unsuccessfully, in Prague.[9] Laurent-Pichat also found a vehicle for radical political commentary by translating the verse of foreign writers. Presenting the poetry of Ferdinand Freiligrath and Alfred Meissner, for example, publicised their commitment to the democratic struggle in their own countries.[10] Laurent-Pichat thus promoted ideas with which he sympathised, but at one remove.

These foreign authors were kindred spirits of Laurent-Pichat. Freiligrath, a friend of Karl Marx, spent many years in exile and his poetry was banned in his homeland. Meissner, born in Austria but raised in Bohemia, joined 'Young Bohemia', the nationalist literary movement. Forced to flee to Paris in 1847, he mixed there with Victor Hugo, George Sand and Alfred de Musset, as well as with Polish émigrés like Adam Mickiewicz.[11] A poem written by Laurent-Pichat in July 1849 suggests that he, too, was a friend of Meissner. Reflecting on the nationalist struggles across the Austrian Empire in that year, it asked whether Kossuth would lead the Hungarians to independence; whether the Poles, 'tossed from exile to exile' like the Jews, would 'reconquer Canaan by force'.[12] The poem concludes:

> It's only a friend, my friend!
> He comes knocking at your door,
> Bringing you
> A jaunty and high-spirited greeting;
> Calmly and courageously he casts
> His voice into the storm, –
> Like a flower into a hurricane!

Untitled in manuscript form, this poem was titled 'To Alfred Meissner' when Laurent-Pichat published it in 1856.[13]

Several 'republican ballads' by Laurent-Pichat also appeared in *Le Propagateur de l'Aube* in 1850–51. These extracts from a longer work show him beginning to grapple with the implications for republicanism of the militancy of urban workers that had shocked many bourgeois in 1848.[14] This issue would be hotly debated in the 1860s as republicanism became a more powerful political force in France. The ideal of class harmony and the promise of limited reform, intended to head off independent mobilisation by workers, would then become common themes among bourgeois republicans.[15] Laurent-Pichat foreshadowed that perspective in 1850–51, perhaps inspired by the idealistic and Romantic republicanism that had exhilarated him in February 1848.

The most significant of Laurent-Pichat's 'republican ballads' was the 'Chronicle of Jacques Bonhomme'. Over one hundred pages long when published in full in 1856, it was written in ten sections between November 1850 and August 1851.[16] 'Jacques Bonhomme', a familiar name for the archetypal French peasant, recounts his suffering at the hands of greedy rural landowners, his cynicism about the Catholic Church and the hardship endured by his wife, Jeanne (another archetype). A crucial section sub-titled 'Le Cadet' (The Younger Brother) appeared in *Le Propagateur de l'Aube* on 17 December 1850. It juxtaposes Bonhomme with 'Jean-François Populus', a swaggering figure representing the urban worker. Populus, the self-proclaimed 'king of February', boasts to Jacques Bonhomme: 'Indeed, the Republic is my great conquest ... / I chased off two reactionary princes: / July [1830] and February [1848] are two fine stripes I've won.'[17] Significantly, the ballad makes no mention of the uprising of June 1848. But Jacques Bonhomme, the wise older brother, warns the younger upstart to be 'patient': 'Let's make ourselves respected ... We've made them fear us; we must make them envy us.' After all, as Jacques Bonhomme declares, 'When your heart is good, your conscience clean, even with an empty stomach, you're worth more than many.'[18]

Laurent-Pichat had yet to make the acquaintance of the artisanal republicans whose electoral campaigns he would finance in the 1860s.[19] His patronising stance reflected not only the gulf of understanding between the classes but also the lingering anxiety of many bourgeois republicans about workers' expectations and potential militancy. Louis Ulbach adopted a similar perspective in his fictional letters to another imaginary urban worker, 'Jacques Souffrant', which appeared in *Le Propagateur de l'Aube* around the same time. He likewise affirmed the importance of 'patience and labour' as the conditions on which 'the people' could claim 'rights [and] liberties'.[20] But events had already undermined the argument that good behaviour would give 'the people' what they sought: a 'democratic and social' republic – their rallying cry in 1848.

While Laurent-Pichat's lengthy chronicle urged social order and at least tolerance of the regime, it criticised priests, condemned the exploitation of peasants and urban workers, and expressed scorn for both past rulers and others keen to try the crown for size. It is not surprising, therefore, that *Le Propagateur de l'Aube* was shut down, along with hundreds of other republican papers, following the coup d'état of December 1851. Laurent-Pichat's writings contributed to that closure.

La Revue de Paris and the politics of censorship

After the closure of *Le Propagateur de l'Aube*, Laurent-Pichat had made his way to *La Revue de Paris*, which became the main outlet for his journalism between 1852 and 1858.[21] A leading Parisian monthly, *La Revue de Paris* was far more prestigious than a provincial newspaper and it was more literary in focus. It published 'illustrious names' like Théophile Gautier, Honoré de Balzac, George Sand, Alphonse de Lamartine and Charles Baudelaire.[22] That Laurent-Pichat was admitted to the eminent literary company of *La Revue de Paris* illustrates his growing literary reputation and his expanding friendship networks in literary circles. His contributions included verse, fiction, book reviews and commentary. Most of the poems that would feature in his collection *Chroniques rimées* in 1856 first appeared there. Some of his short stories, later published as *Cartes sur la table*, were serialised in *La Revue* in 1853 and 1854, while his first novel, *La Païenne,* was also serialised there between December 1856 and April 1857.[23]

Laurent-Pichat joined the editorial board of *La Revue* in January 1853, taking his place alongside Théophile Gautier, Maxime Du Camp and Louis de Cormenin (who soon withdrew). He surely played a role in creating the position of Director of *La Revue*, to which his friend Louis Ulbach was appointed in October 1853.[24] Laurent-Pichat's invitation to join the editorial board was probably due in part to his wealth: his support was equivalent to a line of credit in case of necessity. In 1856 *La Revue* was incorporated as a limited partnership, with Du Camp and Laurent-Pichat as joint owners.[25] From February 1856, Laurent-Pichat's name appeared alone as Managing Editor of *La Revue*. Du Camp and Ulbach continued to play important roles behind the scenes and a committee shared the editorial burden. As Managing Editor, however, Laurent-Pichat was legally responsible for ensuring that the censorship regulations were observed.

La Revue declared itself to be 'a purely literary work' so it was not required to post a security bond.[26] But it was required to avoid politics as well as 'political and social economy', which were defined very broadly.[27] Given the constant risk of prosecution, the editorial committee exercised caution about what they published. In March 1856, for instance, they rejected an article by a 'Monsieur Thoré', noting: 'The exceptional position in which this honourable writer finds himself in the context of the legislation that currently governs the press seems not to allow the proposed article to be published.' The author was probably Théophile Thoré, a veteran political activist who had been proscribed by the regime and was living in Belgium.[28] To have published such a writer would have been to invite prosecution.

Laurent-Pichat's own contributions to *La Revue* also reflected caution about legal requirements. He carefully avoided confronting the regime directly. For instance, his short story 'Le Secret de Polichinelle', serialised there in 1854, was set in the aftermath of the uprising of June 1848; its theme was the injustice of the repression that followed that uprising.[29] But the story condemned past events and a regime no longer in power. Similarly, in his novel *La Païenne*, democratic ideas were associated with America rather than with France. Both works passed uncensored.

The authorities acted, however, when Gustave Flaubert's novel *Madame Bovary* was serialised in *La Revue* in late 1856.[30] Maxime Du Camp, a close friend of Flaubert, had been keen to publish the novel, but he was no less alarmed than Ulbach and Laurent-Pichat on reading the text.[31] Flaubert was hostile to making changes and eventually distanced himself from the version that appeared in

La Revue, from which more than seventy-one passages were cut. Nevertheless, in January 1857, Laurent-Pichat was charged, along with Flaubert and the printer, Auguste-Alexis Pillet, with 'affronting public and religious morality and offending moral standards' by publishing the book.[32]

This prosecution is a cause célèbre in literary history. The novel's stylistic innovation, its vivid portrayal of stultifying bourgeois provincial life and a woman's fatal rejection of social norms have seen it declared a turning point in literature; its unsuccessful prosecution has been hailed as a landmark in the struggle for freedom of literary expression.[33] While *La Revue de Paris* cautiously welcomed the literary innovation of *Madame Bovary*, however, it seems unlikely that the editors were defending freedom of literary expression in publishing it, given the substantial cuts they made to the book. Ulbach, for one, found the work 'strange'; it offended his 'artistic taste'.[34] Nor was publication likely intended as a deliberate challenge to sexual mores, even if debate at the trial centred on passages the prosecutor deemed offensive.

The editors' decision to publish the novel was part of a broader political battle against the Empire and its political ally, the Catholic Church, as well as its regime of censorship. Publishing even an edited version of the novel, with its unsparing portrait of the family and the Church, allowed a critique of bourgeois and clerical hypocrisy, although that critique remained more cautious than Flaubert himself had intended.[35] The editors certainly believed that their prosecution for 'moral' infringements was merely a pretext for a politically motivated attack on a publication known for its republican and 'advanced' views.[36] *La Revue* had already been warned twice before this incident. However, the judge accepted the defence case that the novel, with the ghastly death of Emma Bovary, presented a moral warning rather seeking to titillate. The defendants were acquitted.[37]

La Revue de Paris was nevertheless on the censors' watch list, and political infractions, which required no court case, proved an easier target than moral ones. In January 1858, *La Revue*'s 'Fortnightly Chronicle' included a section by Laurent-Pichat headed 'Political Review'. As Laurent-Pichat's private papers note, this was 'one of the main articles targeted by the suppression decree of January 1858'.[38]

This 'Political Review' defended key republican principles in what amounted to a condemnation of the Empire. While Laurent-Pichat focused, as usual, on examples drawn from other countries, his message was transparent. He argued, first, for the inevitable decline of autocracy by comparing the 'great countries, [that] after apparently fruitless revolutions, seem to slumber in indifference', with Piedmont and Belgium, small nations whose 'growing energy' he attributed to 'the development of their institutions, founded on liberty'. Similarly, contrasting what he saw as the declining fortunes of Russia with the rise of England and the United States, he proclaimed 'the growing prosperity of free States, the moral ascendancy of their governments, the extension of their influence'. By implication, given the suppression of liberties under the Empire, France was out of step with 'the march of ideas' and was falling into decline both materially and morally. Furthermore, by raising the issue of clerical interference in recent elections in Piedmont, Laurent-Pichat not only reminded readers of France's pivotal role in supporting the papal states against the Italian nationalists, but also implicitly criticised the close ties between the Empire and the Church in France. Like his sardonic portrait of priests in his earlier chronicle of Jacques Bonhomme, this was a clear statement of the anticlericalism that Laurent-Pichat would later express even more vigorously.

Laurent-Pichat deliberately tempted fate in this column, particularly in a literary journal that was required to eschew politics. Reaction was swift, and *La Revue de Paris* was suppressed on 18 January 1858.[39] Laurent-Pichat paid a high price financially. A friend wrote to him from Angers: 'What you tell me, sir, about having made a loss of 80,000 francs pains me enormously. I deeply regret [the disappearance of] *La Revue de Paris*, which nothing can replace'.[40] Most would have been bankrupted by that outcome, although Laurent-Pichat was not. Nor was he deterred from continuing to support the voice of opposition. Three years later, however, as another investment in the republican press teetered on the brink, he was still smarting from this blow to his finances and his optimism.

'Shifting ideas': the politics of literature and the arts

As he moved into the literary and political society of mid-nineteenth-century Paris, Laurent-Pichat found friends and associates among those who shared his passionate view that literature, along with painting and sculpture, should serve a moral – and thereby political – purpose. It should be an expression of principles and beliefs. 'Think as you live, otherwise be silent', he had written in 1847.[41] This aphorism guided both his own literary activities and his expectations of others. He reiterated in 1862: 'I demand that every poet have an elevated, living ideal, whether that be called virtue, morality [or] religion. I call it duty'.[42] Similarly, he wrote that 'A novel must be a study of morals or of characters. A lesson must emerge from the plot.'[43] The programme of his new literary journal, *La Réforme littéraire*, likewise declared: 'The true writer must possess a moral ideal and impose himself, in a certain fashion, on those he addresses.'[44]

These views positioned Laurent-Pichat unequivocally in a major nineteenth-century divide between the artistic radicals who championed 'art for art's sake' – the view that art should be judged solely in aesthetic terms rather than by its use value – and those (like him) who emphasised the social role and responsibility of the arts.[45] A social perspective in literature underpinned contemporary trends in realism and naturalism, which laid bare the daily realities of life and analysed social values and practices. Laurent-Pichat's perspective was closer to that of Lamartine and Hugo, however, than to that of Balzac or Zola. He remained in the tradition of the Romantics, whose social aspirations, tinged with spiritual values, made them 'apostles of the emancipation of the people and of social revolution'.[46] For him, the arts had a political role: they should help to redress social injustice.

In assigning this political role to the arts, Laurent-Pichat also followed in a republican tradition shaped by belief in social progress. Many republicans were influenced by the philosophy of 'positivism', which proclaimed that societies gradually evolved from a metaphysical stage when religious ideas dominated, to a 'positive' stage when knowledge derived from science and rational thought would prevail. Republicanism, based on principles of liberty and democracy, was seen as the inevitable product of this historical process.[47] As Laurent-Pichat wrote: 'From all directions peoples are advancing towards these three terms: Unity, Independence, Liberty. Liberty is the end point.'[48] If some writers (like Flaubert, in *Madame Bovary*) emphasised the struggle for creative 'liberty' – freedom from the strictures of the classical tradition – Laurent-Pichat's emphasis on 'liberty' was more political. He assigned the arts a major role in the struggle for 'liberty' and the Republic.

In the emerging democratic society of the mid-nineteenth century, according to Laurent-Pichat, the arts should drive progress, 'express[ing] only representations and symbols that exalt Justice and Liberty'.[49] They should engage with contemporary issues rather than seeking inspiration in the past. He set the example himself, continuing to eulogise the struggle of European peoples for nationhood.[50] As in his youth, Laurent-Pichat again praised Byron, who had been prepared to die for Greek independence, and dedicated his 1859 novel, *La Sibylle,* to the Italian patriots seeking independence from Austria: 'I have written these pages with profound tenderness', he declared. 'I have put into them all my affection for the independence of a nation that I love'.[51]

Laurent-Pichat applied similar ideas to the visual arts, about which he was also passionate. He set out his ideas principally in *L'Art et les artistes en France*, as well as in his published commentaries on the annual Salons in Paris and Lyon. Like many republicans, he extolled François Rude's sculpture 'Departure of the Volunteers of 1792': it was 'conceived by the soul of a citizen', he declared, and expressed the virtues of patriotism in the new age.[52] Similarly, he admired paintings, like those of Jean-François Millet and other painters of the Barbizon School, whose 'naturalist' style was based on direct observation of contemporary subjects and ordinary people.[53] Laurent-Pichat urged both writers and painters to reflect on the issues raised by advancing industrialisation, which provided dramatic subject matter for the arts. Like his contemporaries Eugène Sue and George Sand, Laurent-Pichat saw workers as important subjects for literature:

> Those who are inspired by the wonders of industry, will find energetic and original heroes in the people, the centaurs of matter, athletes of the new struggles, tamers of the steam monsters ... Who is it that reins them in, climbs on their backs and applies the brake? – It's the worker. The poetry of such combats demands to be expressed. It's a new world for the imagination; it is the most beautiful poetic utopia.[54]

Laurent-Pichat went further than many, however, in his passionate insistence on the moral duty of writers, whom he charged with providing examples of righteous behaviour, positive moral choices and just political struggles:

> Seeking justice for the oppressed nations, Poland and Italy, summoning everyone's pity for the sufferings of the workers, warning the people about revolution, feeling sympathy for those who suffer, always throwing himself into the midst of formidable conflicts and murderous struggles ... I think that is a fine role for the poet.[55]

In particular, Laurent-Pichat urged writers and painters to help shape the ideas and aspirations of the masses, whom he saw as politically naïve. His stance remained paternalistic. Poets should mix with the people 'in order to explain to them in a manly fashion the secret of their suffering, to share their sufferings and applaud them lovingly, to speak to them of their country, of humanity, to give the great concepts they love their true meaning, an immortal form'.[56]

The reception of Laurent-Pichat's ideas on the moral role of literature and the arts highlighted the political issues that were at stake. Conservative critics poured scorn on his ideas and argued that the solution to social problems lay in a return to traditional social hierarchy based on religion and monarchy.[57] However, many on the Left shared Laurent-Pichat's views. Eugène Pelletan likened Laurent-Pichat to famous Revolutionary generals, calling him 'the Hoche or Marceau of poetry'.[58] Nevertheless, as responses to Laurent-Pichat's *Chroniques rimées* indicate, caution prevailed in the decades that followed 1848. Reviews in progressive newspapers praised Laurent-Pichat for addressing social issues and admired his portrait of the patient and longsuffering peasant, Jacques Bonhomme. They were silent, however, on the figure of Jean François Populus, the urban revolutionary.[59] The danger of prosecution surely governed their responses, but so too did lingering concern among bourgeois republicans about popular radicalism. Many shared Laurent-Pichat's caution and his message of restraint.

Laurent-Pichat himself remained passionate about his moral duty as a writer. As he noted in 1862: 'I am reproached with demanding that the poet be a man of politics and with demanding social convictions from him! ... It's dignity that I demand of poets; it's honour; it's strength.' But he also argued that without commitment to a cause, a poet could only 'move around words, not shift ideas'.[60] Since he himself certainly sought to 'shift ideas', he was unrepentant

Figure 3.1 Léon Laurent-Pichat, *c.* 1860.

about his own politicised writing, even if it deterred 'the great mass of readers'. 'We will continue to place our pen at the service of liberty,' he declared.[61]

'At the service of liberty': the republican press in the 1860s

In 1859, Laurent-Pichat wrote to his fellow republican activist Jules Ferry, soliciting his contributions to the periodical *La Libre Recherche*: 'We dream of a weekly paper, devoted to pure criticism, until the day when we can fly a daily political flag. When will that be?'[62] His use of the plural form was not a rhetorical flourish but highlighted the co-operative effort of a group of republicans to promote their political message through this periodical. Journalists worked across multiple titles and relied on circles of friendship to keep republican papers alive. Laurent-Pichat's experiences with *Le Propagateur de l'Aube* and *La Revue de Paris* – both closed by the government – had already indicated that the right to 'fly a daily political flag' still lay in the future. But despite the weight of censorship and surveillance, journalism remained one of the main avenues for promoting the republican cause and affirming a republican identity. A battle of wits was engaged: as each newspaper or periodical was suppressed or driven out of existence, friendship networks ensured that another was opened as republicans regrouped to continue the struggle. Laurent-Pichat was a pivotal figure in that journalistic network.

Books and newspapers published outside France played an important role in republican struggles against the Empire in the 1860s and helped to maintain links between republicans at home and abroad. Those writing outside France were also beyond the reach of the French censors and hence were free to pillory the Emperor and his regime, as Victor Hugo did to devastating effect in *Napoleon the Small*.[63] A game of cat and mouse pitted French writers attacking the Empire from without against French officials endeavouring to intercept contraband literature entering the country.[64] Laurent-Pichat made sure to purchase a copy of *Napoleon the Small*, along with other banned republican works, when he visited Switzerland in 1862, gleefully noting that they passed through customs undetected.[65]

As well as subscribing to several German-language newspapers, Laurent-Pichat wrote for a number of publications produced outside France.[66] He was a correspondent for *Le Confédéré de Fribourg*, financed by Jean-Baptiste Charras, one of six republican representatives in the French National Assembly proscribed at the coup d'état. Another exiled representative, Pascal Duprat, edited *La Libre Recherche* in Brussels.[67] In writing to Ferry in 1859, Laurent-Pichat was trying to enlist more correspondents for this paper. He explained: '*La Libre Recherche* is the raft on which almost all the shipwrecked souls of *La Revue de Paris* have taken refuge. You see that we waylay everyone. Belgium is free; we write in Belgium.'[68] Laurent-Pichat also served on the administrative committee of *L'Association*, another publication based in Belgium, which was founded in 1864 as a mouthpiece for the co-operative movement.[69] His fellow-contributors included Charles-Louis Chassin (who also wrote for *Le Confédéré de Fribourg*), Eugène Despois (who would later join Laurent-Pichat at *La Réforme littéraire*) and Henri Lefort, a militant republican banished following the coup d'état (and brother-in-law of Laurent-Pichat's sister Herminie). Laurent-Pichat and Lefort would co-operate on a number of republican projects over the years.

The most influential of these foreign-based papers, *L'Indépendance belge*, was also based in Brussels, where it was edited in the 1860s by Marseilles-born Léon Bérardi. The paper had many foreign contributors, including French *proscrits*, and it had more than 2,500 subscribers in France in 1865, including Laurent-Pichat.[70] To the annoyance of French Interior Minister Victor de Persigny, it was 'awaited impatiently in Paris every day'.[71] But the threat of seizure at the border hung over it constantly, and the editor exercised some self-censorship. In 1862, for instance, Bérardi declined to publish an article by Laurent-Pichat on divisions within the French government: 'Publishing it would inevitably lead to the paper being seized in Paris'.[72]

Laurent-Pichat also supported the cause of 'liberty' during the 1860s by aiding the literary and journalistic ventures of others. Since his time at *La Revue de Paris*, authors had brought him their books hoping he would write a review; others brought him manuscripts hoping he would support their publication.[73] They paid Laurent-Pichat homage and asked him to preface their works.[74] Given his wealth, he was approached regularly for subventions. Some proposals, such as the plan by *La Petite Bibliothèque* to publish cheap literary editions, took his fancy; others he rejected.[75] He was also asked on numerous occasions to purchase or invest in newspapers and periodicals, including *La Gazette des beaux-arts* and *L'Echo des provinces*.[76] He carefully recorded the amounts when he did contribute but rejected many such approaches. Laurent-Pichat was clearly sceptical, for instance, when M. de Morville, who sought funding for *Le Message,* claimed that it would 'realise 40 thousand in four years!'[77] Similarly, proposals to establish mass-circulation newspapers probably seemed like poor investments, and did not accord with Laurent-Pichat's interest in political and literary questions.[78]

Laurent-Pichat nevertheless donated his time and his literary skills, as well as his money, to a number of newspapers and periodicals during the 1860s. His friend François Favre pointed out in 1862, on hearing that he was ill: 'You work too hard, and even while travelling or on vacation you have perhaps tried to continue the forced labour that you subject yourself to in Paris.'[79] Laurent-Pichat served on the editorial board of *La Critique française,* founded in 1860, which set out to 'reflect the intellectual movement of the era as in a mirror': an impossible task under the censorship laws.[80] He contributed one thousand francs to help rescue the struggling *Courrier du dimanche* in early 1862, and gave the editors of the ephemeral *Tablettes de Pierrot* a guarantee for 180 francs for their printer.[81] He responded positively when Alphonse Peyrat requested support to establish *L'Avenir national* in November 1864, purchasing shares as well as contributing articles for the paper. He was perhaps attracted by the paper's strongly anticlerical and even 'Jacobin' tone.[82]

Laurent-Pichat's most significant journalistic roles in this period were with the periodicals *La Correspondance littéraire* and *La Réforme littéraire.* He was actively involved from 1861 with *La Correspondance littéraire,* directed by Ludovic Lalanne, and his name appeared on the masthead.[83] But his prominence may have owed more to his financial support than his literary contributions, which were limited to book reviews. In October 1861, he promised to contribute one thousand francs for 'arrears' and the same sum during the year ahead to ensure the periodical's success.[84] His donations continued in subsequent years. He recorded in April 1865, shortly before *La Correspondance littéraire* shut down, that he had given the managing editor a thousand francs to pay the printer.[85]

Laurent-Pichat was a key figure at *La Réforme littéraire* from its inception.[86] Enlisting subscribers for the new periodical proved difficult, however, and he perhaps feared losing money as he had on *La Revue de Paris*. After an unproductive afternoon visiting potential subscribers in November 1861, he recorded: 'One subscription. If we seek our two thousand in this manner, it will take a long time. Bitterness of *La Revue de Paris*, I remember you!'[87] Despite messages of support and offers to contribute, the periodical did not flourish and Laurent-Pichat again sought Jules Ferry's support for the 'poor little thing' that was 'growing slowly in the shade'.[88]

Laurent-Pichat authored the address 'To the reader' that opened the first issue of *La Réforme littéraire* in January 1862, setting the tone for a periodical with high-minded aims: 'to defend progress and seize the ideal', to promote literature that had 'confidence in its purpose', and to restore a sense of moral duty to literary criticism.[89] While this was a serious literary review, however, it took a clearly republican line and its radical tone, certain to attract police attention, perhaps frightened off subscribers. The contributors were a 'who's who' of republican activists. They included Laurent-Pichat's longtime friend Louis Ulbach and emerging friends like Etienne Arago and Auguste Scheurer-Kestner, as well as the notable republicans Paul-Armand Challemel-Lacour, Eugène Pelletan, Victor Chauffour and Eugène Despois. Victor Hugo's name appeared, when Laurent-Pichat presented extracts from *Les Misérables*. Henri Lefort was secretary of the review, and contributed a biography of the well-known revolutionary Armand Barbès.[90]

La Réforme littéraire gave coverage to controversial ideas, as when it reviewed Clémence Royer's translation of Darwin's *Origin of Species*. Laurent-Pichat himself took every opportunity to keep political issues to the fore, even daring to refer to the coup d'état and the repression that followed. His report on an 'Excursion to Geneva and Veytaux', for instance, was ostensibly a travel narrative. But the itinerary was highly symbolic for republicans: Geneva and Veytaux were sites of pilgrimage, sheltering the exiled leaders Jules

Barni and Edgar Quinet respectively. Laurent-Pichat's articles put his encounters with those revered figures centre stage.[91]

In a provocative move in 1862, Laurent-Pichat re-published in *La Réforme littéraire* some poetry from the student newspaper *Le Travail*, whose editors had had the temerity to organise a demonstration at the Bastille to commemorate the Revolution of February 1848. Introducing these verses, Laurent-Pichat proclaimed: 'This is an opportunity for us to demonstrate our sympathies for a paper, several of whose editors have just been arrested'. He took care to disqualify himself from judging 'the political side of the question' but expressed sympathy for 'those in need of support and consolation', a hollow justification.[92] His colleagues were alarmed: 'Laprade heard that I had been arrested. He came to see if it was true ... Duboy, and also Hérold, think that I'm going to be hauled before the magistrate's court for the article I wrote on the students'.[93] Surprisingly, perhaps, he was not. But in August 1862, when *La Réforme littéraire* had been in existence for barely eight months, the printer refused to accept it any longer 'for reasons of personal safety'.[94]

Consistent with Laurent-Pichat's determination to keep the cause of 'liberty' to the fore, his contributions to the newspaper *Le Phare de la Loire* were also highly provocative. This paper was reputedly one of the most radical of the republican organs. Officially warned in 1862 and again in 1863, it was then suspended for two months. Perhaps it owed its survival to the fact that, in the royalist region around Nantes where it was published, it counterbalanced the more numerous monarchist papers.[95] As well as publishing on literature, Laurent-Pichat addressed political topics in *Le Phare*. Again, he came back to the fate of Poland and the ongoing struggle in Italy.[96]

In this provincial area dominated by conservative forces, republican readers of *Le Phare de la Loire* were no doubt receptive to the anticlerical views that Laurent-Pichat expressed in its pages. Republicans had long been outraged by the Emperor's support for the papacy: most egregiously, Napoleon III had sent French troops to protect the Papal States against the Italian nationalists. Republicans were further outraged by the papal encyclical 'Quanta Cura' (condemning modern errors) of December 1864, which rejected 'progress, liberty and modern civilisation'.[97] It denounced freedom of thought and expression, secular education and the separation of Church and State: ideas sacred to republicans. Writing in *Le Phare*, Laurent-Pichat was highly critical of this encyclical: 'It damns, reproves and condemns civilisation. We have faith in civilisation ... We therefore reject the encyclical and distance ourselves from its defunct doctrines, in order to advance in confidence and in liberty ... To us, it's a choice between life and death'. He wrote two more critiques of the encyclical in the weeks that followed.[98]

But Laurent-Pichat completely overstepped the mark in October 1865 when he published an extract from a satirical verse by Marc Monnier entitled *Paillasse* (Whore). Published in Geneva and banned in France, it parodied France's relationship with the Pope. The extract that Laurent-Pichat inserted in *Le Phare de la Loire* referred directly to the encyclical. The character Arnolphe, described as a monk but standing for the Pope, states:

> It's I who am the true whore!
> /.../
> I have come to declare to you:
> That the monk's habit has the scent of amber,
> That spring arrives in December,
> That peace reigns between kings,
> Finally that two times two is three.
> But if anyone ever has the temerity
> To tell you, on the contrary,
> That the monk's habit sometimes smells foul,
> That December is a vile month,
> That kings are known to wage war,
> Finally that two times two is four,
> He will roast paralysed in hell
> /.../
> Believe blindly what I tell you
> And you will go to Paradise.[99]

Twelve days later, Laurent-Pichat noted in his diary: 'Etienne [Arago] came to get me. [Received a] writ for the prosecution of *Le Phare*.'[100] In November, Laurent-Pichat and the managing editor of the paper, Evariste Mangin, were tried in Nantes, charged with: '1. Having aroused hatred and contempt for the government of the Emperor; 2. Having held the Catholic religion in derision' by publishing this piece. On 21 November, they were found guilty on both counts. Laurent-Pichat was fined one thousand francs and sentenced to three months in prison; Mangin received a fine of five hundred francs and a month in prison.[101] On 20 December 1865, Laurent-Pichat reported to Sainte-Pélagie, where political prisoners were held, to serve his sentence.

In the 1850s and 1860s, Laurent-Pichat gradually emerged onto the national stage as a writer of some repute. His publications and activities were reported in the press and his image became familiar to the reading public. He was also a writer with a strong political agenda, who was well embedded in networks of republican journalism. His friendships in these circles would strengthen through his period of imprisonment and underpin his ongoing activities as writer and political figure into the 1870s.

Through his publishing activities, Laurent-Pichat articulated his passion for republican principles, a passion that eventually – perhaps inevitably – led to a prison sentence. In going to prison in 1865, Laurent-Pichat paid his dues to the republican cause like many other prisoners. But his contribution to that cause in the 1860s was far from ordinary. Without Laurent-Pichat's remarkable and diverse role – as journalist, subscriber, patron, financial supporter and editor – the strength and resilience of the opposition press as the voice of 'liberty' under the Empire would have been greatly reduced.

Notes

1 'Panthéon Nadar', *Messager des théâtres et des arts*, 14 Aug. 1853.
2 Bellanger et al., *Histoire générale*, II, pp. 13–28; 249–83; Price, *French Second Empire*, pp. 355–64; Iouda Tchernoff, *Le Parti républicain sous le Second Empire, documents et souvenirs* (Paris: A. Pedone, 1906), chapters 8, 14.
3 Léon Laurent-Pichat, preface to *Les Poètes de Combat* (Paris: Collection Hetzel, 1862), p. 4.
4 See Claude Bellanger, 'Journalistes républicains sous le Second Empire avec des documents inédits', *Etudes de presse*, nouvelle série, 6:9 (1954), 3–11.
5 Christophe Charle, *Le Siècle de la presse, 1830–1939* (Paris: Editions du Seuil, 2004), pp. 91–4; Bellanger et al., *Histoire générale*, II, pp. 219–73; Irene O. Collins, *The Government and the Newspaper Press in France, 1814–1871* (Oxford: Oxford University Press, 1959), esp. pp. 111–28.

6 AN 248AP/1: A. Enfantin to LLP, 19 Nov. 1851. On *L'Illustration*, see Bellanger et al., *Histoire générale*, II, pp. 300–301.
7 Gustave Vapereau, *Dictionnaire universel des contemporains*, 3e édition (Paris: L. Hachette, 1865), pp. 1754–5; Adolphe Bitard, *Dictionnaire général de biographie contemporaine française et étrangère* (Paris: A. Lévy et Cie, 1887), p. 500.
8 Charle, *Le Siècle de la presse*, p. 94.
9 LLP, 'Les Deux momies', *Propagateur de l'Aube*, 25, 28–31 May, 1–11 June 1849; also in Léon Laurent-Pichat, *Commentaires de la vie* (Paris: Alphonse Lemerre, 1868), pp. 205–331, where it is dated 1850.
10 LLP, 'Feuilleton', *Le Propagateur de l'Aube*, 31 (1850), nos 24 (29 Jan.), 73 (29 March), 171 (25 July).
11 www.britannica.com/biography/Ferdinand-Freiligrath; 'Alfred von Meissner', in Henry Garland and Mary Garland (eds), *The Oxford Companion of German Literature*, 3rd edn, online 2005: www.oxfordreference.com
12 BHVP, 17, fos 94–5: LLP, untitled, 19 July 1849. This poem carried an epigraph from Freiligrath.
13 'A Alfred Meissner', in LLP, *Chroniques rimées*, pp. 255–63.
14 LLP, Feuilleton, *Le Propagateur de l'Aube*, 17 Dec. 1850; 10 Feb. 1851.
15 Stone, *Sons of the Revolution*, pp. 56–8; Price, *French Second Empire*, pp. 339–43 and chapter 12; Tchernoff, *Le Parti républicain*, chapter 12.
16 LLP, 'Chronique rimée de Jacques Bonhomme', in *Chroniques rimées*, pp. 111– 233.
17 *Ibid.*, pp. 193–201 (195–6).
18 *Ibid.*, p. 201.
19 See chapter 5.
20 L. Ulbach, *Lettres à Jacques Souffrant, ouvrier* (Paris: Garnier Frères, 1851), p. ix, originally in *Le Propagateur de l'Aube*, Jan.–June 1851. These letters were fictional replies to L. Ulbach, *La Politique à l'atelier: Lettres de Jacques Souffrant, ouvrier* (Troyes: Vigreux-Jamais, 1850), originally in *Le Propagateur de l'Aube*, June 1850.
21 See Michael Palmer, 'Revue de Paris, La,' in France (ed.), *New Oxford Companion*, p. 696.
22 T. Gautier, 'Liminaire,' *Revue de Paris*, Oct. 1851, p. 10.
23 Léon Laurent-Pichat, *La Païenne* (Paris: A la librairie nouvelle, 1857).
24 The final pages of each issue list the personnel. The catalogue of the BnF does not name Laurent-Pichat as an editor; nor does the entry on *La Revue de Paris* in France (ed.), *New Oxford Companion*, p. 696.

25 'Société en commandite pour l'exploitation de la Revue de Paris … 25 fév. 1856', *Revue de Paris*, April 1856.
26 Gautier, 'Liminaire', *Revue de Paris*, Oct. 1851, p. 11.
27 Bellanger et al., *Histoire générale*, II, pp. 283–304; Collins, *The Government and the Newspaper Press*, pp. 116–17.
28 BHVP, MS-FS-07-0011, vol. 14 (hereafter BHVP, 14), fo 12: Minutes, editorial committee, 4 March 1856. On Thoré, see A. Saint-Ferréol, *Les Proscrits français en Belgique: ou la Belgique contemporaine vue à travers l'exil* (Brussels: C. Muquardt, 1870), p. 65; Nord, *Republican Moment*, p. 192.
29 LLP, 'Le Secret de Polichinelle', *Revue de Paris*, Oct.–Dec. 1854. Also in *Cartes sur la table*, pp. 1–305.
30 *Revue de Paris*, Oct.–Dec. 1856.
31 Dominick LaCapra, *Madame Bovary on Trial* (Ithaca, NY: Cornell University Press, 1986), pp. 21–2.
32 William Olmsted, *The Censorship Effect: Baudelaire, Flaubert, and the Formation of French Modernism* (Oxford: Oxford University Press, 2016), pp. 42–3; Flaubert to Laurent-Pichat, 7 Dec. 1856; Flaubert to Louis Bouilhet, 12 Dec. 1856; Maxime Du Camp to Flaubert, 14 July 1856, in Gustave Flaubert, *Correspondance*, II (July 1851–Dec. 1858), édition établie, présentée et annotée par Jean Bruneau (Paris: Gallimard, 1980), pp. 649–51, 869; and notes pp. 1327–1330, 1460.
33 LaCapra, *Madame Bovary*; Christine Haynes, 'The politics of publishing in the Second Empire: The trial of *Madame Bovary* revisited', French Politics, Culture and Society, 23:2 (2005), 1–27; Diana Knight, '*Madame Bovary*', in France (ed.) *New Oxford Companion*, pp. 482–3.
34 Quoted in LaCapra, *Madame Bovary*, p. 22.
35 LaCapra, *Madame Bovary*, pp. 7, 18–19.
36 *Ibid.*, p. 22; Maxime Du Camp, *Souvenirs littéraires*, quoted in Haynes, 'The politics of publishing', p. 14.
37 *Gazette des tribunaux*, 9 Feb. 1857, copy in BHVP, 14, fo 22. See also Gustave Flaubert, Madame Bovary, mœurs de province, *suivie des réquisitoire, plaidoirie et jugement du procès intenté à l'auteur avec introduction, notes et variantes par Edouard Maynal* (Paris: Garnier frères, 1957), pp. 397–9; Diana Knight, '*Madame Bovary*', in France (ed.) *New Oxford Companion*, pp. 482–3.
38 BHVP, 14, fo 4: 'Articles écrits par Monsieur Laurent-Pichat dans la *Revue de Paris* du mois d'octobre 1851 au mois de février 1858' (apparently in the hand of Laurent-Pichat's daughter, Geneviève).

39 BHVP, 14, fo 18: 'Acte entre Laurent-Pichat et Maxime Du Camp relatif à la liquidation de la société en commandite pour l'exploitation de *La Revue de Paris*', 6 April 1858.
40 AN 248AP/1: Leroyer de Chantepie to LLP, Angers, 22 April 1862.
41 LLP, 'L'Homme a besoin de croire', in his *Libres Paroles* (Paris: Comptoir des imprimeurs unis, 1847), p. 47.
42 LLP, Les Poètes de combat (Paris: Collection Hetzel, 1862), p. 4.
43 LLP, La Païenne (Paris: Librairie nouvelle, 1857), preface, p. i.
44 LLP, preface to *La Païenne*, pp. i–ii; *ibid.*, 'Au lecteur', *La Réforme littéraire*, no. 1 (19 Jan. 1862).
45 Raluca Batranu, 'L'écrivain et la société: Le discours social dans la littérature française, du XVIIIe siècle à aujourd'hui', Thèse de doctorat, Communauté Université Grenoble Alpes, 2017, pp. 144–57; Brian Rigby, 'L'art pour l'art', in France (ed.), *New Oxford Companion*, p. 48.
46 Jean-Claude Yon, *Histoire culturelle de la France au XIXe siècle*, nouvelle édition revue et augmentée (Paris: Armand Colin, 2021), pp. 59–63, 152–6 (62).
47 Tchernoff, *Le Parti républicain*, pp. 168, 188–90, 300–301; Georges Weill, *Histoire du parti républicain en France, 1814–1870* (Paris: Félix Alcan, 1928), pp. 166–9, 185, 255, 349; John Eros, 'The positivist generation of French republicanism', *Sociological Review*, 3 (1955): 255–73.
48 LLP, *Les Poètes de combat*, p. 158.
49 Léon Laurent-Pichat, *L'Art et les artistes en France* (Paris: Dubuisson et Cie, 1859), p. 40; LLP, *Les Poètes de combat*, pp. 178–9. See Yon, *Histoire culturelle*, p. 51.
50 LLP, *Les Poètes de combat*, pp. 66–9, 121–50; Léon Laurent-Pichat, *Le Poète anonyme de la Pologne, Sigismond Krasinski* (Paris: Imp. Dubuisson et Cie, 1861).
51 LLP, *Les Poètes de combat*, pp. 66–7; Léon Laurent-Pichat, *La Sibylle* (Paris: A la librairie nouvelle, 1859), pp. 1–3.
52 LLP, *L'Art et les artistes*, pp. 117, 122.
53 Léon Laurent-Pichat, *Notes sur le Salon de 1861* (Lyon: Imprimerie du Progrès, 1861), pp. 60–61; John Houre, 'Naturalism' and 'Realism', in *The Oxford Companion to Western Art*, ed. Hugh Brigstocke (Oxford: Oxford University Press, 2001), pp. 510, 619; Susan Foley, '"A great and noble painting": Léon Gambetta and the visual arts in the French Third Republic', *French History and Civilisation*, 4 (2011), 106–17.
54 LLP, *Les Poètes de combat*, p. 181. See Batranu, 'L'écrivain et la société', pp. 159–64; Yon, *Histoire culturelle*, pp. 109–10.
55 LLP, *Les Poètes de combat*, p. 252.

56 Ibid., p. 180.
57 Comte Armand de Pontmarin, review of LLP, *Chroniques rimées*, in *L'Assemblée nationale*, 2 Aug. 1856. See also reviews of LLP, *La Païenne*, in *Journal des débats politiques et littéraires*, 22 Nov. 1857; *Le Figaro*, 15 May 1857.
58 E. Pelletan, review of LLP, *Chroniques rimées* in *La Presse*, 16 July 1856.
59 *Le Siècle*, 25 May 1856; *Charivari*, 12 March 1856. On Bonhomme and Populus, see p. 68.
60 LLP, *Les Poètes de combat*, pp. 4, 14.
61 LLP, preface to *La Sibylle*, p. 3.
62 Médiathèque de Saint-Dié-des-Vosges (MSDV): M-247, VII, C42 (50): LLP to Jules Ferry, 29 March 1859.
63 See Victor Hugo, *Napoléon le Petit* [Brussels, 1852], 9th edn (Paris: J. Hetzel, 1871).
64 See Tchernoff, *Le Parti républicain*, pp. 137–40. On ingenious smuggling methods, see Saint-Ferréol, *Les Proscrits français*, I, pp. 227–8.
65 LLP, Journal, 20 Jan. 1862.
66 Laurent-Pichat's subscriptions to German-language newspapers (often unnamed, but including *Welt Zeitung*, *Wiener Lloyd* and *Die Debatte*) are noted in his journal: e.g. 22 May, 29 June 1865; 10 Feb. 1866.
67 Tchernoff, *Le Parti républicain*, p. 71, p. 72 and note 1; p. 137 and note 1; p. 143; Weill, *Histoire du parti républicain*, pp. 273, 288; Maurice Engelhard, 'La Contrebande politique sur la frontière du Rhin', *Revue alsacienne*, 1882, 116–23.
68 MSDV: LLP to J. Ferry, 29 March 1859.
69 *La Presse*, 5 Nov. 1864; Tchernoff, *Le Parti républicain*, p. 435.
70 Nord, *Republican Moment*, p. 192; Saint-Ferréol, *Les Proscrits français*, I, p. 195; LLP, Journal, 2 June 1862.
71 Bellanger et al., *Histoire générale*, II, p. 275; Pierre Van den Dungen, 'Influences et présence françaises dans la presse belge, 1830–1870', in Marie-Ève Thérenty and Allain Vaillant (eds), *Presse, nations et mondialisation au XIXe siècle* (Paris: Nouveau Monde éditions, 2010), pp. 97–114.
72 AN, 248AP/1: [Léon] Bérardi to LLP, Brussels, 26 May 1862. A letter to Bérardi dated 12 Jan. 1858 indicates that LLP had been a subscriber for some years.
73 For example, LLP, Journal, 28 Nov. 1862; 20 Oct., 5 Dec. 1863; 24 March, 8 Nov. 1864; 9 Feb. 1865. See also AN 248AP/1: letters of Charles de Mouy (1857–1865) and Eugène Noël, 24 June 1864.

74 J.-G. Ponzio, *Les Chants du peuple*, préface de LLP (Nîmes: Imp. de Clavel-Ballivet, 1864); René Ponsard, 'Les Emigrants', dedicated to LLP, in *La Rive gauche*, 26 Feb. 1865.
75 LLP, Journal, 21 May, 5 Sept. 1863; 24 Feb., 28 May 1864; 12 June 1865.
76 *Ibid.*, 7 May 1863; 1 May 1865. Also 24, 28 Oct. 1861.
77 *Ibid.*, 10, 11, 27 Jan. 1862.
78 *Ibid.*, 28 Oct. 1863 (Arnould Frémy); 7 Nov. 1863 (Ulysse Parent).
79 AN 248AP/1: François Favre to LLP, Paris, 7 Sept. 1862.
80 *La Critique française: Revue philosophique et littéraire* (1860–1864). Jean-François Vaudin names LLP as an editor, and summarises the aims of the periodical, in Jean-François Vaudin, *Gazettes et gazetiers: Histoire critique et anecdotique de la presse parisienne, deuxième année* (Paris: E. Dentu, 1863), pp. 242–5.
81 On the *Courrier du dimanche*: LLP, Journal, 30 March, 2 April 1862; on *Les Tablettes de Pierrot*, 14 Dec. 1865.
82 *L'Avenir national* (Jan. 1865–Oct. 1873). See LLP, Journal, esp. 4 Nov. 1864; 26 Feb., 18 April, 15 June 1865; Bellanger et al., *Histoire générale*, II, pp. 322–3, 337.
83 *La Correspondance littéraire: critique, beaux-arts, érudition* (1856–1865).
84 LLP, Journal, 24, 28 Oct. 1861.
85 *Ibid.*, 28 April 1865.
86 *La Réforme littéraire* (Jan.–Aug. 1862): meetings of the committee are mentioned regularly in LLP's journal from late 1861 and throughout 1862.
87 LLP, Journal, 18 Nov. 1861.
88 MSDV: LLP to J. Ferry, no. 3, undated [annotated: 'among letters from spring 1862']. LLP noted letters of support from Garnier-Pagès and Maxime Du Camp (Journal, 24, 26 Jan 1862), and offers to contribute from A. Lefêvre and A. Arnould (Journal, 3 Dec 1861; 5 Jan. 1862).
89 LLP, 'Au lecteur', *La Réforme littéraire*, no. 1, 19 Jan. 1862.
90 Tchernoff, *Le Parti républicain*, pp. 343–5.
91 LLP, 'Excursion à Genève et à Veytaux', *La Réforme littéraire*, no. 2, 26 Jan. 1862; no. 3, 2 Feb. 1862.
92 Léon Laurent-Pichat, 'Le Reptile: poésie extradite du journal *Le Travail*', *La Réforme littéraire*, no. 7, 2 March 1862. On *Le Travail*, see Nord, *Republican Moment*, p. 34; Tchernoff, *Le Parti republicain*, pp. 345–6.
93 LLP, Journal, 5 Dec. 1862.

94 Emile Reyneau [managing editor], *La Réforme littéraire*, no. 33, 31 Aug. 1862. See Tchernoff, *Le Parti républicain*, p. 265.
95 Bellanger et al., *Histoire générale*, II, pp. 262, 314–15; Weill, *Histoire du parti républicain*, pp. 363–4.
96 *Le Phare de la Loire*, 22 Sept. 1862; 23 Feb., 31 March 1863.
97 Quoted in Charles Sowerwine, *France Since 1870: Culture, Politics and Society*, 3rd edn (Houndmills: Palgrave Macmillan, 2018), p. 42.
98 *Le Phare de la Loire*, 6, 14, 17 Jan. 1865.
99 *Ibid.*, 13 Oct. 1865. See Marc Monnier, 'Paillasse' (1865), in *Théâtre des marionnettes*, préface de Victor Cherbuliez (Geneva: F. Richard, 1871), pp. 191–222, and editor's note, pp. 263–4. The references to December evoke the coup d'état of December 1851.
100 LLP, Journal, 25 Oct. 1865.
101 *Le Phare de la Loire*, 17, 18, 21 Nov. 1865.

4

'Pure happiness': shaping a bourgeois family for the Republic, 1851–75

In the 1850s and 1860s, as Laurent-Pichat gained prominence as a republican journalist and writer, he was also establishing himself as a family man. The family he established was, in most respects, typically bourgeois, its patterns of consumption, aesthetics and sociability reflecting his substantial wealth. However, the family was unusual in that Laurent-Pichat never married. His family life was not based, therefore, on the 'conjugal heterosexuality' that would become a defining feature of republican masculinity during the Third Republic.[1] Rather, his household first comprised his mother and his sister Herminie. Later it comprised his mother and his daughter, who (like him) was born out of wedlock. It then became a joint family in which he and his daughter lived with his sister Rosine, her husband and their daughter. Laurent-Pichat's determination to create an intimate family, though an unconventional one, reflected his childhood sense of isolation and his deep desire for a warm and affectionate family of his own. That determination throws into relief the critical place that family occupied in bourgeois emotional life, self-identity and social mores, as historians have argued.[2]

Laurent-Pichat's family life also highlights the critical place of the family in republican thinking at mid-century. As Philip Nord and Judith Stone have demonstrated, republicans were not simply concerned with how to transform the State. Rather, as they examined the disastrous failure of the Second Republic, they were convinced that the successful establishment of a Third Republic depended upon the regeneration of private life. They emphasised the role of the family in implanting the values essential for a Republic to flourish.[3] As Eugène Pelletan put it, 'private virtue supports public virtue'.[4]

Figure 4.1 Geneviève Leroi, Mme Deslandes, mother of Léon Laurent-Pichat, *c.* 1860.

The family life of Léon Laurent-Pichat provides a glimpse not of a theoretical or fictional family such as republican writers Jules Michelet and Eugène Pelletan imagined, but of family life as it was lived among the republican bourgeoisie during the Second Empire. Despite its unconventional basis, the life of this family indicates that little distinguished such republican families from other bourgeois families. Indeed, by living in a thoroughly bourgeois fashion, republicans like Laurent-Pichat set out to show the established elites that republicans were 'not savages', as Edmond Adam put it, and had the potential to govern.[5] Laurent-Pichat's family, like other bourgeois families, was affectionate and child-centred; the children were raised to take their places in the bourgeois world. But the bourgeois world to which they aspired would also be republican. Children were imbued with republican values and loyalties. This chapter shows how the daughters of a republican family of this era were raised to become suitable wives for republican men, as republican theorists envisaged. Moreover, since the intimate family was embedded in a vibrant republican sociability, this chapter also demonstrates how republicans created a foundation for the intersection of family life and political life that would facilitate republican activities during the Second Empire and early Third Republic. That intersection will be explored in the remainder of this book.

Assembling a family

Whereas most men established families by marrying and producing children, Laurent-Pichat assembled a family unit from his maternal kin. Late in 1851, soon after recognising him officially as her son, his mother moved into Laurent-Pichat's apartment at 46, rue Jacob, in the heart of the Left Bank, where he had been living since late 1848. Presumably she brought her youngest child, Herminie, aged twelve.[6] Rosine was already married to Amédée Beaujean. Nineteen-year-old Achille, embarking on a career in the family distillery, joined the household of his uncle.[7] Laurent-Pichat's household consisted, therefore, of his mother, his younger sister and himself.

A decade later, when Laurent-Pichat's daily journal began in October 1861, both Achille and Herminie were also married.

But Laurent-Pichat, thirty-eight years old, had not married, although he had become the father of a daughter in 1856. His single status was unusual for a man of his social standing in this era. Founding a family was the expected pattern in bourgeois circles and only 11.4 percent of men born, like him, in the early 1820s, remained unmarried.[8]

A variety of personal factors may have contributed to Laurent-Pichat's remaining single. His family background, first of all, meant that he was not embedded in the extended family structure that created pathways to bourgeois marriage. He had neither the web of cousins as potential partners, nor the elderly aunts and other relatives who undertook discreet investigations into suitable families and set the marriage machine rolling.[9] But Laurent-Pichat's decision not to marry surely reflected his own inclinations and attachments as well. His youthful passion for Henri Chevreau might suggest that he felt no attraction for marriage. He did develop intense relationships with women, but these women were not potential spouses. This was true not only of his sister Rosine but also of the Princesse de Beauvau, his lover and the mother of his daughter, whose religious faith ultimately proved an insurmountable hurdle.

Laurent-Pichat's illegitimacy may also have remained an impediment, despite his adoption by Pichat, and he himself may have been unwilling to endure scrutiny of his background by seeking a wife. Had he sought to marry, he risked revealing his mother's past and exposing her to public humiliation. Perhaps most significantly, he needed to find a wife who, with her family, would accept his prenuptial child. Geneviève's presence raised inheritance issues, as well as emotional issues, for any prospective union.

That Laurent-Pichat remained unmarried and fathered a child out of wedlock appears to confirm stereotypes about the bohemian lives of mid-century republicans. Among the rising generation of republican leaders, it was well known that a number, including Léon Gambetta, Eugène Spuller and Paul-Armand Challemel-Lacour, were living in 'free unions'; Jules Ferry would only marry in 1875, aged forty-three.[10] Edmond Adam lamented, according to his wife Juliette, that 'there will be no wives and widows in the coming republic'.[11] Without wives and widows, not only would the salutary influence of womanly virtue be absent, but so would the family hearths around which republicanism would be instilled in children.

Despite being unmarried, Laurent-Pichat was committed to family life with all that implied in republican thinking. At one with many of his peers in savouring the pleasures and emotional ties of family, he embraced the delights of 'home' which, as John Tosh argues, denoted not merely a 'pattern of residence' but 'a profound attachment', 'a state of mind'.[12] The respectable bourgeois man was understood to be both a successful public figure and a good husband and father enmeshed in a web of domestic affections.

Laurent-Pichat's daughter 'Marie-Geneviève' (known simply as Geneviève) was born on 2 August 1856, but the loss of the original birth certificate – probably destroyed, like many others, in the fires of 1871 – means that the official records of her birth are fragmentary.[13] The identity of Geneviève's mother remained a carefully guarded family secret. She is never named in public documents, such as Geneviève's later marriage certificate. If Laurent-Pichat kept a diary at that time, it has not survived, and his later diaries are intensely discreet about this major event in his life.

Geneviève's daughter Eugénie, known to the family as Ginette, later recorded what she was told about her mother's history: that Geneviève's mother was Ludmille Komar, Princesse de Beauvau.[14] Komar was the second wife of Charles-Just de Beauvau-Craon, fourth Prince de Beauvau, who had been an officer in the army of Napoleon I and became a Senator under Napoleon III.[15] The Prince was nearly thirty years older than Komar, a Polish Countess who was a patron of the decorative arts. The painter Ernest Hébert initially introduced Laurent-Pichat to the couple at a spa in Germany, and it soon became apparent that he and the Princesse shared many cultural interests.[16] This was evident in 1862, for instance, when Laurent-Pichat coached her for her role in the play *Henri III*, later attending the performance with his mother, Rosine and Amédée.[17] Frequent references in Laurent-Pichat's diary leave no doubt that he shared a close relationship with the Princesse de Beauvau, although he always referred to her formally as 'Mme de Beauvau' in his journal. Only many years later, on learning of her death, did Laurent-Pichat write 'Ludmille' in his diary.[18]

The death of the Prince de Beauvau in 1864 freed his widow to remarry. Rosine apparently believed that the Princesse visited Rome in 1865 in order to facilitate a marriage with Laurent-Pichat, though on what basis is unclear.[19] That the Princesse did so nevertheless indicates the depth and seriousness of their attachment.

Figure 4.2 La Princesse de Beauvau-Craon.

But marriage between a devout Catholic aristocrat like the Princesse and a deeply anticlerical republican was always unlikely. Indeed, religion would eventually sever their bond in 1877.[20] By 1861, the relationship between Laurent-Pichat and the Princesse had extended to become a friendship between their two families, despite their political differences. In 1860 and 1861, both the Princesse and her husband wrote letters to the Minister for Public Instruction and Fine Arts seeking promotion for Laurent-Pichat's brother-in-law, Amédée Beaujean.[21] Laurent-Pichat and his family also dined occasionally with the de Beauvau family. Rosine and the Princesse became friends and visited each other with their children.[22]

Geneviève was registered without a family name at birth, preserving both parents' anonymity. History threatened to repeat itself in the life of Laurent-Pichat, whose own child was now denied legally by both father and mother. But again like her father, Geneviève was not abandoned to the foundling hospital at birth. Rather, she was placed in the care of a trusted confidante of the Princesse, Mme Toinette Krash, to whom she became very attached. Both father and mother visited regularly.[23] Geneviève also had a nurse, who would call on Laurent-Pichat several times in later years.[24] The nurse knew that Laurent-Pichat was Geneviève's father, therefore, which indicates that he had accepted paternal responsibility for her from her infancy. The similarities to his own infancy are, again, remarkable.

Laurent-Pichat clearly did not remain impervious to this child who, like himself, had entered the world unexpectedly. Whether he felt pangs of affection for her at birth we cannot know. But the child was named Geneviève after Laurent-Pichat's mother, thus signalling discreetly her welcome into her kin group. With the birth of this second Geneviève, the wheel turned full circle for Geneviève Leroi. Having borne a child out of wedlock whom she was unable to raise, she now had a vital role in raising her motherless grandchild.

Little Geneviève was brought into the family in 1861, when she turned five, and the process of integrating her began. In mid-1862, Laurent-Pichat noted: 'Since yesterday, [we've been] attempting to get Geneviève to call my sister <u>aunt</u>.'[25] But Geneviève was much older before she learned about her parentage. She learned her mother's identity only after the death of both her parents.[26] Only in 1871, when she was fifteen, was her relationship with Laurent-Pichat acknowledged explicitly. Until that time, his letters to her were always signed 'Laurent-Pichat' or 'your friend Léon' and Geneviève addressed him as her 'friend'.[27] Nevertheless, there was no shortage of love for Geneviève. Laurent-Pichat had officially acknowledged paternity and given Geneviève his name in June 1861, shortly before her fifth birthday.[28] Indeed, Laurent-Pichat's love for his daughter was always on display. Juliette Adam later reported: 'Pichat absolutely adored his daughter; he spoke of her as a father and a mother in the same breath. I have never known anyone who viewed fatherhood as a more absolute gift of the self.'[29]

Laurent-Pichat and his little family established close family bonds with Rosine, Amédée and their daughter Clémence, who lived nearby at no. 1, rue Jacob.[30] But the death of Geneviève Leroi disrupted this incipient family life. Taken ill on 18 November 1863, she declined rapidly and died on 26 November, aged fifty-seven.[31] Her death was particularly poignant for Laurent-Pichat, given the complex personal history between mother and son. His diary describes his shock and bewilderment: 'One comes and goes with an idea that one can't get used to.'[32] Two days later his journal entry was a single word – 'Burial' – as though he was unable to express his emotions at this loss.

Laurent-Pichat, a single man whose professional and political activities occupied his days and often his evenings, was unable to care for his daughter alone. Besides, a young girl needed a mother to raise and educate her. Geneviève took up temporary residence with her aunt and uncle, but the family sought a living arrangement that would allow Laurent-Pichat to have a paternal presence in Geneviève's life. He had already been searching for more spacious accommodation for the family before the death of his mother. He had looked at a number of houses in 1862 and 1863, making unsuccessful offers on two of them.[33] In March 1864, Laurent-Pichat purchased a large property at 39, rue de l'Université, in the very wealthy seventh arrondissement, for 340,000 francs.[34] After extensive renovations, Laurent-Pichat and Geneviève moved into their new home with Rosine, Amédee and Clémence on 12 November 1864.[35]

Creating a republican bourgeois home

In their new residence, Laurent-Pichat and his family sought to create a bourgeois home where they could live the domestic ideal.

Some studies have argued that the intense emotions associated with 'home' – an 'emotionally heightened space' – helped to delineate a 'private' domain separate from the competitive world of business and politics.[36] But that was not the case for republicans during the Second Empire. Certainly, as the example of Laurent-Pichat illustrates, their homes – like all homes – had private spaces where non-family members did not venture. But if the bourgeois home was open to friendship and sociability, the republican bourgeois home was also open to politics. Under the Empire, when political activities were heavily controlled and mostly illegal, home was a vital site for discussing and debating politics. Home was the site for gatherings that, if held elsewhere, would have been open to prosecution as illegal political meetings. Wealthy republicans, by hosting political friends and colleagues in their homes, made opposition politics possible in the 1850s and 1860s. If family intimacy was nurtured assiduously, therefore, the porousness of 'public' and 'private' in the republican home facilitated the intersections between politics and family life that were frequently on display.

Wealth was the fundamental prerequisite for creating such a home. Laurent-Pichat had inherited his father's fortune in 1838 and was able to live very comfortably without needing to work.[37] In addition to the income from his investments, he benefited over the years from two further windfalls. In 1863, during Baron Haussmann's redevelopment of Paris, Laurent-Pichat was awarded 1,760,000 francs in compensation when the extensive four-storey property inherited from his father, La Rotonde du Temple, was expropriated and demolished (his lawyer had sought three million francs).[38] A second expropriation in 1880, this time of the family's seaside chateau at Beuzeval, would bring him 85,000 francs in compensation.[39]

Such wealth underpinned a luxurious family lifestyle, as the layout and furnishing of the home at 39, rue de l'Université illustrate.[40] The L-shaped four-storey *hôtel particulier* was constructed around a private courtyard, with a coachman's lodge forming a third wing. It had more than ample space to house three adults and two children, with their servants. Indeed, when the girls later married, apartments would be created in the building for each of their families as well.[41] Thanks to Laurent-Pichat's wealth, he and Rosine and her husband enjoyed adjacent apartments in this *hôtel particulier*, each preserving a private space yet living a quasi-nuclear family life in common. Laurent-Pichat's apartment consisted of a salon and dining room, as well as a study and library (which together held about eight thousand books). The bedroom, with its dressing room, had windows onto both the street and the courtyard. That Geneviève lived in the apartment of her aunt and uncle, sharing a bedroom with Clémence, betrays the fact that, outside the normative domestic model, Laurent-Pichat could not raise his motherless daughter himself. By instituting a system of shared parenthood, Laurent-Pichat gave expression to his love for Geneviève and his aspiration to become a *père de famille*, although he could not achieve that ambition in the conventional manner.

For wealthy siblings to cohabit was not unusual in itself. From 1858, for instance, the Hôtel Pereire on the rue du Faubourg St-Honoré – vastly grander than Laurent-Pichat's relatively modest abode – housed three Pereire brothers with their families on separate floors. They had their own living and dining spaces but ate together regularly.[42] Two generations of the Hachette family also shared a *hôtel particulier* on the Left Bank.[43] Laurent-Pichat's arrangement with Rosine and Amédée was a little different. Sisters who presided over the households of their unmarried or widowed brothers were usually unmarried themselves.[44] But Rosine was mistress of both her own and Laurent-Pichat's families, which, in some respects, functioned as a single household.

In the shared spaces of the joint family home, there was a 'small salon' and a 'grand salon', which was sufficiently large to be furnished with two canapés, nine armchairs and a grand piano, as well as with Chinese screens, assorted tables bearing candelabras and lamps, and cabinets full of bibelots. Gatherings of twenty or thirty people – often simultaneously social and political, bringing together republican friends and colleagues – were easily accommodated here.[45] Two further rooms in the shared spaces of the house were designated libraries; all four walls of the larger room had polished walnut cabinets with glass doors. This, too, was a versatile space: 'I prepared my library for this evening … meeting at my place after dinner, about sixty people.'[46] Throughout the house, oriental carpets competed for wall space with paintings by Delacroix, Greuze, Ingres, Boileau and many others.[47] The family clearly favoured the 'old masters', although they attended exhibitions of 'new painters' like Manet as the Impressionists emerged.[48]

If this Parisian home cosseted the family from autumn to spring, the summer house provided a home away from home from late June through September. Laurent-Pichat did not have a family chateau in a village of origin, filled with memories of long childhood summers. But the holiday house he acquired at Beuzeval-sur-mer, on the Normandy coast, became the family's sanctuary. There they constructed and recorded memories of summer holidays as a privileged time in the life of the family.[49]

Beuzeval was less fashionable than the neighbouring resort towns of Houlgate (just across the Drochon river), Trouville and especially Deauville, frequented by the Empire elite.[50] The town's social obscurity may have appealed to Laurent-Pichat, who began to record the family's visits to Beuzeval in 1862. He purchased a house there in 1863, renovating it the following year.[51] The family called it 'the chalet'. Images depict a grand chateau complete with turrets, though it was no more extraordinary than many of the architectural wonders dotting the coast.[52] Simultaneously country estate and family nest, it met the requirements for enacting both the social display of the successful bourgeois and the emotional intimacy of the family.

The house at Beuzeval could easily accommodate the extended family and close friends, as it did during many summers in the 1860s and 1870s.[53] The women and children usually spent several leisurely months on vacation. The men, with careers and businesses to attend to, joined their families for short breaks and weekends, facilitated by the arrival of the railway in 1863.[54] Friends were often invited to holiday as well. They spent their time playing croquet, walking, sketching and playing parlour games. They bathed in the sea almost daily. The girls learned to swim, prompted by both the potential pleasure of the experience and the self-improvement ethos that pervaded their education. In 1871, fifteen-year-old Geneviève confessed that she did not yet 'have the courage to swim using both feet'.[55] In July 1874, however, she wrote: 'I am pleased to inform you that I have made some progress with my swimming, and this morning I launched myself <u>all by myself</u> to float on my back. I hope that's a good result. As for Clémence, she swims on her back, it's quite amazing.'[56] Her father urged her to enjoy sea-bathing as part of the Beuzeval experience. 'Swim! Laugh! Be happy!' he wrote in 1875. 'Bathe – and profit from this sea that knows you. She's an old *nounou*!' The familiar sea, he mused, was protective and welcoming like a nurse (*nounou*) enfolding her charge.[57]

That the family returned to 'the chalet' at Beuzeval for nearly twenty years gave the site ritual significance for them.[58] Laurent-Pichat wrote:

> I know this sea well;
> Its waves leap up before
> The returning family;
> The same skies over our heads;
> The same wind in our hair![59]

It remained in memory an idyllic site of family life, imbued, as Laurent-Pichat wrote to Geneviève, with the 'indelible trace of your childhoods, of the mornings of your life'.[60] While Laurent-Pichat memorialised family holidays at Beuzeval in verse, Rosine captured 'the chalet' in watercolours and Amédée photographed both the house and its inhabitants. Despite the expropriation and demolition of 'the chalet' in 1880, it was preserved and treasured in family culture as a cipher for a happy period of youth and expectation. It remained a private 'site of memory', a souvenir of past happiness which would be passed on to the next generation through rituals of story-telling, as Laurent-Pichat observed in a poem to his family: 'Once upon a time ... tell the story!'[61]

Bourgeois domestic life

The rituals of family life in the nineteenth-century bourgeois home were both enactments of family togetherness, and enactments of emotions like love, sentimental attachment and happiness deemed 'natural' for families. Despite the atypical structure of Laurent-Pichat's family, their family rituals were closely aligned with current bourgeois practices. Indeed, their very atypicality as a family highlights the pivotal place of 'family' in the bourgeois imagination. By living a bourgeois life, wealthy republicans like Laurent-Pichat asserted their social respectability and thus claimed political respectability as well.

Many of the domestic rituals of this family, whether in Paris or at Beuzeval, resembled those practised by other bourgeois families at the time. The family regularly shared an evening meal and, with a table seating sixteen, the dining room was spacious enough to accommodate all the siblings and their families.[62] Birthdays also brought the siblings together.[63] More distant family members like Mme Asselin, their maternal aunt, and Henri Lefort, Herminie's brother-in-law (and a journalist colleague of Laurent-Pichat), frequently ate at the house as well.[64]

New Year was the most important family celebration in the French calendar. This family exchanged tokens of affection and made the customary New Year offerings to the servants.[65] Like other bourgeois families, too, this family spent the afternoon of New Year's Day visiting or receiving the extended family and close friends, affirming the broader web of family attachments and asserting their social qualifications as a bourgeois family. New Year's Day usually culminated (as it did, for instance, in 1875) in a dinner at the rue de l'Université attended by all four siblings and their children. 'We played snakes and ladders', Laurent-Pichat reported.[66] Christmas, by contrast, had not yet become a major family festival in France.[67] Family members exchanged small tokens of affection, but in some years Laurent-Pichat's diary makes no reference to any special events on 25 December.[68]

The family's social activities were also typical of bourgeois sociability in this period. If family meals were common, so too were dinners that brought friends together. Those dinners spilled over into soirées devoted to conversation and sometimes parlour games like charades. Costume balls were regular events. Having appeared as King Louis XIII at a ball hosted by the publisher Hachette in February 1874, Laurent-Pichat transformed into a republican soldier to host his own ball a few weeks later.[69]

Evenings at the theatre, often in the company of friends, were frequent occurrences. The family enjoyed the light entertainment offered at venues like the Porte-St-Martin and the Gaîeté. They also attended opera regularly (Verdi's *Rigoletto* and *Il Trovatore*, Donizetti's *Lucia di Lammermoor* and Mozart's *Marriage of Figaro*, for instance). They saw Gounod's *Romeo and Juliette* three times.[70] The musical tastes of Amédée Beaujean, a musician himself, extended to Handel Oratorios and Wagner's early opera *Rienzi*. He also went to a performance in April 1875 of Bizet's opera *Carmen*, which had been poorly received at its recent première and closed soon after.[71]

The family were often present at 'must see' events in the bourgeois calendar. In June 1868, they managed to obtain tickets for the revival of Victor Hugo's renowned drama *Hernani*. A decade later they saw it again, with the famous duo Mounet-Sully and Sarah Bernhardt playing the leads. They saw that same duo in 1875 in the immensely popular patriotic play *La Fille de Roland*. The family also attended the farewell concert of the renowned singer La Patti in 1870.[72] Such events and activities identified the group as both family-oriented and 'bourgeois', as did their evenings playing patience, whist and bezique (another popular card game).

Family life would not have been possible without the servants, whose presence in the household was a demonstration of bourgeois wealth, civility and leisure. The lifestyle of the family depended upon the labour of those who prepared the meals, laid out the clothing, waited on the guests and attended to the intimate needs of others. The family had a number of servants, as befitted their wealth and the size of the household, although their number and roles are never made clear. Aimable and Fideline Bogaert, employed as valet and housekeeper respectively, moved into the newly renovated residence in January 1864 and remained in service until January 1867.[73] In 1868, 'Ferdinand' and his unnamed wife filled those roles, the Bogaerts returning in 1869. There was also a coachman, Isidore, later replaced by François Roux.[74] Clémence and Geneviève each had a maid, Louise (replaced by Ida) and Félicie. We can assume that Rosine had a maid and Amédée may well have had a valet.[75] In later years, the birth of each grandchild would bring a nurse into the family to breastfeed and care for the infant, with additional nursery staff to care for the older ones. In addition to the cook, there must have been a number of kitchen staff, general servants and housemaids to undertake the essential tasks of cleaning and serving at table, but they are never mentioned in family sources.[76] The value placed on swift and efficient service in this very large house explains the incorporation of the latest technology, speaking tubes (an early form of intercom system), as part of the renovations.[77]

The servants appear only fleetingly in the letters and diaries of family members. That they were referred to by their first names or simply by their roles – the nurse, the cook, the servants – was a mark of the hierarchy of family life. They remain anonymous cogs in the wheel that was the bourgeois household, generally unable to be traced or identified. The servants never tell their own stories. In 1863, for instance, Cyprien and his wife, 'the Fléchier servants', were dismissed and arrested for theft: was the accusation justified?[78] How did 'Ferdinand and his wife' cope, in 1868, with the sudden death of their daughter, from whom they were separated by their employment?[79] Servants had the power to resign, as they did from time to time. But they had little power in the household, even if bourgeois family life would have been impossible without them.

Vacations for the family did not bring respite for the servants because their employers could not holiday without them. Some of the household staff accompanied the family to Beuzeval and local people were employed to assist them. The year 1864 gives an insight into the servants' experience there. 'Fideline and Aimable left [for Beuzeval] at 8 am', Laurent-Pichat noted on 4 July. They had to see to the family's luggage, open the house and prepare a meal. This was a particularly difficult year for the servants because the house at Beuzeval was undergoing renovations. The family nevertheless thought nothing of inviting nine people for dinner. Perhaps this accounts for the exasperation of Fideline and Aimable Bogaert, which was met with incomprehension by their employers: 'An inexplicable scene by Fideline, similar to that of her husband the day before', Laurent-Pichat noted. 'I spoke to Aimable. He has apologised to my sister. It seems that things will be better now'. But we might wonder whether Fideline's illness, which required a visit by the doctor, was a result of the stress of that summer.[80] The family's blissful experience of life at Beuzeval stood in stark contrast to the hard work and frustration of the servants.

Raising bourgeois girls

By the nineteenth century, children had acquired a stellar place in the bourgeois domestic firmament, their happiness and socialisation ranking high in parental concerns.[81] Rosine's daughter, Clémence, and Léon's daughter, Geneviève, were certainly beneficiaries of this trend. They also benefited from the republican desire to ensure that girls received a serious education that would prepare them for important roles as wives of republican husbands. Republicans would be unable to implement a programme of secondary education for girls until they were securely in power from 1879. But republican families like that of Laurent-Pichat, Rosine and Amédée would provide the girls with the best education possible in the 1860s, even if raising girls for independent living was inconceivable in their world.

Clémence and Geneviève were lavished with attention by their family. They were clothed in furs against the winter chill and received gifts large and small: dolls' clothes, new shoes, coral earrings, cabinets for their bedroom.[82] They picked violets in spring in the Bois de Vincennes and made snowballs in winter in the forest at L'Isle-Adam.[83] They went to the theatre to see *Cinderella* and *Peau d'Ane*; they were taken to magic shows and to performances at the Cirque d'Hiver, and were treated to cakes in the Tuileries Gardens.[84] Laurent-Pichat read them stories and constructed cut-out chateaux, and made frequent trips to M. Huret to have Geneviève's broken doll mended.[85] In documenting these child-centred activities in his diary, Laurent-Pichat proclaimed the children's privileged place at the heart of this family: a contrast with the isolation from family that had scarred his youthful sense of identity. His detailed recording of the love and affection lavished on Clémence and Geneviève also asserted his merits as an attentive and conscientious parent.

Like most bourgeois girls in this period, Clémence and Geneviève were educated at home. It seems that her grandmother took Geneviève's education in hand as soon as the child was brought into the family. Laurent-Pichat noted in July 1862, when Geneviève was almost six: 'Geneviève read to me from M. Delapalme's book. She reads very well. Great surprise to me. She had only spelled before.'[86] After Geneviève Leroi's death in 1863, the education of both girls was supervised by Rosine.

Their first lesson was that they must take their education seriously: it was a project with purpose. Laurent-Pichat wrote to ten-year-old Geneviève in 1866: 'It is time to make good use of your time; I'll take this opportunity to advise you not to play, not to laugh and pull faces during your lessons. Some children are punished for all these faults. We employ reason with you; and I am sure you will understand'.[87] He urged self-discipline and compliance on his daughter. Bourgeois norms and expectations were instilled from childhood, though with affection and tenderness. Her father reminded Geneviève on another occasion:

> Some girls and some children are treated more severely than you [...] no gifts, no dolls, no dresses, hats or surprises of any kind. I don't criticise you for what people do for you if you are sensible enough to show yourself worthy, but I do want to say that you are loved and spoiled like no child I know.[88]

As Laurent-Pichat's letter revealed, the education of bourgeois girls was above all an education in bourgeois dispositions and behaviours. Learning to 'govern their hearts and their minds' (in Laurent-Pichat's words), to manage their emotions and thoughts, was as important for their futures as the acquisition of knowledge.[89] Clémence and Geneviève were expected to commit themselves to the fundamental bourgeois value of self-improvement, even though they were given no serious intellectual task in which to progress. This was reinforced during the girls' adolescence. Laurent-Pichat urged them to 'apply' themselves to their sketching and track their progress by saving their drawings. He presented them with sketchbooks to assist in that task.[90]

Letter-writing was an important element of girls' education, and girls were encouraged to practise desired traits such as modesty, cheerfulness and self-restraint, which would draw the approval of others. They also learned the self-censorship that was essential to emotional self-management. If there were moments of unhappiness in her life, if Geneviève had fallings out with Clémence or her aunt, for instance, there is no evidence of this in her letters, which remained on a smooth emotional keel.

In the home, Clémence and Geneviève – like other bourgeois girls – were prepared for lives in bourgeois society. They practised social etiquette by accompanying their parents when they went visiting.[91] They also hosted their friends at home as part of family gatherings.[92] Tutors taught Clémence and Geneviève music. Jules Laurens, who exhibited regularly at the Salon, taught them sketching and painting.[93] They took dancing lessons with several friends from M. Rémond, who was sometimes delayed by his rehearsals at the Paris Opéra. The dancing class expanded in size when the girls' Alsatian friends, Fanny Chauffour, Jeanne Scheurer and Eugénie

'Pure happiness' 107

Risler, were in Paris.[94] Regular ventures with Laurent-Pichat and Rosine to the conservatorium of music, the Cluny Museum, the opera and the annual Salon provided these young women with the cultural capital and general knowledge that would develop their interests and make them intelligent partners of their husbands.[95]

Raising republican girls

In some respects, the education of girls like Clémence and Geneviève, raised in secular republican families, differed little from that of girls in devout Catholic families. They were imbued with many similar ideals and shared the same rites of passage. Yet republicans set out to ensure that their daughters shared their secular values and their appreciation of secular knowledge. This gave their education a distinctive emphasis.

Religious instruction remained an almost universal expectation for girls in the 1860s, republican or not. Practices like confession, which encouraged girls to reflect on their strengths and weaknesses, contributed to their emotional education, teaching them to eradicate not only bad behaviours but emotions like anger, jealousy and self-centredness.[96] Such education went hand in glove with the self-shaping that typified education for bourgeois girls. Moreover, most republican girls, including Clémence and Geneviève, made their First Communions at about age twelve; Geneviève's mother apparently insisted that her daughter do so.[97] By the 1860s, this rite had acquired a secular social cachet, marking the shift from childhood to adolescence. It was an essential ritual in bourgeois society, even in republican circles.[98] Clémence's paternal grandparents travelled from Chablis to attend her First Communion on 18 May 1865 at the Basilica of St Clotilde in Paris. The ceremony was celebrated in true bourgeois style, with a luncheon for fifteen and a dinner for seventeen in the evening. When Geneviève made her First Communion on 14 May 1868, Laurent-Pichat presented her with a watch and carefully recorded the names of the seventeen people who attended the celebratory luncheon.[99]

However, Clémence and Geneviève were not raised to be devout, as girls in Catholic families were. Laurent-Pichat's diary suggests that their religious instruction was largely confined to their preparation for First Communion; their attendance at Mass was irregular and infrequent. Piety is absent from accounts of family life, as is the focus on spiritual growth and sanctity that Catholic literature prescribed.[100] The model of womanhood presented for the girls' imitation, therefore, was bourgeois and secular. Theirs was an education in culture and worldly sociability, and one compatible with a republican world view: it was not an education in Catholic faith and the inner life.

The value that this family placed on a serious education for its daughters was evident from the late 1860s, when the girls were among only two thousand across France who attended the 'Duruy courses'. These courses represented an attempt by Victor Duruy, Education Minister in the Second Empire, to have the State provide some form of secondary education for girls: the only such attempt until the Republican government established secondary schools for girls more than a decade later. The Duruy courses outraged Catholics like Monsignor Dupanloup, for whom the education of 'the French Christian woman' could only be undertaken by the Church: girls should be educated to raise their children in the Catholic faith, not to acquire secular knowledge.[101]

The Duruy courses were essentially lectures, with no formal programme, which girls attended with their mothers or governesses.[102] This education, controversial as it was, thus bore no resemblance to the structured classical programme offered to boys of the bourgeoisie, like the girls' cousin Georges, who attended the Collège Sainte-Barbe.[103] Clémence and Geneviève both attended the Duruy lectures from 1867 to 1869. Geneviève continued attending weekly between November 1869 and mid-May 1870, when the family went on holidays.[104] In July, the outbreak of the Franco-Prussian War halted the courses and ended Geneviève's education. Her cousins Jeanne and Elisabeth Lefort (Herminie's daughters) attended the revived Duruy courses in 1875 and 1876, coming to Paris from L'Isle-Adam to do so.[105] The fact that all the girls in the family around Laurent-Pichat attended the Duruy courses indicates that this family welcomed the opportunity to provide them with the best intellectual formation possible, even if intellectual achievement was not yet prized in girls.

In 1871, when Clémence and Geneviève were aged eighteen and fifteen respectively, a trip to Spain with Rosine and Amédée provided the culmination of their education. They visited galleries, churches and museums in Madrid, Seville and Cadiz. They enjoyed a performance of Verdi's *Rigoletto*, having 'worked on the score a bit' in music lessons.[106] Like their exercises in sketching and watercolours, however, this trip was about more than pleasure. 'Take good note of everything you see', Laurent-Pichat reminded Geneviève. 'In observing everything that happens before you, remember that you will have to tell me about the things I haven't seen'.[107] Geneviève noted the instruction, writing to her father perhaps tongue in cheek: 'Yesterday our day was well spent ... this morning we visited the museum which, to our great pleasure, contained few paintings. I say to our great pleasure because we often find that we have to spend a very long time in each room'.[108] Travel was intended to broaden the girls' minds and reinforce their lessons, but they were expected to work towards the desired outcome.

At the age of nineteen, Geneviève was a source of immense paternal pride to her father. She exhibited, he declared, all the qualities admired in a young woman: her 'precious letter' was 'unaffected, sweet, good, submissive and vivacious, like you, like your heart'.[109] 'To widespread satisfaction, you govern your heart and your mind, and the faculties that depend on them'.[110] In other words, her will and her emotions were successfully under control. Geneviève's proficiency in the arts of bourgeois womanhood also camouflaged her somewhat mysterious origins. By providing his daughter with the best education that money could buy, Laurent-Pichat compensated her as best he could for the social disadvantage occasioned by her illegitimacy. Furthermore, in documenting the girls' lessons and accomplishments in his journal and in his letters, Laurent-Pichat not only expressed his pride in what they had become but proclaimed himself a worthy parent, despite the irregularities in his life and his family relationships.

Celebrating the family

As in many bourgeois families, correspondence played an important role in expressing the emotional life of the family in a tangible form that could be preserved.[111] In childhood, Geneviève and Clémence wrote daily to Laurent-Pichat when they were separated, often on the same sheet of paper, reporting the same events: the expression of attachment was more important than innovative content. As testaments to family connectedness, family letters were often read by several people or read aloud by the assembled family. Family photographs, too, testified to family bonds and visits to photographers were frequent.[112] The 'twelve framed photographs' in Laurent-Pichat's bedroom, like the twenty-eight in his *cabinet de toilette*, were probably family images.[113] Amédée Beaujean became a keen photographer himself and purchased his own equipment, although he needed instruction in the new technology from one of his students.[114]

Laurent-Pichat's practice of composing verse to mark important domestic moments like birthdays gave an intense and perhaps unique flavour to this family's expressions of intimacy. As private family tributes, Laurent-Pichat's verses allowed full reign to the expression of emotion, affirming his love for his family, his delight in observing the development of the children (and later, the grandchildren), and his attempts to come to terms with the passage of time and the process of ageing.

A number of poems celebrate the lives of the cousins, Clémence and Geneviève, illuminating the extent to which they were regarded virtually as sisters within the family. Laurent-Pichat wrote in 1868, when they were fifteen and twelve respectively:

> How old is each of you?
> I don't want to know. /.../
> For me, the two of you are but one. /.../
> You are growing up together:
> That is sufficient for our heart [*sic*];
> You were born together![115]

But Laurent-Pichat was already preparing himself emotionally for the moment when they would leave home:

> When it has sounded, – for the hour is sounding
> When the future approaches, when hope weeps,
> When the children leave, when our trembling heart
> Imagines the perils of that sad and white [wedding] day, –
> When the hour has sounded, the hour when young women
> Become ladies, and simply leave for their new homes,
> What will you preserve of me? What memory

To combine with the present? What dream of the future?[116]

Their growing up aroused bitter-sweet feelings in Laurent-Pichat. Hopes and dreams for their future were mingled with a sense of loss, a premonition of his own mortality and his fear of being forgotten.

As Clémence and Geneviève grew up, Laurent-Pichat's verses became eagerly awaited tributes that they re-read and treasured: 'I received my verses', Geneviève wrote in 1874, when she turned eighteen:

> I asked that they be read on 1 August, as soon as they arrived, then I had them read again on the second [her birthday]. I cannot tell you how charming I found them and what pleasure they gave me ... Each year on 2 August, I tell myself that the last verses received are more charming than all the others, but since the same thing happens each year, I believe I must conclude that it's impossible to make a decision.[117]

The verses were sometimes copied into letters, enabling absentees to experience the celebratory moment vicariously.[118] The family would publish a collection of these verses as a memento to Laurent-Pichat after his death.

Laurent-Pichat's verses did more than commemorate particular moments. They were also testimonials to family life, written to be preserved for posterity. A seventy-two-page account, in verse, of a family holiday, written in mid-1868 is instructive. Laurent-Pichat described his verses as the 'living trace of a month of pure happiness', 'the record of a moment of infinite joy', which would remind the girls of him:

> Later, you will say to yourself if I am no longer there:
> 'His poor heart loved to make rhymes!
> He was our poet! He sang our life,
> /.../
> He was the chronicler of our adventures,
> And it's less talent than feeling that we find there.' [119]

This account would create a shared family memory, enabling the participants to re-live the experience and to remember its author. More than that, the account sought to preserve the emotions of the event, the happiness and joy of family togetherness. The document certainly fulfilled at least some of those purposes. The version that survives in the archive is not that written by Laurent-Pichat himself, but a copy in the hand of his niece, Clémence, who was fifteen in 1868, and who preserved it into adulthood as Laurent-Pichat had hoped.

Laurent-Pichat was deeply invested in family, as were those around him. Despite the irregularity of his domestic arrangements, he eschewed the bohemian stereotype. Rather, he was intent on living and displaying a stable family life, both because he valued family life in itself and because family life was a mark of social and political respectability. Laurent-Pichat and his family sought cultivation and refinement, indulging in bourgeois pursuits like theatre and opera. They conscientiously made time to spend together as a family, sharing intimate occasions and enjoying a range of social activities in common. The holiday home at Beuzeval stood as testament to the passion for family life that this family shared. Their replication of a bourgeois family model based on intimacy and affection demonstrated that, as republicans, they were indeed 'not savages'; rather, they displayed the emotions and attachments dear to many of their bourgeois peers.

The family around Laurent-Pichat also confirms that republican families viewed education as a means to social progress. They educated their daughters in a bourgeois fashion, but with an eye to the future, valuing a serious education, not one confined to polite accomplishments. They welcomed knowledge in girls, not the religious faith emphasised in Catholic families, though the schooling available to girls at the time was limited. No one imagined offering them the same education as boys, since it was taken for granted that they would not live the same lives as boys. Republican women, raised like Clémence and Geneviève, would be cultured and cultivated, equipped with a secular spirit and with knowledge appropriate for the secular world. But they were not raised to be independent women making their own lives: a still-inconceivable possibility. It is revealing that, in the 1868 poem in which Laurent-Pichat imagined the girls leaving home, he imagined their departure as brides. He shared the widespread republican expectation that women were destined for marriage.[120]

The family around Laurent-Pichat was bound together by close ties and linked to others by a strong network of familial loyalties and friendships. Such families provided a secure basis for the sociability that would nurture the Republic in the home, during a period when, outside the home, republican sympathies and republican proselytising were constantly under threat. As the following chapters show, that home-based republican sociability would encompass both men and women, who would co-operate in pursuing the republican dream for several decades. Rather than being a haven from the political domain, the republican home, for this family and others like it, was a deeply politicised space.

Notes

1 Judith Surkis, *Sexing the Citizen: Morality and masculinity in France, 1870–1920* (Ithaca, NY: Cornell University Press, 2006), pp. 13, 161–83.
2 On the sentimental bourgeois family, see Johnson, *Becoming Bourgeois*; Verjus and Davidson, *Le Roman conjugal*; Garrioch, *Formation of the Parisian Bourgeoisie*; Pellissier, *Vie privée*. For a British comparison, see Davidoff and Hall, *Family Fortunes*.
3 Nord, *Republican Moment,* pp. 220–22, 232–7; Stone, *Sons of the Revolution*, pp. 34–40, 47–56.
4 Quoted in Stone, *Sons of the Revolution*, p. 51.
5 Quoted in Juliette Adam, *Nos amitiés politiques avant l'abandon de la Revanche*, 5e édition (Paris: Alphonse Lemerre, 1908), p. 117.
6 APF, GC, notebook, unpaginated. Geneviève Leroi was living on the outskirts of Paris in September 1851 but was residing with Laurent-Pichat two months later: AN MC/ET/XXXIII/1204: 'Reconnaissance d'enfant naturel par Mme Deslandes', 5 Sept. 1851; AN MC/ET/XXXIII/1205: 'Contrat de mariage, Amédée Beaujean/Rosine Deslandes', 26 Nov. 1851.
7 See chapter 8.
8 Florence Laroche-Gisserot, 'Pratiques de la dot en France au XIXe siècle', *Annales ESC*, 6 (1988), 1433–52 (1443); Adeline Daumard, *Les Bourgeois et la bourgeoisie en France depuis 1848* (Paris: Aubier, 1987), p. 208; Pellissier, *Vie privée*, p. 164. See Michelle Perrot, 'Roles and characters', in *A History of Private Life,* IV, pp. 245–9.
9 Martin-Fugier, 'Bourgeois rituals', in *A History of Private Life,* IV, pp. 309–10. For examples of such marriage patterns, see Johnson,

Becoming Bourgeois; Pellissier, *Vie privée*; Verjus and Davidson, *Le Roman conjugal*.
10 Adam, *Nos amitiés*, pp. 310–11; Stone, *Sons of the Revolution*, pp. 74–6; Martin-Fugier, *Salons*, pp. 27–9.
11 Adam, *Nos amitiés*, p. 31.
12 John Tosh, *A Man's Place: Masculinity and the middle-class home in Victorian England* (New Haven, CT: Yale University Press, 1999), p. 4. See also Davidoff and Hall, *Family Fortunes*, p. 358.
13 A reconstructed birth certificate with minimal information is located at AP, naissances: V3E/N1322.
14 APF, GC, notebook, unpaginated.
15 See 'Beauvau-Craon, Charles-Just de', in Adolphe Robert, Edgar Bourloton and Gaston Cougny, eds. *Dictionnaire des parlementaires français depuis le 1er mai 1789 jusqu'au 1er mai 1889*. Paris: 1889–1891. Available at https://numelyo.bm-lyon.fr/f_view/BML:BML_00GOO0100137001103448309; records of the Legion of Honour, AN, Base Léonore, dossier LH/158/66 (1855).
16 Henri Blaze de Bury, 'Etudes et souvenirs: Frédéric Chopin', *Revue des Deux Mondes*, 15 Oct. 1883, 849–78 (861–2); Martin-Fugier, *Salons*, p. 81.
17 LLP, Journal, 1, 27 Feb., 12 April, 20 May 1862. A photograph of the Princesse in costume remains in the private archives of Laurent-Pichat's family.
18 *Ibid.*, 14, 16 Nov. 1881.
19 APF: GC, notebook, unpaginated.
20 See chapter 8.
21 AN F^{17}/20117: Beaujean, personnel file: Prince de Beauvau to the Minister for Public Instruction and Fine Arts, 18 July 1861; draft replies from the Minister to the Prince de Beauvau, 25 July 1861; to the Princesse de Beauvau, 29 Aug. 1854, 29 Dec. 1860.
22 LLP, Journal, 1 Dec. 1861; 20 Jan., 13 Feb. 1863; 17 May, 29 June 1866, etc.
23 APF, GC, notebook, unpaginated.
24 LLP, Journal, 6, 8 April 1869; 6 Sept. 1870; 2 Jan. 1873.
25 *Ibid.*, 23 July 1862. Emphasis original. See also APF: GC, notebook, unpaginated.
26 APF, GC, notebook, unpaginated.
27 BHVP, 7, no. 23: GLP to LLP, 5 Aug. 1871. See Foley, 'Becoming a woman'.
28 AN MC/ET/LXXXIV/1136: 'Reconnaissance d'enfant naturel par Mr. Laurent-Pichat', 29 June 1861.

29 Adam, *Nos amitiés*, p. 324.
30 This was their residential address when their daughter Clémence was born at Le Plessis-Piquet: AD des Hauts-de-Seine: E NUM PLE87: Beaujean, Clémence, 24 June 1853.
31 AP, décès, 6ᵉ arron, V4E 677: Geneviève Leroi, Veuve Deslandes, 27 Nov. 1863; LLP, Journal, 18–28 Nov. 1863.
32 LLP, Journal, 26 Nov. 1863.
33 *Ibid.*, 26 April, 8 May 1862; 11, 13, 15 Jan. 1863.
34 AN MC/ET/LXXXIV/1304: 'inventaire après décès, Léon Laurent-Pichat'; LLP, Journal, 23 March, 1 July 1864. The *hôtel privé* remained in the family until 2016.
35 LLP, Journal, 12 Nov. 1864.
36 See Gammerl, 'Emotional styles', esp. p. 165.
37 See chapter 1.
38 *Rotonde du Temple. M. Laurent Pichat propriétaire* (Paris : Impr. de N. Chaix, [1863]; LLP, Journal, 12 Feb.–1 May 1863.
39 LLP, Journal, 10 Aug. 1880.
40 AN MC/ET/LXXXIV/1304: 'inventaire après décès, Léon Laurent-Pichat'.
41 Geneviève and Charles moved into a ground floor apartment in late 1877; Clémence and Abel moved into a third-floor apartment in December 1878.
42 Davies, *Emile and Isaac Pereire*, pp. 173, 180–85.
43 Jean-Yves Mollier, *Louis Hachette le fondateur d'un empire* (Paris: Fayard, 1999), p. 395.
44 Perrot, 'Roles and characters', in *A History of Private Life,* IV, pp. 222–3; Pellissier, *Vie privée*, pp. 166–70.
45 For instance, LLP, Journal, 4 May; 1, 29 June 1872; 19 March 1883.
46 *Ibid.*, 1 Feb. 1876.
47 Snippets of information about the house are found in Laurent-Pichat's journal. More detailed information is contained in AN MC/ET/LXXXIV/1304: 'inventaire après décès, Léon Laurent-Pichat', and in AN MC/ET/84/1912-04-19-HUGOT: 'inventaire après décès, Geneviève Laurent-Pichat'.
48 LLP, Journal, 23 May 1875; 10 Jan. 1884. See Nord, *Republican Moment*, chapter 7.
49 See André Rauch, *Vacances en France de 1830 à nos jours* (Paris: Hachette, 1996); Alain Corbin, *The Lure of the Sea: The Discovery of the seaside in the Western world, 1750–1840*, trans. Jocelyn Phelps (Cambridge: Polity Press, 1994).
50 Dominique Rouillard, *Le Site balnéaire* (Liège: Pierre Mardaga, 1984), pp. 10–14, 29–35, 76–9.

51 LLP, Journal, 29, 31 July, 3 Aug., 26 Dec. 1863.
52 Lithographs by Charles Gosselin, Jules Laurent and Adolphe-Etienne Viollet-le-Duc (younger brother of the renowned architect Eugène) can be found in Léon Laurent-Pichat, *Heures de fêtes: Album intime* (Nancy: Berger-Levrault et Cie, 1893), pp. 83, 108, 118. On the architecture of the seaside towns of Normandy, see Rouillard, *Le Site balnéaire*, chapters 6 and 7.
53 According to Laurent-Pichat's journal, all four siblings spent a period with their families at Beuzeval in 1862, 1863, 1864 and 1869, for instance.
54 See Martin-Fugier on the 'husbands' trains' timetabled to accommodate men's professional lives: 'Bourgeois rituals', in *A History of Private Life*, IV, pp. 302–3.
55 BHVP, 7, no. 17: GLP to LLP, 10 July 1871.
56 *Ibid.*, no. 50: 27 July 1874. Emphasis original.
57 BHVP, 6, no. 27: LLP to GLP, 16 July 1875; no. 33, 17 July 1876.
58 Martin-Fugier, 'Bourgeois rituals', in *A History of Private Life,* IV, pp. 262–3.
59 LLP, 'A Geneviève', Beuzeval, 2 Aug. 1876, in *Heures de fêtes*, pp. 81–8 (82).
60 *Ibid.*, p. 83.
61 LLP, untitled, 12 Aug. 1879; untitled, 11 July 1880, in *Heures de fêtes*, pp. 105–108; 115–118. See Pierre Nora (ed.), *Les Lieux de mémoire*, 3 vols. (Paris: Gallimard, 1984–1986).
62 AN MC/ET/LXXXIV/1304: 'inventaire après décès, Léon Laurent-Pichat'.
63 LLP, Journal, 23 June 1862.
64 *Ibid.*, 15 Jan., 18 April 1865; 29 April, 18 Dec. 1866, etc. As Achille's marriage contract reveals, Geneviève Leroi's two sisters married two Asselin brothers so 'Mme Asselin' may have been, not just the maternal aunt of the siblings, but Achille's mother-in-law.
65 Laurent-Pichat exchanged small gifts with Rosine, e.g. in 1864 and 1870.
66 LLP, Journal, 1 Jan. 1875.
67 Susan Foley, 'The Christmas tree becomes French: From foreign curiosity to philanthropic icon, 1860–1914', *French History and Civilization,* 7 (2016), 139–57; Martyne Perrot, *Le Cadeau de Noël: Histoire d'une invention* (Paris: Autrement, 2013).
68 No Christmas events were recorded in 1869 or 1870.
69 LLP, Journal, 21 Feb., 14 March 1874.
70 *Ibid.*, 14 May 1868; 14 Feb., 16 May, 21 Nov. 1872; 21 March 1873; 17 Feb. 1876; 14 Nov. 1878.

71 *Ibid.*, 8 April 1869; 7 May 1871; 31 March, 10 Dec. 1874; 28 April 1875.
72 *Ibid.*, 20, 26 June 1868; 1 May 1870; 14 Feb. 1878.
73 *Ibid.*, 19 Jan. 1864; 18 Jan. 1867.
74 *Ibid.*, 1 Feb. 1874.
75 *Ibid.*, 4 July 1864; 15 Sept. 1865; 11 March 1866.
76 *Ibid.*, 20 Oct. 1863; 19 Jan., 4 July 1864; 3 July, 30 Aug., 30 Sept. 1865; 3 Sept. 1866; 18 Jan. 1867, etc. They were seeking a new cook on 22 May 1876.
77 *Ibid.*, 25 Feb, 1 March 1865.
78 *Ibid.*, 11, 18 Jan., 20 Oct. 1863; 4 July 1864.
79 *Ibid.*, 13, 14, 19 Feb. 1868.
80 *Ibid.*, 4, 5, July, 11, 22 Aug. 1864.
81 On child-centred families, see Heywood, *Growing Up in France*, pp. 119–23; Perrot, 'Roles and characters', in *A History of Private Life*, IV, pp. 196–227; Zeldin, *France,* I, pp. 315–42.
82 LLP, Journal, 26 May, 25 Nov. 1862; 16 April 1863; 22 Dec. 1869.
83 *Ibid.*, 26 March 1863; 8 Feb. 1864.
84 *Ibid.*, 16 Feb., 6, 8, 22 June 1862; 25 Jan., 1 April, 6 May, 4 Nov. 1863; 28 Feb. 1865; 29 April, 10 Oct. 1866; 23, 26 Oct. 1867, etc.
85 *Ibid.*, 11 Feb., 31 May 1862; 18 Jan. 1863; 29 Nov. 1864; 11 Feb. 1867, etc.
86 LLP, Journal, 4 July 1862. On girls' education, see Rebecca Rogers, *From the Salon to the Schoolroom: Educating bourgeois girls in nineteenth century France* (University Park, PA: Pennsylvania State University Press, 2005); Lévy, *De mères en filles*.
87 BHVP, 6, no. 1: LLP to GLP, 20 Oct. 1866.
88 *Ibid.*, no. 4, undated ('29').
89 See BHVP, 6, no. 29: LLP to GLP, 31 July 1875.
90 *Ibid.*, no. 17, 29 July 1871; BHVP, 7, nos 36–38: GLP to LLP, 10, 13, 15 July 1873.
91 For example, LLP, Journal, 2 Jan. 1874.
92 *Ibid.*, 4 Jan. 1870. Also 2, 9 Jan. 1872.
93 *Ibid.*, 1 Feb. 1864; 4 July 1867; 21 Dec. 1874; 22 Feb., 12 Oct. 1875; BHVP, 7, nos 1, 44, 48: GLP to LLP, undated, 31 May, 15 July 1874.
94 LLP, Journal, 1 Feb., 5 April, 3 May, 1870.
95 *Ibid.*, entries for May–June 1867; 31 Jan., 21, 28 Feb., 1 Nov. 1869; 7 Jan. 1872.
96 Harrison, *Romantic Catholics*, pp. 31–42; Martin-Fugier, 'Bourgeois rituals', pp. 325–30; Lévy, *De mères en filles*, pp. 81, 103–14.
97 APF, GC, notebook, unpaginated.

98 Harrison, *Romantic Catholics*, chap. 1.
99 LLP, Journal, 18 May 1865; 14 May 1868.
100 On education in piety, see Harrison, *Romantic Catholics*, esp. chapter 4; Lévy, *De mères en filles*.
101 Lévy, *De mères en filles*, p. 170.
102 Rogers, *From the Salon to the Schoolroom*, pp. 202–205; Françoise Mayeur, *Histoire de l'enseignement et de l'éducation. III: 1789–1930* (Paris: Tempus, 1981), pp. 121–2, 140–44.
103 LLP, Journal, 16 Feb. 1871; 4 Aug. 1872.
104 LLP, Journal, 10, 17 April 1867; 13 Jan., 21 April 1869.
105 *Ibid.*, 15, 16 Nov. 1875; 1, 22 Nov. 1876. The courses ceased running in 1878.
106 BHVP, 7, no. 32: GLP to LLP, Cadiz, 6 Sept. 1871.
107 BHVP, 6, no. 19: LLP to GLP, 14 Aug. 1871.
108 BHVP, 7, no. 31: GLP to LLP, Seville, 30 Aug. 1871.
109 BHVP, 6, no. 27: LLP to GLP, 16 July 1875.
110 *Ibid.*, no. 29: 31 July 1875.
111 Cécile Dauphin, *Prête-moi ta plume… Les manuels épistolaires au XIXe siècle* (Paris: Editions Kimé, 2000), pp. 80–81; 115–21; Ruberg, *Conventional Correspondence*, pp. 103–108.
112 See Perrot, introduction to 'The secret of the individual', in *A History of Private Life*, IV, pp. 460–67.
113 AN MC/ET/LXXXIV/1304: 'inventaire après décès, Léon Laurent-Pichat'.
114 LLP, Journal, 16, 17 June 1866.
115 LLP, 'Pour Clémence et Geneviève', 23 June 1868, in *Heures de fêtes*, pp. 17–18.
116 LLP, 'Pour les deux', Beuzeval, July–Aug. 1868, *ibid.*, pp. 19–26.
117 BHVP, 7, no. 51: GLP to LLP, 2 Aug. 1874.
118 BHVP, 6, no. 39: LLP to GLP, 28 Aug. 1877. Here Laurent-Pichat copied to Geneviève the verses he had written for Rosine's birthday.
119 BHVP, MS-FS-07-0009, vol. 12: 'Journal de Clémence Hovelacque, 29 juillet–7 déc. 1868', 72 fos (quotations fo 12).
120 See Stone, *Sons of the Revolution*, pp. 49–56.

5

'Bound together forever': friendship, family bonds and republican solidarity, 1861–70

On 19 December 1865, Léon Laurent-Pichat dined at Le Grand Véfour, a leading Parisian restaurant known for its elegant cuisine and urbane clientele.[1] He listed in his diary the names of his seventeen dinner companions – all men – and added:

> Farewell dinner. Toast by Emmanuel [Arago]. I replied that parties, like families, have spoilt children, that I am one of those, and that, at the very moment I was about to endure suffering, I felt their friendship, which transformed the imprisonment that I was about to undergo into something welcome.[2]

The following day, after a luncheon at home with his family and a few close friends, he recorded: 'Rosine, Amédée, the children, [and] Obermayer drove me to Sainte Pélagie', the prison in the heart of Paris where he was to serve a three-month sentence for a newspaper article deriding Emperor Napoleon III and the Catholic Church.[3]

The events of these few hours highlight the intense emotion with which republican political commitment was imbued under the Empire. In going to prison, Léon Laurent-Pichat underwent a rite of passage that confirmed his republican credentials. In the privacy of his journal, he presented himself as a martyr to imperial oppression. This was a narrative of heroism and sacrifice: one of several such narratives in the republican repertoire. In this narrative, Laurent-Pichat's impending suffering was made tolerable, even 'welcome', by the palpable and sustaining friendship that linked republicans as a family.

In deploying the image of the spoilt child, Laurent-Pichat evoked both a metaphorical and a biological sense of family. Given that, as a child, Laurent-Pichat had felt rejected by his parents, the metaphor emphasised the secure affection in which he now delighted. It illustrated his deep attachment to his friends, a metaphorical family of 'brothers' in which a powerful culture of male sociability prevailed. Constantly under threat of prosecution and imprisonment, these 'brothers' found in friendship a vital personal resource in their political struggle.

Yet the powerful bonds of friendship among republican men did not undermine family attachment. Rather, the two were complementary and reciprocal.[4] The entourage that accompanied Laurent-Pichat to prison – his sister Rosine, his brother-in-law Amédée Beaujean, his daughter Geneviève and his niece Clémence – showed that his immediate family shared his republican faith and the suffering it demanded. Such mutual support, whether within biological or metaphorical families, ensured that individual acts of rebellion were magnified, becoming collective acts of republican resistance. Moreover, friendship was not confined to sites of male camaraderie but inhabited family spaces as well. Since political action on the public stage was banned, the intimate sphere became a site of political engagement where friends and family came together to advance the republican cause.

Friendship and intimacy

The guests at Laurent-Pichat's farewell dinner were drawn from his extensive network of republican friends. That most were journalists is unsurprising, given his leading role in journalism over more than a decade and the importance of the press as a forum for challenging the Empire.[5] Many of the dinner guests had originally come together as contributors, with Laurent-Pichat, to Eugène Carré's short-lived periodical, *La Jeunesse: Journal littéraire,* in 1861.[6] Some had worked with Laurent-Pichat on the literary periodical *La Revue de Paris*. Laurent-Pichat's friendship with two other dinner guests, Arthur Ranc and Charles Delescluze, would soon see him collaborate with them on Delescluze's newspaper, *Le Réveil* (founded in 1868).[7]

Laurent-Pichat's broad intellectual and literary interests extended beyond the boundaries of journalism. Many of the diners at Le Grand Véfour attended Laurent-Pichat's salon, which brought together sixteen or seventeen close male friends and colleagues on Monday (later Tuesday) evenings.[8] A number of those who regularly attended that salon, including Etienne Arago, Eugène Pelletan and Henri Lefort, also attended meetings of the editorial committee of *La Réforme littéraire*.[9] The distinction between salons, editorial meetings and political gatherings was always finely drawn.

Republican salons were sites for discussions of philosophy, art and music, but they were also places where 'the sacred flame of liberty was kept alight' during the Empire.[10] Laurent-Pichat reported a lively argument at the salon of Jean-Baptiste Delestre, for instance, about whether republicans should take the oath of loyalty to the Emperor.[11] The programme at Laurent-Pichat's gatherings, which included readings from literary works and discussions of current ideas, such as those of prominent Italian nationalists Garibaldi and Mazzini, resembled that of the renowned salons hosted by Marie d'Agoult (the author and historian 'Daniel Stern') and later by Juliette Adam.[12]

While Laurent-Pichat held many mixed gatherings, only men attended his Monday evening salon, which he hosted in conjunction with Rosine and Amédée.[13] This regular gathering, like the dinner at Le Grand Véfour, demonstrated the intersection between collegiality and friendship, between work and pleasure. His salon deliberately fostered a distinctly male sociability, offering an opportunity not only for the exchange of ideas but also for the expression and exploration of friendship in a select gathering. In this respect it performed a similar role to the learned societies and *cercles*, as well as to the increasingly popular freemasons' lodges, though in a less formal and ritualised environment.[14] Similarly, the international congresses that Laurent-Pichat and his colleagues attended in the 1860s were not only sites for sharing republican ideas and aspirations, but also sites of male camaraderie. Laurent-Pichat looked forward to meeting up with Auguste Scheurer-Kestner at the Berne congress in August 1865, for instance, but he wrote: 'It's not the congress that interests me: it's you – and the group of friends – will you still be there [when I arrive]?'[15]

Laurent-Pichat's correspondence provides glimpses into the emotional tenor of his male friendships at this time. The letters show that men sought the companionship of others for whom they felt love and affection, expressing that emotion directly, sometimes effusively. The men's shared interests included politics, since republicans gravitated towards other republicans. Their friendships were sites for what Richard Godbeer describes as 'male emotional labour', creating and nurturing the bonds of sympathy as the bases of collective action.[16] But they were not simply pretexts for instrumental political alliances. The friendships among French republicans under the Empire were based on strong emotional attachment, like those that Godbeer found among republicans in the early American Republic.[17] They were valued relationships in their own right, from which the friends drew emotional sustenance. The emotional quality of their friendships, in turn, gave strength to their political alliances.

The letters to Laurent-Pichat from François Favre, fellow journalist and republican, reveal a warm and trusting relationship between them from at least 1861.[18] They also reveal the links that bound each of them to Louis Ulbach and to Etienne Arago, a journalist and writer of popular melodramas. Favre wrote a lengthy letter in November 1861 seeking a loan of 1,500 francs to clear the debts accumulated during his exile in Belgium. He had already approached Arago but, as he noted, 'the thousand francs we lent Ulbach made it impossible for Etienne to help me at this moment'. This, he explained, had forced him to call on 'your good friendship'. The precarity of a career in republican journalism, which was subject to constant threat of prosecution, was hinted at in this account. If friendship enabled Favre to request a loan from Laurent-Pichat, however, Favre also expressed the fear that the request might imperil that friendship: 'You will never know what bitterness accompanies this request for assistance ... and what fear of disturbing the most secure relationship and the most solid friendship.'[19] The mutual support embedded in male friendship nevertheless enabled him to appeal to that bond.

Laurent-Pichat was wealthy, unlike most of his friends. Etienne Arago was the son of the treasurer at the Perpignan Mint.[20] François Favre's father had been a wine merchant in Lyon, but by the 1860s was dependent on his son. Not only did Favre lack an inheritance, but the 'imperious duty' of caring for his father had also prevented him from seeking a wealthy wife. He provided a revealing insight into the considerations underpinning bourgeois marriage in this period – even among republicans – when he explained to

Laurent-Pichat: 'I could not ask a woman who was rich, compared to me, to assume the burden of an eighty-year-old man who needs a lot of care ... So I took a wife for whom marriage was beneficial.'[21] Eugène Pelletan might have lived in comfort from a paternal inheritance but as a rebellious son who had rejected Catholicism he had been cut out of his father's will.[22]

Laurent-Pichat apparently did come to Favre's rescue in 1861. Favre remained a friend and dinner guest over many years and felt sufficiently confident to request other loans.[23] While contemporary norms ensured that none of the friends used the intimate *tu* to each other, Favre always addressed Laurent-Pichat as 'dear friend'. He expressed his 'deepest attachment', sent his 'most affectionate greetings', and signed off 'very affectionately' or 'in good friendship'.[24] These may have been formulaic greetings, but they repeatedly affirmed the men's friendship, and they testify to the emergence of more expressive epistolary practices among male friends by this period.[25]

Letters also formed a central component of Laurent-Pichat's developing friendship with Auguste Scheurer-Kestner, who came from a wealthy family of Alsatian industrialists. They first met at Sainte-Pélagie prison in 1862; Scheurer-Kestner was an inmate and Laurent-Pichat was visiting Eugène Pelletan. Laurent-Pichat declared that making Scheurer-Kestner's acquaintance was the highlight of 1862, and the feeling was apparently mutual. At Christmas that year, Laurent-Pichat sent Scheurer-Kestner a portrait of himself, as requested, recalling fondly 'our handshakes in that little room perched high' in the building at Sainte-Pélagie: 'nothing is sweeter to me than these swallow's memories'. The origins of their friendship gave it particular intimacy, according to Laurent-Pichat: 'A friendship born in prison cannot fade away. Friendship loves the shadows and prospers in them – like ivy'. He repeated this sentiment on several occasions, insisting through his repetition on the special bond between them: 'I ... met you and got to know you at Ste-Pélagie and through you those close to you – and thus we are bound together forever, in our dreams, in our actions, in our silence, in our hearts!'[26]

If friendship was sometimes lived as a relationship between 'brothers', it was a multifaceted relationship that linked not only the men, but also those around them, in bonds of attachment.

Rather than being practised in male-only spaces outside the family, friendship in these republican circles was very much a family affair. Friends valued and reinforced the intimate family ties that were an important dimension of bourgeois men's lives and a mark of their worth. Men presented themselves to each other not just as 'friends' (though that was important) but – according to circumstance – as sons, fathers and husbands; they shared an emotional connection that was homosocial, but that shaped and was shaped by their other relationships. In their letters, therefore, male friendships were often intertwined with family relationships. Similarly, in their social interactions, the boundary between family intimacy and male sociability was fluid, creating a flexible and open environment in which personal relationships could flourish.

In writing to Laurent-Pichat, François Favre frequently sent his greetings to Rosine and Amédée Beaujean, with whom he dined on occasion. Similarly, the friendship between Laurent-Pichat and Auguste Scheurer-Kestner integrated strong male sociability with inter-familial tenderness. Laurent-Pichat's letters invariably contained greetings from his entire family to Mme Scheurer-Kestner and the children: 'You are all there in our conversations and those who are farthest away are not the least present'.[27] While exchanging family greetings was a form of politeness, it was inspired by a deeper conviction about the precious nature of family life and its inter-relationship with political life. Laurent-Pichat wrote to Scheurer-Kestner in 1863:

> How are your children? Well, I hope? And Madame Scheurer too. Once someone has met you, they don't forget you, and they want to know that you are happy at least at home. The other family, the one outside the home, is suffering; but the home [*foyer*] requires peace and quiet. That consoles us for the patience necessary [in the struggle].[28]

Laurent-Pichat's letters to Scheurer-Kestner reveal the growing intimacy of their friendship over time. He initially opened his letters 'Dear Sir and friend', positioning himself as a respectful admirer of Scheurer-Kestner. He was flattered to receive a note informing him of the birth of Scheurer-Kestner's second daughter in 1863: 'Allow me to offer you my best wishes and congratulations.... Thank you for thinking of me'.[29] By the time Scheurer-Kestner sent condolences to Laurent-Pichat on the death of his mother later that year, their friendship had become a relationship between equals, one that nurtured the spirit and sustained emotional health:

> I do not thank you [for your condolences]; I expected this sincere expression of your kind sympathy: but I want to tell you how much good it has done me. There are some forms of grief that friends cannot console, but they support us in the ordeal and prevent us from succumbing to desolation.[30]

Scheurer-Kestner's letter of sympathy has not survived, unlike that of François Favre, which achieved intimacy not only by acknowledging his friend's grief but also by evoking his own:

> If I didn't write to you on the occasion of the death of madame your mother, let me tell you how much I shared your sorrow. I carry in my thoughts a distant grief, the memory of which is as intense, despite the years that have passed, ... as the day of separation. Those who have experienced these heartbreaks know how painful they are and I don't believe there are any consolations for them but the precious and careful preservation of the memories that are dear to us.[31]

Favre and Laurent-Pichat were linked here as bereaved sons who vicariously shared each other's suffering. Further, Favre's preparedness to describe intimate experiences and expose his personal feelings confirms that his relationship with Laurent-Pichat was not just strategic, designed to advance a shared political interest, but had a deeply personal and emotional component.

Even when the testimony of correspondence is lacking, Laurent-Pichat's social interactions provide revealing insights into his intimate male friendships. Despite the absence of correspondence between them, it is certain that Laurent-Pichat, Louis Ulbach and Etienne Arago were close friends. Otherwise, it is unlikely that they would have worked together so frequently on political ventures. Nor would they have chosen each other as travelling companions, as they did in 1863.[32] The friends supported each other's activities and often dined in each other's homes. When Ulbach was too ill to complete a promised newspaper article, his wife appealed to Laurent-Pichat to complete it for him.[33] Ulbach even took refuge at Laurent-Pichat's home for more than two months during the Paris Commune of 1871, when he was in danger of arrest.[34]

Scattered entries in Laurent-Pichat's journal document the familial warmth of his exchanges with Ulbach and Arago over many years. We catch a glimpse of Etienne Arago playing with Geneviève and Clémence after dinner, 'like an uncle'.[35] We see Laurent-Pichat, accompanied by Ulbach and Arago, shopping for dolls for the children in Bâle. We see him visiting Ulbach on New Year's Day, bringing a present for his daughter's doll. We see his concern to know whether the toys sent to Scheurer-Kestner's daughters had arrived intact.[36] A shared experience of fatherhood gave added intimacy to Laurent-Pichat's relationships with Scheurer-Kestner and Ulbach. When Scheurer-Kestner's second daughter, Suzanne, was born in 1863, Laurent-Pichat's congratulatory note emphasised the paternal feeling they shared: 'I have tasted my measure of your joy and I tell you that as simply and sincerely as possible.'[37] Suzanne later remembered her father as strict and authoritarian, but Laurent-Pichat saw in him a tender and loving father like himself.[38]

Not all Laurent-Pichat's friends were political activists; nor were they all fathers. Gustave Nadaud, for instance, conducted his politics by other means as a composer of popular songs and a leading light at the singing society *La Goguette de la Lice chansonnière*. But his enduring relationship with Laurent-Pichat, too, highlights the familial dimension of friendships among the men in this social circle. Nadaud was best known for his ribald verses about seduction and sex workers.[39] This hints that male friends sometimes enjoyed the freedom to indulge in risqué humour in male-only environments. However, Nadaud was a frequent guest at Laurent-Pichat's dinner table and holidayed with the family at Beuzeval, where he often sang for them.[40] Again, this friendship was not confined to the social institutions of male camaraderie. Rather, the boundary between male sociability and family sociability was fluid and flexible, and Nadaud willingly crossed from one to the other when the opportunity arose.

Another close friend of Laurent-Pichat, Léonce Anquez, also avoided political action. As a teacher employed by the State, he had been required to swear an oath of loyalty to the Emperor: political action would have meant dismissal.[41] While no letters survive between them, Anquez's participation in family rituals over twenty-five years reveals the intimacy of his relationship with

Laurent-Pichat and his family. He visited the house frequently and, like Nadaud, took holidays with them; in 1868, he was invited to Geneviève's First Communion and the celebratory dinner that followed.[42] Writing to his daughter some years later, Laurent-Pichat described the interaction between Anquez and two-year-old Mimi, Laurent-Pichat's great-niece:

> We were delighted at Mimi's behaviour towards Anquez, singing to please him – Anquez, who had so many dolls' tea parties with Clémence [Mimi's mother] when she was a child; ... Mimi kissed him, let herself be kissed, was cuddly and sweet, she who says – No! – so well. Our friend was enraptured. It was a well-deserved reward.[43]

By harking back to the childhood of Clémence and Geneviève, both now married, Laurent-Pichat provided a revealing glimpse of Anquez's place within the family over many years.

Both Anquez and Nadaud were bachelors, like Etienne Arago and Laurent-Pichat himself. We might have expected their relationships with each other to have been quintessentially male and homosocial. Yet the evidence suggests that those relationships were embedded in a familial intimacy in which they all took delight. Nor was the experience of fatherhood a prerequisite for enjoying an affectionate relationship with children or indulging in family pastimes. The culture of masculine sentiment allowed men to engage with other men's families and children; it gave men's relationships a transparency and warmth that exceeded the demands of politics, enabling them to provide lifelong support to each other.

Friendship and political opposition

Republican opposition, as Roger Price has noted, was 'the product of a founding "myth" and of a shared political culture, language, and symbolism'.[44] It was also the product of friendship, since friendship both supported those suffering under political repression and facilitated the sharing of ideas and strategies of resistance. The 'salutary terror' that had ensured minimal opposition to the coup d'état may have eased, but surveillance and prosecution throughout the 1850s continued to make opposition difficult. Republican organisations were illegal and political gatherings were banned.

Even a decade after the coup, therefore, the dead hand of repression still weighed heavily on republicans. François Favre wrote to Laurent-Pichat (in Beuzeval) from an unseasonably cold Paris in July 1861: 'This November temperature is not enough to console us for the misfortunes of the present moment. Who can be assured of sleeping in his bed, on seeing the pathetic bases on which the accusations against Greppo or several others are based?'[45] Laurent-Pichat wrote to Jules Ferry in similar terms in 1862:

> Miot arrested. Greppo arrested.... Gonesco arrested.... Searches at the home of Martin-Bernard. It's a shoddy terror stunt [*coup de terreur raté*]. And these six or seven hundred arrests don't include the students seized [demonstrating] at the Bastille or at their homes. There is great unrest.[46]

While a few revolutionary republicans were prepared to countenance violence, the great majority sought a parliamentary path to the Republic. They participated in Empire elections – despite the limits on republican campaigning and the promotion of handpicked official candidates – to achieve that goal. Moderate republicans remained very cautious opponents of the Empire, with cautious agendas for change. Radicals, including Laurent-Pichat and his friends, were frustrated at the slow pace of change. As the elections of 1863 approached, they wanted to challenge sitting republicans who were too ready, they believed, to support the government.[47] Moreover, a number of them, like Laurent-Pichat, wanted to support worker candidates in the elections.[48] Laurent-Pichat's diary for March and April 1863 reports 'stormy' meetings and 'discontent' about this issue and reveals his ongoing affiliation with men like Henri Lefort, Charles Delescluze and Etienne Arago.[49]

The issue of worker candidates was again on the agenda for the by-elections of February 1864. Laurent-Pichat remained strongly in favour – the minority position – and on this occasion outlined his views in a letter to Scheurer-Kestner. His critics, he wrote, argued that the workers could not be relied upon to support a republican agenda, but those same critics allowed considerable latitude to bourgeois republicans in their dealings with the Empire. The issue, for Laurent-Pichat, was to give the workers confidence in the republicans: 'It would be fatal if the workers could one day say that they sought the support of the radicals, that they requested it and that it was not forthcoming'.[50]

Consistent with his position, Laurent-Pichat helped finance the campaign of the engraver Henri Tolain in the by-elections of 1864. Tolain, in collaboration with Henri Lefort and others, had recently published the 'Manifesto of the Sixty' defending workers' rights, including their right to self-representation: a concept still inconceivable to many bourgeois.[51] Laurent-Pichat's journal records several visits by worker delegates during the campaign and, on 8 April, notes his meeting with 'the printer Blot, to whom I paid the costs of Tolain's electoral campaign and the balance of Blanc's'.[52] According to Henri Lefort, who acted as the workers' go-between with bourgeois republicans, Laurent-Pichat contributed eight thousand francs.[53] As a result of this payment, he was investigated for belonging to an unauthorised association. He was interrogated but not charged.[54]

The republicans' endurance as an opposition force, despite the constant threat of prosecution, owed a great deal to their friendship networks. These personal bonds ensured that friendship became a resource, a radical force enabling republican action. Friendship not only provided emotional and social support, but also modelled republicans' shared vision of social connectedness in an idealised Republic based on 'liberty, equality and fraternity'.[55] They suffered together, but they also shared a common hope. Thanks to these bonds, republicans devised creative modes of opposition that avoided prosecution. They rallied around each other's efforts, volunteering for committees and donating time as well as money to each other's ventures.

Friendship networks underpinned the success of the public lectures that provided one opportunity to express republican solidarity in a legal way.[56] Those organised by Albert Le Roy and Prosper-Olivier Lissagaray at the rue de la Paix were among the most popular. Held three times per week, they were 'family talks, animated by the spirit and the heart', according to one sympathetic report.[57] 'Due to the friendship that linked me with M. Albert Le Roy I was invited to be involved in these talks', wrote Laurent-Pichat. 'All the speakers at these lectures were my friends.'[58] Like Louis Ulbach, who also participated in the lecture programme, many of these men also regularly attended Laurent-Pichat's salon.

Political subjects were forbidden at the rue de la Paix and Laurent-Pichat spoke on poetry. However, the clearly republican character of these lectures ensured that the police remained vigilant. Individual speakers like Eugène Pelletan were banned and prosecuted (he had declared in the *Courrier du dimanche* that the Austrians were freer than the French) and the talks were eventually shut down.[59] Pelletan's friends rallied around as he struggled to pay his fine, a sale of Pelletan's books attracting a 'who's who' of the republican movement. Indeed, the preview of the book sale was shut down, too, as a cover for an illegal political gathering.[60]

Another imaginative republican campaign that remained within the law was built around the tercentenary of Shakespeare's birth in April 1864. Louis Ulbach, Etienne Arago and Laurent-Pichat joined a committee with friends of Victor Hugo to create an event to mark that anniversary, separate from the official event.[61] They planned a banquet in Shakespeare's honour for six hundred paying guests, presided over by Hugo. The republican political agenda behind the banquet was only barely concealed. An empty presidential armchair at the proposed banquet was intended to draw attention to the fact that Hugo was still in exile as a prominent opponent of the Empire. The banquet was banned, along with another organised by the English community in Paris, sparking international indignation.[62] Even though this act of republican resistance was aborted, therefore, the international condemnation of arbitrary power represented a victory.

The assassination of Abraham Lincoln in April 1865 provided yet another opportunity for French republicans to promote their cause by hitching it to a prominent event, and again Laurent-Pichat and his friends were involved. Republicans genuinely grieved for Lincoln, whom they regarded as a beacon of progressive thought, a defender of individual liberties and democratic government.[63] Henri Allain-Targé (another friend of Laurent-Pichat) wrote to his mother: 'This evening I am as sad as if one of my own family were dead. The wretched slavers have assassinated Lincoln!', a man of 'virtue and honour', who, in decreeing an end to slavery, had attacked 'the most hideous plague that the spirit of tyrannical domination has ever invented.'[64]

But in mourning Lincoln as a virtuous republican hero, French republicans also seized the opportunity to attack the Empire and promote their cause. They commissioned a gold 'medal of liberty', funded by popular subscription, to be presented to Lincoln's widow.[65] The medal would 'glorify the hero of American democracy, affirm the principles for which this great and decent man was martyred', Laurent-Pichat proclaimed.[66] The medal's design honoured Lincoln's opposition to slavery and his devotion to the American Republic. It simultaneously condemned the French Emperor, who had overthrown the Second Republic and reinstituted slavery (abolished by that Second Republic) in the French colonies. The Lincoln medal project kept the Republic to the fore, demonstrating again how friendship could be shaped into a weapon against the Empire.

Mourning republican friends

Given the importance of friendship in sustaining the republican struggle, the deaths of friends and colleagues drew grieving survivors together in solidarity. The sudden death in January 1865 of Jean-Baptiste Charras, a major republican leader aged only fifty-five, was one such moment, revealing much about how republicans incorporated grief and mourning into their culture of mutual support and friendship. Charras was a charismatic figure, a career soldier who had risen to the rank of colonel but who had been expelled from the army and proscribed following the coup d'état of 1851. Like Hugo, he had rejected the amnesty in 1859 and remained in exile in Bâle. Despite his absence from France, Charras had retained his prominence in the French republican movement and his death sent shock waves through the republican community. For Laurent-Pichat and his close friends, the loss was personal as well as political. Charras was married to Mathilde Kestner, sister of Scheurer-Kestner's wife, Céline. Laurent-Pichat had known the broader family since at least 1863, when he had travelled to Bâle with Arago and Ulbach to meet them.[67] This death thus added a particular poignancy to Laurent-Pichat's relationship with Scheurer-Kestner; they were now united, Laurent-Pichat declared, as 'friends in sorrow and brothers in despair'.[68]

Attendance at a republican burial could be an act of defiance in itself and the authorities policed funerals carefully.[69] The funeral of republican Ernès Durran in October 1861 highlighted the stand-off that could result. Durran had died in poverty and was buried in a common grave. About fifty republicans assembled on one side; opposite stood the priest and the police, 'watchful of what was happening' lest a republican protest develop.[70]

Since Charras died in Switzerland, his funeral could make an explicit political statement, albeit one that most French republicans would only read about in the newspaper. Laurent-Pichat and Etienne Arago were among the 'long columns of republican men, mostly political exiles', who followed Charras's coffin at Bâle in 1865.[71] Press reports emphasised the 'innumerable crowd' and the intense emotion of the event. Arago, for instance, who had first met Charras during the Revolution of 1830, struggled to deliver his tribute owing to 'the emotion of a long and true friendship'.[72] By insisting on the widespread 'anguish' and 'grief' of the republican family, reports highlighted the sincerity of republicans' attachment to Charras and the extent of their loss.

Charras chose a civil burial: a republican protest against the Catholic Church's anti-republican politics and its control of burial practices in France. The funeral orations provided a secular liturgy of suffering and hope to replace their religious equivalents. The speeches at the graveside not only mourned Charras, therefore, but also sought to comfort and rally the bereaved. By reciting Charras's political virtues, the orators aimed to restore hope and maintain the spirit of resistance among those left behind. Charras's brother-in-law, Victor Chauffour-Kestner, declared: 'We owe this grave more than tears: we must seek here a lesson, an encouragement to do good'.[73] In that vein, speakers lauded Charras's merits as a republican: his 'unwavering steadfastness, absolute devotion to the political faith', his deep sense of 'Duty'. 'Every time his name is uttered it will signify: courage, perseverance, honour, victory!'[74]

Secular eulogies were increasingly common at bourgeois funerals. In proclaiming the good character and virtue of the deceased, republicans participated in the practices of emulation that helped to create a specifically bourgeois culture prizing individual virtue over ancestry.[75] However, republican funerals departed from the standard bourgeois pattern in that republicans did not remain silent about politics. The political virtues of the deceased were vital to the republican sense of identity and their task of rallying survivors to stay the course. The model of heroism presented in republican eulogies therefore highlighted the visibility of men's public action in the republican struggle.

Familial virtue, which ranked high in bourgeois estimates of good character, was also an essential quality in republican men: if political 'duty' was lauded, therefore, so too was tenderness. In praising Charras, Victor Chauffour-Kestner celebrated 'the noble and tender heart who loved the Fatherland with a love at once so virile and so passionate'.[76] Etienne Arago celebrated the 'familial tenderness, so delicate and so noble, which produced in him all the greatness and all the consideration of a husband, a son, a brother'.[77] Republican men needed to fight publicly for their goal. But that republicans were family men, embedded in relationships that were not defined simply by politics, was equally important. Moreover, to be a family man was to be a solid citizen, not a hot-headed youth enamoured of revolution. This claim was vital to the movement's emerging self-narrative as a serious political force capable of government.

While bourgeois women rarely received funeral orations, Etienne Arago's eulogy for Marie-Reine Rolland, Mme Lefebvre, shows how republicans occasionally attempted to incorporate women into their narratives of heroism. In 1851, Mme Lefebvre and her husband had accompanied their two sons into exile, where Arago had made the family's acquaintance. When Mme Lefebvre died in 1862, Arago paid tribute to her suffering for the republican cause: 'Adieu to the valiant woman! Adieu to the faithful wife! Adieu to the devoted mother! Adieu to the *citoyenne* [citizeness]!' Arago praised Mme Lefebvre's domestic virtues but he also acknowledged her civic contribution. By describing her as a 'valiant' woman, Arago endowed her with courage and endurance; by describing her as a *citoyenne*, he attributed to her an investment in the republican cause. However, he declared: 'The Fatherland was the dream of her nights, devotion to family the reality of her days'.[78] Her civic role remained a 'dream', not a 'reality'. Convinced of gender difference, yet conscious of women's entitlements within a Republic that espoused equality of citizens, republicans would struggle for some decades to define the duties and rights of a female citizen. Eugène Pelletan, for one, simply evaded the issue as 'a question for the future'.[79]

Figure 5.1 Léon Laurent-Pichat in prison attire, 1866.

Sainte-Pélagie: friendship, family and steadfastness

Sainte-Pélagie prison was ostensibly a place of punishment. For Second Empire republicans, however, the building was visible testimony to their steadfastness, solidarity and resistance. Republican prisoners remained living embodiments of dissent, admired and supported by their friends and communities. Sainte-Pélagie thus became a site of republican pilgrimage, but one intended to laud the living not to commemorate the dead. It was a hub of sociability to which republicans flocked, moving freely among the political prisoners as though on a regular round of visiting. Laurent-Pichat conveyed that gregarious atmosphere in reporting his visit to Sainte-Pélagie on 12 April 1862:

> Visit to Pelletan at Ste-Pélagie. Fleury was there. I went upstairs with him to see Scheurer; Mme Scheurer was there with Mme and Mlle Hingray. I called on Pelletan on the way down. Chaudey, his wife and son were there. I walked Fleury back and spent some time with him. Mme Fleury and her two daughters were there, with Arnaud de l'Ariège.[80]

Laurent-Pichat visited Eugène Pelletan, as well as Scheurer-Kestner, many times between March and June 1862; he visited other prisoners as well. He was therefore no stranger to Sainte-Pélagie when he presented himself to the Director on 20 December 1865 to begin his own sentence. He wrote to Scheurer-Kestner the following day: 'My first thought was of you. I made your acquaintance here, and this building [*pavillon*] is precious to me'.[81] He thus recited once again the genealogy of a personal friendship nurtured by the men's shared suffering as prisoners for the republican cause.

Laurent-Pichat's status and wealth ensured that he was allocated the finest cell in the building, with two large windows.[82] He installed curtains to divide up the space: a sketch he sent to Scheurer-Kestner showed how he had created a miniature bourgeois apartment with an antechamber, a living room, a bedroom, a *cabinet de toilette* and a small room with a commode.[83] A photograph from the time shows Laurent-Pichat sporting a beard and wearing rough prison clothing rather than elegant bourgeois attire (see figure 5.1). He ate restaurant meals instead of prison fare, however, and his valet came daily to bring his letters and restock the wine supply. He spent his evenings replying to his correspondence.[84] As a political prisoner, Laurent-Pichat was free to read, to write and to visit other inmates during the day, as well as to receive books, newspapers and gifts from outside. He adorned his cell with photographs of his mother and the children, as well as one of Jean-Baptiste Charras.[85] The deprivation of liberty was no doubt a hardship but, for political prisoners convicted of publishing offences, prison discipline was not punitive in this period.

The sociability that Laurent-Pichat had described when reporting his visits to Pelletan in 1862 also characterised his own imprisonment. His diary records streams of callers, and he reported to Scheurer-Kestner that he had on average ten visitors per day. These included Scheurer-Kestner himself and a number of other friends and fellow-militants.[86] Family solidarity was highlighted by the daily visits of Rosine, Amédée, Geneviève and Clémence. At least one family member kept him company for lunch; family dinners were 'not quite within the rules', but the Director turned a blind eye and the dinners continued regularly.[87] Family solidarity extended to Laurent-Pichat's other siblings and their families, while even the in-laws of his siblings made the effort to visit him.

These family visits illustrate that republican children were not sheltered from the consequences of the family's politics. At twelve, Rosine's daughter Clémence was the oldest child in the family. Geneviève was nine and the other cousins were all younger. They were nevertheless initiated into the prison regime, which was part of the cultural and emotional experience of republican opposition. That this could help reproduce republican loyalty across generations was demonstrated in early 1866, when Auguste Scheurer-Kestner and his wife, Céline Kestner, paid a visit to Laurent-Pichat at Sainte-Pélagie.

Céline had been a child of ten when the coup d'état was unleashed on 2 December 1851. Her father, Charles Kestner, and her sister's husband, Victor Chauffour-Kestner, were arrested and imprisoned along with the other republican Deputies. Mme Kestner tried to keep news of the arrests from her youngest children. She wrote to her husband: 'Céline is very ill today. I'm waiting for the doctor. She was a little delirious in the night. It's the effect of the emotion caused by the arrest of our loved ones, which she learned with the heart of a woman but which reacted on her child's body.'[88] Céline had been traumatised by the arrest of her father, but according to her mother, even at age ten her 'heart' had understood what was at stake: she embraced the family's attachment to the republican cause. Now in 1866, aged twenty-four, she proclaimed her identity as a republican by making the pilgrimage to Sainte-Pélagie to visit Laurent-Pichat.[89]

Scheurer-Kestner reported that his days in Sainte-Pélagie were among the happiest of his life.[90] Laurent-Pichat certainly enjoyed many moments of camaraderie there, too, extending and reinforcing his republican network. He became friendly with Jules Miot, whose arrest he had lamented to Jules Ferry in 1862 and who was serving a three-year sentence for belonging to a secret society.[91] New arrivals – including many convicted journalists – soon joined them. They spent their evenings together and regularly issued dinner invitations to one another. Despite being imprisoned for their republican activities, Laurent-Pichat and his friends assembled unhindered to '[drink] to the Republic' on 24 February: anniversary of the founding of the Second Republic in 1848.[92]

Laurent-Pichat's social group in Sainte-Pélagie expanded further on 2 March 1866 with the imprisonment of a group of students – admirers of perennial revolutionary Auguste Blanqui – who had been convicted for holding a republican demonstration at the Bastille.[93] They joined Laurent-Pichat's daily walks with friends in the prison courtyard, and the evenings of discussion in Laurent-Pichat's room. The experience of one of the students, Debroz, illustrates that imprisonment was indeed a republican rite of passage. Laurent-Pichat recorded: 'Debroz, Jaclard and two others came to invite me to go to their quarters tomorrow at four o'clock to <u>give Debroz his spurs</u> [.] Having been sentenced to two months, and completed one month, he's <u>on his horse</u>'. Laurent-Pichat accepted the invitation and dined with the group the following day.[94]

The rapprochement between these 'young men' and Laurent-Pichat is perhaps surprising. What did they see in him? They were probably familiar with his radical journalism and his developing reputation for supporting the workers' cause, which suggested he was a kindred spirit. Perhaps they basked in the attention of a respected republican figure. What did he see in them? As supporters of Blanqui, their politics were more radical than his. Blanqui's belief in deploying secret societies to instigate a popular uprising was totally at odds with Laurent-Pichat's pursuit of democracy through open politics.[95] Besides, Blanqui demanded followers and Laurent-Pichat was not a follower.[96] Significantly, he never visited Blanqui; when he encountered him on visits to Sainte-Pélagie his reaction was non-committal.[97] Yet Laurent-Pichat's social circle in Sainte-Pélagie included several Blanquists as well as the students, so he was not averse to discussion and engagement. Laurent-Pichat described the students to Scheurer-Kestner:

> They are very charming, very fiery, very young, in the full flowering of the grand passion, the first glorious blooming of the beautiful flower of radicalism! One feels sensible in their company, that is to say old; but they have such ardour and such personality.[98]

As someone whose own radical acts were committed with the pen, Laurent-Pichat admired the young men's bravado in deliberately confronting the authorities. They evoked a youthful nostalgia in the now middle-aged radical.

Laurent-Pichat was released from Sainte-Pélagie on 19 March 1866. Those friends who had farewelled him at Le Grand Véfour three months earlier celebrated his return with another dinner.[99] Not only did he slip back comfortably into family routines and social life, but he also resumed his former activism. He was soon writing again for the republican press and providing support to an array of newspapers, including *La Revue encyclopédique*, *La Libre Pensée*, *La Pensée nouvelle*, and *La Coopération*.[100] His speedy return to republican social and political life highlighted the futility of prosecution as a means of suppressing republican activities.

In May 1868, the 'liberal' Empire allowed a loosening of the laws around the press and public assembly; an explosion of public meetings and new opposition newspapers followed.[101] The ongoing prohibition on discussing religion and politics was largely ignored by republicans, however, so prosecutions continued unabated. In April 1869, Jules Favre would count 118 prosecutions for press offences over the preceding thirteen months, with sentences totalling ten years' imprisonment and more than 135,000 francs in fines.[102]

Laurent-Pichat made a modest contribution to those totals when he was jailed again for an article in *Le Phare de la Loire*, where he had declared in February 1868 that France was beginning to resemble 'the Russian regime': all citizens were treated as guilty; they were harassed and subject to interrogation 'on no other grounds than a vague suspicion ... or holding an unpopular political opinion'. Found guilty of defaming the authorities and disturbing public order, he was sentenced to one month in prison and a fine of one thousand francs.[103] His sentence confirmed that freedom to recognise the government remained very limited in the 'liberal' Empire.

Laurent-Pichat entered the Hospice Dubois to serve his sentence on 15 May 1868. As if the authorities recognised the pointlessness of the exercise, the regime at the Hospice Dubois was even more relaxed than at Sainte-Pélagie. Again, Laurent-Pichat was surrounded in prison by other republicans, most notably Alfred Naquet (future author of the republican divorce law, who was serving fifteen months for belonging to a secret society). As well as receiving numerous visitors, Laurent-Pichat was also permitted to take day release. He often dined at his home, returning to the Hospice late at night; he even made a day trip to visit his sister Herminie at L'Isle-Adam. Again, his imprisonment barely interrupted his social life or his political activities.[104]

Released from prison again on 14 June 1868, Laurent-Pichat was largely absent from Paris for the next three months. He and his family spent July at the seaside and August in the Pyrenees. After three weeks with Amédée Beaujean's parents in Chablis, the family then travelled to Thann to visit their Alsatian friends, the Kestners and the Rislers. They were welcomed on 4 October by Camille Risler and his son Charles: 'We played, we amused ourselves, especially in the evening. Geneviève and Clémence were caught up in the excitement. A wonderful welcome. As always.' Over the following days, the extended family – the widowed Mme Charras, Camille and Charles Risler, Auguste Scheurer-Kestner and his wife Céline, and Céline's sister, Hortense – entertained their guests with carriage rides and croquet. The evenings were spent playing parlour games. Even charades had a political edge in this political family: on one occasion, as Laurent-Pichat recorded, the solution was 'Liberty'; a few days later, it was 'Alsace'.[105] As well as providing enjoyment and strengthening family ties, their games reinforced the political opinions that united them in republican solidarity.

Republican friendship, enmeshed in family ties, was splendidly on display in this gathering. Such friendship was a constant source of succour, providing a web of personal support that sustained individuals in the ongoing political struggle. As this example demonstrated, friendship stretched, amoeba-like, across family borders, creating a broad zone bathed in politics where republicanism was absorbed, sustained and reproduced. Laurent-Pichat and his family basked in the security of their ties to this republican community of friends and were also generous contributors to its reserves of sociability and affection.

Notes

1 Rebecca L. Spang, *The Invention of the Restaurant: Paris and modern gastronomic culture* (Cambridge, MA: Harvard University Press, 2000), pp. 238–9.
2 LLP, Journal, 19 Dec. 1865. Present were '[Charles] Delescluze, Etienne [Arago], Emmanuel [Arago], [Eugène] Carré, [Charles-Louis] Chassin, [Charles] Quentin, [?] La Tour, [François] Favre, [?] Belin, [Antonin] Lafont, [Eugène] Courmeaux, [?] Léclouché, [? uncertain], Amédée [Beaujean], [Arthur] Ranc, [Alphonse] Fleury, [Jules] Mottu, [Eugène] Despois.'
3 *Ibid.*, 20 Dec. 1865. For a discussion of the offending article (*Le Phare de la Loire*, 13 Oct. 1865), see chapter 3.
4 On the complementarity of family and friendship ties, see Macías-Gonzáles, 'Masculine friendships', 416–35.
5 See chapter 3.
6 Published weekly, *La Jeunesse: Journal littéraire*, appeared only eight times, 8 June–27 July 1861 (BnF catalogue).
7 See chapter 6.
8 The Monday evening gatherings continued (with breaks over the summer months) until 1865, when they were held on Tuesdays. On republican salons, see Martin-Fugier, *Salons*; Grévy, *La République des Opportunistes*.
9 LLP, Journal, 15 Dec. 1861.
10 Nord, *Republican Moment*, p. 124.
11 LLP, Journal, 19, 25 Nov., 29 Dec. 1861.
12 Tchernoff, *Le Parti républicain*, pp. 216–17; Martin-Fugier, *Salons*, pp. 30–33. On Garibaldi and Mazzini: LLP, Journal, 19 Nov. 1861.
13 BHVP, 14, fo 104: 'Discours de M. de Mahy' [funeral oration].

14 See Harrison, *The Bourgeois Citizen*; Agulhon, *Le Cercle*; Nord, *Republican Moment*, chapter 1; Grévy, *La République des Opportunistes*, chapter 10. See also Hoffmann, 'Civility, male friendship', 224–48.
15 AN 276AP/1: LLP to Scheurer-Kestner, undated ('16th').
16 Godbeer, *Overflowing of Friendship*, pp. 12–13.
17 *Ibid.*, chapter 5.
18 AN 248AP/1: 22 letters from François Favre, 1861–85.
19 AN 248AP/1: François Favre to LLP, 26 Nov. 1861. See Vapereau, *Dictionnaire universel*, p. 566.
20 Michel Mourre, *Dictionnaire encyclopédique d'histoire*, nouvelle édition (Paris: Bordas, 1996), pp. 357–8.
21 AN 248AP/1: Favre to LLP, 1 Nov. 1871.
22 Stone, *Sons of the Revolution*, p. 25.
23 AN 248AP/1: Favre to LLP, 1 Nov. 1871; 13 July 1883.
24 For example: AN, 248AP/1, 7 Aug. 1862; 9 Dec. 1865; 8 Sept. 1871.
25 Marie-Claire Grassi, *Lire l'épistolaire* (Paris: Armand Colin, 1998), pp. 54–6; Macías-Gonzáles, 'Masculine friendships'.
26 AN 276AP/1: LLP to Scheurer-Kestner, 23 Dec. 1862; undated ('29th'); undated; undated ('22nd').
27 *Ibid.*, 10 Dec. 1869.
28 *Ibid.*, undated (in pencil: '1863').
29 *Ibid.*, 6 Jan. 1863.
30 *Ibid.*, undated (in pencil: '1863').
31 AN 248AP/1: Favre to LLP, 3 Dec. 1863.
32 LLP, Journal, 23 Sept. 1863.
33 *Ibid.*, 24 Jan., 21 March, 4 April, 2 May, 20 Nov. 1862; 28 Jan., 4 Feb. 1864, etc.
34 See chapter 6.
35 LLP, Journal, 30 Oct. 1863. The girls were aged seven and ten.
36 LLP, Journal, 23 Sept. 1863, 4 Jan. 1864; AN 276AP/1: LLP to Scheurer-Kestner, '31' [Jan. 1866?].
37 *Ibid.*, 6 Jan. 1863.
38 Suzanne Gobron, *Les Mémoires de Suzel: Journal de ma vie, quelques souvenirs, annotés et illustrés par Olivier Dornès* (Paris: Le Trigramme, 2002), p. 95.
39 See Marie-Véronique Gauthier, 'Sociétés chantantes et grivoiserie au XIXe siècle', *Romantisme*, 68 (1990), 75–86.
40 According to LLP's journal, Nadaud holidayed with the family at Beuzeval in 1862 (11–30 July), 1867 (22 July until at least 20 Aug.) and 1869 (26 July–29 Aug.) In 1869, he sang on at least eight occasions. Anquez also joined the family at Luchon in 1868 (6 Aug.–4 Sept.)

41 Isabelle Havelange, Françoise Huguet, Bernadette Lebedeff-Choppin, 'Anquez, Henri-Louis-Léonce', in *Les Inspecteurs généraux de l'instruction publique. Dictionnaire biographique, 1802–1914* (Paris: Institut national de recherche pédagogique, 1986), pp. 130–31.
42 LLP, Journal, 14 May 1868.
43 BHVP, 6, no. 79: LLP to GR, 14 Oct. 1877.
44 Price, *French Second Empire*, p. 317.
45 AN 248AP/1: Favre to LLP, Paris, 12 July 1861.
46 MSDV, LLP to Ferry, undated, annotated 'among letters from spring of 1862'.
47 Tchernoff, *Le Parti republicain*, pp. 363–9.
48 *Ibid.*, pp. 390–97; Price, *French Second Empire*, pp. 365–72.
49 LLP, Journal, 29, 31 March, 6 April 1863.
50 AN 276AP/1: LLP to Scheurer-Kestner, 9 March [1864]. For workers' criticisms of the republican election campaign, see Henri Tolain, *Quelques vérités sur les élections de Paris (31 mai 1863)* (Paris: E. Dentu, 1863).
51 'Manifeste des Soixante', *L'Opinion nationale*, 17 Feb. 1864.
52 *Ibid.*, 8 April 1864. He reports many meetings with workers during February and March 1864.
53 Tchernoff, *Le Parti républicain*, pp. 407, 409. LLP's journal notes several donations to worker candidates.
54 LLP, Journal, 8 April, 2 July 1864. See AN 248AP/1: Notes on Laurent-Pichat's interrogation, written over a letter from Favre, 21 July 1864. See also *Le Procès des treize en premier instance* (Paris: E. Dentu, 1864).
55 On the political significance of republican friendship, see Godbeer, *Overflowing of Friendship*, chapter 5.
56 Robert Fox, 'Les Conférences mondaines sous le Second Empire', *Romantisme*, 65 (1980), 49–57.
57 Anatole de la Forge in *Le Siècle*, 2 June 1861.
58 LLP, preface to *Les Poètes de combat*, pp. 1–2. This volume published his talks at the rue de la Paix.
59 LLP, Journal, 28 Feb. 1862. Stone, *Sons of the Revolution*, p. 41; Nord, *Republican Moment*, p. 193. Paul-Armand Challemel-Lacour and Jules Vallès were also banned: Tchernoff, *Le Parti républicain*, p. 327.
60 LLP, Journal, 20 Dec. 1861; 1, 28 Feb., 1, 18, 19 March 1862; MSDV, LLP to Scheurer-Kestner, undated.
61 LLP, Journal, 4, 11, 12, 14, 15, 18, 19 April 1864.
62 Marie-Clémence Régnier, 'Shakespeare's 1864 jubilee in France: A crown for two writers, William Shakespeare and Victor

Hugo', in Christa Jansohn and Dieter Mehl (eds), *Shakespeare Jubilees: 1769–2014* (Münster: LIT Verlag, 2015), pp. 111–27.

63 Michael Vorenberg, '*Liberté, égalité*, and Lincoln: French readings of an American president', in Richard Cartwright and Jay Sexton (eds), *The Global Lincoln* (Oxford: Oxford University Press, 2011); Olivier Frayssé and Laurence Grégoire, 'The French Masonic tributes to Abraham Lincoln', *American Studies Journal*, 60 (2016), online version, 27 Sept. 2019: DOI 10. 18422/60-10. LLP attended a memorial ceremony for Lincoln on 29 May 1865 (Journal).

64 H. Allain-Targé to Mme Allain-Targé, undated [April 1865], in Allain-Targé, *La République sous l'Empire: Lettres, 1864–1870* (Paris: Bernard Grasset, 1939), pp. 22–5 (23).

65 Benjamin Gastineau, *Histoire de la souscription populaire à la médaille Lincoln* (Paris: Librairie internationale, 1865). See also AN 248 AP/1: ten letters from Charles Thomas to LLP, 9 Oct. 1866–17 Sept. 1867.

66 *Le Phare de la Loire*, 2 Aug. 1865. LLP received a note of thanks from Mrs Lincoln: Journal, 28 Jan. 1867.

67 LLP, Journal, 11–19, 21–24 Sept. 1863.

68 AN 276AP/1: LLP to Scheurer-Kestner, undated ('21'). Charras's death seems the most likely inspiration for this letter.

69 Avner Ben-Amos, *Funerals, Politics and Memory in Modern France, 1789–1996* (Oxford: Oxford University Press, 2000), pp. 87–110; Price, *French Second Empire*, pp. 326, 335–6.

70 LLP, Journal, 23 Oct. 1861. See LLP's letter recommending Durran to Jules Ferry: MSDV, 29 March 1859.

71 LLP, Journal, 23–25 Jan. 1865; *Volksfreund* (Bâle), quoted in *L'Enterrement d'un proscrit (25 janvier 1865), discours prononcés par MM. Chauffour-Kestner, Edgar Quinet, Etienne Arago, et Ch.-L. Chassin*, 3ᵉ édition (Fribourg: Impr. de C. Marchand, 1865), p. 1.

72 *L'Enterrement d'un proscrit*, pp. 1–2.

73 V. Chauffour-Kestner in *ibid.*, p. 2.

74 Edgar Quinet, 'Discours sur la tombe de Charras, 25 janvier 1865', in *Le Livre de l'exilé, 1851–1870: après l'exil, manifestes et discours, 1871–1875* [1895], (Geneva: Slatkine reprints, 1989), pp. 580–83; C.-L. Chassin in *L'Enterrement d'un proscrit*, p. 2.

75 James Arnold, '"*Il fut bon père*": The *Institut de France*, funeral eulogies and the formation of bourgeois identity in early nineteenth-century France', *French History*, 29:2 (2015), 204–24.

76 V. Chauffour-Kestner, in *L'Enterrement d'un proscrit*, p. 2.

77 Etienne Arago, in *L'Enterrement d'un proscrit*, pp. 2–3.

78 Etienne Arago, *Quelques mots prononcés au cimetière de Montmartre, le 21 janvier 1862 sur la tombe de Madame Lefebvre (née Marie-Reine Rolland) par M. Etienne Arago* (Paris: Imp. de A. Augros, 1862).
79 Eugène Pelletan, *La Femme au XIXe siècle* (1869), quoted in Stone, *Sons of the Revolution*, p. 51.
80 LLP, Journal, 12 April 1862.
81 AN 276AP/1: LLP to Scheurer-Kestner, 21 Dec. 1865.
82 LLP, Journal, 30 Nov, 17 Dec. 1865.
83 AN 276AP/1: LLP to Scheurer-Kestner, 13 [Feb. 1866]. See Émile Couret, *Le Pavillon des princes: Histoire complète de la prison politique de Sainte-Pélagie depuis sa fondation jusqu'à nos jours* (Paris: E. Flammarion, 1895), pp. 12, 201.
84 LLP, Journal, 22 Dec. 1865; AN 276AP/1: LLP to Scheurer-Kestner, 1 Feb. 1866.
85 LLP, Journal, 23, 29 Dec. 1865; 6 March 1866; AN 276AP/1: LLP to Scheurer-Kestner, 7 Jan. 1866.
86 AN 276AP/1: LLP to Scheurer-Kestner, 7 Jan. 1866; 1, 13 [Feb. 1866]; LLP, Journal, 8, 12 Feb., 13, 16 March 1866.
87 LLP, Journal, 25 Dec. 1865.
88 BHVP, 1, fo 141: Eugénie Kestner to Charles Kestner, undated but annotated 'December 1851'.
89 LLP, Journal, 16 March 1866.
90 A. Scheurer-Kestner, *Souvenirs*, quoted in Tchernoff, *Le Parti républicain*, p. 336, note 1.
91 LLP, Journal, 26, 29 Dec. 1865; 2 Jan. 1866. On Jules Miot, see https://maitron.fr
92 LLP, Journal, 24 Feb. 1866.
93 Laurent-Pichat lists the men as Edmond Levraud, [Ernest] Granger, G[abriel] Brideau, V[ictor] Jaclard, Debroz and [Emile] Villeneuve: Journal, 13 March 1866. See the entries on these men in https://maitron.fr Debroz's first name is never given, even by Maitron.
94 LLP, Journal, 15, 16 March 1866. Emphasis original.
95 M. Dommanget, *Blanqui et l'opposition révolutionnaire à la fin du Second Empire* (Paris: A. Colin, 1960).
96 On republican proselytising in Sainte-Pélagie, and especially on the role of Blanqui, see Tchernoff, *Le Parti républicain*, pp. 336–9.
97 LLP, Journal, 3 June 1862; 5 March 1863: 'saw Blanqui'.
98 AN 276AP/1: LLP to Scheurer-Kestner, 5 March 1866.
99 LLP, Journal, 19 March 1866.

100 *Ibid.*, 24 April 1866; 10, 14, 17 May 1867.
101 Tchernoff, *Le Parti républicain*, pp. 495–526; Martin Phillip Johnson, *The Paradise of Association: Political culture and popular organizations in the Paris Commune of 1871* (Ann Arbor, MI: University of Michigan Press, 1996), chapter 1.
102 Tchernoff, *Le Parti républicain*, p. 521.
103 *Le Phare de la Loire*, 12 Feb. 1868 (the offending article); 1 April 1868 (the judgment).
104 LLP, Journal, 15 May–14 June 1868.
105 *Ibid.*, 4–14 Oct. 1869.

6

'The revolution was so beautiful and pure': family, friendship and trauma, 1868–71

Léon Laurent-Pichat wrote to his Alsatian friend Auguste Scheurer-Kestner in September 1869:

> Are you coming to Paris this winter? That would certainly be very useful: a letter says very little. An evening's conversation says a lot more. We will spend a morning or an evening with Delescluze. On that subject, have you read his book *From Paris to Cayenne*? I make everyone here read it ... It's a book that will endure. I can't tell you how much it has taken hold of me.[1]

While this letter highlights the friendship between Laurent-Pichat and Scheurer-Kestner, it also reveals Laurent-Pichat's admiration for Charles Delescluze, whose book he so highly recommended. That book detailed the sufferings of political prisoners transported to the infamous penal colony in French Guiana after the coup d'état of 1851. Laurent-Pichat, who had co-operated with Delescluze on several republican projects in the 1860s, shared the book's condemnation of the Empire. In 1871, however, Delescluze and Laurent-Pichat would find themselves on opposite sides of a major republican divide: Delescluze became a leader of the revolutionary Paris Commune that challenged the Government of National Defence and he died on the barricades. Laurent-Pichat, despite his criticisms of that government, could not accept insurrection. Remarkably, the two friends' respect and sympathy for each other survived the breakdown of their political alliance.

The crisis-filled years of 1870 and 1871 had devastating impacts on many, not least on republican families and friends. War with Prussia, declared in July 1870, while a military disaster, brought the welcome arrival of the Third Republic. But the question of how to end the conflict and establish the Republic divided republicans. As foreign war gave way to civil war with the Paris Commune, the republican movement fractured. The Commune severed relations between revolutionaries and the conservative republicans in the Government of National Defence. It also put to the test the links between revolutionary republicans like Delescluze and those radicals, like Laurent-Pichat, committed to taking a parliamentary path to the Republic.

Laurent-Pichat's first-hand account of the Paris Commune casts light on the emotional weight that friendship carried during this critical period. His relationship with Delescluze, in particular, illustrates how personal suffering and political trauma were enmeshed during the crisis of 1871, as they had been for French Revolutionaries in the 1790s. Marisa Linton has shown that friendships became 'deadly' during the French Revolution, because personal friendships were distrusted as a threat to the common good.[2] However, the nineteenth-century understanding of friendship as an intense emotional connection between individuals enabled the bonds of affection between Laurent-Pichat and Delescluze to endure, despite the political gulf that opened between them.[3] Neither Laurent-Pichat nor Delescluze abandoned their relationship. Indeed, Laurent-Pichat mourned his friend long after Delescluze was killed and the crisis had passed. The divisions opened up by the Commune, however, would leave their mark on the republican movement as it attempted to construct a secure Republic in its aftermath.

Friends and allies

True to his promise that they would 'spend an evening with Delescluze' when Scheurer-Kestner came to Paris, Laurent-Pichat and his family hosted a dinner party for their friends in January 1870. This dinner brought to their home Delescluze, Scheurer-Kestner and his wife Céline, Charles Floquet and his wife Hortense (sister of Céline) and several republican journalist colleagues.[4] Clémence and Geneviève and Scheurer-Kestner's twelve-year-old daughter, Jeanne, were also included.

Laurent-Pichat's friendship with Charles Delescluze was already well established by 1870. His journal notes Delescluze's presence at 'gatherings of friends' from the early 1860s, often in the company of Etienne Arago and Henri Lefort.[5] Laurent-Pichat became literary editor of Delescluze's newspaper, Le Réveil, in 1868. During Delescluze's lengthy prison term for press offences – from 26 January 1869 until 15 August 1869 – Laurent-Pichat not only visited him regularly but also played an active role in running the newspaper.[6] In June 1869, for instance, he was at its offices almost daily. Moreover, as his journal shows, Laurent-Pichat was a major financial supporter of Le Réveil, donating more than twenty-three thousand francs between 1868 and 1870.[7] Laurent-Pichat's last recorded contribution – two thousand francs – was made on 8 September 1870.

Laurent-Pichat's contributions to Le Réveil consisted mainly of book reviews and reports on the annual Salon. The books he reviewed were carefully chosen. Some were works by republican friends, like Jean-Baptiste Charras's posthumous History of the Campaign of 1815. Laurent-Pichat described it as a literary 'monument consecrated to all those who have died for liberty in a foreign land'.[8] The review was also a personal tribute to a friend: 'I'm reading the first volume of Charras', he told Scheurer-Kestner. 'I'm going to discuss it. It's nothing less than fidelity to a friend. The ivy has grown on his tomb: I am one of those ivies of memory, the most faithful.'[9] Other reviews allowed him to take direct aim at the Empire. Concluding three long articles on Alain Morel's study of Napoleon III, for instance, he summed up: 'Where are we now? At the hour of settlement, the hour of accounting, the hour of facts, the hour of figures, the hour of truth, the hour of justice!'[10]

Laurent-Pichat's art criticism in Le Réveil, too, remained strongly political, as it had been since the 1840s. He continued to emphasise the social and political responsibility of artists. Commenting on a painting at the 1870 Salon that portrayed Protestants fleeing France after the Revocation of the Edict of Nantes in 1685, he wrote:

> When we see paintings like this, we look forward to the time when our artists will depict republican fugitives after 2 December [1851], the scenes at Cayenne, political prisoners thrown into ships laden with galley-slaves. In provincial towns, scenes of the massacres that accompanied the coup d'état, the acts of violence, will be hung on the walls of official buildings alongside portraits of the generals and prefects who committed these crimes against liberty and justice.[11]

Le Réveil was at the forefront of a republican campaign in late 1868 to raise funds for a monument to Alphonse Baudin, a republican Deputy killed resisting the coup d'état. Ignoring government threats, *Le Réveil* published the names of donors, including 'the editors of *Le Réveil*'. It also published the notice of prosecution.[12] The trial opened on 13 November 1868 and drew many spectators.

Laurent-Pichat recorded: 'From 9am till 6pm in the 6th Chamber of the Police Correctional [court], the case of Delescluze, Peyrat, Quentin etc.'[13] But Laurent-Pichat was not in court the following day, which proved to be a landmark day for republicans: Léon Gambetta's speech as Delescluze's defence lawyer caused a sensation. Although his client was convicted, Gambetta's intervention was widely seen as marking not only the arrival of a new generation of republican leaders, but also the beginning of the end of the Empire.[14] The friendship between Laurent-Pichat and Gambetta would gradually strengthen as they co-operated in the republican cause over the following years.

The elections of May 1869 illustrated the political affinity between Laurent-Pichat and Delescluze at that time. Having turned down the suggestion that he stand as a candidate for Le-Pont-de-Beauvoisin (in south-eastern France), Laurent-Pichat joined the electoral campaign in Paris.[15] He aligned himself with the 'democratic union', the Republican Left around Delescluze. The democratic union favoured running radical candidates even against sitting republicans, as in 1863, charging those sitting members with being too compliant with the regime.[16] Laurent-Pichat attended a number of electoral meetings in March and April, often at the home of Leclanché, a close friend of Delescluze, whom Laurent-Pichat had known since at least 1862.[17] Those meetings also attracted Laurent-Pichat's friends Etienne Arago and François Favre, as well as other colleagues from *Le Réveil*, and Alphonse Peyrat, editor of the like-minded republican paper *L'Avenir national*. Laurent-Pichat had celebrated the anniversary of 1848 with these same friends on 24 February.[18] If the radicals in the democratic union disagreed with conservative republicans on some questions, however, they were not united among themselves. Alphonse Peyrat had been tasked with drawing up the radical programme but, as Laurent-Pichat noted: 'After dinner, [I went] with Rampal to Leclanché's place. The programme was withdrawn. An unexpected scene caused by Peyrat'.[19]

The 1869 elections revealed the increasing strength of republicanism in urban areas like Paris, where opposition candidates secured three times as many votes as the official candidates. But urban republicans were outnumbered by rural voters supportive of the Emperor, and by monarchists who preferred the Empire to the republicans. Worse was to come when the Emperor's new constitution was put to a plebiscite on 8 May 1870. Under its terms, the Emperor would not be responsible to the Legislative Body and would retain his plebiscitary powers. Republicans campaigned for a 'no' vote. As Laurent-Pichat predicted to Scheurer-Kestner, the large towns voted 'no' but the overall result was a resounding 'yes', the government attracting three million more votes than it had in the May 1869 elections.[20] Laurent-Pichat's dinner on 25 June with Delescluze and other friends from *Le Réveil* was probably a sombre affair.

War and family suffering, 1870–71

The Emperor's fortunes would soon plummet despite his triumph in the election and the plebiscite. In July 1870 France declared war on Prussia over a dynastic dispute concerning the vacant Spanish throne. Within two months, the French armies suffered a series of dramatic defeats. They culminated at the battle of Sedan on 2 September, when both the commander-in-chief, Marshal Patrice Mac-Mahon, and Emperor Napoleon III himself were forced to surrender. The Empire collapsed.[21] The French population was nevertheless faced with war and invasion. Personal accounts, like that of Laurent-Pichat, complement official reports on public opinion and morale, providing a glimpse into how families coped during this traumatic period.[22]

Laurent-Pichat was holidaying with his sisters and the children at Luchon, in the Pyrenees, as the war unfolded.[23] When the 'disastrous news about the army' began to filter through, guests started leaving. But there was a question about where to go as the Prussians advanced towards Paris. Laurent-Pichat's sister Herminie and her family made their way to Amiens.[24] Amédée arranged safe haven for Rosine and the girls with his parents at Chablis. On 25 August, Rosine took Clémence and Geneviève to spend the duration of the war there; Laurent-Pichat and Amédée headed back to Paris. The family would be separated for nearly six months.

The French public watched the unfolding military disaster with anger and dismay. At Luchon, guests had reacted to news of the army's defeat at Wissembourg with a spontaneous rendition of the Marseillaise, the banned republican anthem.[25] When news of Sedan circulated in Paris on 4 September, crowds invaded the Legislative Body calling for the Republic. A similar popular movement had already greeted the news in a number of provincial cities. The Republic was installed by popular acclaim and an interim Government of National Defence assumed power. But the war with Prussia continued. By 19 September, Paris was under siege, the Prussians endeavouring to starve the city into submission.[26]

Families with few financial resources were hard hit. Unable to leave Paris, they were not only exposed to bombardment but they also endured serious privations. Laurent-Pichat's journal confirms the claim that divisions between rich and poor were accentuated during the siege, as food supplies and firewood dwindled and a black market sprang to life.[27] Despite requisitioning and rationing, Laurent-Pichat was able to purchase 'a good cheese from Holland', mortadella sausage, smoked beef, and luxuries like cooking oil. When Laurent-Pichat dined at the home of Juliette and Edmond Adam, he recorded: '[We] ate beef from Australia with potatoes, ham and asparagus.'[28]

Like other bourgeois families that sent the women and children to safety, Laurent-Pichat's family faced the pain of separation, as he confided to Scheurer-Kestner.[29] They initially believed that this would be short-lived. Laurent-Pichat wrote to Geneviève: 'Perhaps the month of September that is beginning will bring us some respite and if you don't come here maybe I'll be able to go to Chablis'. A week later, he reiterated: 'In a little while, I am very confident, we shall be reunited'.[30] But his confidence was misplaced. For some families, such as that of professor Victor Desplats, the separation stretched beyond a year.[31]

The disruption of the postal service created great anxiety and heightened the emotional burden of separation. Even telegrams took up to two months to arrive and many never arrived at all.[32] Letters that did get through were greatly treasured. 'You miss me, dear Geneviève. You don't know how much I miss you, how much I miss all of you,' Laurent-Pichat declared. 'Write to me when you have a moment. It does me so much good to know that someone is thinking of me.'[33] Geneviève wrote in February: 'In the months since we have seen you, not a day passes when we don't think about where you are, what you are doing, and if you are worrying about us. We haven't suffered at all, though we've had some very sad moments.'[34] Geneviève and Clémence repeatedly expressed their affection and reminded Laurent-Pichat not to neglect his health. They urged him to let the servants, Aimable and Fideline, take care of him. Geneviève suggested: 'Follow the example of Monsieur Fifi [the dog], who accepts all the attention he is given'. 'When you have to spend the night outdoors [on watch], make sure you take a very warm blanket to snuggle into'.[35]

Laurent-Pichat was a member of the National Guard, like his brother and many of his friends. Much of Laurent-Pichat's time was spent exercising and performing guard duty with his unit. He assured the family that, apart from sore feet and not being in control of his own time, he was very well.[36] The opening of the National Guard to workers and employees in September 1870 saw Laurent-Pichat's male servants, Aimable and Isidore, join as well. They brought him meals so that he did not have to eat in 'dreadful canteens'.[37] Laurent-Pichat dined regularly with his brother Achille. But stalwart friends largely composed his social world and filled the emotional gap in his life. Etienne Arago and Léonce Anquez were foremost among them. Others, including Charles Delescluze, Louis Ulbach, Charles Floquet, Victor Schœlcher and Ludovic Lalanne, also continued to appear regularly in his journal.[38]

Laurent-Pichat's poetry gave him solace in this period of separation. During December 1870 and January 1871, he wrote lengthy verses inspired by a copy of the Revolutionary Calendar of 1793 that his friend Anquez had found in a print collector's shop. His verses drew parallels between the earlier period of upheaval and the one he was living through. He dedicated them to Rosine, writing: 'During your indefinite absence / These meagre verses sustained me.'[39] The thought of loved ones, especially of his cherished sister Rosine, remained a vital support.

Republicans divided

Laurent-Pichat's daily journal entries were usually summary. The entry for 4 September 1870 – when the Republic was proclaimed in Paris – was no exception: 'Day of celebration. Overthrow [of the Empire] and Republic'. He was more expressive in a letter to Geneviève two days later: 'Yes, my dear Child, I was very happy on the day of 4 September. The revolution was so beautiful and pure, it was something to see, if you were in Paris. The sight of such excitement lives in one's memory! Not a moment's danger! Not a shot fired! Nothing.' But he added: 'Now I hope that what follows will be worthy of this beginning. If it weren't for these dreadful Prussians, it would be splendid. But the nightmare is there; we have to cast it off.'[40] The 'purity' of Laurent-Pichat's revolution, and the excitement of the moment, were soon tarnished by republicans' divergent expectations. Political differences emerged, shaking or shattering friendships in the process.

The Government of National Defence was dominated by the most conservative republicans, a number of whom had been regularly criticised, as members of the Legislative Body, for compromising with the Empire. They were wary of their more radical colleagues and fearful of popular unrest. The government moved quickly to fill important posts and keep the country running. Etienne Arago was appointed Mayor of Paris, tasked with naming provisional mayors of the Paris districts until elections were held. Arago approached Laurent-Pichat to become mayor of the seventh arrondissement. But as Laurent-Pichat recorded in his journal, 'I told [Lalanne] about the proposition and my hesitations. We went together to the Hôtel de Ville. I refused.'[41]

Laurent-Pichat's hesitations may have been practical. He had no desire to be a full-time administrator, organising public assistance, supervising the rationing system and running soup kitchens.[42] François Favre, who became mayor of the seventeenth arrondissement, wrote to Laurent-Pichat: 'Since my installation, since the proclamation of this dear Republic, I haven't had time to go and see you or even to write to you ... I haven't seen any of my friends. I'm a prisoner in my arrondissement, only leaving the *mairie* for a few rapid visits to the Hôtel de Ville.'[43]

Perhaps Laurent-Pichat's hesitations were political as well. The government excluded as mayors those whose revolutionary tendencies had been on show in the political clubs in the late 1860s.[44] Laurent-Pichat was acceptable by that standard but some of his friends, like Charles Delescluze and Arthur Ranc, were among the most radical elements of the republican movement. Perhaps he decided to wait and see what unfolded.

Despite refusing the position of mayor, Laurent-Pichat soon accepted appointment to the 'council of hospices', which met almost daily to distribute funds for the care of the sick and wounded.[45] He also accepted the invitation to join the 'commission for the publication of papers from the Tuileries': papers abandoned by Empire officials as the regime suddenly collapsed. In joining this commission, Laurent-Pichat was in the company of friends like Etienne Arago, Arthur Ranc and Edmond Adam. Wealthy republican art collector, Henri Cernushi, claimed responsibility for Laurent-Pichat's appointment to this body.[46]

The 'three Jules' in the Government of National Defence – Jules Favre, Jules Simon and Jules Ferry – believed that the war was unwinnable and that France had to accept whatever terms Prussia would offer. They began negotiating in secret, fearful of revolt in Paris.[47] Most Parisians, however, blamed incompetent leadership for the army's defeats and were loath to surrender. Laurent-Pichat reported to Geneviève on 12 September: 'Delbousquet has just come in. He is furious. He is ranting about these old fossils running the army. His tirade is continuing as I write to you'.[48] An ongoing series of heavy French defeats, most notably General Bazaine's surrender at Metz on 27 October with 100,000 men, fuelled public rage and suspicion of treachery. Rather than surrendering to the siege, Parisians raised money for the manufacture of four hundred cannons to defend the capital. Laurent-Pichat contributed to four such collections, donating 750 francs.[49]

When the government finally confirmed the rumours of Bazaine's surrender, and acknowledged that erstwhile monarchist Adolphe Thiers had been sent to negotiate an armistice with Bismarck at Versailles, the result was explosive. A brief and enigmatic entry in Laurent-Pichat's diary attests to the popular mood: 'News about the Hôtel de Ville. We went there. All the [National Guard] battalions, their rifle butts in the air. The commune, the Republic, total confusion.'[50] An angry crowd had occupied the Hôtel de Ville, and while some called for 'the Republic', others called for 'the Commune': harking back to 1792, they wanted the municipal government of Paris (the 'Paris Commune') to take charge of the city's affairs and organise its defence.

This was a moment of insurrection, the beginning of a serious divide between the Government of National Defence, dominated by republicans, and many of its republican constituents. But as Laurent-Pichat's journal illustrates, the significance of the event was unclear to observers. Jules Ferry and General Trochu brought in mobile units from Brittany and loyal National Guard units from bourgeois districts of Paris to restore order. They would do so again when ongoing rumours about an armistice produced further unrest on 22 January 1871.[51] These demonstrations, while quickly suppressed, highlighted the growing divisions among republicans.

If the government's secret negotiations with Prussia enraged Parisians, they were also denounced by leading republicans. Georges Clemenceau (mayor of the eighteenth arrondissement) placarded the walls to condemn this government 'treason'. Both Clemenceau and Etienne Arago were forced to resign as mayors for complicity with the rebels. Edmond Adam also resigned from his post, insisting that Ferry had broken his word not to prosecute protesters.[52] Jules Ferry, who had now assumed Arago's role as mayor of Paris, sought to defuse resentment by calling municipal elections. Laurent-Pichat was again invited to stand for mayor of his arrondissement but again he refused.[53]

The final agreement with Bismarck in February 1871 included not only the occupation of parts of France until a 200 million franc indemnity was paid, but also the surrender of Alsace and part of Lorraine to the newly created German Empire and a victory march through Paris by Prussian troops, even though Paris had never surrendered to the siege. Laurent-Pichat's letter to his Alsatian friend Scheurer-Kestner on 26 February – the day that the peace deal was signed at Versailles – reflected the shock and fury of many on learning its terms:

> We are saved and lost. And when the truth becomes known, too late, alas! people will be unable to comprehend the pitiful cowardice of the wretches who held our fate in their hands. I am crushed. The siege was nothing. I was apart from my loved ones, that was the only suffering I felt. Shame did not tarnish my hopes, my illusions. Today, a blood-soaked peace, delivered on a bed of gold, wrapped in bloodied swaddling and sullied by humiliation, that is what threatens us; it's this evening; it's tomorrow. They are looking for the time to produce it; they're hesitating, and rightly so. The Prussian is there – the usurer

crowned with laurels, the vermin frolicking in our sunshine. I am suffering with you, dear friend, and deeply, believe me.[54]

Laurent-Pichat's emotion overflowed: shame and anger directed at the republican government; hatred and scorn for the Prussians; empathy and pain shared with his Alsatian friend about to lose his homeland. The personal and the political were deeply intertwined in this despairing note that marked his lowest emotional point. Men like Ferry who had so recently been comrades and friends in the struggle for the Republic were now 'they', the opponent. But he embraced the colleagues who continued to reject a humiliating peace at any price, concluding his letter: 'Best wishes to Clemenceau and Delescluze'.

When the peace terms were put to the Assembly convened at Bordeaux, the Alsatian representatives walked out; a few others including Gambetta joined them in solidarity. But the majority acquiesced, to Laurent-Pichat's despair. He wrote again to Alsace, this time to Camille Risler: 'There was no protest from this gathering! ... Is the world so small-minded? Are we so diminished?' His thoughts were with his friends whose lives had been upended:

> What will become of you all? You are the most sorely sacrificed and the most unfortunate ... Mme Kestner and Mme Charras will be widowed twice over. And your young women! Arriving at the happiest of ages and encountering such distress! Do not comfort them; it's their soul that is wounded; it's their national virtue that is bleeding; but take care of the health of this dear group.[55]

Having already lost their husbands, the older women had now lost their homeland as well. Those friends would all choose to retain their French citizenship, and the friendship that linked them to Laurent-Pichat would be reinforced by a shared devotion to the cause of recovering Alsace and Lorraine for France.

There was, however, a bright side to the armistice. Even before it was officially signed, the mail service resumed. Moreover, the possibility beckoned of the family's return to Paris. Laurent-Pichat remained cautious, writing to Geneviève on 8 February: 'I would like to have a secure itinerary to suggest to you. But ... nothing has been ordained in the armistice (from our side) for those wanting to return to Paris'. He worried about 'pillaging soldiers, blocked and destroyed roads', urging wisdom and prudence.[56] On 10 February, however, he and Amédée threw caution to the wind and made the difficult journey to Chablis, where they arrived at 9:30 pm. 'The joy of reunion', Laurent-Pichat noted. 'Conversation in which everyone wanted to talk at once'. After a 'day of chatting by the wood-stove', they all left for Paris on 13 February.[57]

The Paris Commune, March–May 1871

A great deal has been written about the Paris Commune, its politics, its social aspirations and its suppression.[58] A personal account like that of Laurent-Pichat provides keen insights into the emotional tenor of the event. If it highlights the dilemma faced by dedicated republicans who now found themselves in conflict with other republicans, it also reveals the enduring power of friendship in a period of traumatic suffering. Even though Laurent-Pichat became politically estranged from Delescluze over the Paris Commune, the two remained friends.

Bismarck's terms for the armistice required France to hold national elections within twenty-one days. This allowed little time for parties to draw up and publicise lists of candidates. As Laurent-Pichat observed, too, the cordon around Paris prevented republicans from campaigning outside the capital.[59] Almost all those elected in Paris on 8 February 1871 were republicans, but in regional electorates the monarchists' promise to end the war proved attractive. Laurent-Pichat wrote to Scheurer-Kestner: 'I am very happy to hear you've been elected. Paris has performed very well but the provinces are still very monarchical'.[60] The National Assembly that would govern the fledgling Republic consisted of four hundred monarchists and one hundred and fifty republicans.[61]

This Assembly passed a series of measures intended to bring Paris to heel, further enraging Parisians. One law ended pay to the National Guard, who then rejected government authority and elected a Central Committee to whom they reported instead. On 18 March, when the government sent troops to take control of the cannons that Parisians had purchased to defend the city, the National Guard and the populace united in resistance. The national government fled to Versailles and revolutionaries established themselves in the Hôtel de Ville. The Paris Commune now governed the city. But in May, the national government launched a military attack on Paris, which suppressed the Commune with enormous bloodshed. Both the Paris Commune and its vicious repression bitterly divided republicans even years later.

In the days leading up to the Commune, Parisians going about their daily lives had only a fragmented picture of events unfolding in the city. This had already been evident during the war. In October 1870 and again in January 1871, Laurent-Pichat had had difficulty making sense of what was happening. 'All is confusion', he had noted in October.[62] Nor did he recognise the significance of the army's failed attempt, on 18 March 1871, to seize the cannons paid for by Parisians. His journal entry for that day noted simply: 'the call to arms [*rappel*] sounded; affair of the cannons of Montmartre'. He continued nonchalantly: 'Toinette came to lunch; went for a walk with the children'. Nothing suggests that he saw this event as the beginning of overt hostilities between Paris militants and the central government, which refused all subsequent efforts by republican moderates to negotiate a solution.[63]

Even if Laurent-Pichat did recognise the significance of events, he did not always confide that to his journal. He recorded impassively in his journal on 19 March that the National Guard had occupied the Right Bank and that 'Tony [Moilin was] mayor of the sixth arrondissement'. But Moilin was not the elected mayor. He had occupied the *mairie* on behalf of the local vigilance committee: one of a series of occupations by revolutionary elements pressuring for new municipal elections.[64] The *mairie* in Laurent-Pichat's own seventh arrondissement had likewise been occupied by Raoul Urbain and militants of the Club républicain socialiste, although if Laurent-Pichat knew that he did not mention it.[65] Confusion had turned to silence for Laurent-Pichat, and both were a long way from the joy of 4 September. His silence is not transparent, but it suggests that Laurent-Pichat did not support this radical challenge to duly elected officials.

His actions on 22 March certainly testify to his disquiet about civil unrest and violence. While taking an afternoon walk, he and his family came upon a frightening incident at the Place Vendôme, where militants opposing the Commune confronted National Guardsmen, leaving two Guardsmen dead and seven wounded.[66] Laurent-Pichat went home and collected his firearm: ' [I] spent from

5pm until 11 the following day in the courtyard of the *caisse des dépôts et consignations*', guarding the resources of the council of hospices. He does not explain if he feared looting by reactionaries or by Communards.

Elections for the Paris Commune were held on 26 March, despite the opposition of the Versailles-based national government. Whether Laurent-Pichat voted he does not say; many abstained. The elections produced a Commune dominated by an unwieldy mix of revolutionary republicans of various kinds, including Charles Delescluze. Mayor Raoul Urbain was also among their number and red flags were hoisted over public buildings in the seventh arrondissement, domain of the wealthy bourgeoisie. Supplementary elections in early April, however, saw a clean sweep by opponents of the Commune, further highlighting the political divisions in Paris. The radical newspaper *Le Rappel* put forward Laurent-Pichat's name as a candidate in April but, like a number of other proposed candidates, he refused to stand.[67] If Laurent-Pichat had previously been at odds with the conservative republicans who had negotiated a humiliating peace deal, this abstention confirms his distance from the revolutionary elements of the Commune, among whom his friend Delescluze was a leading figure.

Laurent-Pichat remained silent about the revolutionary clubs that blossomed in Paris, a further indication of his distance from the revolutionary movement. The Club républicain socialiste met daily in his own seventh arrondissement. Yet Laurent-Pichat's only recorded visit to a club was to the Club de St-Sulpice, which met at the church of that name. On 10 May the church was the scene of a major, if peaceful, confrontation between the congregation and club members for control. Probably prompted by curiosity, Laurent-Pichat attended that club a few days later, reporting: 'A big crowd, very calm'.[68]

Laurent-Pichat's distance from the revolutionary republicans was reflected, too, in his support for friends and colleagues who fell out with Commune officials. Louis Ulbach, for one, came under suspicion in March for protesting against the closure of the conservative newspaper *Le Figaro*. On 19 April, Ulbach's satirical weekly, *La Cloche*, was suspended; orders were given for his arrest. But he had taken refuge at the home of Laurent-Pichat on 23 March and would remain there until 30 May.[69] It seems likely that

Delescluze's friendship with Laurent-Pichat protected Ulbach from further action, as well as protecting Laurent-Pichat from reprisals for having harboured him. That friendship certainly explains how Laurent-Pichat was able to help free writer and journalist Mario Proth, imprisoned in April 1871: at the behest of Proth's friends, Laurent-Pichat 'went to find Delescluze' and Proth was released. It was probably Delescluze, too, who facilitated the release of the wine merchant Cédille, a neighbour of Laurent-Pichat, whose wife came to thank him for his help.[70] These personal interventions required courage, but Laurent-Pichat's friendship with Delescluze remained intact.

Versailles forces began to bombard the fortifications of Paris on 3 April. This gave urgency to a project by former mayors of the city, joined by lawyers, journalists and businessmen, to secure a truce between the Versailles government and the Paris Commune. Laurent-Pichat had already demonstrated both his desire to defend the rights of the city and his abhorrence of violence. After attending a meeting organised by Charles Floquet on 4 April, he signed the manifesto of the 'League of the Republican Union for the Rights of Paris', published in *Le Rappel* the following day.[71] But it rapidly became clear that third-party negotiation was futile; it was opposed by both sides.

The Paris Commune was regarded by the government as a revolutionary uprising and Versailles troops were intent on the total elimination of its supporters when they entered the city on 22 May 1871. The vicious repression of the Commune in what became known as 'the Week of Bloodshed' left thousands dead, many summarily executed and thousands more imprisoned or rounded up for deportation.[72] The emotional intensity that marked Laurent-Pichat's – and his family's – experience of 'the Week of Bloodshed' was echoed, therefore, in the intensity and volume of Laurent-Pichat's writing. If his journal entries were generally summary, the five days during which the Commune was crushed, from Monday 22 to Friday 26 May, occupied six pages of his journal. Whereas he had often remained silent about developments during the early phases of the Commune, 'the Week of Bloodshed' brought an outpouring of ink as he detailed the unfolding horror visible from his windows. Then, on Saturday 27 May, he wrote four lines: his journal returned to the typically brief summary of daily events as though he had woken from a nightmare, all his emotion spent.

Laurent-Pichat's narrative of the recapture of the city by troops of the Versailles government echoes established reports, its repetitions and disorder perhaps suggesting his dismay, or the imperative to record what he observed before memory failed. It is particularly compelling in its immediacy and evocative power, revealing the powerful emotions that gripped him as an eyewitness. His account emphasises the sensory impact of the experience. While he noted the smell of gunpowder pervading the house, the sounds of warfare dominated the early part of his narrative as Communards tried to hold out against the army on 23 May.[73] A 'bursting shell struck the wall of the courtyard at 7:30 am'. He recorded bullets whistling, 'fusillades from every side', cannons resounding, 'windows breaking everywhere'. The family could hear shouting and arguing among the 'few insurgents' on a barricade outside their house before 'silence descended'. 'The street was deserted. Suddenly it was filled with soldiers'. The following day, too, Laurent-Pichat recorded: 'We heard the assault on the barricade in the rue du Bac', a few doors away. Again, a sudden exchange of gunfire 'sent us back under the couch. Geneviève's legs failed her. Clémence was seized by fear as well'.[74]

If the sounds of violence were terrifying, so, too, was the visual impact of the battle for Paris. The city was illuminated by fire, its blazing landmarks visible from Laurent-Pichat's home. 'The fires concern us more than anything else', he wrote.[75] Moreover, the sight of violence – the killing witnessed from the windows – was profoundly shocking. The army had occupied Laurent-Pichat's courtyard and officers had taken up residence in his porter's lodge. Rather than being a place of refuge, his property was a site of conflict and execution.

Accounts of extrajudicial killings on his doorstep dominated Laurent-Pichat's journal on 24 May. The courtyard became a holding point for prisoners. 'On the steps, under the awning, prisoners were huddled together'. Some were summarily executed, like the National Guardsman shot on the footpath outside his house. More commonly, he reported prisoners being hauled away for execution on the barricades, their deaths staged to 'prove' that they were dangerous insurgents:

> A locksmith from the [nearby] rue de Verneuil, tall, with a black beard, in his shirtsleeves and wearing soiled cotton trousers, was brought [here] by a sailor and dragged to the barricade on the rue de Poitiers where he was shot. A National Guardsman [*fédéré*], captured bearing arms, was shot on the same spot.[76]

In several cases, Laurent-Pichat was able to give names to the victims: 'The young inspector of prisons who lived a number 58, Georges Michel, an upholsterer ... was taken and shot during the night'. Again, 'an old man, a photographer from the rue du Bac near the grocer Rousseau-Jacob, named Titus Albitès .... After a few words, taken out and shot'. Later, the army 'removed the body from the courtyard, the one on the footpath and those on the barricade; they washed away the traces of blood'.[77] The luck that determined life or death on 24 May was reflected in Laurent-Pichat's own experience. He and Ulbach had tried unsuccessfully to have two young prisoners freed; they were only released when Amédée Beaujean identified one as his former student.

It is not clear from Laurent-Pichat's account whether he personally knew the men whose names he reported, but militants often fought in their own local areas.[78] Laurent-Pichat's descriptions, with their small details of clothing and appearance, suggest some compassion: these were not the 'monsters' whose behaviour he would soon condemn. The locations he mentions – the rue de Verneuil, and the barricades on the rue du Bac and the rue de Poitiers – were all close by. The fighting there was within earshot, if not directly visible. At least some of Laurent-Pichat's information, however, came from the officers who had occupied his porter's lodge and who controlled proceedings in the courtyard. Laurent-Pichat who, a few days earlier, could meet with Delescluze, was now regarded affably by the officers intent on eliminating Delescluze and his ilk.

It was through his contact with the officers that Laurent-Pichat learned the fate of some leading Communards: 'The officers told us that Assi has been captured, that Billioray has been shot, that Delescluze is on the run'.[79] But Delescluze was not on the run. Wearing the red sash of an official of the Paris Commune he would climb onto one of the last remaining barricades at the Place du Château d'Eau to face death in the closing hours of the insurrection.[80] The circumstances of his death evoke Delacroix's portrayal of 'Liberty Leading the People', depicting the Revolution of 1830. It might be fanciful to speculate that Delescluze deliberately modelled his death on this archetypal revolutionary image, which had been returned to public display during the Second Republic, but he certainly chose to control the time and circumstances of his own death rather than to place that choice in the hands of his enemies.

The joy of 4 September had been destroyed, and not by the Prussians. The final pages of Laurent-Pichat's account of the Paris Commune are dominated by anger and bitterness, both at the sight of Paris in flames and at the political violence. Some fires were the result of the army's shelling of Communard positions; others were deliberately lit by Communards either as a symbolic gesture or as a tactical manoeuvre.[81] While he noted the 'seething gossip'[82] about the fires, however, Laurent-Pichat believed the now discredited rumour that the Communards had deployed *pétroleuses* – female arsonists – to burn the entire city. He mused bitterly on the scenario that had been averted by the defeat of the Commune, 'the sad parody [of revolution] concluding with a scene from melodrama':

> The battle would have been fought amidst the rubble, in a raging inferno: a real Martyns![83] The horrible and the monstrous, conceived by ham actors! Savages from the drinking houses! Redskins of the cabaret! Envy! Hatred! Brutality! Ignorance! Pride![84]

News that his friend, the journalist Gustave Chaudey, had been summarily executed by the Commune's Public Prosecutor, Raoul Rigault – a young revolutionary with a reputation for violence – filled Laurent-Pichat with sadness and probably confirmed his hostile opinion of the Commune.[85]

Laurent-Pichat reiterated that opinion in a letter to Scheurer-Kestner in early June: 'The malcontents, the eager ones, the hard nuts, the down-and-outs, those who hang around cafés and cabarets, the would-be politicians on the make, the devotees of absinthe, such have been by chance the masters of a town like Paris, for two months'. He fumed: 'How they have dishonoured a worthy cause by unspeakable excesses. Fanaticism, hatred, envy, madness, everything was in the mix…. What led these men astray? The fierce passion for power'.[86]

This damning portrait echoed the racist and class-based stereotypes of the day and resembled the condemnations of the Versailles press, who also labelled the Communards criminals, drunkards, cannibals and madmen.[87] Scheurer-Kestner shared his criticism, writing later:

> It will be difficult in the future to understand the effect produced on a great many republicans by the beginning of the Parisian insurrection, the character of which was denatured and tarnished so much

by what came later. At first I couldn't help but wish it success. It was only when I saw Pascal Grousset present himself as minister for foreign affairs that I realised I was dealing with madmen.... I began to ask myself how men whom I had long held in high esteem could have become accomplices [of this 'crime'.][88]

Laurent-Pichat's ire was directed at the militants leading the Commune, not at the rank and file: he would be prominent among those arguing for an amnesty for Communards as early as 1872. Nevertheless, even though Delescluze remained a key commander, issuing orders to the end, Laurent-Pichat's judgement of Delescluze was shaped by his personal grief. Bitter and sad, refusing to hold his old friend responsible, Laurent-Pichat accused him of weakness rather than malevolence: 'Delescluze, while looking like he was in command, obeyed that Central Committee, gave the lie to his own ideas and convictions so as to look like he was still the master. Another day and he would have been crushed by them'.[89]

Laurent-Pichat's condemnation of the Commune did not mean that he was a friend of Versailles. He painted a caustic portrait of savagery among the Communards' opponents, describing an officer, 'nephew of General Bruat', 'on a tour of inspection, making his horse traverse the barricades strewn with corpses, a flower in his buttonhole'.[90] The republicans of the Versailles government – his former colleagues – invited his scorn as well. There was a note of distaste in Laurent-Pichat's description of Ferry, who passed by after the Commune was crushed 'wearing his tricolour scarf and his tricolour sash', emblems of his allegiance to the Versailles government.[91] His disdain for Jules Simon, expressed in a letter to Scheurer-Kestner, was even more pronounced:

> The fury of victory is so great that Jules Simon was on the point of sacking a teacher, an acquaintance of [Communard] Pascal Grousset, who had asked [Grousset] for a favour (not for himself) by writing: my dear friend.... This is the level of nonsense to which they have fallen.[92]

Simon's stance suggests that, for some in the government, friendship itself, rather than the action it motivated, became suspect in this political conflict, as it had been at the height of the Terror in 1793.[93]

The Paris Commune represented a Rubicon for republican friendships; some survived the crossing, others did not. Laurent-

Pichat's friendship with Jules Ferry never recovered from Ferry's pursuit of a more conservative republican agenda and the brutality it required at that moment. While Laurent-Pichat and Scheurer-Kestner shared with Ferry an aversion to the Commune's revolutionary aspirations, they desired negotiation, not the slaughter from which Ferry did not resile.[94] Laurent-Pichat's friendship with Auguste Scheurer-Kestner emerged from this crisis strengthened by shared political views and aspirations. Similarly, Laurent-Pichat's longstanding ties with Etienne Arago and Henri Lefort proved solid and enduring. It was thanks to friendship, too, that Laurent-Pichat sheltered Louis Ulbach, despite the danger posed by uncompromising militants like Raoul Rigault.

Laurent-Pichat's friendship with Charles Delescluze also endured despite their serious political disagreement over the Paris Commune. The emotional capital that the two men had invested in their relationship ensured that they could take diametrically opposed positions in 1871 and maintain their sympathy towards each other. Moreover, Laurent-Pichat's ties to Delescluze survived Delescluze's death. Not only did Laurent-Pichat help wind up the legal affairs of *Le Réveil* (in which he himself had a financial interest) but he gave financial support to Delescluze's family.[95] With Scheurer-Kestner and Charles Floquet, Laurent-Pichat provided a pension for Delescluze's sister, and later gave money for the funeral costs of both Delescluze's sister and brother.[96]

The Commune created a gulf between those who saw it as the means to achieve a purer democracy which, they imagined, would become a model for the whole country, and those like Laurent-Pichat and Scheurer-Kestner, who saw it as an insurrection against a republican government which, whatever its failings, had been legally elected. Laurent-Pichat's concept of a republican 'revolution' was not the armed struggle of the Commune but the events of 4 September 1870: the bloodless triumph of the popular will, achieved in a spirit of joy and without violence. He retained his youthful Romantic republicanism. His condemnation of the Commune's 'revolution' aligns him with the majority of republicans, especially those of a bourgeois background, who sought regime change via the ballot box but did not accept a revolutionary transformation of society driven by a minority.[97] Laurent-Pichat's journal, with its studied silences and its record of his anguish and angry incomprehension, illustrates the conflicted response of many Parisians, particularly of republican activists forced to take sides.

By-elections for vacancies in the National Assembly were announced for 2 July 1871. Both Laurent-Pichat and Scheurer-Kestner were candidates. Republican electoral committees sprang to life again to draw up their lists. Laurent-Pichat reported attending numerous political meetings and donating to several republican committees.[98] He also visited leading republican newspapers seeking their support.[99] On 29 June, *Le Siècle* published the list of candidates endorsed by the General Committee of the rue Turbigo on behalf of the arrondissements of the Seine. The list included Laurent-Pichat and Scheurer-Kestner, as well as a number of their friends. The candidates' joint manifesto noted that they were 'not in complete agreement on certain questions with the head of the executive power [Adolphe Thiers]', but they agreed to support him given the monarchist threat and desired conciliation between 'the diverse nuances of republican opinion'.[100] Laurent-Pichat and Scheurer-Kestner, along with Léon Gambetta, were also included on the list of the 'radical committee'.[101] Candidates' fortunes fluctuated over two days of counting. On 5 July Laurent-Pichat noted in his diary: 'I am 17th this morning with ninety-nine thousand votes ... bouquet from I don't know whom ... card to Gambetta.' He finally garnered more than 103,000 votes and Scheurer-Kestner 108,000.[102] On 8 July 1871, the two friends took their places in the Assembly as part of the circle around the radical republican leader Léon Gambetta.

Notes

1 AN 276AP/1: LLP to Scheurer-Kestner, 22 Sept. 1869.
2 Marisa Linton, 'Fatal friendships: The politics of Jacobin friendship', *French Historical Studies*, 31:1 (2008), 51–76; Linton, *Choosing Terror*.
3 Vincent-Buffault, *L'Exercise de l'amitié*, pp. 77–8, 122; Counter and White, 'Introduction: The soul's sentiment', 1–5.
4 LLP, Journal, 22 Jan. 1870.
5 LLP, Journal, 16 March 1862; 17 Nov. 1863, etc.
6 *Le Réveil*, 13 May 1869. See Marcel Dessal, *Un Révolutionnaire Jacobin Charles Delescluze, 1809–1871* (Paris: Marcel Rivière et Cie, 1952).

7 Ibid., p. 250.
8 Review of Lieutenant-Colonel Charras, *Histoire de la Campagne de 1815. Waterloo* (*Le Réveil*, no. 214, 26 Dec. 1869).
9 AN 276AP/1: LLP to Scheurer-Kestner, undated [1870].
10 Review of A. Morel, *Napoléon III, sa vie, ses œuvres et ses opinions* (*Le Réveil*, nos 181–183, 23–25 Nov. 1869).
11 'Feuilleton: Salon de 1870, treizième article', *Le Réveil*, no. 378, 11 June 1870. Laurent-Pichat wrote fourteen articles on each of the 1869 and 1870 salons.
12 *Le Réveil*, 5, 12 Nov. 1868.
13 LLP, Journal, 13 Nov. 1868.
14 Tchernoff, *Le Parti républicain*, pp. 526–31; Dessal, *Un Révolutionnaire Jacobin*, pp. 235–40.
15 LLP, Journal, 11 March 1869.
16 Tchernoff, *Le Parti républicain*, pp. 532–46.
17 LLP, Journal, 16 March 1862. On Leclanché and his relationship with Delescluze, see Dessal, *Un Révolutionnaire Jacobin*.
18 LLP, Journal, 24 Feb., 8, 12, 13, 21 March, 22 April 1869.
19 *Ibid.*, 24 March 1869. On divisions within the democratic union, see Tchernoff, *Le Parti républicain*, p. 536.
20 AN 276AP/1: LLP to Scheurer-Kestner, 3 April 1870.
21 Geoffrey Wawro, *The Franco-Prussian War: The German Conquest of France, 1870–1871* (Cambridge: Cambridge University Press, 2003); Michael Howard, *The Franco-Prussian War* (London: Routledge, 2021).
22 On public opinion as reflected in army records and Prefects' reports, see Stéphane Audoin-Rouzeau, *1870: La France dans la guerre* (Paris: Armand Colin, 1989).
23 LLP, Journal, 6–30 July 1870.
24 *Ibid.*, 11 Aug. 1870; BHVP, 7, nos 10, 13: GLP to LLP, 20 Sept. 1870, 2 Feb. 1871; *ibid.*, no. 4 verso: Clémence Beaujean to LLP, 8 Sept. 1870.
25 LLP, Journal, 6 Aug. 1870.
26 On the events of this period, see Wawro, *The Franco-Prussian War*, chapters 10 and 11; Jean-Yves Mollier and Jocelyne George, *La Plus Longue des Républiques, 1870–1940* (Paris: Fayard, 1994), pp. 24–32.
27 On Paris during the siege, see Bertrand Taithe, *Defeated Flesh: Welfare, warfare and the making of modern France* (Manchester: Manchester University Press, 1999), pp. 101–29. For similar findings about siege situations, see Mark M. Smith, *The Smell of Battle, the Taste of Siege: A sensory history of the Civil War* (Oxford: Oxford University Press, 2014), chapter 4.

28 LLP, Journal, 17 Oct., 2 7, 14, 18, 26 Nov. 1870; 4, 8 Jan., 5 Feb. 1871.
29 AN 276AP/1: LLP to Scheurer-Kestner, 26 Feb. 1871.
30 BHVP, 6, nos 10, 12: LLP to GLP, 30 Aug., 6 Sept. 1870.
31 David A. Schafer, *The Paris Commune* (Houndmills: Palgrave Macmillan, 2005), p. 29.
32 LLP, Journal, 1 Dec. 1870; 12 Jan. 1871; BHVP, 7, no. 13 verso: C. Beaujean to LLP, 2 Feb. 1871.
33 BHVP, 6, no. 10: LLP to GLP, 30 Aug. 1870.
34 BHVP, 7, no. 13: GLP to LLP, 2 Feb. 1871.
35 *Ibid.*, nos 3, 6: 31 Aug., 13 Sept. 1870; no. 6 verso: C. Beaujean to LLP, 13 Sept. 1870.
36 BHVP, 6, no. 15: LLP to GLP, 18 Sept. 1870.
37 BHVP, 6, no. 15: LLP to GLP, 18 Sept. 1870; LLP, Journal, 16 Sept., 10 Oct., 3 Dec. 1870. On the expansion of the National Guard, see Schafer, *The Paris Commune*, pp. 33–4.
38 For instance, 7, 10 and 18 Sept., 6, 20 Oct., 25 Nov., 12 Dec. 1870.
39 BHVP, 17, fos 184–205: LLP, 'A Mme R. Beaujean, 31 janvier 1871'.
40 BHVP, 6, no. 12: LLP to GLP, 6 Sept. 1870.
41 LLP, Journal, 5 Sept. 1870.
42 Taithe, *Defeated Flesh*, pp. 114–29.
43 AN 248AP/1: Favre to LLP, 18 Sept. 1870.
44 Taithe, *Defeated Flesh*, p. 103; Schafer, *The Paris Commune*, pp. 31–5.
45 LLP, Journal, 30 Sept., 5, 17 Dec. 1870. On the *'council of hospices'*, see Taithe, *Defeated Flesh*, pp. 64–7.
46 LLP, Journal, 2, 5, 27 Oct. 1870.
47 Sowerwine, *France Since 1870*, pp. 13–14.
48 BHVP, 6, no. 14: LLP to GLP, 12 Sept. 1870. I have been unable to identify Delbousquet.
49 LLP, Journal, 22, 28 Oct., 4 Nov., 17 Dec. 1870.
50 *Ibid.*, 31 Oct. 1870.
51 Robert Tombs, *The Paris Commune 1871* (London: Longman, 1999), p. 60; LLP, Journal, 22 Jan. 1871.
52 Dessal, *Un Révolutionnaire Jacobin*, pp. 301–5.
53 LLP, Journal, 3 Nov. 1870.
54 AN 276AP/1: LLP to Scheurer-Kestner, 26 Feb. 1871.
55 BHVP, 7, fos 17–18: LLP to Camille Risler, 5 March 1871.
56 BHVP, 6, no. 16: LLP to GLP, 8 Feb. 1871.
57 LLP, Journal, 10–14 Feb. 1871.
58 A vast literature dates from the time of the Commune itself. Among recent general studies, see Tombs, *The Paris Commune 1871*; John Merriman, *Massacre: The life and death of the Paris Commune*

(New York: Basic Books, 2014); Jacques Rougerie, *La Commune de 1871*, 2ᵉ édition corrigée (Paris: Presses universitaires de France, 1992).
59 BHVP, 6, no. 16: LLP to GLP, 8 Feb. 1871.
60 AN 276AP/1: LLP to Scheurer-Kestner, 16 Feb. 1871.
61 Mollier and George, *La Plus Longue des Républiques*, pp. 34–43; Sowerwine, *France Since 1870*, pp. 14–15.
62 LLP, Journal, 31 Oct. 1870; 22 Jan. 1871.
63 On those efforts, see Mollier and George, *La Plus Longue des Républiques*, pp. 40 –53.
64 See 'Moilin, Tony', in https://maitron.fr/; [P.-O.] Lissagaray, *Les Huit journées de mai derrière les barricades* (Brussels: Bureau du Petit Journal, 1871), pp. 287–91.
65 Johnson, *Paradise of Association*, pp. 95–8. See 'Urbain, Raoul', in https://maitron.fr.
66 P.-O. Lissagaray, *Histoire de la Commune de 1871* [1876] (Paris: François Maspéro, 1972), pp. 134–40; LLP, Journal, 22 March 1871.
67 LLP, Journal, 9 April 1871. On these elections, see Dessal, *Un Révolutionnaire Jacobin*, pp. 342–3.
68 Johnson, *Paradise of Association*, pp. 169, 229–30; LLP, Journal, 13 May 1871.
69 Bitard, *Dictionnaire général*, p. 500; LLP, Journal, 23 March, 30 May 1871.
70 LLP, Journal, 1, 2, 3 April, 15 May 1871.
71 LLP, Journal, 5 April 1871; *Le Rappel*, 5 April 1871; Jeanne Gaillard, 'Documents: Les papiers de la Ligue républicaine des Droits de Paris', *Le Mouvement social*, 56 (1966), 65–87; Philip G. Nord, 'The Party of conciliation and the Paris Commune', *French Historical Studies*, 15:1 (1987), 1–35. The manifesto, with the signatories, is reproduced in Benoît Malon, *La Troisième défaite du prolétariat français* (Neuchâtel: G. Guillaume fils, 1871), pp. 232–4.
72 Estimates of numbers killed vary widely. See Tombs, *The Paris Commune 1871*, pp. 179–80; Schafer, *The Paris Commune*, pp. 90–100; Merriman, *Massacre*, p. 253.
73 LLP, Journal, 24 May 1871.
74 *Ibid.*, 23, 24 May 1871.
75 *Ibid.*, 23 May 1871.
76 LLP, Journal, 24 May 1871.
77 *Ibid.*
78 Bertrand Taithe, 'Neighbourhood boys and men: The changing spaces of masculine identity in France, 1848–1871', in Christopher Forth and Bertrand Taithe (eds), *French Masculinities: History, culture and politics* (Houndmills: Palgrave Macmillan, 2007), pp. 67–84 (77).

79 LLP, Journal, 23 May 1871.
80 Lissagaray, *Histoire de la Commune de 1871*, pp. 350–54. On Delescluze's death, see Dessal, *Un Révolutionnaire Jacobin*, pp. 410–12 and note 145.
81 Tombs, *The Paris Commune 1871*, pp. 11, 168; Dessal, *Un Révolutionnaire Jacobin*, p. 397.
82 LLP, Journal, 24 May 1871.
83 Nicolo Martyns was a well-known composer of comic opera.
84 LLP, Journal, 24 May 1871.
85 *Ibid.*, 26 May 1871. On this incident, see Schafer, *The Paris Commune*, p. 92. On Rigault, see Taithe, 'Neighbourhood boys and men', p. 79; 'Rigault, Raoul Georges Adolphe', in https://maitron.fr
86 AN 276AP/1: LLP to Scheurer-Kestner, 9 June 1871.
87 Mollier and George, *La Plus Longue des Républiques*, p. 44; Tombs, *The Paris Commune 1871*, p. 191.
88 A. Scheurer-Kestner, *Souvenirs*, quoted in Dessal, *Un Révolutionnaire Jacobin*, p. 337.
89 AN 276AP/1: LLP to Scheurer-Kestner, 9 June 1871.
90 LLP, Journal, 24 May 1871.
91 *Ibid.*, 25 May 1871.
92 AN 276AP/1: LLP to Scheurer-Kestner, 9 June 1871. See 'Grousset, Paschal, Jean, François', in https://maitron.fr
93 Linton, 'Fatal friendships', esp. pp. 75–6.
94 Gaillard, *Jules Ferry*, pp. 247–51.
95 LLP, Journal, 28 July, 17 Dec. 1871; 21 Jan., 28 Feb., 24 March, 12, 22 May, 20 June, 20 July 1872; 3 April 1874.
96 *Ibid.*, 2 Aug. 1875; 1, 16 Nov. 1876; 29 April 1879.
97 Nord, 'The Party of conciliation', 31–2.
98 LLP, Journal, 1 July 1871.
99 *Ibid.*, 18 June 1871.
100 *Le Siècle*, 29 June 1871.
101 A. Jamet, *Le Flambeau républicain: études démocratiques et sociales*, 10e livraison [1871], 20 pp. According to Jamet, Laurent-Pichat featured on five lists and Scheurer-Kestner on three.
102 *Ibid.*, p. 9.

7

'Steadfast and enduring fidelity': friendship and honour in the fledgling Republic, 1871–76

The National Assembly in which Laurent-Pichat took his seat in July 1871 was the site of an intense struggle to secure – or overturn – the Republic. Republicans remained in the minority. But the monarchists were divided behind two different contenders for the throne, while the Bonapartists were hamstrung by the recent collapse of the Empire and the fact that the Prince Imperial was an adolescent. Monarchists and Bonapartists were united, however, in their hostility to the Republic.

In late 1872, the monarchists made an unsuccessful attempt to overthrow the conservative republican government led by Adolphe Thiers.[1] In May 1873, they succeeded, installing Marshall Patrice Mac-Mahon, Duc de Magenta, as head of the government. France remained a nominal Republic only because the monarchists could not agree on who should take the throne. Efforts to restore dynastic rule were not finally defeated until January 1875, when a series of delicately worded clauses saw a republican constitution accepted by the majority in the National Assembly.[2]

Friendship remained an invaluable resource for republicans in this difficult period. As Laurent-Pichat's republican networks reveal, too, many friendships remained intimate emotional connections that transcended politics and drew entire families together. If Laurent-Pichat's careful cultivation of friendship stood him in good stead in the Assembly, so too did his capacity to maintain polite relations with his political opponents. His roles in the Assembly demonstrate that Laurent-Pichat was widely trusted and respected. Indeed, the broad respect in which he was held saw him elected a Life Senator by his peers in 1875. Moreover, thanks to the bonds of friendship and trust that he nurtured, Laurent-Pichat helped to ensure the successful operation of the code of honour that regulated

Figure 7.1 Portrait of Léon Laurent- Pichat, by Ernest Hébert [1865].

the numerous conflicts between political opponents. Respected as an honourable man himself, Laurent-Pichat was well placed to mediate in disputes, in most cases negotiating a peaceful resolution of conflict.

Friendship, respect and republican solidarity

Laurent-Pichat's friendship circles remained diverse as he assumed his new role in the National Assembly. The friends of his youth still feature regularly in his journal during the 1870s. His visits with

Louis Ulbach continued, for instance, though less frequently than in earlier years. The marriage of Ulbach's daughter Marie in January 1874 brought a flurry of visits, as Laurent-Pichat and his family met the prospective husband and arranged for a generous gift.[3] François Favre also remained a regular presence in Laurent-Pichat's daily journal. Favre once again turned to his friend for support during financial hardship in November 1871.[4] There is no record of Laurent-Pichat's response to this request, but the journal, and Favre's correspondence, indicate that their friendship continued as in the past. Laurent-Pichat prided himself on unwavering fidelity to his friends as well as to the republican cause. His friendships linked past and present, illustrating both the enduring quality of many of his personal relationships and the evolution of his friendship circles along with his political activism.

While Louis Ulbach and François Favre were absorbed in their careers as journalists and writers, Laurent-Pichat's daily contacts in the 1870s were mainly with other politicians. Republican social networks both in and outside the Assembly, networks based on camaraderie and friendship, provided the main structures through which Laurent-Pichat pursued his political goals. Family connections also proved significant. On his first day as an elected representative at Versailles in July 1871, for instance, Laurent-Pichat dined with several colleagues including Jules Rathier, who came from Chablis.[5] Laurent-Pichat had family ties to this region through his brother-in-law Amédée Beaujean. Those ties, as well as political affiliation, ensured that his relationship with Rathier would not only prove enduring, but would become a lasting friendship between the two families.

Laurent-Pichat first attended the Republican Circle of the Seine, a fee-paying club with restricted membership, on 8 November 1871, a week after it was founded. Its membership was a 'who's who' of the republican elite and included a number of Laurent-Pichat's longstanding friends. They met at the Circle for dinner or went there to read the wide range of newspapers it provided.[6] Laurent-Pichat was also a member of the Family Circle (*Cercle des familles*), one of the groups that had supported his candidature in July 1871.[7] This organisation assisted the families of imprisoned Communards. Laurent-Pichat contributed one hundred francs to that cause each time he collected his monthly parliamentary allowance of 745 francs; he continued donating to these families even after the Family Circle was shut down by the authorities in March 1873.[8] Many of Laurent-Pichat's friends, including Etienne Arago, Auguste Scheurer-Kestner and François Favre, belonged, like him, to both the Republican Circle and the Family Circle.[9]

While membership lists of the republican factions were not kept until 1882, Laurent-Pichat's journal indicates that most of his close friends in this period were also, like him, members of the Republican Union led by Léon Gambetta.[10] This was the most radical republican faction and was labelled the 'Extreme Left', but it occupied that position only because the revolutionary republicans had either been killed in the Paris Commune or were now in prison or in exile.[11] Its members were not averse, however, to provocative political actions, as when they resurrected the project of building a monument to Alphonse Baudin, the republican Deputy killed resisting the coup d'état in 1851. Having raised funds for the memorial before the Franco-Prussian War, in 1872 they commissioned a design from sculptor Aimé Millet and purchased a plot in the Montmartre cemetery.[12] The monument was completed in November, just as conservatives were attempting to unseat Thiers. As Millet wrote to Laurent-Pichat: 'Everything depends, I know, on what happens over the next few days in the Chamber ... Stand firm, gentlemen of the Left, because you are the real conservatives and saviours of the country'.[13] The inauguration of the memorial finally took place on 3 December 1872, in daring proximity to the anniversary of the coup d'état on 2 December.[14] Projects like this served to rally radicals and remind conservatives that the battle was far from conceded.

Laurent-Pichat lunched with his friends in the Republican Union between sessions at Versailles and relaxed with them after evening meetings. As he recorded on one occasion: 'Meeting at the rue de la Sordière. [I went] with Rathier and Lefèvre, to the Café de la Paix on the boulevard, where Adam joined us. We played dominos'.[15] Laurent-Pichat's journal also reports frequent meetings with his close ally Léon Gambetta. Ever the *bon vivant*, Gambetta was the life of the party and the last to leave.[16] He and Laurent-Pichat lunched or dined together regularly, and Gambetta gave the family sweets at New Year.[17] Laurent-Pichat was also one of the group of friends who were with Gambetta on 11 June 1874 when, during an orchestrated anti-republican riot, a Bonapartist zealot struck Gambetta in the face with his cane. Laurent-Pichat testified in the legal proceedings that followed.[18]

Despite his lengthy career in journalism and his close ties to Gambetta, Laurent-Pichat apparently did not write for Gambetta's paper, *La République française*. Articles were not signed, but Gambetta hand-picked the contributors for their expertise in politics, science or international affairs. He aimed to make it the leading republican political organ, syndicated in the provinces to spread the republican message.[19] Laurent-Pichat's forte remained poetry, and the volume of verse he published in 1880 would contain many items written in the 1870s.[20] But while his literary interests did not suit the agenda of *La République française*, Laurent-Pichat often visited the offices of the newspaper, usually in the evenings when the next day's edition was being prepared. Politics was surely on the agenda, although these gatherings had a social dimension as well. Laurent-Pichat noted on one occasion: 'With Adam, Gambetta and Lefèvre, returned via the boulevard, stopped for sorbets and beer'.[21] His experience demonstrates how friendships in the Republican Union were a resource, both emotional and political, sustaining republicans personally and providing camaraderie in their work for the Republic.

That Laurent-Pichat enjoyed the respect and trust of his republican colleagues was evident in the roles he played in the National Assembly during these years. He found his niche, not as an orator, but as a man behind the scenes, active in committees, writing and working for the cause, and supporting that cause with his financial acumen and resources. Laurent-Pichat was soon elected to leadership roles in the Republican Union, becoming vice-president in June 1873 and joining the Union's administrative committee in December. When he became President of the Republican Union in May 1875, he noted with pride that the vote was unanimous.[22]

Presiding over the Republican Union was largely honorary. The same could not be said of joining parliamentary commissions, the main vehicles for conducting the Assembly's business and thus a major site for the political contest between republicans and conservatives. Laurent-Pichat's election to a variety of commissions showed that he was respected, not just by those in the Republican Union, but across a broad spectrum of his colleagues. About fifty commissions investigated projects and produced reports for the Assembly to consider. The commissioners were elected from standing committees (*bureaux*) whose members were chosen by lot. Between 1871 and 1875, the fifteen *bureaux* were selected at the beginning of the parliamentary session and renewed every four months.[23] But even if republicans were balloted into the *bureaux*, it was difficult to get them elected to commissions (especially, perhaps, radicals from the Republican Union), given that republicans were still a minority in the Assembly.

Laurent-Pichat joined his first commission only weeks after entering the Assembly.[24] He was elected to a number of other commissions over the years, including several dealing with major public loans for which financial astuteness was vital.[25] He became secretary of another commission investigating matters of local government.[26] With his election in 1875 to the *commission de permanence*, Laurent-Pichat joined a small group of twenty-five that kept a watching brief on affairs when the Assembly was not in session.[27] Serving on this commission had obvious drawbacks, as Laurent-Pichat's friend Jules-Antoine Lissajous recognised: 'I've seen with pleasure that you've been appointed to the *commission de permanence*! You are trapped then! No vacation during the vacation? I'll be able to come and see you in Paris – you can offer me lunch'.[28] Laurent-Pichat's daughter had mixed feelings as well, given that his new responsibilities would disrupt family vacations. But as she noted, 'You can console yourself by thinking that you are doing your duty.'[29]

The two members of the Republican Union on the *commission de permanence* – Laurent-Pichat and Charles Lepère – endeavoured to hold the government to account during the parliamentary recess when, despite the new constitution of January 1875 that had established the Republic, repression of republican activities continued apace. In August 1875, for instance, Laurent-Pichat tabled a report and questioned Interior Minister Louis-Joseph Buffet (whom Gambetta labelled 'the black viper') about the sacking of the republican town council of Béziers.[30] Buffet stonewalled and denied, leading the politically alert Rosine to comment to her brother Laurent-Pichat: 'Still Buffet's same old tactics'.[31]

Like the National Assembly, the *commission de permanence* was dominated by conservative and centrist forces and was chaired by the President of the Assembly, the Duc d'Audiffret-Pasquier. It was an achievement for members of the Republican Union to make it onto the *commission* at all, given the weight of conservative votes and the generally hostile attitude towards those allied with Gambetta. Audiffret-Pasquier himself had attacked the Republican Union in the Assembly in December 1872, accusing its members of supporting the 'brutal despotism of the multitude' and being hostile to 'religion, family, property and fatherland'.[32] That a significant number in the *bureaux* – 305 of 374 – were prepared to vote Laurent-Pichat onto the *commission de permanence* suggests that he himself was well regarded, therefore, even if many remained wary of the political aspirations of the Republican Union. Laurent-Pichat recorded proudly: 'Named a member of the *permanence* by 305 votes'.[33]

Political conflict and *affaires d'honneur*

Laurent-Pichat's role in resolving disputes between his political colleagues offers further evidence of his good standing in the Assembly and testifies to his extensive friendship links in republican circles. Disputes between politicians, or between politicians and journalists, were frequent in the hostile political environment of the early 1870s. Such disputes were often matters of honour (*affaires d'honneur*): incidents in which an individual believed his integrity, truthfulness or courage had been attacked. Since honour was fundamental to masculine self-identity, a challenge to one's honour had to be contested because manhood itself was at stake.[34] A duel might well be the result.

Robert Nye estimates that, on average, two hundred duels took place annually between 1875 and 1900, with as many as three hundred in periods of major political crisis.[35] The importance of political duels in this period is attested to by Arlette Schweitz's biographical dictionary of politicians representing the Paris region, which includes each man's duelling record in his political history.[36] Schweitz identifies 109 duels, the vast majority occurring between the 1870s and the 1890s. She notes, however, that the record of a number of politicians could not be established with certainty.[37]

Press reports provide the main source of information on duelling. These reports were shaped by a range of considerations, but not by the desire to create a reliable record. Laurent-Pichat's daily journal is particularly valuable, therefore, in providing an intimate perspective on duelling from inside political circles. It confirms that politicians were frequently at odds over matters of honour but suggests, contrary to the stereotype, that few of those conflicts resulted in duels. Of the eighteen incidents in which he himself was involved either as offended party or as witness (he declined to play a role in several others), only four proceeded to combat.

Laurent-Pichat played a key role in ensuring that disputes among his colleagues were settled peacefully. His diary illustrates Robert Nye's argument that the duel occupied the extreme end of a 'rule-ordered continuum' of social etiquette that governed bourgeois men's behaviour.[38] These rules enshrined dignity and self-control, as well as courage, as markers of bourgeois manhood. While political debate in the early Third Republic was renowned for the *affaires d'honneur* it provoked, therefore, the fact that the vast majority of disputes over honour did not result in duels highlights the mechanisms for promoting self-restraint and politeness, and thus preventing conflict. Moreover, Laurent-Pichat's journal provides a rare insight into the processes of negotiation by which most disputes were resolved. The ritualised mechanisms for resolving disputes, like the ritualised practices of duelling, formed part of the code of honour, and their purpose was to avoid combat.

In illuminating those mechanisms, Laurent-Pichat's journal provides a rare insight into the under-appreciated role of the 'seconds' or witnesses (*témoins*) in ensuring the peaceful settlement of disputes. It also highlights the importance of friendship in the selection of those witnesses. The French term *témoin* conveys the seriousness and responsibility of this role more fully than the English term 'second'. The witness was not just a support person but the one who 'bore witness', testifying publicly to the facts of the encounter. Integrity, discretion and good manners were therefore vital. The witnesses (each man had two) were charged with conducting preliminary negotiations in search of a resolution that left both men's honour intact without resort to arms. If no resolution was reached, the witnesses officiated over the duelling process, following established practices for the choice of terrain, weapon and conditions of combat. The witnesses for the two disputants were also responsible for producing a joint report that was published in the newspapers. This public testimony was crucial to the defence of 'honour': the account usually concluded by declaring that 'honour had been satisfied'. If fighting a duel was a display of the combatants' honour, the witnesses' honour was at stake in the management of proceedings.[39]

Laurent-Pichat's republican friendship networks and his reputation as a trustworthy man explain the frequency with which his colleagues turned to him in matters of honour. A man needed full confidence in the reliability and skill of his witnesses, and he often sought trusted friends for this role. This is evident in the experience of Laurent-Pichat himself. When he was insulted in the Assembly by the Duc Decazes in 1873, Laurent-Pichat turned to his close friend Auguste Scheurer-Kestner as witness. Similarly, when his integrity was impugned by a journalist in 1875, he turned to another longstanding friend and eminent republican, Edmond Adam.[40] Adam, in turn, sought Laurent-Pichat's assistance when a Bonapartist newspaper attacked his wife Juliette (who was also a personal friend of Laurent-Pichat) in December 1876.[41] Charles Floquet likewise asked Laurent-Pichat to be his witness when his wife was insulted in *Le Figaro* in 1879. Floquet was not only a friend but also the husband of Hortense Kestner, and thus part of a family to which Laurent-Pichat was closely attached by friendship, and into which he had married his daughter Geneviève in 1877.[42] Léon Gambetta, too, placed his faith in Laurent-Pichat's friendship and negotiating skills. He appealed to Laurent-Pichat to support their mutual friend and colleague, Arthur Ranc, in 1873; he himself then sought Laurent-Pichat as witness in 1874 when he was challenged by the Bonapartist Alfred Haentjens.[43] In all, Laurent-Pichat acted as witness for another man on sixteen occasions between 1872 and 1881. The majority were his friends; others were perhaps inspired to seek his assistance by his success in dispute resolution. Reliable, trustworthy and widely respected, Laurent-Pichat made an ideal witness.

For politicians, unlike journalists, a momentary loss of self-control, an ill-spoken word in the Assembly, could result in a challenge. The witnesses for the two disputants would attempt to negotiate a resolution. The most important consideration for both parties in the dispute was to save face. The *affaire d'honneur* between Laurent-Pichat and the Duc Decazes in 1873 illustrates the process at work. During a debate over the Catholic Church's control of education, Decazes accused Laurent-Pichat of using 'cowardly' words: a charge that impugned his honour. Laurent-Pichat asked his friends Henri Lefèvre and Scheurer-Kestner to 'seek an explanation' from Decazes, as he recorded in his diary. The witnesses for Decazes were expecting their visit. After several hours, the four witnesses produced a revised account of the incident for the *Journal officiel de la République française* (the record of parliamentary proceedings), which declared that the words spoken by both Laurent-Pichat and Decazes 'were lost amid the noise and agitation' in the Assembly.[44] Since the words were unheard and unrecorded, Laurent-Pichat's honour remained intact; since Decazes had not been forced to withdraw, his honour was also unsullied. Both men saved face.

In other cases, too, negotiation produced a 'clarification' that eliminated the perceived offence and resolved the dispute. When Laurent-Pichat and Edmond Adam acted as witnesses for a colleague in February 1873, for instance, they soon reported that 'everything was explained'.[45] Similarly, when Gambetta faced a challenge for calling the Bonapartist Alfred Haentjens a liar, Laurent-Pichat and Michel Renaud managed to establish that Gambetta had 'misheard' Haentjens, but achieving that solution required two days of negotiation with Haentjens' witnesses.[46]

Laurent-Pichat's diary also shows that, when negotiation proved difficult, the witnesses might recruit an adjudicator to pronounce on the merits of each disputant's case. Laurent-Pichat and Antonin Proust adopted that approach when trying to resolve a dispute between two republicans in 1875. That was also the tactic when Laurent-Pichat and Georges Clemenceau acted for the republican Georges Perin in his dispute with the Bonapartist journalist Louis Grégori. Grégori refused to accept the verdict and a duel resulted. However, the processes of *politesse* were preserved as the two republican witnesses, Laurent-Pichat and Clemenceau, sent cards to the monarchist adjudicator to thank him for his role.[47]

Journalists were often deliberately provocative or sensational in their attacks on politicians.[48] They even attacked the wives of politicians, which was regarded as particularly reprehensible and was sure to result in a challenge by the politician, duty-bound to defend his wife. Having made their point and got good copy, journalists were often ready to withdraw their accusations. Laurent-Pichat elicited a 'satisfactory note' from *Le Figaro* that 'ended the matter' concerning Mme Floquet; similarly, he 'composed a note' that was accepted by the journalist who had slandered Juliette Adam.[49] Laurent-Pichat even managed to achieve a resolution in a particularly difficult case, when the wife of republican Nicholas Parent spat in the face of a conservative journalist who had insulted her husband. Her shocking act defied both gender expectations and standards of civility. Moreover, according to the protocols of the code of honour, Mme Parent's physical assault entitled the offended man to set all the conditions of the contest. By acceding to all the man's demands and acknowledging the justice of his case, Laurent-Pichat and his colleague managed to settle the dispute without bloodshed.[50] The Parent case, like those concerning Juliette Adam and Hortense Floquet, nevertheless illustrates that, whether women insulted men or were insulted by them, they remained pawns in a contest between men, since honour remained a male prerogative.[51]

While most incidents were resolved by the witnesses, some did proceed to physical combat and here friendship was particularly important. The four actual duels at which Laurent-Pichat assisted were largely symbolic encounters and none caused serious injury. The shift over time towards 'first blood' duels (rather than duels to the death) and command duels by pistol (where a shot was fired on command, with no time to take aim) had ensured that this was so.[52] Laurent-Pichat reported only 'light wounds', therefore, in noting the outcomes of these affairs.[53] As he recorded of the contest between Georges Perin and Louis Grégori: 'The encounter took place by the main road [in the countryside] at 10 am. No rain. No sunshine. Nobody. A good outcome for us. We returned to Lille.'[54]

Laurent-Pichat acted as witness at one of the most famous duels of the early Third Republic, that between republican Arthur Ranc and Bonapartist Paul de Cassagnac in July 1873. Both men were well known for their aggressive journalism. Ranc was also republican representative for the Rhône at the time. He had fled into exile in June when an investigation was launched into his participation in the Paris Commune: part of a wave of anti-republican attacks. As Gambetta wrote to Ranc, 'I am the target as much as you, don't doubt that'.[55] Indeed, de Cassagnac had vilified Ranc not only as 'the friend of arsonists and murderers' but as 'the right-hand man of

Gambetta'.[56] This duel was politically significant, which was why Gambetta called on Laurent-Pichat's friendship in asking him to serve as Ranc's witness. Laurent-Pichat travelled to Luxembourg, where the contest was to be held.

Laurent-Pichat's account of this duel differs markedly from the others he reports. Not only is it lengthy, occupying eighteen pages in his journal, but it is also written as a narrative, with a detailed travelogue and snippets of dialogue between the participants. At first glance, it seems that Laurent-Pichat was considering publication. However, a passing reference to 'the report that you [*tu*] will see in the newspapers' provides the clue that this account was intended for someone closely related to him, almost certainly Rosine, who followed politics closely. This was yet another indication that brother and sister shared political insights, and that politics were keenly discussed in the home. In this case, Rosine may even have been invited to read his journal.

Had Laurent-Pichat published his version of events he would surely have precipitated another duel, given his unflattering portrait of de Cassagnac: 'He claimed that he had only fought because Ranc had doubted his courage. He said it to his witness to convey to us and approached Ranc himself, can you imagine, and said it to him!' By approaching his opponent, de Cassagnac broke the rules of engagement. His behaviour on the duelling ground, in Laurent-Pichat's view, did not meet the standard of honour expected of a gentleman: 'It's the [three] musketeers, it's all bragging,' Laurent-Pichat wrote. 'He has no moral sense but is not wicked'.[57] Ranc received a small cut on the arm. The official transcript of the duel reported, however, that since Ranc's injury 'made it absolutely impossible for him to continue the combat, the witnesses declared that honour had been satisfied'.[58] The desired outcome had been achieved.

Honour was central both to concepts of masculinity and to political culture in the 1870s. Laurent-Pichat's involvement in *affaires d'honneur* illustrates how those two elements came together. His reputation as a man of honour, along with his immense capacity for friendship, facilitated his own integration into the political world of the National Assembly. That his parliamentary colleagues turned to Laurent-Pichat as their witness in *affaires d'honneur* affirmed him as reliable and trustworthy. In witnessing to the honour of others, therefore, Laurent-Pichat simultaneously testified to his own honour: the quality on which a man's reputation rested.

Intimate friendship

Laurent-Pichat derived deep emotional satisfaction from his many political friendships. Some of these relationships, moreover, transcended their political contexts. Like the close friendships of his youth with Henri Chevreau and Louis Ulbach, they became deeply personal and intimate bonds for which Laurent-Pichat used the word 'love'. Studies of other close friendships between political allies, especially in periods of intense political struggle, have shown that they were markedly homosocial, nurtured in the spaces and activities of male political solidarity.[59] Laurent-Pichat's close friendships are particularly interesting, however, because they were grounded in family, both structurally and emotionally.

Laurent-Pichat's relationship with Auguste Scheurer-Kestner, which had gradually strengthened during the 1860s, continued to exhibit deep affection. 'Your letter is as cheerful as good health and as delightful [*bon*] as friendship', Laurent-Pichat wrote to him in August 1874.[60] Their joint political struggle inevitably had an emotional dimension, through the shared pleasure of small victories and the shared misery of defeats.[61] But as during the Second Empire, their emotional bonds remained at once political, personal and familial. During parliamentary vacations, when Laurent-Pichat left Paris with his family, he relied on Scheurer-Kestner to keep him abreast of political developments. He wrote from Switzerland in August 1872: 'I know nothing about what is happening. If you receive this letter in time, in Paris, please do me the kindness of replying to Zurich, poste restante.'[62] Laurent-Pichat felt free to make light of their political opponents in the privacy of his correspondence with Scheurer-Kestner. He shared snippets of gossip about the monarchists he encountered at Cauterets, a spa resort near the popular pilgrimage site of Lourdes, quietly indulging his anticlerical sentiments: 'I've run into de Larcy ... Chesnelong is here! Martin d'Auray and the priests! The priests! This proximity to Lourdes is a curse.'[63] Similarly, he was keen for news about the latest Paris scandal when General Bazaine – convicted of treason in

1873 after surrendering to the Prussians with 100,000 men during the Franco-Prussian War – escaped from prison in 1874.⁶⁴

Laurent-Pichat had asked Scheurer-Kestner to act as his witness in his *affaire d'honneur* with the Duc Decazes in January 1873, testifying to his high esteem for his friend. His respect derived not only from his friend's personal qualities, but also from his family connections. Auguste Scheurer had become 'Scheurer-Kestner' through his marriage in 1854 to Céline Kestner, daughter of Charles Kestner and Eugénie Rigau. Laurent-Pichat was in awe of this entire family; four of the five Kestner daughters married leading republican activists. Not only were this family staunch republicans but, as wealthy and powerful industrialists from Alsace, they also possessed the social and cultural capital that Laurent-Pichat – blessed with wealth but without family connection – had had to acquire by his own individual efforts.⁶⁵

Moreover, Scheurer-Kestner was always associated, for Laurent-Pichat, with his deceased hero, Jean-Baptiste Charras, husband of Céline's sister, Mathilde Kestner. Laurent-Pichat's holiday in Switzerland in 1872 with Rosine and the girls concluded with a 'pilgrimage to the tomb of Charras', as he informed Scheurer-Kestner: 'it is no bad thing to complete [the voyage] with a sad thought.'⁶⁶ In 1874, Laurent-Pichat again identified Charras as the common denominator in his friendship with Scheurer-Kestner, though he did so now without naming Charras: 'You must be at Thann, at a family gathering, full of memories, of sadness, and dare I say of hope. I have my sweet little part in that past: I gained there the right to love you.'⁶⁷ This formulation suggests that, for Laurent-Pichat, the bond uniting him to Scheurer-Kestner was not simply an impulse or an attraction. A 'right' implies a moral entitlement: to deny it is unjust. Laurent-Pichat claimed the 'right' to Scheurer-Kestner's friendship on the basis of their shared affection for Charras; shared suffering at his death, shared memories and history. From Laurent-Pichat's perspective, his friendship with Scheurer-Kestner was a chosen friendship, or even 'a brotherhood of choice'.⁶⁸ But if choice was the essential component of friendship, Laurent-Pichat justified that choice on moral grounds. By emphasising the justice of his claim, he expressed his faith that his friendship with Scheurer-Kestner was reciprocated.⁶⁹

Laurent-Pichat's letters to Scheurer-Kestner were intimate testaments to friendship and its shared pleasures. If their friendship was a political alliance that enabled them to support each other as republicans, it was also an emotional attachment, a valued personal bond: 'We possess the gift of steadfast and enduring fidelity. I am a wordy man (*un bavard*). You are a serious man, a chemist, and ... you find the time to reply to an honest dreamer, like me. So you are excellent.'[70] As a 'wordy man', Laurent-Pichat was perhaps more forthcoming in his expression of attachment than was his friend, whose letters have not survived in Laurent-Pichat's papers. Laurent-Pichat remained the 'romantic', the man of emotion, of his youth. Yet the invitation to intimacy that was offered by Laurent-Pichat's declaration of friendship did not fall into a void.[71] Scheurer-Kestner replied to Laurent-Pichat's letters, acknowledging the friendship and the emotion in which it was embedded. Their friendship continued to intensify over the following years.

Friendship, family ties and republican politics

Male friendship and family ties were deeply integrated in Laurent-Pichat's circles. While his expressions of attachment to Scheurer-Kestner certainly evoke the 'emotive fraternalism'[72] that often bound male political allies, therefore, those male bonds did not remain detached from men's other relationships but intersected and overlapped with them. As in the 1860s, a letter from the Scheurer-Kestner household was always 'greeted with enthusiasm' in Laurent-Pichat's household in the 1870s.[73] The women exchanged visits, and family dinners were frequent when all were in Paris. There are no extant letters to testify directly to the relationships between the women, but Laurent-Pichat's letters to Scheurer-Kestner always included an exchange of greetings between the women and children: 'Take care to remember me to everyone around you. We send most cordial and friendly greetings from all of us to all of you.' Again, he noted: 'My sister is asking if you have mentioned Madame Scheurer; Clémence and Geneviève are asking me, too, about your daughters; in other words, they would like to know the details that you have omitted.'[74]

It is certainly true that Laurent-Pichat's calendar was filled with the male gatherings, hotbeds of political discussion, that typified republican sociability.[75] But what is more remarkable is how frequently women and adolescent children were part of the company. Two family dinners among many illustrate this point. A dinner at Scheurer-Kestner's home in Paris on 29 January 1873 was primarily a family affair. The family matriarchs, Mmes Kestner and Charras, were present. So were Laurent-Pichat, Amédée and Rosine, with Clémence and Geneviève. So was the hero of the Franco-Prussian War, Colonel Denfert-Rochereau, with his wife and their daughter Pauline.[76] Similarly, the guests who joined Laurent-Pichat's family for dinner on 15 March 1873 included not only leading figures from the Republican Union – Eugène Spuller, Georges Clemenceau, Henri Allain-Targé – but 'M. and Mme Scheurer and Mademoiselle Jeanne, Denfert[-Rochereau], his wife and daughter',[77] and they were joined later in the evening by colleague Jules Rathier, his wife and their daughter Marguerite. Family life and political life were inextricably intertwined in republican circles like this one, and such gatherings were by no means unusual. Women were an integral part of republican sociability, involved as hostesses but also sharing the political aspirations of the men. Similarly, the presence of young people in this company, like their visits to Sainte-Pélagie prison, socialised them into the republican world, introduced them to the political issues of the moment and helped ensure the reproduction of republican loyalties.

The deep integration of family life and politics is further evident in family correspondence. Geneviève's exchange of letters with her father reflects an environment in which political discussion between parents and growing children played a prominent role in daily life. Laurent-Pichat's election in July 1871 meant that the family left for a holiday in Spain without him because the Assembly was slow to complete its business. 'It's the taxes', Laurent-Pichat explained to fifteen-year-old Geneviève, writing a lengthy passage on the budget question dividing the Assembly. He then recovered himself: 'Dear child, I've just made you read two very boring pages.' He suggested she seek an explanation from family friend Léonce Anquez, who was travelling with the family. But he added: 'Poor girl, if I continue like this you will be condemned to this political chatter. But you should get used to it straight away.'[78] Now that he had been elected to the Assembly, politics was inescapable even on holidays. Besides, politics would be an integral part of Geneviève's life as a republican woman.

The correspondence offers glimpses of Geneviève's maturing political consciousness. She reassured her father in 1874: 'You don't bore me at all in talking politics; I don't know why you think that. What interests you interests us too, and since it's politics that is separating us, it's the least we can do to concern ourselves with it. Tell me about it then and try to make me a little more serious.'[79] Here the well-raised young woman deferred to the concerns of her father, adopting the appropriate gender position as well as the appropriate stance for a child. As a letter-writer, she presented herself to her reader as she thought he would like her to be, thus strengthening her relationship with her father. But as gestures of attachment, the letters between father and daughter also reveal their desire to reach out to each other, to share a relationship of trust and familiarity. In his earlier letter on the budget, Laurent-Pichat had sought not only to explain a serious question to his daughter, but also to have her understand politics and share the preoccupations of his life; Genevieve, in turn, reached out to him to express her willingness to do so.[80]

The wives of a number of Laurent-Pichat's republican colleagues took their daughters (their sons were usually in school) to witness the debates in the Assembly, as Rosine Beaujean took Clémence and Geneviève.[81] These visits provided another opportunity to socialise the young in republican issues and republican loyalties. But in initiating their daughters into the life of the Assembly, republican women also expressed their own keen interest in politics. Women's engagement with the political fortunes of the Republic was serious and enduring. They were deeply concerned as the conservatives tried to topple Thiers' government in November 1872, for instance, and anxious to witness events first-hand: 'Travelled [to Versailles] with Mme Floquet, her husband, Mme Kestner, M. and Mme Louis Blanc, M. and Mme Brelay', Laurent-Pichat noted, mentioning a host of republican stalwarts.[82] Gambetta's lover, Léonie Léon, was often in the gallery to hear him speak, as was Juliette Adam.[83] Women could not participate directly in the political debate, but they could participate vicariously through their presence.

Rosine Beaujean was far from alone, then, in her fascination with politics. As early as 1862, she had gone with her brother to hear republican Deputy, Ernest Picard, and she was present on many other occasions as well.[84] The close relationship between Laurent-Pichat and his sister, and Rosine's intense observation of politics, ensured her familiarity with personalities and tactics. Laurent-Pichat introduced Rosine to his colleagues and she visited and was visited by those colleagues and their wives.[85] Her interest in politics also inspired Laurent-Pichat's detailed account of the duel between Ranc and de Cassagnac, which was almost certainly written for her.[86] Rosine read the political press, as in 1875, when she mentioned articles 'in *Le Siècle* and in *Dix-Neuvième Siècle* and *La République [française]*'.[87] No doubt this was not the only day she immersed herself in those papers, and it is highly likely that she discussed such articles with her brother.

Rosine's political passion and her close political alliance with Laurent-Pichat were on display in May 1873, when the conservatives succeeded in defeating Thiers and installing Marshall Mac-Mahon as head of the government. Laurent-Pichat shared that disastrous moment not only with his colleagues, but also with Rosine who, like him, was on tenterhooks as events unfolded. His journal recorded:

> Session at 9 am; Thiers' speech; lunch at *Le Petit Vatel* with Rathier, Lefèvre, Gambetta, M. and Mme Scheurer [and others]. Second session at 2 pm. Thiers defeated. Telegram to Rosine. Dinner at *Le Petit Vatel* ... Third session. Nomination of Mac-Mahon. Return by the midnight train with Rathier. Rosine was waiting for me.[88]

Laurent-Pichat's first act was to telegram his sister, who he knew would be expecting news. Rosine's midnight sojourn suggests her desire to discuss these events and their political significance. It also attests to the anxiety of all republicans, women and men, at the looming reaction. Moreover, this incident illustrates that, in maturity, Rosine still played the role of confidante to Laurent-Pichat that she had in their youth. Political men had long sought intelligent and perceptive women as sounding boards, advisors and emotional supports. Some men – like Scheurer-Kestner and Jules Ferry – found confidantes in their wives. The unmarried Gambetta turned to Léonie Léon. Laurent-Pichat, also unmarried, found his confidante in his sister Rosine, with whom his emotional intimacy had remained undiminished since his youth.[89]

A radical republican in the Senate

The respect that Laurent-Pichat enjoyed among his republican colleagues and within the National Assembly more broadly was evident in December 1875, when he garnered sufficient votes from across the political spectrum to be elected a Life Senator. As Life Senator, he acquired enhanced status and respect. He immediately exerted his influence in Paris to try to ensure a victory of radical republicans in the 1876 elections. Furthermore, as he took his seat in the Senate in March 1876, he unashamedly pushed the radical republican agenda.

The constitution of 1875 that established the Third Republic provided for a Senate of three hundred members, including seventy-five chosen for life by the National Assembly from among its sitting members. The seventy-five were elected from lists drawn up by the political groupings, each individual requiring an absolute majority of votes. Some three hundred Deputies put their names forward for inclusion on those lists.[90] Laurent-Pichat did not do so voluntarily, as a letter to Geneviève six months later reveals: 'I am regarded as fortunate and therefore as happy. You know that I would have preferred to be a deputy.'[91] The distinction between Life Senator and Deputy was one between a secure and therefore 'fortunate' position, and one responsible to the electorate and thus less secure. But many republicans regarded a Senate as undemocratic and had been dismayed when Gambetta had accepted its creation: he had done so in order to ensure that the constitution enshrining the Republic would be accepted by the conservatives. Laurent-Pichat's reluctance to become a Life Senator reveals his own democratic sentiments and his desire to remain in the lower house, the heart of government and the main site of political contest.

Gambetta persuaded Laurent-Pichat to stand for election as Life Senator: he probably found it useful to have Laurent-Pichat and Scheurer-Kestner, two of the main financiers of the republican cause, on the Republican Union list.[92] Gambetta's comments on Edmond Adam, also on that list, might well have applied to Laurent-Pichat: 'thanks to his elevated and universally respected character, and to his position in Parisian society, indeed to the esteem that his adversaries of every rank constantly afford him, he seems to me destined to succeed.'[93]

The main conservative grouping (the Centre-Right Orleanists) had assumed that they would emerge victorious from these elections, but the outcome was a surprise: Gambetta's shrewd negotiations with the Extreme Right and the Bonapartists (all keen to defeat the Orleanists) ensured that the Left secured fifty-seven senators and the Extreme Right ten. Only eight Life Senators were elected from the conservative list. Of the fifty-seven on the Left's list, the majority were from the Centre-Left, but seven were elected from the more radical Republican Union, including Scheurer-Kestner, Edmond Adam and Laurent-Pichat.[94]

Voting by list diluted the weight of personal qualities in these elections but having 'the esteem of [one's] political adversaries' remained a factor.[95] This may have benefited Laurent-Pichat, given his cultivation of respectful relationships in the Assembly and his work on the parliamentary commissions. Like most of those from the Republican Union, he was elected towards the end of the process, in sixty-seventh position. Following the seventh ballot, on 16 December, he recorded: 'I have been elected with 309 votes, the [necessary] majority being 296 ... I sent some telegrams. I received a congratulatory note from *La République [française]*.'[96]

As a Life Senator, Laurent-Pichat occupied an eminent position in Paris. He was immediately called upon to chair electoral meetings ahead of elections for the remaining Senate seats and the legislature. Laurent-Pichat took the opportunity to spell out what he stood for and to advance the cause of radical republicanism by drawing up a programme to put to the candidates. While it was called the 'Laurent-Pichat programme', it closely resembled the Belleville Programme that Gambetta had accepted in 1869. Indeed, Laurent-Pichat's programme embodied the principles of republicanism as they had long been understood by the Left of the republican movement: freedom of assembly and association; freedom of the press; free, compulsory and secular primary education; compulsory military service for all; separation of Church and State; tax reform; and the election (rather than appointment) of mayors and municipal councils. An amnesty for Communards was added to this agenda and was to become one of Laurent-Pichat's prime concerns.[97] More conservative republicans sometimes contested Laurent-Pichat's agenda, however, and electoral meetings were often fiery.[98]

While republicans won overwhelmingly in Paris in January–February 1876, nationally the conservatives gained a slim majority in the Senate with a total of 154 of the 300 seats. The elections for the Chamber of Deputies, however, were a national triumph for the republicans. They won 340 seats to the conservatives' 155, with a small number unaligned in the Centre. Ninety-eight of the republicans were radicals.[99] Ever polite, and a diligent networker, Laurent-Pichat spent several evenings writing cards to the many republican colleagues and friends who had been successful.[100]

With a huge majority in the lower house, the Republic appeared secure, even without a Senate majority and even with a monarchist President in Mac-Mahon. Radicals were clearly in a minority, however, despite Laurent-Pichat's efforts. The government was headed by Centre-Left republicans determined to hold their radical colleagues in check. Laurent-Pichat's friend François Favre advised treading carefully: 'You and your colleagues are charged with founding the Republic [but] I remain convinced that one cannot be too moderate in order to attain the goal so wished for and so long desired'.[101] But Laurent-Pichat was determined to pursue the radical agenda. An amnesty for Communards was his top priority, as it was for many in the Republican Union. It was a point of principle. For Laurent-Pichat, it may also have been inspired by the memory of his friend Charles Delescluze. But it was highly controversial, given that the Commune was widely condemned even by many republicans.

Laurent-Pichat and several colleagues immediately began drafting a bill for a general amnesty, which was presented simultaneously in the Chamber and the Senate on 21 March 1876. It caused uproar in the Chamber and was rejected out of hand by the Centre-Left government.[102] It indicated, however, that the terms of the political debate had changed with the republican majority. As Victor Hugo declared in the Senate debate on 22 May: 'If you vote for amnesty, the issue is closed; if you reject amnesty, the issue is just beginning.'[103] As indeed it was. 'A brilliant and excellent session', noted Laurent-Pichat, despite a heavy defeat for the Republican Union.[104] Not until mid-1880 would the radicals manage to achieve the amnesty they sought, and Laurent-Pichat would support the campaign until that victory.

Laurent-Pichat's role in politics in the 1870s illuminates the challenges politicians faced in constructing a parliamentary system based on democratic processes. They needed to create new 'rules of engagement' that allowed open debate and intense disagreement without such disagreement becoming life-threatening. Laurent-Pichat held strong convictions, embracing the radical programme of the Republican Union. Even for his political opponents, however, he was a man whom one could trust, as his role on the commissions and his mediating role in many affairs of honour attest. Once elected, he quickly established himself as reliable, polite and true to his word. He reached out beyond his own circle to practise the bourgeois civility that, though not always observed, was essential to the functioning of the National Assembly, and he was well respected in return.

Laurent-Pichat's political interactions in these years also demonstrate the centrality of friendship to his personal and professional life. His capacity for deep and sincere friendship had been evident since his youth and remained unabated. Laurent-Pichat greatly valued his friends and cultivated amicable ties with his political colleagues, enabling him to fulfil the demands of honour on their behalf. Some of his friendships, like that with Auguste Scheurer-Kestner, continued to exceed the limits of political camaraderie, transcending the confines of 'emotive fraternalism' and encompassing the men's families. This familial dimension of republican friendship gave it a particular emotional quality distinct from the fraternal affect that more frequently characterised nineteenth-century political alliances. The power of the emotional bond between families enabled friendship to play a major role in sustaining republicans in the slow process of installing the Republic.

Notes

1 J.P.T. Bury, *Gambetta and the Making of the Third Republic* (London: Longman, 1973), pp. 102–34.
2 LLP, Journal, 29–30 Jan. 1875; 2, 12, 23–25 Feb. 1875. See Jacques Chastenet, *Histoire de la Troisième République*, I: *Naissance et jeunesse* (Paris: Hachette Littérature, 1952), pp. 171–89.
3 LLP, Journal, 28 Nov. 1873–77 Feb. 1874.
4 AN 248AP/1: Favre to LLP, 1 Nov. 1871.
5 LLP, Journal, 8 July 1871.
6 Grévy, *La République des Opportunistes*, pp. 180–83, 355 n. 73.
7 LLP, Journal, 15, 20 July; 21 Aug. 1871.
8 *Ibid.*, 12, 26 March 1873.
9 *Ibid.*, 19 July 1872.

10 On membership lists, see Grévy, *La République des Opportunistes*, p. 362, n. 4.
11 *Ibid.*, pp. 63–4, 216–19; Bury, *Gambetta*, pp. 38–40, 120–21.
12 LLP, Journal, 5 March, 3, 4, 25 Nov. 1872; 2, 4 March 1873; AN 248 AP/1: Aimé Millet to LLP, 27 Feb., 2 July 1872.
13 AN 248AP/1: Aimé Millet to LLP, 27 Nov. 1872.
14 *La République française*, 4 Dec. 1872.
15 LLP, Journal, 4 Nov. 1873. See Jérôme Grévy, 'Les cafés républicains de Paris au début de la Troisième République. Étude de sociabilité politique', *Revue d'histoire moderne et contemporaine*, 50:2 (2003), 52–72; Grévy, *La République des Opportunistes*, pp. 171–80.
16 LLP, Journal, 14 March 1874.
17 *Ibid.*, 31 Dec. 1873.
18 *Ibid.*, 10–13 June; 12 July 1874. See Bury, *Gambetta*, pp. 191–2.
19 See Claude Bellanger et al., *Histoire générale de la presse française*, III: *De 1871 à 1940* (Paris: Presses universitaires de France, 1972), pp. 222–4; Grévy, *La République des Opportunistes*, pp. 150–60.
20 Léon Laurent-Pichat, *Les Réveils: Poésies* (Paris: Alphonse Lemerre, 1880).
21 LLP, Journal, 18 Aug. 1873.
22 *Ibid.*, 6 June, 5 Dec. 1873; 28 May, 8 Nov. 1875.
23 Guy Chapman, *The Third Republic of France* (New York: St. Martin's Press, 1962), appendix VII, p. 386.
24 LLP, Journal, 2 Aug. 1871.
25 *Ibid.*, 10 March, 3, 4, 15–19, 21, 24 Dec. 1874; 16 March 1875. *La République française*, 12 March 1874, 18 March 1875; *Rapport fait au nom de la 29e commission d'intérêt local, sur le projet de loi tendant à autoriser la ville de Grenoble (Isère) à contracter un emprunt de 600,000 francs, par M. Laurent-Pichat (19 décembre 1874)* (Versailles: Impr. de Cerf et fils, undated), 5 pp.
26 LLP, Journal, 9, 15, 20, 23 Feb. 1877.
27 *Ibid.*, 19 March 1875. *Annales de l'Assemblée nationale: compte rendu in extenso des séances, annexes (1871–1875), séance du 29 juillet 1875*, p. 201; also reproduced in *La République française*, 31 July 1875.
28 AN 248AP/1: J.-A. Lissajous to LLP, 21 March 1875.
29 BHVP, 7, nos 57, 58: GLP to LLP, 30 July, 1 Aug. 1875; BHVP, 6, no. 28: LLP to GLP, 26 July 1875.
30 *La République française*, 21 Aug. 1875. On Buffet, see Bibliothèque de l'Assemblée nationale [BAN], MS 1777, 76: 31/50: Léon Gambetta to Léonie Léon, 16 June 1876.
31 BHVP, 7, no. 63: Rosine [Beaujean], postscript to GLP's letter to LLP, Chablis, 21 Aug. 1875.

32 This is Bury's summary of Audiffret-Pasquier's speech, in *Gambetta*, p. 125.
33 LLP, Journal, 29 July 1875; *La République française*, 31 July 1875.
34 François Guillet, 'Le duel et la défense de l'honneur viril', in Alain Corbin (ed.), *Histoire de la virilité*, II: *Le Triomphe de la virilité: le XIXe siècle* (Paris: Seuil, 2011), pp. 83–124.
35 Robert A. Nye, *Masculinity and Male Codes of Honor in Modern France* (New York: Oxford University Press, 1993), esp. pp. 183–7; William Reddy, *The Invisible Code: Honor and sentiment in Post-Revolutionary France* (Berkeley, CA: University of California Press, 1997).
36 Schweitz, *Les Parlementaires*.
37 *Ibid.*, pp. 16 (Edmond Adam), 152 (Charles-Roger Cloutier), 284 (Emile Goussot), 333 (Anatole de La Forge).
38 Nye, *Masculinity and Male Codes of Honor*, chapter 9 and pp. 127–8.
39 *Ibid.*, pp. 142–4.
40 LLP, Journal, 9 Jan. 1873; 6, 7 July 1875; *Le Soir*, 5 July 1875.
41 LLP, Journal, 23, 25, 26 Dec. 1876.
42 *Ibid.*, 28 Oct. 1879.
43 *Ibid.*, 7 July 1873; 21, 23 Jan. 1874.
44 *Journal officiel de la République française*, 10 Jan. 1873, pp. 153–61 (160).
45 LLP, Journal, 17 Feb. 1873.
46 *Ibid.*, 21, 23 Jan. 1874. See Bury, *Gambetta*, p. 191 and n. 3.
47 LLP, Journal, 28 Jan.–8 Feb. 1875; 11–16 Oct. 1874.
48 Nye, *Masculinity and Male Codes of Honor*, pp. 146, 173–5, 187–95; Bellanger et al., *Histoire générale*, III, pp. 137–41.
49 LLP, Journal, 28 Oct. 1879; 23, 25, 26 Dec. 1876.
50 *Ibid.*, 20, 25 Dec. 1875.
51 Radical feminist Arria Ly would seek to end this prerogative. See Andrea Mansker, *Sex, Honor and Citizenship in Early Third Republic France* (Houndmills: Palgrave Macmillan, 2011).
52 Nye, *Masculinity and Male Codes of Honor*, pp. 142–3, 195; Guillet, 'Le duel et la défense de l'honneur viril', pp. 117–18.
53 LLP, Journal, 7 July 1872; 7 July 1873; 15 Oct. 1874; 8 Feb. 1875.
54 *Ibid.*, 15 Oct. 1874.
55 L. Gambetta to A. Ranc, 15 June 1873, in Arthur Ranc, *Ranc: Souvenirs, correspondence, 1831–1908* (Paris: Edouard Cornély et Cie, 1913), p. 213.
56 Quoted in Bury, *Gambetta*, p. 159, n. 1.
57 LLP, Journal, 7 July 1873.
58 Reproduction of the *procès-verbal* in *Ranc: Souvenirs*, p. 230.

59 Godbeer, *Overflowing of Friendship*; Macías-González, 'Masculine friendships'.
60 AN 276AP/1: LLP to Scheurer-Kestner, 29 Aug. 1874.
61 On the emotional context of political action, see Forster, 'Radical Friendship'.
62 AN 276AP/1: LLP to Scheurer-Kestner, 27 Aug. 1872.
63 *Ibid.*, 29 Aug. 1874.
64 *Ibid.*, 14 Aug., 22 Sept. 1874. See Chastenet, *Histoire de la Troisième République*, I, pp. 165–6; Bury, *Gambetta*, pp. 357–8.
65 Sylvie Aprile's thesis on Auguste Scheurer-Kestner remains unpublished at the time of writing: 'Auguste Scheurer-Kestner et son entourage, étude biographique et analyse politique d'une aristocratie républicaine' (Thèse, Université de Paris I, 1994).
66 AN 276AP/1: LLP to Scheurer-Kestner, 27 Aug. 1872.
67 *Ibid.*, 29 Aug. 1874.
68 Godbeer, *Overflowing of Friendship,* pp. 156–7.
69 On choice and friendship, see Counter and White, 'Introduction: The soul's sentiment'.
70 AN 276AP/1: LLP to Scheurer-Kestner, 22 Sept. 1874.
71 See Vincent-Buffault, *L'Exercise de l'amitié*, pp. 54–5.
72 Macías-González, 'Masculine friendships', 419–20.
73 AN 276AP/1, LLP to Scheurer-Kestner, 27 Aug. 1872, 29 Aug. 1874, 7 Aug. 1876, etc.
74 AN 276AP/1: LLP to Scheurer-Kestner, 29 Aug., 22 Sept. 1874; 2, 7 Aug. 1876.
75 Grévy, *La République des Opportunistes*, pp. 185–6; Nord, *Republican Moment*.
76 LLP, Journal, 29 Jan. 1873.
77 LLP, Journal, 15 March 1873.
78 BHVP, 6, no. 22: LLP to GLP, 10 Sept. 1871.
79 BHVP, 7, no. 49: GLP to LLP, 20 July 1874.
80 On the role of letters in relationship-building, see Bossis, 'Methodological journeys through correspondence', 63–75; Dauphin et al. (eds), *Ces bonnes lettres*; Foley, 'Becoming a woman'; Susan Foley, ' "Your letter is divine, irresistible, infernally seductive": Léon Gambetta, Léonie Léon and nineteenth-century epistolary culture', *French Historical Studies*, 30:2 (2007), 237–67.
81 For instance, LLP, Journal, 22 Feb. 1872; 6 March 1874; 12 March 1875; 19 June 1876, etc.
82 *Ibid.*, 28 Nov. 1872.
83 Foley and Sowerwine, *A Political Romance*.

84 LLP, Journal, 17 June 1862; 22 Feb. 1872; 12 Nov. 1873; 6 March 1874, etc.
85 Ibid., 29 Jan. 1873; 5 Jan. 1874; 8 Jan. 1876, etc.
86 Ibid., 12 Nov. 1873.
87 BHVP, 7, no. 63: Rosine Beaujean, postscript to GLP's letter to LLP, 21 Aug. 1875.
88 LLP, Journal, 24 May 1873.
89 See Horowitz, *Friendship and Politics,* for many examples of women confidantes in the early nineteenth century. On Gambetta and Léonie Léon, see Foley and Sowerwine, *A Political Romance.*
90 J.-M. Mayeur, 'Naissance des inamovibles', in Mayeur and Corbin (eds), *Les Immortels du Sénat,* pp. 15–31; Patrick Chamonard, 'Un recrutement politique exceptionnel: l'élection des soixante-quinze premiers sénateurs inamovibles (9–21 déc. 1875)', in Alain Faure, Alain Plessis et Jean-Claude Farcy (eds), *La Terre et la Cité: mélanges offerts à Phillipe Vigny* (Paris: Créaphis, 1994), pp. 283–309.
91 BHVP, 6, no. 33: LLP to GLP, 17 July 1876.
92 Grévy, *La République des Opportunistes,* p. 234.
93 L. Gambetta to Juliette Adam, 13 Nov. 1875, in Léon Gambetta, *Lettres de Gambetta 1868–1882,* recueillies et annotées par Daniel Halévy et Emile Pillias (Paris: Bernard Grasset, 1938), no. 255.
94 See Mayeur, 'Naissance des inamovibles'; Bury, *Gambetta,* pp. 258–62.
95 Mayeur, 'Naissance des inamovibles', p. 22.
96 LLP, Journal, 16 Dec. 1875.
97 www.senat.fr/senateur-3eme-republique/laurent_pichat_leon1497r3.html. Accessed 8 September 2020; Grévy, *La République des Opportunistes,* pp. 234–5. Some versions of the 'Laurent-Pichat programme' include the lifting of the state of siege and the return of the Assembly to Paris, e.g. Mario Proth, *Charles Floquet* (Paris: A. Quantin, 1883), pp. 27–8.
98 LLP, Journal, 4, 11, 17, 21, 23, 26 Jan. 1876; 1, 5, 14 Feb. 1876.
99 Chastenet, *Histoire de la Troisième République,* I, pp. 209, 211–13.
100 LLP, Journal, 20–22 Feb. 1876.
101 AN 248AP/1: Favre to LLP, 28 Dec. 1875.
102 LLP, Journal, 8, 10, 12, 21 March 1876.
103 Quoted in *La République française,* 24 May 1876, p. 1.
104 LLP, Journal, 22 May 1876; *La République française,* 24 May 1876.

8

'Such hope is in the air': bourgeois marriage and republican politics, 1851–80

Wednesday 20 [June 1877] ***

<u>Geneviève's marriage</u> ... At 11:15 the Kestner family and our family arrived ... We left for the town hall. Wonderful ceremony ... we returned to the house. I left for Versailles by the 1:35 pm omnibus. The decree of dissolution [of the Assembly] was read. Discussion was deferred until tomorrow. I left for home by train and omnibus at 3:35 pm.[1]

The entry in Laurent-Pichat's journal for the day of his daughter's marriage was highlighted twice over, stressing the importance of both the date and the event it marked. This was a moment of triumph for him and for Geneviève. Despite her illegitimacy, which placed her at a disadvantage in bourgeois society, Laurent-Pichat had shepherded her into a successful marriage alliance. Her acceptance into an elite republican family also confirmed his own acceptance as a suitable friend and family ally, despite his murky origins.

Laurent-Pichat was forced, however, to cut short his presence at the wedding celebrations of his only child in order to attend a crucial sitting of the Senate. Geneviève's marriage coincided with the constitutional crisis of 1877. On 16 May, President Mac-Mahon had dismissed the republican Prime Minister and replaced him with a monarchist, despite the large republican majority in the Chamber of Deputies. Mac-Mahon then called on the Senate to dissolve the Assembly and prorogued proceedings for a month. Many regarded these acts as a coup d'état.[2] The Senate gathered to debate the dissolution on 20 June, hence Laurent-Pichat's early departure from the wedding celebrations. Debate was adjourned and, after two further sessions, the vote was finally taken on 22 June. 'I voted against the dissolution', Laurent-Pichat wrote. 'I returned home without waiting for the count'.[3] The newspaper that evening confirmed the expected outcome: the Senate had approved the dissolution.

The concurrence of the two events of 20 June, while coincidental, aptly represented the deep interconnection between family life and political life in these staunchly republican families. In the circles around Laurent-Pichat, as in other sectors of the bourgeoisie, families sought marriage partners of comparable wealth and status for their children.[4] They also sought to ensure the happiness of the couple. In addition, the choice of marriage partners in republican circles was shaped by politics, since that choice had the power to advance the republican cause. This combination of financial, emotional and political imperatives was evident in the marriages within Laurent-Pichat's family.

Bourgeois marriage: inclination and family interest

The pioneering work of Adeline Daumard in the 1960s, based on notarial and fiscal sources, showed the care with which families of the Parisian bourgeoisie oversaw the selection of marriage partners for their children. While Daumard argued that most marriages over time became 'real unions', she reserved judgement on 'the question of sentiments, about which we know nothing'.[5] Family interest and individual 'sentiments' were not necessarily at odds. Rather, as Christopher Johnson has argued, 'the interaction between the two lies at the heart of understanding the dynamics of families and the structuring of kinship in any society'.[6] A number of other studies have also highlighted the blending of family interest and individual choice in marriage-making.[7]

However, our picture of the balance between interest and emotion in marriage-making is shaped by the surviving sources. Adeline Daumard herself, after examining correspondence and wills, later argued that 'most marriages in bourgeois and aristocratic society were marriages of convenience ... But [they] could also be marriages of inclination'.[8] The marriages in Laurent-Pichat's extended family often appear to favour family interest over affection, but that impression is nuanced where intimate sources have survived. Moreover, these marriages demonstrate that 'interest' had a strong political dimension for republicans in this period. By drawing in new contributors, marriage strengthened the family's forces for the political struggle, which was lived in the intimate sphere as well as in public life. Marriage created new nodes of republican commitment, new centres in which the republican faith was lived day by day and from which the collaborative project of republicanism could be pursued by the extended family. In these families, the expectations of marriage by both young people and their parents were shaped by that understanding. They sought marriages that would offer emotional satisfaction within the parameters of the family's financial and political interests.[9]

Little information remains about how Rosine Deslandes, the eldest of Laurent-Pichat's surviving siblings, came to marry Amédée Beaujean in November 1851. No letters between the couple survive. The marriage may have been intended to counteract the intense emotional bond between Laurent-Pichat and his sister.[10] In that case, Rosine's personal feelings would probably have been subordinate to her family's concern to bring an inappropriate attachment under control and avoid scandal. Whether she and Amédée knew each other before becoming betrothed we do not know.

On the other hand, records of the marriage in July 1858 between Laurent-Pichat's brother, Achille, and Juliette Asselin (known in the family as Victorine) suggest that both 'interest' and 'inclination' were involved.[11] As a marriage of cousins, it followed a well-established bourgeois practice.[12] Their mothers were sisters and they would have known each other from childhood, so there may well have been an element of 'inclination' in their union. But the marriage also suited the families' interests. At the time of his marriage, Achille was not only working for his uncle, Juliette's father, but also living in his household. This marriage was probably arranged by the aunts and uncles who protected their investments in the family distilling business through this endogamous union.[13]

The marriages of both Rosine and Achille also illustrate the families' careful weighing up of wealth and social status in forming such alliances. Like many couples in the professional bourgeoisie, Rosine and Amédée would owe their financial security to the wife's dowry. Rosine's family assembled a dowry valued at 51,000 francs; Laurent-Pichat promised a further 30,000 francs, with interest, over a decade. This sum made possible an extremely comfortable living for the couple and placed them in the ranks of the very wealthy.[14] Indeed, all the marriages in this family illustrate great wealth, given that a family of urban workers could expect to earn about 2,500 francs per year.[15]

Amédée Beaujean brought to his marriage with Rosine Deslandes not wealth but 'prospects', another commodity valued in bourgeois circles but difficult to calculate. His parents promised him 20,000 francs as a marriage settlement, although only 4,000 francs were paid at the time of the marriage; the remainder was to be paid – with interest – over seven years: a not uncommon arrangement. As professor at an elite Parisian lycée, Amédée could expect advancement. But while his earnings would remain modest, his profession gave him social status. He received public recognition as author of an abbreviated version of the multi-volume Littré dictionary, which won him a medal in 1877 from the 'society for the encouragement of works useful to education' and the Legion of Honour in 1878.[16] These 'prospects' of accomplishment could only be anticipated by the Deslandes family in 1851 but were accepted as valuable contributions to marital resources.

Nevertheless, the Deslandes family looked to protect its superior financial investment in this union, again revealing attention to their 'interests'. In the overwhelming majority of marriages among the nineteenth-century Parisian bourgeoisie, the couple opted for 'community of property' arrangements, combining their wealth. The marriage between Rosine and Amédée, however, was contracted under the dowry system in which the wife's property remained inalienable. This protected her family's assets but limited the possible financial gains. Only 2 percent of marriages among the Parisian bourgeoisie were based on this system at mid-century.[17]

Laurent-Pichat played no formal role in arranging the marriages of Rosine or Achille: he was a relative newcomer to the family at the time. But in 1859, aged thirty-five, Laurent-Pichat was head of a household comprising his widowed mother and his youngest sibling, twenty-year-old Herminie. He took the lead in finding a husband for his sister. This marriage, too, illustrated the careful management of the family's interests.

Herminie's marriage to the notary Siagre-Emile Lefort (known as Emile) exhibited, once again, a strategy of bourgeois wealth management: the wife brought cash, the husband professional skills and social status. Herminie's dowry was valued at more than 100,000 francs. It was surely a family investment in the union, as Rosine's had been, although no amounts are individually attributed in this contract. Emile Lefort was heavily indebted from purchasing his practice and, like many notaries starting out, benefited from his wife's large dowry. But like Amédée Beaujean, he had 'prospects': his professional skills promised wealth to come.[18]

This was the first marriage in the family that was also deliberately envisaged as a political alliance. Laurent-Pichat had the Lefort family's political credentials in mind when he wrote to Jules Ferry: 'I am busy with a marriage that will unite my sister to the brother of a young patriot exiled on Jersey. I am pleased with this union which consolidates [political] commitment through marriage.'[19] Emile was the brother of Henri, a republican colleague and friend whom Laurent-Pichat likely knew since their days at the lycée Charlemagne, where Henri Lefort acquired a youthful reputation for his republican views. Henri Lefort was prosecuted many times for his political activities, spending time in prison and in exile.[20]

'Interest' took on added meaning in this marriage, then, designating not merely the financial compatibility between the two families but also their social and political affinity. The signing of the marriage contract, a family celebration, was also a celebration of republican solidarity and friendship. The event was attended by former Deputies of the Second Republic – Jules Simon, Hippolyte Carnot and Barthélemy Saint-Hilaire – who would all play significant roles in the Third Republic. Some of Laurent-Pichat's republican friends, including Louis Ulbach, Eugène Pelletan and Auguste Millard, were also present, along with a number of republican journalists, writers and painters.

Whether Rosine or Herminie played a role in choosing their husbands is unknown. At the very least, women were usually given the right to refuse and sometimes posed conditions.[21] In deeply political families, the women themselves might embrace marriage to advance the family's interests, as Hortense Kestner did in marrying the rising republican star Charles Floquet in 1869. Her sister explained:

By becoming the wife of Floquet, she wants not only to become the adored wife of a man she loves, but even more the companion of a good soldier of our future struggles. It is certain that our new brother carries the political tradition of our family and friends in his heart and that the only thing he will love with as much passion as his wife will be the Republic.[22]

According to this account, Hortense Kestner considered family interest at least as much as personal satisfaction in contemplating the marriage, or rather, she saw the two as one and the same.

Nothing suggests that Rosine and Herminie Deslandes brought political aspirations of this kind to their marriages. But men, too, had to be careful about expressing republican sentiments in the 1850s and 1860s. As a State employee, Amédée Beaujean was required to swear allegiance to the Emperor in order to keep his position. His professional file, with its letters from prominent Empire figures requesting advancement for him, illustrates the extent to which employment and promotion still depended on patronage.[23] As a young notary seeking to build a career in a State-controlled profession, Emile Lefort also did well to be silent.

However, in January 1870, before the Empire collapsed, Lefort published a pamphlet eulogising the French Revolution and the Declaration of the Rights of Man and the Citizen as the bases of French law: a wholeheartedly republican view.[24] Amédée Beaujean's republican credentials also became evident in the 1870s. His abbreviated *Dictionary of the French Language* was the product of his collaboration with Emile Littré, a republican Deputy and Life Senator who promoted the philosophy of 'positivism' in republican circles.[25] The friendship between Beaujean and Littré was both scholarly and republican. It seems highly likely, therefore, that Beaujean and Laurent-Pichat shared a common political outlook, even under the Empire when Beaujean could not share his brother-in-law's political activities.

Forging marriage alliances in the Republic

As the republicans came to power in the 1870s, marriage remained central to advancing and consolidating the political cause. Intermarriage among republican families was therefore not uncommon. Longstanding republican activist Jean-Jules Clamageran, for instance, married Adèle Hérold, daughter of a renowned republican *salonnière* and sister of politician Ferdinand Hérold; Henri Allain-Targé's daughter, Geneviève, married Jules Ferry's brother, Charles. Similarly, in the Grévy family, where three brothers all became significant republican politicians, children married within the republican network: Jules Grévy's daughter, Alice, would marry Daniel Wilson, a republican Deputy; Albert Grévy's son, Léon, would marry Louise Labiche, the daughter of a Senator like himself.[26] The marriages of Clémence Beaujean and Geneviève Laurent-Pichat were therefore not unique as alliances cementing republican connections. These marriages also illustrate how young people shaped their expectations to the family's interests.

Clémence Beaujean, aged 22, married 32-year-old Alexandre-Abel Hovelacque in January 1875.[27] The Hovelacques, originally from Lille, were not part of the family's regular social circle. Yet on 12 November 1874 both M. and Mme Edouard Hovelacque, and that evening their son, known as Abel, called on Laurent-Pichat and his family. The following morning, Rosine, Amédée and Clémence visited the Hovelacques.[28] These visits marked the beginning of the marriage arrangements.

This was very much a republican family alliance. Its origins probably lay in a visit to Laurent-Pichat two weeks earlier by Mme Babaud-Laribière, widow of a Second Republic Deputy who had become Prefect of the Charente in 1870. Mme Babaud-Laribière was also the sister of Léonie Khnopff, who was married to Abel's uncle, Emile Hovelacque.[29] It appears that Mme Babaud-Laribière played the role of marriage broker on behalf of Abel's family. She did so very successfully. Three days after the Hovelacque and Beaujean families met, Laurent-Pichat recorded: 'Went to the Hovelacques' place. General presentation ... It is all decided and is progressing speedily'.[30]

As a prominent member of republican high society, Laurent-Pichat was the fulcrum on which this marriage proposal initially rested. His niece was a valuable match for Abel Hovelacque, a republican with professional and political aspirations, who, after a period on the Paris municipal council would be elected a Deputy for Paris in the 1880s. A colleague of eminent anthropologist Paul Broca, Hovelacque would be appointed Professor of Linguistic

Anthropology in the Paris School of Anthropology – a hotbed of republicanism – in 1876, specialising in language and its links to racial hierarchy. While the work of this School has since been discredited for the racist assumptions that underpinned it, it was highly regarded at the time.[31] The swift response of Clémence's parents to the initiative of Mme Babaud-Laribière indicates that they welcomed Abel as a suitable husband for their daughter. As was common in bourgeois circles, a two-month courtship allowed the couple and their extended families to become acquainted.[32]

The marriage contract reveals that both families committed significant assets to this union. Unlike Rosine and Amédée, Clémence and Abel married under 'community of property' arrangements: their assets and any future gains became joint property. This was the choice of 90 percent of the Parisian bourgeoisie, and a sign that both families were invested emotionally, not merely financially, in the marriage.[33] Abel and his family brought some 422,000 francs to the union. Clémence was a very wealthy young woman, declaring cash and shares in her own name worth 155,000 francs.[34] Laurent-Pichat's generosity to her mother two decades earlier had paid dividends, and he had also given Rosine money for Clémence when he was compensated for the acquisition of La Rotonde du Temple in 1863.[35] Her parents now gifted Clémence as dowry a four-storey *hôtel particulier* on the rue Bellechasse in the fashionable and expensive seventh arrondissement. They had paid 165,000 francs for the house in 1867; in 1875, it was earning more than 10,000 francs per year in rent.[36]

The financial underpinnings of this marriage highlighted the two families' bourgeois credentials. So did the elaborate celebrations around the signing of the marriage contract: a vital component of bourgeois marriage arrangements.[37] One hundred and forty-six names were appended to the contract. Along with the two extended families, longstanding family friends – Léonce Anquez, Etienne Arago, Louis Ulbach – featured among them. The remaining names were a 'who's who' of republicanism. They testify that, by 1875, the republican elite spanned the political, cultural and professional domains of French society: *tout Paris* was becoming republican. Twenty-four republican Deputies and five members of municipal or general councils were among the signatories. The presence of nine doctors (including society doctor Samuel Pozzi and the bridegroom's colleague Paul Broca) highlights the prominent role played by medical men in the early Third Republic.[38] Equally prominent were members of the literary and intellectual elite: publishers, newspaper editors, *hommes de lettres* (some designated as members of the Académie française or the Institut français) and professors from various lycées, along with artists, architects and lawyers. Laurent-Pichat was very pleased with the event: 'Lots of people ... it finished about 1 am. All our friends came.'[39] The marriage was celebrated two days later by eminent republican Arnaud de l'Ariège. Overall, this marriage was a republican triumph.

Two years later, in June 1877, Laurent-Pichat's daughter Geneviève married Charles Risler. This, too, was a thoroughly republican marriage. Charles Risler's grandfather (Charles Kestner), four of his uncles and his brother-in-law (Jules Ferry) were or had been republican politicians. Laurent-Pichat's republican status made Geneviève a suitable wife for Charles, while Charles's eminent republican connections, as well as the friendship between the families, were attractive to Laurent-Pichat. The marriage was also an alliance of the very wealthy. Laurent-Pichat endowed Geneviève with 10,000 francs in furniture and a five-storey building on the rue Gaillon: in the less salubrious second arrondissement, its apartments earned only 4,000 francs per year. The Rislers, father and son, contributed 60,000 francs in cash to the union, to which Charles added shares in industrial concerns and in French and American railway companies valued at more than 365,000 francs. Like most bourgeois couples, Charles and Geneviève joined their assets in 'community of property'.[40]

Family 'interest' was well served by this union, therefore, as it had been by the marriage of Clémence and Abel. But it is highly likely that Geneviève's marriage, unlike that of her cousin, also had a strong element of personal choice. Information about most of the marriages in the family comes only from the official records but, in Geneviève's case, a trove of intimate sources reveals the high degree of affection invested in this union and the intricate intersection between affection and political interest.

Whereas Clémence met her husband only two months before their marriage, Geneviève had known Charles from childhood; their fathers had been friends since about 1862. Laurent-Pichat also counted Charles's grandmother, Mme Eugénie Kestner, as a friend.

Figure 8.1 Geneviève Laurent-Pichat, *c.* 1876?

He made many visits over the years to the small Alsatian town of Thann, where Charles, a chemist, helped manage the family's industrial plant and dye business. Laurent-Pichat found him a sensible and pleasant young man.[41] The extended families socialised in Paris each winter, and in summer they met at the seaside: a favourite site for allowing the young to mingle with 'suitable' potential spouses.[42] Mme Charras (Charles's aunt, and widow of the friend Laurent-Pichat deeply admired) hosted the entire extended family at Villers-sur-mer, only four kilometres from Laurent-Pichat's place in Beuzeval.[43]

There is some evidence that personal attraction between Geneviève and Charles played a role in their marriage. From the summer of 1873, Geneviève's letters to her father from Beuzeval suggest her growing friendship with Charles Risler. She wrote of playing croquet, bathing, taking long walks and socialising with a group that included 'Mr Risler' and his sister Eugénie.[44] She also asked her father: 'Can you bring one or two photos of each of us …? People are asking to see them'.[45] Photographs are pre-eminently mementoes of a person who is absent. Perhaps Geneviève was modestly suggesting that 'people' – like Charles – wanted photos of her to keep after the holiday ended: another hint that this marriage was driven at least in part by the couple's attraction to each other.

If personal attraction did inspire this union, however, it would have counted for little had either spouse been unacceptable to the other family. In most circles, Geneviève's illegitimacy would have been a serious barrier. Charles's family were already aware of it, since they knew that Laurent-Pichat was unmarried. Mme Kestner had raised her daughters to be freethinkers, suggesting a readiness to question social and religious prejudices and to rank individual character over social expectations. In the Kestner circle, Geneviève's personal qualities and the republican bond the families shared proved decisive.

Laurent-Pichat was nevertheless careful to ensure that he had the approval of Mme Kestner, the family matriarch, before making any plans. He recorded in his journal on 12 April 1877: 'Visited Mme Kestner. Mmes Floquet and Charras [her daughters] went out for a walk. I stayed with Mme Kestner'. The following day he noted: 'Conversation with Geneviève. Visit to Ch. Risler. … To Mme Kestner's place and to Risler's [i.e. Charles's father] first'.

Mme Kestner was known to prevent unions that she believed were not in the family's interest. Georges Clemenceau's suit for Hortense Kestner in the 1860s had not been welcome: Clemenceau may have been a committed republican and would eventually become President of the Council of Ministers (Prime Minister), but he was seen as a hothead.[46] Hortense would marry the less impetuous but equally promising Charles Floquet, a future President of the Chamber of Deputies and Prime Minister himself. Jules Ferry took care to recognise Mme Kestner's authority when courting Charles's sister, Eugénie Risler, in 1875. Shrewder than Clemenceau, Ferry wrote respectful and admiring letters not only to the woman he hoped to marry, but also to Mme Kestner, addressing her as his 'maternal friend' or his 'dear Providence': he wanted to persuade them both of his devotion to Eugénie.[47] The senior women in the family then persuaded Eugénie Risler that this match (with a man twenty-seven years her senior and socially her inferior) was a good one.[48]

That Mme Kestner approved the marriage between Charles and Geneviève was soon evident. Numerous visits and family dinners brought members of the two families together and, by acknowledging Rosine as de facto 'mother' of Geneviève and incorporating her into these exchanges, Charles's family discreetly acknowledged and accepted Geneviève's irregular origins.[49] The formal engagement on 29 April 1877 gave the official seal of approval to the union. Laurent-Pichat recorded in his journal: 'In the evening Geneviève received a magnificent bracelet from Mme Kestner, a fan from Mme Charras, and a bouquet of flowers from Mme Ferry [Charles's sister], as well as a splendid bouquet from Charles'. As was customary, too, Charles sent Rosine a gift, a 'magnificent vase', acknowledging the quasi-filial relationship that he was about to enter with her.[50] Through these gifts, Charles's family welcomed Geneviève as a worthy family member.

A week before the wedding, Laurent-Pichat hosted a grand dinner for the extended family and his republican friends. Gambetta reportedly proposed the toast to the young couple.[51] Nevertheless, even in republican circles, it appears that the social impact of illegitimacy could not be entirely eliminated. This may explain why the marriage celebrations of Charles and Geneviève differed significantly from those of Clémence and Abel. Laurent-Pichat's status among the republican elite had played a major role in allowing Clémence to attract a host of republican luminaries to her nuptials in 1875. The same was not true for his own daughter, whose marriage celebrations in 1877 were modest. Whereas the signing of Clémence's marriage contract had attracted more than one hundred guests, a comparable event for Geneviève on 13 June 1877 was an intimate gathering of family, close friends and political colleagues of Laurent-Pichat.[52] And whereas Clémence's many guests appended their names to the marriage contract, Geneviève and Charles had only their extended families as signatories even if, in Charles's case, that family was a powerful republican cohort.[53]

The contrast between the two signing ceremonies highlights the discretion with which Geneviève's marriage was celebrated. The legal formulas of both the marriage contract and the wedding certificate could not be evaded: they described Geneviève as the 'recognised'– not the 'legitimate' – daughter of her father, making obvious her birth outside wedlock. Moreover, the marriage certificate noted that her mother's name was 'not declared', drawing attention to the secrecy of her birth and to her mother's absence from the ceremony.[54] Whether to avoid awkward questions or protect Geneviève from gossip, those invited to the wedding rituals were all family members or long-term friends. The celebrity figures of Clémence's celebration were absent.[55]

The contrasting wedding ceremonies of Geneviève and Clémence also highlight a major fault line within the republican elite: religious observance. This fault line also helps to explain the absence of the Princesse de Beauvau from Geneviève's wedding: she totally opposed her daughter's marriage to a non-believer.[56] Anticlericalism was not yet the explosive issue it would become in the 1880s once the republicans in power began to legislate to reduce the power of the Catholic Church, but many republicans, including Laurent-Pichat, strongly opposed the Church's intervention in secular matters and its claim that papal authority took precedence over that of states and governments. Republicans showed an interest in the Gallican movement, which sought a French Church independent of Rome. This attracted them to renegade priests critical of the papacy, like the excommunicated Father Hyacinth Loyson, whose lectures at the Cirque d'Hiver in April 1877 attracted a sell-out crowd. Laurent-Pichat's family attended in the company of many republicans, including Céline Scheurer-Kestner, Louis Ulbach and Etienne Arago: '*Tout Paris* was there', Laurent-Pichat recorded.[57] The republican elite – including Gambetta, Mme Charras, the Ferrys and Laurent-Pichat's family – also met Loyson at the famous salon of Madame Yung.[58]

Civil marriage was required by law, but that formality was often accompanied by a religious ceremony even in republican circles. Laurent-Pichat reported attending nuptial Masses for a number of his republican friends and acquaintances, including the children of Emmanuel Arago and the brother and daughter of Henri Allain-Targé.[59] Laurent-Pichat's niece Jeanne Lefort also had a nuptial Mass, as he commented: 'Abbé Milière married them and brought politics into his sermon.'[60] It is surprising, nevertheless, that Clémence had a nuptial Mass when she married Abel Hovelacque in 1875.[61] Hovelacque belonged to a number of organisations that embraced a positivist world view, including the Society of Anthropology, the Voltaire Society, and a group devoted to 'scientific materialism'. He was also a freemason. His family origins were Catholic, however, and he had attended a Jesuit college.[62] This suggests that his family may have desired a religious marriage. Given social expectations, Rosine and Clémence may also have desired a religious ceremony.

The wedding of Geneviève and Charles, on the other hand, was limited to the civil ceremony. There is little evidence that Geneviève was ever devout, even though (like most girls) she made her First Communion and was confirmed, and sometimes went to Mass with Rosine and Clémence. More importantly, a civil ceremony suited Geneviève's father and husband, neither of whom were believers. Outraged by this union, however, not only did the devout Princesse refuse to attend Geneviève's marriage, but she never spoke to Laurent-Pichat again.[63]

Just as the Princesse feared, Geneviève was marrying into a secular republican family and, perhaps worse, one whose religious background, insofar as it acknowledged one, was Protestant rather than Catholic. Charles's sister, Eugénie, had insisted on a civil ceremony when she married Jules Ferry, even though Ferry was prepared to have a religious marriage.[64] The secular marriage rituals of Geneviève and Charles thus reflected the culture of the two families, who were becoming aligned. The different rites surrounding the marriages of Geneviève and Clémence highlight the diversity of bourgeois republican culture at that time. They also highlight the role of families not only in shaping marriage alliances, but also in influencing the manner in which marriages were formalised.

Love and tenderness

Family correspondence provides an intimate glimpse of the marriage of Geneviève and Charles, which is lacking for the other couples in the family. That correspondence, which reveals moments of interaction between the couple as well as others' perceptions of their relationship, emphasises the affection between them and their attachment to each other. Their marriage certainly established an alliance between two like-minded republican families, but it was also a 'marriage of inclination', bringing together two people who took pleasure in each other's company. It illustrates the blending of family interest and individual choice in nineteenth-century marriage-making.

Following their wedding, Geneviève and Charles spent a month in Paris before joining the family at Beuzeval for the summer holidays.[65] The families keenly observed the first days of their marriage and were soon congratulating themselves on a successful alliance. Laurent-Pichat reported to Charles's father in July: 'There aren't enough hours in the day for Charles and his wife to fill … They're ready for anything, so long as they are together.'[66] In September, he wrote to Mme Kestner:

> I see that the first steps of our young newlyweds have been satisfactory … Yes, they are launched, and under a lucky star. It will be a pleasure for me to follow their progress, in full confidence. For their life seems so securely established, on such sound and well-balanced foundations, that there is nothing to fear for their future except accidents of health, and in that regard too appearances are promising.[67]

Laurent-Pichat went further, reaching out to Charles's father, Camille Risler, to bring the two families closer together: 'Let's devote ourselves to living in unison, united and strong'.[68]

By transforming a young woman into an adult, marriage not only established a new relationship of intimacy between her and her husband but also transformed her relationships with her birth family. Both Geneviève's changing relationship with her father and her relationship with her new husband were on display as she and Charles left Beuzeval in late August to begin married life. While each of those relationships was marked by great tenderness, Geneviève was nevertheless pained by separation from the family that had formed her world since infancy.

Geneviève wrote to her father the day after their departure: 'I was very upset to leave you yesterday. I watched the tops of your hats for as long as I could, but eventually they all disappeared. Everything was fine until Trouville'. Then, after boarding the train for Paris, 'your daughter presented her husband with the spectacle of bursting into tears, to which Charles, as a good husband, replied by shedding a few tears as well'. Geneviève reported Charles's compassionate reaction, giving an insight into the personal relationship between the couple: 'My husband was very kind to me. He consoled me very affectionately, because he understands that I have never left you before and that it was painful for me to be separated from you'.[69] Laurent-Pichat's love for his daughter, and his recognition of their changed relationship, was evident in his reply: 'Dear child, you know quite well that we are not separated and that you could not find in life a more reliable and more tender protector when you are absent'.[70] She was still his 'child', but she now had a 'protector' other than him.

The daily togetherness of Beuzeval was replaced for Laurent-Pichat and Geneviève by the poignant togetherness of the letter.[71] 'This daily chat, as you know, is a great joy for me', her father assured Geneviève. 'I am with you while I write; I think of you with each word; I am happy if I have a little news to deal with in my pages'. Letter-writing provided an alternative – if also inadequate – means for father and daughter to be present to each other. While they were both delighted by the marriage, their letters exhibited an undercurrent of sadness and longing: 'With one letter on its way, I begin another', he wrote. 'I chat with you, I think of you, and time is sweeter to me'.[72] His letters were a jumble of thoughts: 'That only demonstrates my desire to let you know about the multitude of insignificant details that life is made of.'[73] Rosine, too, wrote affectionately to Geneviève, barely concealing her sorrow:

> I have nothing to write to you, my dear, that you cannot learn from Léon's letters; but ... we think of you much too often for your absence not to be a little hard to bear. It seems quite strange to me that we go walking without you; we sketch without you; we read without you; ... it takes full confidence that you have been well received, are well cared for, well loved, to make us accept that you don't miss all of that as we do.[74]

After a brief sojourn in Paris, Geneviève and Charles headed to Thann to visit his family, and Geneviève described to her father the warm and affectionate welcome she received there. Over the following weeks, Laurent-Pichat received from Charles's family many letters singing Geneviève's praises.[75] He replied to Charles's father, Camille Risler: 'You finally see that I did not deceive you and that I did not exaggerate when I described Geneviève's perfections to you'.[76]

The sentiments these letters expressed may have been heartfelt, but they also sought to strengthen family ties and affirm the new family connection. Laurent-Pichat was delighted by a glowing tribute from Victor Chauffour and another from Mme Charras: 'It's a letter that I'll keep ... It's a sweet and precious testament that has aroused my paternal pride'.[77] Likewise Mme Floquet wrote to Rosine, lauding Geneviève's virtues and Rosine's role in fostering them. Laurent-Pichat was extremely moved by this recognition of Rosine, which subtly both acknowledged Geneviève's illegitimacy and erased its significance. He wrote to Geneviève: 'This letter can add nothing to the sentiments I feel for your aunt, who deserves all your affection, but I will never forget it.'[78] Both the newlyweds and their families, therefore, saw themselves bound in a web of affection. Marriage was a 'family affair', and this family placed a premium on love and affection.

United to save the Republic

Republican aspiration was embedded within marriages in these families and formed part of their *raison d'être*, as they created new nodes of republican affiliation that reinforced the broader family's networks and advanced its goals. The constitutional drama of May 1877 was experienced as a crisis, therefore, by the entire family.

They all had a stake in the political outcome just as they all had a stake in the new family alliances.

Indeed, if the crisis drew the immediate family together, it also invoked Laurent-Pichat's political bonds with the extended family into which Geneviève had now married. Angered by President Mac-Mahon's dismissal of the republican government, Laurent-Pichat expressed his intense political emotion in poetry. He found consolation in the memory of his hero, Jean-Baptiste Charras, Charles's uncle, who had faced an even worse defeat in the violent coup d'état of December 1851. 'I have shaped my life to your teachings', he wrote. 'During such dreadful, troubled days, / One must cling fast to dignity: it's the polar star'. Laurent-Pichat claimed to have learned from Charras that he should control his passions, act with honour and integrity, even when his opponents did not.[79]

Once the conservative-dominated Senate approved the dissolution of the Assembly on 22 June, new elections were scheduled for mid-October. Laurent-Pichat and the entire family threw themselves wholeheartedly into the campaign to ensure an overwhelming victory. Laurent-Pichat's letters to Geneviève (in Thann) throughout September and into October were filled not only with outpourings of affection, therefore, but also with political discussion.[80] The elections – critical to the survival of the Republic – competed with Geneviève for Laurent-Pichat's attention.

Laurent-Pichat returned briefly to Paris from Beuzeval on 20 September to consult Léon Gambetta, leader of the Republican Union, about how best to contribute to the republican campaign. As he explained to Geneviève, he wanted to 'remain worthy' of his privileged position as Life Senator.[81] Both he and Gambetta realised that the elections would be won or lost in the provinces, as did their opponents. The new monarchist government launched a fear campaign against the republicans, singling out Gambetta for particular venom. Elements of the Church hierarchy also mobilised against the republicans. Pastoral letters read from the pulpit advised voters how to cast their ballot. This was a battle not only over the composition of the government but also between competing visions of France.[82]

Laurent-Pichat travelled to the Chablis region to assist family friend Jules Rathier, the Republican Union candidate for Tonnerre, who was up against both a moderate republican and a

Bonapartist.[83] Lodging with Amédée Beaujean's staunchly republican family, Laurent-Pichat set about fostering Rathier's candidature and 'spurring [him] on'. 'I am working for the destruction of a Bonapartist', he informed Geneviève. As well as writing numerous letters, he sent newspapers 'en masse' into Rathier's electorate.[84] Laurent-Pichat's national status enabled him to play a vital role: 'Everyone in the district looks on me as a special delegate, armed with special powers ... to ensure that Rathier is successfully elected, and that exaggerated illusion does him no harm'.[85]

The republican campaign in Tonnerre was decidedly a family affair. Amédée Beaujean's father, Eusèbe, chaired electoral meetings in his capacity as acting Mayor of Chablis; Laurent-Pichat reported Eusèbe Beaujean's unflinching anticlerical views: 'No concessions! The priests have been granted whatever they demanded because no one had the courage to refuse them! There's no time to lose. We must take everything from them as quickly as possible!'[86] Amédée's uncle, Léonce Pic, distributed republican newspapers in nearby villages. During a visit in April 1877, Laurent-Pichat had worried about the rural vote in this electorate, observing to Scheurer-Kestner: 'Here, in Chablis, opinion is favourable ... Rathier is liked and carries influence, but outside Chablis, the villages escape him'. Pic reported in early October, however, that Rathier could now expect about half the vote in some villages.[87]

Geneviève and Clémence, close friends of Rathier's daughter Marguerite, were keenly interested in his candidature, too. Geneviève wrote to her father: 'I had resolved to re-establish our little trio with [Marguerite] and Clémence. I hope that will happen this winter, and that good elections will bring the whole family back to Paris'. She was relieved when the moderate republican withdrew his candidature and recommended Rathier to his supporters, virtually guaranteeing Rathier's success.[88] But Geneviève's interest in the contest was not only an expression of the family's republicanism: Marguerite's personal prospects hinged on the election of her father, since the daughter of a member of the Chamber of Deputies was a more appealing marriage partner than the daughter of a local winegrower. Laurent-Pichat, too, knew what was at stake. If Rathier won, 'a marriage is almost assured', he wrote. 'Being back in circulation again [in Paris] can only be favourable to [Marguerite's] future'.[89] Family and political fortunes were intertwined in multiple ways in this campaign.

With election day approaching, the political contest intensified and Laurent-Pichat turned his mind to tactics:

> I will advise [Rathier] to stay at Tonnerre, handy to the printer of his newspaper, like an artillery man at his cannon, for the five days that precede the election (the time reserved for dirty tricks), with people ready to put up his posters ... so as to respond if there are last-minute placards when they think no response is possible.[90]

Laurent-Pichat also responded to requests from other republican candidates who believed his name would assist their campaigns. Charles-Félix Frébault, the candidate in Laurent-Pichat's own electorate in Paris, called for his support. Laurent-Pichat highlighted the impact of coercion and intimidation even there:

> A committee needs to be formed and posters put up on the walls. We have few people available to take public action, because ... the brave folk of our arrondissement aren't disposed to take initiatives and their hesitation is understandable, because reactionary pressure still has power over the small businesses of our neighbourhoods.[91]

Laurent-Pichat returned to Paris on 5 October for a meeting in that electorate, which he reported as a triumph:

> My meeting at the Pré-aux-clercs was perfect. About two thousand people. You couldn't move. When I entered everyone stood and greeted me with five or six shouts of 'Long live the Republic!' They made me preside and when I took the chair I was applauded. Everything went calmly. At one point I feared there'd be tumult, but they heeded my advice and I managed the meeting to everyone's satisfaction.[92]

Laurent-Pichat forwarded to Geneviève and Charles the report of the meeting in *La Petite République française*, describing it as 'brief but accurate'.[93] It contrasted the orderliness of the republican meeting with the tumult of the Bonapartist gathering the previous evening.[94]

Laurent-Pichat wrote detailed letters about the elections to Geneviève and Charles because they were still in Thann and largely reliant on correspondence for information. Geneviève wrote on one occasion: 'I frequently think of my native land and of you all'.[95] Her sense of estrangement was more than a figure of speech. Since France's defeat in the war of 1870–71, Alsace had been part of the German Empire and its inhabitants had been forced to choose between French and German citizenship. Charles's family remained proudly French while retaining their property and business interests on what had become German soil. Geneviève and Charles were indeed in a 'foreign land'. Their delayed return from what had been envisaged as a short honeymoon visit threatened their participation in the critical French elections of October 1877.

Geneviève wrote to her father on 21 September: 'You will know from the letter I wrote to my aunt yesterday that Madame your daughter has taken it into her head to take precautions. The situation isn't at all serious, and I hope that in a few days I will be absolutely well.' In subsequent letters she elaborated on her nausea, diet and bed rest, and the care with which she was surrounded. Clearly, she believed she was pregnant and so did her father. He wrote to Charles: 'I am so happy at your letter that I could embrace passers-by in the street and tell them what you have told me'.[96]

However, the pregnancy was short-lived. Barely a week after receiving the joyful tidings, Laurent-Pichat recorded: 'Bad news from Thann.' 'The accident has taken place, in good circumstances'.[97] Complete bed rest was prescribed for Geneviève. This placed her father in a dilemma because the elections were so important: 'I would love to be with you; .... I am not there – and it's not from lack of desire ... I have been very troubled and full of remorse for several days.' Laurent-Pichat decided, however, that he could never replace 'the goodness or the experience' of the excellent nurses who surrounded his daughter.[98] Charles's consideration and attentiveness at this time again suggest the affection between the couple. He read to her; he sketched her portrait; he played cards with her. Charles was 'the best husband imaginable', Geneviève wrote. 'He deserves all the praise that is showered on him'.[99]

In early October, Geneviève became more anxious about not being permitted to travel. 'I had hoped that we could leave Thann on the 13th so that Charles could vote on the 14th ... but I am a little afraid that we will be forced to wait three or four days longer, out of prudence'. While other members of the family departed for Paris, the couple spent election day alone in Thann, except for the servants. But their thoughts were on France. 'We won't know anything until tomorrow. I am deeply upset to have kept Charles here on such a serious and important day. But we are both being very sensible, and my dear husband hasn't shown an instant's regret that he couldn't be useful to his country this year [by voting]'.[100]

In Paris, too, all thoughts were on the election. Laurent-Pichat began his letter of 14 October: 'I have just voted. The weather is wonderful. Such hope is in the air. Having done my duty, I am filled with serenity and confidence'. He paid a visit to the Kestner household and to the Hovelacques, observing that Abel's father Edouard did not share his son's radical views: 'He will vote for [republican] Grévy, I don't doubt that, but he reads *Le Figaro* and allows himself to be worried by the stupidities and lies of the despicable crooks who write for that paper'. His thoughts were on Rathier in Tonnerre, as well as on the seventh arrondissement in Paris: 'Success [there] would indicate what Abel could expect in our neighbourhood if he decides to stand in the municipal elections'.[101] Clearly that possibility was already under discussion.

The next day saw a flurry of telegrams and letters as the votes were tallied and the republican victory was confirmed. The results for the family were positive: Charles's uncle, Charles Floquet, increased his vote; his brother-in-law, Jules Ferry, won his seat but with a reduced majority. Both Rathier in Tonnerre and Frébault in Paris were successful, so Laurent-Pichat could feel satisfied with the contests in which he had played a role. But he noted, 'My old friend Henri Chevreau was defeated in the Ardèche'.[102] He still followed Chevreau's fortunes and, despite their political estrangement, still remembered him as his friend.

Geneviève replied from Thann: 'Yesterday was such an emotional day, soothed a little by your telegrams ... I believe there is cause to be satisfied even if the majority is not as great as we had hoped'. She celebrated the election of Monsieur Rathier, adding: 'I am certain that Charles's vote could not have got Monsieur de la Forge elected, but all the same, I am not reconciled to the fact that my poor husband was unable to do his duty'.[103] Geneviève and Charles finally returned to Paris with the doctor's blessing on 22 October.

Geneviève remained silent about the loss of her pregnancy. In the lead-up to the elections, her letters had focused on the political implications of her condition. 'I am quite upset that Charles cannot vote', she had written. 'I am disrupting everything. I'd really like to have been in Paris on election day, too, such an exciting day ... But we'll forget all our troubles if the election results are good, won't we?'[104] Geneviève constantly presented a stoic face to the family, as a republican wife whose personal sufferings were of less importance than the political cause. While she was 'deeply upset' that Charles could not vote, therefore, she never expressed any emotion about her own personal loss.

Geneviève's reaction reflected her education as a bourgeois woman, trained to avoid self-indulgence and to think first of others. Besides, her responses are known only from her letters to her father, whom she always sought to please. What she and Charles expressed privately remains unknown. Charles's reactions, as reported by Geneviève, prioritised not the political struggle but Geneviève's wellbeing. If she presented herself first and foremost as a republican wife, she presented Charles first and foremost as a loving husband.

Bourgeois families took great care to find compatible matches for their children, none less so than republican families for whom a successful marriage offered the prospect of both ensuring their children's future and advancing the republican cause. The unions of Clémence and Abel and of Geneviève and Charles each created a new nucleus of republican sentiment. That both men would soon stand as republican candidates in the municipal elections shows that the hope invested in those marriages was not misplaced, either for the family's future or for the Republic. As republican alliances, inspired by a blend of personal affinity and family interests, these marriages rapidly proved successful.

It is impossible to know whether the marriage of Clémence and Abel was emotionally fulfilling, though there is no evidence that it was not. The official sources suggest that republican interests and social status were paramount, but the picture remains partial and incomplete. Our picture of the marriage of Geneviève and Charles is enriched, on the other hand, by intimate sources indicating that their union was successful in personal terms. Charles was a suitable republican husband for Geneviève, but he was above all a person whom Geneviève – and her father – saw as a good husband. In identifying Charles's personal qualities to her father, Geneviève noted traits that revealed his emotional empathy. Charles was kind, affectionate, attentive and considerate. These qualities affected Geneviève directly and made for her happiness. In singling them out in her husband, she indicated her own personal satisfaction in the union. Intimate sources provide an added perspective on this marriage, revealing its intricate mingling of family interest and personal considerations. The marriage of Geneviève and Charles suggests, further, that the social impediments posed by extra-marital birth could be overcome or ignored by bourgeois families. Geneviève's successful social integration through marriage raises the question of whether other bourgeois children born out of wedlock were also quietly shepherded into society, despite social norms that tended to exclude them.

Notes

1 LLP, Journal, 20 June 1877. Emphasis original.
2 On the constitutionality of the dismissal, see Chastenet, *Histoire de la Troisième République,* I, pp. 226–8.
3 LLP, Journal, 22 June 1877.
4 Martin-Fugier, 'Bourgeois rituals', in *A History of Private Life,* IV, pp. 309–10; Elizabeth C. Macknight, *Aristocratic Families in Republican France, 1870–1940* (Manchester: Manchester University Press, 2012); Cyril Grange, 'Les réseaux matrimoniaux intra-confessionnels de la haute bourgeoisie juive à Paris à la fin du XIXe siècle', *Annales de démographie historique,* 109 (2005), 131–56.
5 Adeline Daumard, *La Bourgeoisie parisienne, 1815–1848* (Paris: S.E.V.P.E.N, 1963), quote p. 336.
6 Johnson, *Becoming Bourgeois,* p. 18 and n. 61.
7 Pellissier, *Vie privée*; Macknight, *Aristocratic Families*; Leonore Davidoff, *The Best Circles: Society, etiquette and the season* (London: Croom Helm, 1973), esp. pp. 49–50.
8 Adeline Daumard, 'Affaire, amour, affection: Le Mariage dans la société bourgeoise au XIXe siècle', *Romantisme,* 68 (1990), 33–47 (45). See also Daumard, *Les Bourgeois et la bourgeoisie en France depuis 1848.*
9 Denise Davidson, '"Happy" marriages in early nineteenth-century France', *Journal of Family History,* 37:1 (2012), 23–35.
10 See chapter 2.
11 AN MC/ET/LXXXIV/1114: contrat de mariage, Achille Deslandes/ Juliette Asselin, 29 July 1858.
12 See Johnson, *Becoming Bourgeois;* Pellissier, *Vie privée,* p. 133; Grange, 'Les réseaux matrimoniaux'.

13 Pellissier, *Vie privée*, p. 124; Daumard, 'Affaire, amour, affection', 35. On 'marrying in' versus 'marrying out' of the family, see Johnson, *Becoming Bourgeois*, pp. 301–3.
14 AN MC/ET/XXXIII/1205: contrat de mariage, Amédée Beaujean/ Rosine Deslandes, 26 Nov. 1851. See Florence Laroche-Gisserot, 'Pratiques de la dot', 1445.
15 Sowerwine, *France Since 1870*, p. 9.
16 AN F^{17}/20117: Emile Ambroise Amédée Beaujean, personnel file; Base Léonore: LH/155/34, no. 20675: Legion of Honour (5 Aug. 1878); BHVP, 6, no. 62: LLP to Geneviève Risler [GR], 21 Sept. 1877.
17 Daumard, *La Bourgeoisie parisienne*, pp. 332–3.
18 AN MC/ET/LXXXIV/1118: contrat de mariage, Emile Lefort/ Herminie Deslandes, 31 March 1859.
19 MSDV: LLP to Jules Ferry, 29 March 1859.
20 Tchernoff, *Le Parti républicain*, p. 360, n. 1; 'Lefort, Henri', in https://maitron.fr
21 Pellissier, *Vie privée*, pp. 125–6; Daumard, 'Affaire, amour, affection', 41.
22 Quoted in Sylvie Aprile, 'Bourgeoise et républicaine, deux termes inconciliables?' in Alain Corbin, Jacqueline Lalouette and Michèle Riot-Sarcey (eds), *Femmes dans la cité, 1815–1871* (Paris: Créaphis, 1997), pp. 211–23 (215).
23 On patronage, see Reddy, *The Invisible Code*, chapter 4.
24 Emile Lefort, *De la Loi et les droits et devoirs qu'elle apporte. Conférence faite par M. Em. Lefort, notaire, Président de la Commission d'organisation de la Bibliothèque populaire de L'Isle-Adam, le 16 janvier 1870* (Beaumont-sur-Oise: Imp. de C. Frémont, 1870), 20 pp.
25 Jacqueline Lalouette, 'Littré, Maximilien Paul Emile', in Mayeur and Corbin (eds), *Les Immortels du Sénat*, pp. 399–402; Amédée Beaujean, *Petit dictionnaire universel ou Abrégé du dictionnaire français d'E. Littré, augmenté d'une partie mythologique, historique, biographique et géographique*, 3e édition (Paris: Hachette, 1877).
26 See the entries on theses figures in Mayeur and Corbin (eds), *Les Immortels du Sénat*, and Schweitz, *Les Parlementaires*.
27 AP, Mariages, 7e arron: V4E 3294, 50: Alexandre-Abel Hovelacque/ Clémence Beaujean, 26 Jan. 1875.
28 LLP, Journal, 12, 13 Nov. 1874.
29 On François-Saturnin-Léonide Babaud-Laribière, see Robert, Bourloton and Cougny, eds, *Dictionnaire des parlementaires français*, available at https://numelyo.bm-lyon.fr/f_view/BML:BML_00GOO0100137001103448309 Accessed May 2022. On the

Babaud-Laribière family's connection to the Hovelacque family, see LLP, Journal, 20 March 1882.
30 LLP, Journal, 15 Nov. 1874.
31 'Hovelacque, Abel Alexandre', in Schweitz, *Les Parlementaires*, pp. 314–16; Sowerwine, *France Since 1870*, p. 41; Piet Desmet, 'Abel Hovelacque et l'école de linguistique naturaliste: l'inégalité des langues permet-elle de conclure à l'inégalité des races?', *Histoire Epistémologie Langage*, 29:2 (2007), 41–59.
32 Martin-Fugier, 'Bourgeois rituals', in *A History of Private Life*, IV, p. 312.
33 Daumard, *La Bourgeoisie parisienne*, pp. 332–3.
34 AN MC/ET/XVIII/1403: Contrat de mariage, Abel Hovelacque/ Clémence Beaujean, 20 Jan. 1875.
35 LLP, Journal, 13 May 1863.
36 *Ibid.*, 22 Jan. 1867.
37 See Martin-Fugier, 'Bourgeois rituals', in *A History of Private Life*, IV, pp. 312–13. The contract was officially signed on 20 January; guests appended their signatures at the social ceremony on 23 January.
38 Jack D. Ellis, *The Physician-Legislators of France: Medicine and politics in the Early Third Republic, 1870–1914* (New York: Cambridge University Press, 1990). On Pozzi, see Julian Barnes, *The Man in the Red Coat* (London: Jonathan Cape, 2019).
39 LLP, Journal, 23 Jan. 1875.
40 AN MC/ETLXXXIV/1237: contrat de mariage, Charles Risler/ Geneviève Laurent-Pichat, 15 June 1877.
41 BHVP, 7, fos 1–2, 5–6: LLP to Camille Risler, 16 Dec. 1867; undated ('15').
42 Pellissier, *Vie privée*, pp. 134–5; Daumard, 'Affaire, amour, affection', 45; Davidoff, *The Best Circles*, pp. 49–50. On seaside vacations as opportunities for match-making, see Perrot, 'Roles and characters', in *A History of Private Life*, IV, pp. 180–87.
43 BHVP, 7, no. 38: GLP to LLP, 15 July 1873.
44 *Ibid.*, nos 40, 42: 19, 25 July 1873; nos 46, 48–50: 10, 15, 20, 27 July 1874. See also Clémence Beaujean's letters to her uncle, Laurent-Pichat, undated and attached to Geneviève's letters, nos 48 and 49.
45 BHVP, 7, no. 42: GLP to LLP, 25 July 1873.
46 Michel Winock, *Clemenceau* (Paris: Perrin, 2007), p. 41.
47 AN 418 AP/1, 456MI: Jules Ferry to Mme E. Kestner, 17, 19 Aug. 1875.
48 Gaillard, *Jules Ferry*, pp. 82–8, 103–4.
49 LLP, Journal, 14, 17 April 1877.
50 *Ibid.*, 14 June 1877.

51 *Ibid.*, 13 June 1877; APF: GC, notebook, unpaginated. This notebook puts the dinner on 17 June, but the lists of guests in LLP's diary suggest 13 June as more likely.
52 LLP, Journal, 13 June 1877.
53 The witnesses for Charles were his grandmother, Mme Eugénie Kestner; his aunts Mathilde (widow of Jean-Baptiste Charras), Céline (with her husband Auguste Scheurer-Kestner) and Hortense (with her husband Charles Floquet); his widowed uncle, Victor Chauffour (with his daughter Fanny) and Charles's sister, Eugénie, and her husband Jules Ferry.
54 AP, Mariages, 7e arron., V4E 3314: Charles Risler/Geneviève Laurent-Pichat, 20 June 1877.
55 LLP, Journal, 20 June 1877.
56 APF, GC, notebook, unpaginated.
57 LLP, Journal, 15, 20, 21 April 1877.
58 *Ibid.*, 2 Feb. 1878.
59 *Ibid.*, 3 May, 6, 9 Nov. 1875; 6 May 1878.
60 *Ibid.*, 30 Oct. 1879.
61 *Ibid.*, 26 Jan. 1875.
62 'Hovelacque, Abel Alexandre', in Schweitz, *Les Parlementaires*, pp. 314–16.
63 APF: GC, notebook, unpaginated.
64 Gaillard, *Jules Ferry*, p. 93.
65 LLP, Journal, 17 June 1877.
66 BHVP, 7, fos 21–2: LLP to Camille Risler, 27 July 1877.
67 *Ibid.*, fos 46–7: LLP to Mme Charles Kestner, 17 Sept. 1877.
68 *Ibid.*, fos 23–4: LLP to Camille Risler, 4 Sept. 1877.
69 *Ibid.*, no. 77: GR to LLP, 27 Aug. 1877.
70 BHVP, 6, no. 39: LLP to GR, 28 Aug. 1877.
71 On the practices of family correspondence, see Dauphin et al. (eds), *Ces bonnes lettres*, introduction, pp. 131–60.
72 BHVP, 6, nos 56, 62: LLP to GR, 15, 21 Sept. 1877.
73 *Ibid.*, no. 62: 21 Sept. 1877.
74 *Ibid.* no. 47: Rosine Beaujean to GR, appended to LLP's letter to GR, 6 Sept. 1877.
75 BHVP, 7, no. 80: GR to LLP, 31 Aug. 1877; BHVP, 6, no. 43: LLP to GR, 2 Sept. 1877.
76 BHVP, 7, fos 23–4: LLP to Camille Risler, 4 Sept. 1877.
77 BHVP, 6, nos 50, 54: LLP to GR, 9, 13 Sept. 1877.
78 *Ibid.*, no. 69: 1 Oct. 1877.
79 LLP, 'A Charras: après le 16 mai' [July 1877], in LLP, *Les Réveils*, pp. 123–37.

80 BHVP, 6, nos 54, 63, 69: LLP to GR, 13, 24 Sept., 1 Oct. 1877.
81 *Ibid.*, no. 59: 19 Sept. 1877.
82 Mollier and George, *La Plus Longue des Républiques,* pp. 82–5; Chastenet, *Histoire de la Troisième République*, I, pp. 226–33; *La République française,* 7 Oct. 1877.
83 BHVP, 6, no. 59: LLP to GR, 19 Sept. 1877.
84 *Ibid*, no. 65: LLP to Charles Risler, 26 [Sept. 1877]; *ibid.*, nos 67–9: LLP to GR, 27, 29 Sept., 1 Oct. 1877.
85 *Ibid.*, no. 70: LLP to GR, 2 Oct. 1877.
86 *Ibid.*, nos 64, 67: LLP to GR, 26, 27 Sept. 1877; *ibid.*, no. 65: LLP to Charles Risler, 26 [Sept. 1877].
87 AN276 AP/1: LLP to Scheurer-Kestner, 7 April 1877; BHVP, 6, no. 69: LLP to GR, 1 Oct. 1877. The marriage certificate of Clémence Beaujean identifies Pic as her paternal great-uncle.
88 BHVP, 7, nos 86, 89: GR to LLP, 19, 26 Sept. 1877; BHVP, 6, nos 55, 66: LLP to GR, 14, 27 Sept. 1877.
89 BHVP, 6, no. 64: LLP to GR, 26 Sept. 1877.
90 *Ibid.*, no. 70: LLP to GR, 2 Oct. 1877.
91 *Ibid.*
92 *Ibid.*, no. 72: LLP to GR, 7 Oct. 1877.
93 *Ibid.*, no. 73: LLP to GR, 8 Oct. 1877.
94 See *La Petite République française,* 9 Oct. 1877.
95 BHVP, 7, no. 81: GR to LLP, 4 Sept. 1877. Emphasis original.
96 *Ibid.*, no. 87: GR to LLP, 21 Sept. 1877; BHVP, 6, no. 65: LLP to Charles Risler, 26 [Sept. 1877].
97 LLP, Journal, 27, 28 Sept. 1877.
98 BHVP, 6, no. 68: LLP to GR, 29 Sept. 1877.
99 BHVP, 7, nos 88, 90, 93, 94: GR to LLP, 23 Sept., 5, 14, 16 Oct. 1877.
100 *Ibid.*, no. 93: GR to LLP, 14 Oct 1877.
101 BHVP, 6, no. 79: LLP to GR, 14 Oct. 1877.
102 *Ibid.*, no. 81: LLP to GR, 15 [Oct. 1877].
103 BHVP, 7, no. 94: GR to LLP, 16 Oct. 1877.
104 *Ibid.*, nos 90, 91: GR to LLP, 5, 10 Oct. 1877.

9

'The task is magnificent and enormous': family politics in the 'Republic of republicans', 1877–85

Between October 1877 and January 1879, electoral victories gave republicans control of both houses of the Assembly and thousands of municipalities across France. They moved quickly to cement the Republic in place, restoring Paris's role as capital and seat of government, legalising the Marseillaise and making 14 July the national day. During the 1880s, France's institutions were increasingly run by republicans on republican principles and a major republican legislative agenda was enacted. A significant cultural shift occurred, embedding the Republic in the national psyche. France became a 'Republic of republicans'.[1]

Philip Nord has demonstrated that the organisations of civil society had played, and continued to play, a vital role in making these victories possible by gradually instilling republican values and institutions in the community.[2] Laurent-Pichat's networks illustrate, further, that family and friendship links underpinned those organisations, facilitating their growth and impact; moreover, those links were themselves vital to the republicanisation process. Families, in particular, provided occasions, spaces and networks for co-operative action by men and women for the Republic. Rather than being a private space outside politics, the realm of home and family was a site of political engagement. It also became an important site for managing the political differences that emerged among republicans once the Republic was securely installed.

While republican culture, like bourgeois culture more broadly, was strongly gendered, its gender boundaries nevertheless allowed for co-operative activity in the promotion of republican goals, at least in families like Laurent-Pichat's. A masculine republican

Figure 9.1 Léon Laurent-Pichat, *c*. 1880.

culture, nurtured in masonic lodges, anticlerical gatherings and political meetings, flourished alongside other domains in which both women and men worked for the cause. Exploring how the women and men of these families engaged with republicanism as the 'Republic of republicans' came into being illustrates both the gender differences that marked their lives and their shared experiences of republican activism. It highlights, moreover, that as republican men moved into positions of power, the so-called intimate and political

Family patronage and male camaraderie

The 'republicanising' of institutions and their personnel from the late 1870s created opportunities for republican men. Laurent-Pichat's family illustrates that, while talent and skill were important, personal contacts, family networks and male friendship played vital roles in the distribution of positions and thus the exercise of power. The family saw an opportunity for the young men – Clémence's husband Abel Hovelacque and Geneviève's husband Charles Risler – to launch political careers in the municipal elections of January 1878. As the elections approached, Laurent-Pichat lobbied influential figures, including the local Deputy, Charles-Félix Frébault, who had recently sought Laurent-Pichat's help to retain his seat in the legislative elections.[3] Laurent-Pichat chaired public electoral meetings for his two protégés and hosted private gatherings at the house. Abel's father-in-law, Amédée Beaujean, often attended these meetings, emphasising the family's investment in the campaign.[4]

Abel Hovelacque won handsomely on 6 January, becoming a municipal councillor for the seventh arrondissement in Paris. Charles, however, was unsuccessful. His candidature was perhaps hampered by his delayed return from Thann due to Geneviève's miscarriage.[5] But he also lacked the status and experience of Hovelacque, who was not only a professor at the Paris School of Anthropology, but also a regular contributor to Gambetta's newspaper and a practised public speaker, with good contacts in political and scientific circles. Perhaps Charles, just twenty-nine, was also seen as too young. Laurent-Pichat adjudged it a 'noble defeat ... under the circumstances' and supported Charles when he again stood unsuccessfully in a by-election in September.[6]

When the position of mayor of the seventh arrondissement became vacant in 1881, Laurent-Pichat saw yet another opportunity for Charles to enter public life. Republican heavyweights including Ferdinand Hérold (Prefect of the Seine, who appointed mayors of that Department) urged Laurent-Pichat to accept the position himself. But Laurent-Pichat instead lobbied the Prefect on Charles's behalf: 'I spoke to Hérold and explored fully the question of the mayoralty. I refused. He is thinking about Charles Risler but only as adjunct. He wants Wurtz in the town hall.'[7] Charles-Adolphe Wurtz, an eminent chemist and professor at the medical school, duly became mayor, with Risler as one of his assistants. In April 1882, Risler succeeded Wurtz as mayor of the seventh arrondissement, a post he was to hold until 1919.[8]

Laurent-Pichat's patronage proved vital to the successful implantation of both Charles Risler and Abel Hovelacque in public office. Together, the three men formed a powerful bloc in the seventh arrondissement, furthering the family's republican influence. Laurent-Pichat retained a close political affinity with Hovelacque, whose radical vision for the Republic he shared. It seems that Hovelacque repaid Laurent-Pichat's patronage. One-third of the Senate was due to be replaced in 1881 through a process of indirect suffrage. Hovelacque almost certainly played a role in Laurent-Pichat's nomination as one of the electors voting on behalf of the Paris municipal council, which was dominated by radical republicans.[9]

Laurent-Pichat's reputation as a radical, and Hovelacque's support, also likely explain Laurent-Pichat's appointment as one of five jurors to select a statue of the Republic for the Place du Château-d'Eau, renamed the Place de la République.[10] The Paris municipal council, rather than the national government, had taken the initiative in creating a monument to the Republic, and the jurors chose a radical representation for display. The winning entry by the Morice brothers captured the democratic aspirations of the French Revolution. Controversially, the Republic, represented by the female figure of Marianne, wore the Phrygian bonnet: a radical emblem deployed during the French Revolution and harking back to classical antiquity, where it had been worn by freed slaves. Marianne was surrounded by figures representing Liberty, Equality and Fraternity and by a series of bas-reliefs depicting key moments in France's revolutionary history from 1789, through 1830 and 1848, to 1870. The crisis moments of June 1848 and 1871 were not represented. The monument thus depicted France's path towards democracy as a unifying project unfolding with teleological momentum. While not officially inaugurated until 1883, the statue was enshrined with fanfare on 14 July 1880, the first official Bastille Day, marking the symbolic triumph of the Third Republic. 'Abel left early to get a good place' at the festivities, Laurent-Pichat noted, while the whole family went to see the fireworks.[11] Hovelacque presented Laurent-Pichat with a model of one of the unsuccessful entries in the statue competition. The family installed it above the gate on that date as a personal celebration of the Republic.[12]

Republicanism was a world view, not merely a form of political organisation. The men of Laurent-Pichat's family shared that world view, which formed the basis for their political co-operation. Anticlericalism and freemasonry, two pillars of male republican allegiance in this period, brought them together and linked them with their republican colleagues in male-defined spaces and activities, deploying masculine solidarity for a shared cause.[13]

In 1878, as members of the Voltaire Society, the men of the family were heavily involved in events marking the centenary of Voltaire's death. Voltaire was widely admired by republicans for his defence of freedom of thought and his resistance to Church power in secular life. That resistance, known as anticlericalism, was rapidly becoming a republican touchstone for this generation.[14] Voltaire's centenary inspired an official commemoration by the republican government. But Laurent-Pichat joined Abel Hovelacque and Charles Risler, as well as Amédée Beaujean, at a second event funded primarily by the Paris municipal council, which attracted delegates from municipalities across France. Hovelacque was prominent on the organising committee.[15]

According to the advance publicity for this second event, France was engaged in a war pitting Catholic France, 'with Rome for its capital', against 'secular France, the France of [17]89': 'All those who associate themselves with [this Voltaire celebration] will affirm that they are descendants of the Revolution. All those, on the other hand, who refuse to participate ... are the avowed or silent, conscious or unwitting, accomplices of the Jesuits'.[16] As a leading radical republican, Laurent-Pichat was invited to preside the event and his address echoed its anticlerical theme. Voltaire had defended 'liberty, justice and reason', he declared. 'The past was a terrain of struggle; the present is a terrain of struggle. All the enemies of Voltaire are the enemies of the Republic.'[17] If the absence of women branded the event male, so did the belligerent message of the centenary celebration and its performance of anticlericalism in a public space. In encouraging republican men to emulate the heroism of their revolutionary forebears, the Voltaire celebration became both a call to arms and an assertion of republican manhood.

Freemasonry was a major source of support for republicanism and lodges were sites of male camaraderie.[18] All the men of the family joined lodges but the women showed no interest, although the number of women in the movement was slowly increasing.[19] The men came to freemasonry by different routes, illustrating its diverse appeal. Like many of this 'positivist' generation, Abel Hovelacque was a dedicated materialist who embraced freemasonry as a like-minded movement. Having joined the lodge *Les Amis de la tolérance* in July 1878, he would co-found a short-lived lodge, *Le Matérialisme scientifique*, in 1886.[20] Charles Risler, on the other hand, embraced freemasonry as a vehicle for his revanchist patriotism. A native of Alsace, he fought in the Franco-Prussian War and was taken prisoner following the siege of Neuf-Brisach.[21] Charles joined the lodge *Alsace-Lorraine*, installed in Paris in September 1872.[22] As eminent republican Alphonse Crémieux declared at the installation ceremony: 'The very title of the Lodge that we are establishing today is a political protest.'[23] Charles, the most dedicated freemason of the family, also belonged to the lodge *La Clémente Amitié*. He attended regularly and was appointed a Venerable in December 1878.[24]

Laurent-Pichat, too, found friends and allies in freemasonry, although, like a number of other republicans, he was not very active in the lodge.[25] He became an 'apprentice' of *La Clémente Amitié* in December 1876 but took his association no further until Charles initiated him in February 1879. Perhaps his initiation was a mark of family solidarity rather than of masonic zeal. However, in 1882 he co-founded a new lodge, *La Fédération maçonnique*, with Abel Hovelacque and Charles Risler.[26] Family ties and masculine camaraderie in the republican cause thus brought the men together in freemasonry as in the Voltaire Society.

Men and women together

Freemasonry and anticlerical organisations represent the archetypically male face of politics in the early Third Republic. But other political activities brought men and women together in support of the republican cause. Family networks provided hubs through which they co-operated in that endeavour. Educational reform was a key area of co-operation, since women and men shared the belief that a system of free, compulsory and secular education was fundamental to securing the Republic. Such education would instil democratic principles and encourage 'freedom of thought' rather than acceptance of received truths.[27] Consistent with gender norms, however, men and women worked in tandem, rather than together, for the cause of secular education.

Republican men pursued the struggle for secular education primarily through the education league (*ligue de l'enseignement*). Founded in 1866, the league was a product of the early-nineteenth-century movement to create a bourgeois and specifically male civil society.[28] A network of 'circles' affiliated to the league established schools that offered education inspired by a commitment to 'freedom of conscience and the equality of citizens'.[29] Laurent-Pichat was a member of the league by 1872, when he was among a group of radical Deputies – all league members – who accepted a million-strong petition for free and compulsory primary schooling; the petition had been rejected by the National Assembly, then dominated by conservatives. Laurent-Pichat remained a member of the Paris 'circle' of the league into the 1880s.[30] He was a regular donor to a school in the third arrondissement of Paris, as well as assisting schools in the seventh and ninth arrondissements.[31]

Laurent-Pichat's work for education reform was partly a function of his role as an elected representative and prominent community figure. Parisians approached him seeking donations for the secular schools, as well as for the 'people's libraries' that made reading material available to the masses. He donated money, chaired conferences and attended fundraising events.[32] He was invited to open the new municipal school in Chablis in 1881 not only because he was well known there through his links with the Beaujean family, but also because of his national standing as a Senator.[33]

The roles played by Abel Hovelacque and Charles Risler in the drive for republican education also derived in part from their public positions. Primary education was a municipal responsibility under the Republic. As a municipal councillor from 1879, Hovelacque thus shared responsibility for implementing the republican education programme legislated in 1880–82.[34] So did Risler once he became mayor.[35] Moreover, Risler's work in education was also grounded in his commitment to Alsace, because the *Association Générale d'Alsace-Lorraine* (of which he was a founding member in 1871) not only fed and clothed the children of impoverished Alsatian exiles, but also educated them. As a member of the administrative committee of this association from 1876, Risler shared legal and financial responsibility for such projects.[36]

Women in this family circle also embraced secular education wholeheartedly: a mark of their republican faith. But where the men's educational activities were extensions of their political activism, the women's involvement was consonant with the charitable and philanthropic role that had long been assigned to elite women.[37] They now gave that philanthropic impulse a republican twist through the secular 'Society for vocational education for women' (*Société pour l'enseignement professionnel des femmes*), founded by Elisa Lemonnier in the 1860s. The curriculum of the Lemonnier schools combined general education with preparation for employment in the luxury trades. By 1877, the Society ran four schools in Paris with five hundred students.[38]

Rosine, Clémence and Geneviève, along with other women of the family circle, worked for these schools for at least twenty years. Their efforts were strongly supported by the men. Laurent-Pichat noted in his diary in 1871 that he had paid subscriptions for both himself and Rosine to Lemonnier's society. He and his sister were personally acquainted with Julie Toussaint, who had succeeded Lemonnier as Secretary-General of the Society in 1865; they were friendly, too, with Pauline Kergomard, born into a prominent Protestant republican dynasty, the Reclus family, and author of a major work on maternal education. Kergomard, too, was a devoted admirer of Elisa Lemonnier and would play a major role as Inspector of Schools under the republican government.[39] The Mme Paulin to whose school Laurent-Pichat also donated on several occasions is difficult to identify. But the praise she earned, alongside Toussaint, in the memoirs of renowned Communard Louise Michel places her squarely in the republican cohort.[40]

Rosine first ran a stall at the annual fête for the vocational schools in 1873, and she continued to do so for many years. Her stall specialised in so-called 'Etruscan vases'. Along with Clémence and Geneviève, she began taking painting lessons in April 1874 and devoted many hours to producing vases for the fête. Painting on porcelain had been taught in the vocational schools since Lemonnier's time. It appears that Rosine not only raised money for the schools, but also advised or even assisted with lessons.[41]

Rosine's work for the vocational schools illustrates the familial context that had long marked female philanthropy.[42] Clémence and Geneviève were her main assistants. When they were unable, as mothers of infants, to help with the two-day fête in 1882, Rosine's sister-in-law, Victorine, stepped into the breach.[43] But just as the men's republican activities relied on both family networks and friendship networks, so too did the women's work for the vocational schools. Rosine was appointed to the committee of the professional schools in 1873. This brought her into the company of, for instance, Louise Simon, who along with her husband, former republican Prime Minister Jules Simon, took an interest in women's issues.[44] Close family friends Mmes Millard, Rathier and Gosselin, along with their daughters Marguerite Rathier and Suzanne Gosselin, also worked alongside Rosine at the fête. A wider group of republican women, including those in the family network, also ran stalls (as Mme Floquet did) or collected money for the schools. The men actively supported the women's fundraising efforts. Laurent-Pichat recorded giving donations to Mmes Floquet and Scheurer-Kestner, among others, and his purchases at the annual fête usually totalled three or four hundred francs.[45] Painters Jules Laurens and Ernest Hébert (who painted Laurent-Pichat's portrait) donated works for sale. Antonin Proust (no relation to Marcel), a leading republican who would become Arts Minister in Gambetta's government in 1881, made his donation in 1875 by joining the women for a morning to paint 'etrusqueries'.[46] The men's active participation in the women's endeavours illustrates that, while men and women worked separately for the secular education movement, their 'separate spheres' were also porous, allowing considerable interaction and co-operation.

Relieving the suffering of needy Alsatian exiles, who had fled to France when Alsace became part of the German Empire, provided another site of shared activity for men and women in this family, some of whom were Alsatians themselves. The cause was especially dear to Charles Risler, hence his lengthy service to the *Association Générale d'Alsace-Lorraine* (AGAL) from 1871. AGAL assisted impoverished émigrés but also served, as Risler noted, 'to maintain the links of solidarity and fraternity between Alsace-Lorraine and republican France'.[47] Keeping those links alive was essential to the hope of reunifying the 'Lost Provinces' of Alsace and Lorraine with France.

The women of this family played a significant role in AGAL, too, but through a separate 'ladies' committee'. In 1872, under its inaugural president, Mme Eugénie Kestner, grandmother of Charles Risler, that committee initiated what became the central event on AGAL's calendar and its main fundraiser: its annual Christmas tree celebration. This event, which celebrated Alsatian culture in music and song, expressed participants' French patriotism and distributed aid to needy families. It became a regular feature of Parisian Christmas festivities and attracted huge crowds, playing a major role in introducing the Christmas tree into France.[48] During the 1870s, seven family members followed Mme Kestner onto the ladies' committee: three of her daughters, two nieces, her granddaughter Eugénie Ferry, and her grandson's wife, Geneviève Risler.[49]

Again, men and women co-operated in the Christmas tree event as a joint endeavour. Men assumed financial responsibility, as required by law; women organised the event, solicited donations of goods, prepared parcels according to age and sex and oversaw their distribution at the ceremony: no small feat when they catered for as many as four thousand children in the 1880s.[50] Laurent-Pichat recorded the many evenings that Geneviève and Charles devoted to organising and running the event. He also detailed the broader community support it attracted. Not only did the family attend on a regular basis, but so did other republican dignitaries.[51] In 1874 Laurent-Pichat noted the presence of a host of leading republicans: 'Went to the Christmas of the Alsatians and Lorrainers.

In a [theatre] box with Gambetta, Adam, Castelnau, Tiersot, Tirard; next to us were L[ouis] Blanc, Barni and his wife. A huge crowd.'[52]

Women's activities, as products of their acculturation into philanthropy, arose in a different context from men's activities. But this did not mean that women's endeavours were apolitical, an expression of a different world view.[53] Far from it. Women's choice of 'causes' to support, like secular vocational education for girls, expressed a political perspective. They set up and ran secular schools in competition with the Catholic schools. That various municipalities, including Paris, began to open their own vocational schools for girls based on the programme of the Elisa Lemonnier schools highlights their solid republican credentials.[54] Similarly, fundraising for impoverished Alsatian émigrés through the Christmas tree event had echoes of conventional bourgeois philanthropy. But that was re-imagined as part of the republican project. Through the hands of AGAL's women, the Republic bestowed gifts on her needy children, exhibiting the practices of 'solidarity' that were beginning to characterise republican social welfare.[55]

Fostering the republican cause was not just 'men's work', therefore, and even less the sole pursuit of men in politics or civil society. Women played a vital role and, in some circumstances, such as in the vocational schools for young women, were better placed than men to undertake the task. The spheres were no doubt 'separate' in some respects, but they were more porous than has often been thought. Co-operation across 'separate spheres', facilitated by family and friendship networks, proved an invaluable asset to the republican cause.

Affirming family unity

On 30 January 1879, following the resignation of President Mac-Mahon, Jules Grévy was elected President of the Republic by the National Assembly. He was the first republican to hold this office. This was a landmark day, therefore, completing the republican conquest of power. Amédée Beaujean and Charles Risler accompanied Laurent-Pichat to the session, keen to witness the moment.[56] A few days later, President Grévy asked William Waddington to form a government; Waddington appointed Jules Ferry Minister for Public Instruction and Fine Arts. Mme Kestner hosted a celebratory dinner where the family marked the elevation of one of their own to high office.[57]

Jules Ferry was the family's most successful political figure. His marriage to Eugénie Risler in 1875 had been a major family event; Laurent-Pichat had attended with Geneviève. Laurent-Pichat had known Eugénie since she was a child and had close friendships with her family. Once his daughter Geneviève married Eugénie's brother, Charles Risler, in 1877, Geneviève and Charles formed a close relationship with Eugénie and Jules Ferry, the couples socialising and taking holidays together. Geneviève was firmly part of the Risler/Kestner family by 1879, therefore, and she was invited to the celebratory dinner for Ferry. Whether Laurent-Pichat was invited is unclear.

Jules Ferry dominated national politics between 1879 and 1885, years that saw the embedding of the Republic and the implementation of fundamental republican legislative reforms. He would lead the government himself as President of the Council of Ministers (Prime Minister) on two occasions (September 1880–November 1881; February 1883–March 1885). As Minister for Public Instruction and Fine Arts almost continuously for six years, Ferry shaped the republican education system. He held several other portfolios as well and would oversee a vast expansion of the French Empire.

Laurent-Pichat supported much of Ferry's programme but nevertheless harboured a more radical vision of the Republic. He had been distant from Ferry since the Franco-Prussian War and the Commune, when Ferry's role in the Government of National Defence had been a source of conflict. The appointment of Waddington, a Centre-Left republican, and Ferry's acceptance of a ministry in that government, may have rankled with Laurent-Pichat. Like many others, Laurent-Pichat would have expected Grévy to appoint Léon Gambetta, who headed the largest group in the Chamber. Republican principles suggested as much. But Grévy's deep antipathy to Gambetta, and/or the conviction that government belonged in the hands of the cultivated classes rather than the 'new social strata' that Gambetta personified, saw him ignored.[58] Laurent-Pichat remained close to Gambetta and a member of Gambetta's Republican Union, serving another term as its president in 1880.[59] Ferry was a leading figure in the less radical Republican Left faction, as was Jules Grévy before he became President. Grévy's appointment of Waddington and Ferry's place in the ministry thus highlighted the moderate tenor of the ministry, which did not reflect the composition of the Chamber.[60]

That Laurent-Pichat and Ferry had different expectations of the Republic was evident as soon as the Waddington ministry was installed. Laurent-Pichat again joined the push from the Left, led by Louis Blanc in the Chamber and Victor Hugo in the Senate, to demand an amnesty for the Communards.[61] The Republican Union had urged this throughout the 1870s and Laurent-Pichat's first act as Senator in 1875 had been to join others to work on an amnesty bill that proved unsuccessful.[62] The government of which Ferry was a part accepted only a partial amnesty in 1879 but, following sustained pressure from the Left, would be forced to acquiesce in July 1880.[63]

Family life and political life, personal loyalties and political loyalties, were never fully separate in Laurent-Pichat's family. Their intersection is demonstrated repeatedly in family correspondence, which played a vital role in sustaining affectionate ties even as political differences emerged. Indeed, that was one of the primary functions of the correspondence. Letters played a positive role, both by what they declared and by what they omitted. By proclaiming unity, their expressions of attachment created and testified to family cohesion; by eliding discord, their silences were also expressions of the aspiration to harmony.

From the time Ferry arrived in office, Laurent-Pichat's family letters constantly affirmed his affection for and attachment to the Risler/Kestner family that now included both Jules Ferry and his own daughter. He found words of praise for Ferry whenever possible in writing to Charles Risler, who was both his own son-in-law and Ferry's brother-in-law.[64] He wrote respectfully to Mme Kestner, Ferry's grandmother-in-law, evoking their shared political interests, and he reminisced warmly to Charles's father, Camille Risler, about their early acquaintance.[65] Laurent-Pichat sent his greetings to Charles's aunts, Mmes Charras and Scheurer-Kestner, via Geneviève, who was holidaying with them.[66] His letters were carefully calibrated to indicate the appropriate mixture of respect and familiarity, from his 'very warm friendship' with Camille Risler to the 'respectful attachment' that bound him to Mme Charras.

In exhibiting his sense of family, and the emotional and political bonds uniting them, Laurent-Pichat constantly displayed his desire to maintain good relations.

While Laurent-Pichat felt little affinity with Ferry, his friendships with other men in the family were particularly important to him, and vital in consolidating interfamilial links. His friendship with Scheurer-Kestner had intensified during the 1870s, and its strength was revealed in the single surviving letter between them from 1881. Echoing the 'steadfast and enduring friendship' that he had celebrated in 1874, it affirmed their bonds even more strongly, using the intimate form of speech (*tutoiement*) then reserved for close family. To be invited by another to use intimate speech was a mark of deep attachment, and this is the only letter to a friend in Laurent-Pichat's correspondence that does so. Yet Laurent-Pichat had apparently slipped into *tutoiement* when speaking to Scheurer-Kestner, without such an invitation and without warning. This demanded explanation:

> I was paying tribute to friendship ... The impulse which led me to address you as *tu* [*te tutoyer*] one evening is my guarantee of affection ... I don't regret anything, not even having spoken yesterday. I showed you who I am, and I have received your letter, which I am keeping and which I value.[67]

Laurent-Pichat's affection for Scheurer-Kestner had prompted him spontaneously to abandon polite formality for the speech of intimacy, the speech of brothers. That he now used the intimate form in his letter suggests that, rather than protesting, Scheurer-Kestner had reciprocated, affirming in turn the closeness of their friendship.

Family unity was also firmly on display as the so-called 'Ferry Laws' of 1880–82 passed through the National Assembly. These laws instituted free, compulsory and secular primary schooling for all children as well as secondary education for girls. As President of the Council of Ministers and Minister for Public Instruction and Fine Arts, Jules Ferry took overall responsibility for this suite of laws that formed a major plank in the edifice of the Republic. The laws attracted broad support among republicans and became Ferry's enduring legacy. However, one provision of those laws – 'article seven' – prohibited 'unauthorised [religious] congregations' from teaching in or running educational institutions of any kind. It aroused passionate opposition from some conservative republicans, who branded it an attack on individual liberty, as well as opposition from Catholics.[68] Article seven was defeated in the Senate: Amédée and Charles were again witnesses to that dramatic moment. The government finally instituted article seven by decree: a highly unusual last resort.[69]

The family's support for Ferry as he shepherded this legislation through the Assembly was frequently on display. When the first bill was introduced to the Chamber on 16 June 1879, Charles Risler visited Ferry to hear his impressions, and the matter was surely a subject of conversation two days later when Geneviève hosted a large family dinner, attended (among others) by Laurent-Pichat, the Ferrys, the Floquets, Mmes Kestner and Charras. Once Geneviève left Paris for the summer holidays, Laurent-Pichat's letters kept her up to date on the progress of the legislation.[70]

Laurent-Pichat seized on the opportunity provided by the education laws to shore up his relationship with Ferry and ensure that his relationship with his daughter was not jeopardised by political tensions. He threw his weight publicly behind Ferry's legislation. As President of the Polytechnic Association, which offered free vocational education to workers, he invited Ferry to present the Association's annual awards in July 1879.[71] In his presidential address at the function, Laurent-Pichat declared: 'We must all ... support the courageous minister who has launched the supreme combat, who has taken up the challenge that ignorance poses to human progress.' Describing the struggle over education as another instalment of the French Revolution, he added: 'The task is magnificent and enormous and we are counting on you, Minister, to accomplish it.'[72] Ferry's speech to the five thousand people in attendance was greeted with an 'explosion of applause and prolonged cheering.' Ferry declared that such displays proved France was with him, giving him strength to endure the constant calumnies.[73] This was but one of many enthusiastic gatherings that Ferry would address over the following months, as his letters to his wife from southern France in September 1879 attest.[74]

The award ceremony of the Polytechnic Association revealed the priority placed on family harmony even as national politics took centre stage for family members. In offering Ferry a forum to speak, Laurent-Pichat sought to affirm family links and cultivate good relationships, as well as to advance the republican education laws. Ferry, too, after some prevarication, revealed his desire to foster family goodwill. The event almost provoked a family crisis because, despite Laurent-Pichat's work in organising it, Ferry tried to withdraw at the last minute. Laurent-Pichat recorded: 'Charles Ferry came by. I went to see Jules who didn't want to come. I persuaded him. A wonderful meeting. Ferry must be pleased. I returned home exhausted'.[75] Ferry's withdrawal would have been a serious embarrassment to Laurent-Pichat. But in the event Laurent-Pichat's invitation provided a supportive forum for Ferry and showed him to be Ferry's ally on this legislation. His letters to Geneviève and to Charles (absent on military service) were at pains to assure them of that fact. He wrote to Charles: 'Ferry ... had a great success and I knew what the effect would be. I had made enquiries; Ferry had a good day that displayed his skill and his popularity.'[76] He also explained to Geneviève that he had refused to reinsert into the published version of his speech a vehemently anticlerical passage that Ferry had earlier asked him to delete: he would have been 'badly affected in Ferry's eyes' had he done so.[77]

In displaying his good faith to Geneviève and Charles, Laurent-Pichat's goal – and the fundamental purpose of these letters – was to reinforce family bonds. References to Eugénie Ferry in the letters heightened this emphasis on family attachment. Addressing Geneviève, Laurent-Pichat credited Eugénie with persuading her husband to attend the ceremony: 'I beseeched Madame Ferry. Your excellent Eugénie understood and was perfect.' Similarly, Laurent-Pichat wrote to Charles: 'I hope Geneviève has told you about the letter from your sister [Eugénie Ferry] which expressed her gratitude that I had insisted with her husband.'[78] By underlining his respect and affection for Charles's sister, who was also a close friend of Geneviève, he emphasised his respect for Ferry and his commitment to the family network, as Eugénie had done, too, by writing to Laurent-Pichat. The event was a success, therefore, not only in giving positive publicity to Ferry's legislation, but also in consolidating family unity on behalf of the Republic. It was thanks to family ties and the emotional connections they created that Laurent-Pichat and Ferry co-operated on this occasion. Intimate relations not only complemented but also actively supported the political struggle.

Political differences and family cohesion

While Laurent-Pichat and Jules Ferry were united on education, their different visions of the Republic would create tension between them in the 1880s. Whether they were of one mind on the colonial question remains unclear. It seems likely that Laurent-Pichat initially took the colonies for granted, like most of his republican colleagues. In republican thinking, colonisation was part of the 'mission' to extend the gains of the French Revolution to other peoples. Simultaneously, of course, it allowed France to benefit from labour, resources, products and markets that would enhance French grandeur, at great cost to the colonised. When the republicans came to power in the 1870s, France already had an extensive colonial empire. Apart from Algeria, regarded by the French as an extension of France, the colonies were far from the metropole and from popular consciousness.[79]

Insofar as there was a political debate on colonisation in France in the 1870s, it focused not on the morality of colonisation but on whether the colonies should have political representation in the French National Assembly. This had long been opposed by conservatives.[80] The Third Republic restored colonial representation and, in response to another conservative attack in 1875, Laurent-Pichat identified himself with that cause: 'Today we saved colonial representation.'[81] There is no evidence, however, that he pondered the question of who was now represented under the Republic's laws. Those laws restored citizenship to all adult males in the 'old colonies'. As the example of Guadeloupe illustrates, however, the number of black voters remained small for several decades. The Deputies were elected largely by white men and thus largely represented their interests.[82]

The colonial representatives were not just fellow Deputies of Laurent-Pichat, but republican colleagues who socialised with him and his family.[83] Most were fellow-members of Gambetta's Republican Union. César de Mahy, from La Réunion, was elected its secretary in January 1874; Victor Schœlcher, representative for Martinique, became its president in 1876 and again in 1880.[84] Laurent-Pichat became firm friends with de Mahy. He and his family often visited Laurent-Pichat's home and they were invited to Clémence Beaujean's wedding in 1875. Laurent-Pichat (an admirer of Abraham Lincoln) also had an affinity with Schœlcher, author of the decree that had abolished slavery in 1848 and France's most prominent abolitionist. Schœlcher was also a great admirer of the black Haitian revolutionary leader, Toussaint-Louverture.[85] Laurent-Pichat would hear Schœlcher lecture on Toussaint-Louverture in 1879.[86]

There is no evidence that Laurent-Pichat mixed socially with Count Suzanne Melvil-Bloncourt, although the Count called on Laurent-Pichat on at least one occasion.[87] Melvil-Bloncourt played a major role in Transatlantic antislavery movements but is far less well known than Schœlcher. Born in Guadeloupe, son of a French count and a freed woman of African descent, he completed his education in France, participating as a student in the Revolution of 1848. Melvil-Bloncourt referred to himself as a 'man of colour' and vigorously defended the equality with whites of those he called 'blacks and mulattos'. He was elected in 1871 to represent Guadeloupe in the National Assembly. But any attempt he might have made to represent the interests of black citizens or people of colour in Guadeloupe was cut short, along with his parliamentary career, when he was threatened with prosecution as a Communard. He fled into exile in 1874 and was sentenced to death *in absentia*. Laurent-Pichat donated to a fund to help Melvil-Bloncourt survive.[88]

Jules Ferry's colonial policies would become a major source of division among republicans in the 1880s. Many radicals rejected not the colonial venture itself, but its alleged mishandling by Ferry. Laurent-Pichat was silent on the major parliamentary decisions as governments led by Ferry pursued a policy of colonial expansion. He was present but made no note in his journal when the Senate warmly applauded Ferry's announcement of the treaty of Bardo, by which France established a 'protectorate' over Tunisia in May 1881.[89] His journal was also silent in November that year when the Extreme Left in the Chamber forced Ferry's resignation for having exceeded his mandate in Tunisia.

The sudden death of Léon Gambetta on 31 December 1882 exposed the political differences between Laurent-Pichat and Jules Ferry. Gambetta's death led to the implosion of the Republican Union. Its more conservative members moved into Ferry's orbit; others – like Laurent-Pichat – moved towards the Radical Left

Figure 9.2 Ginette (R) and Charlotte (L) Risler, granddaughters of Léon Laurent-Pichat.

faction. They wanted to 'maximise' republican reforms, rather than settle for the minimum of change, as Georges Clemenceau put it. One of their demands was for the abolition of the Senate, or at least a major limitation on its powers.[90] At stake was the constitutional compromise – the upper house – by which Gambetta had managed to secure the Republic in 1875. Radical republicans like Laurent-Pichat aspired to return to the democratic principles of the Belleville programme; conservative republicans like Ferry feared the consequences for the Republic and resisted major constitutional revision.

That Laurent-Pichat sympathised with the Radical Left by 1883 is clear, given his leading role in the 'Republican League for the Revision of the Constitution'. He was elected president at its inaugural meeting on 15 March (a meeting that Abel Hovelacque also attended).[91] He signed the manifesto that accused the government of pursuing only 'illusory reform': 'What we seek is the triumph and the affirmation of the principles of the French Revolution, a return to the Declaration of the Rights of Man and the Citizen, the unleashing of universal [male] suffrage'.[92] The League's precise aims remained vague and its own members were divided. Bertrand Joly suggests that it ceased meeting in May 1884.[93] However, Laurent-Pichat's journal indicates that the League continued for another year: his final monthly subscription of one hundred francs was paid on 14 April 1885.

For Ferry, League members were 'termites' undermining the constitution.[94] That the League's campaign stood in opposition to Ferry was highlighted by the comments of the leftist newspaper *Le Rappel*. Describing Laurent-Pichat as 'the honourable senator whose ever-firm convictions provide an example to his colleagues, and perhaps, to some, a reproach', it contrasted him with Ferry, 'who has joked, on more than one occasion, about the revisionist league' and its 'ineffectual campaign', but whose 'pretended revision' gave the lie to that claim.[95] That 'pretended revision', passed in August 1884, removed the position of Life Senator but left the Senate intact. Some radicals, like Laurent-Pichat, remained dissatisfied.

As Laurent-Pichat's political differences with Ferry became more pronounced, he continued to ensure that his relationship with his daughter was not jeopardised. He found unexpected allies in that task in his grandchildren. The birth of children, while binding Geneviève more closely into her husband's family, also strengthened the ties between that family and her birth family and Laurent-Pichat called on the children as symbols of what united them.

Charles and Geneviève spent the summer of 1880 at Sèvres, remaining there for the birth of their first child in October. Their numerous visitors included Gambetta, who was holidaying at nearby Ville-d'Avray.[96] Laurent-Pichat spent a month at Sèvres, keeping Geneviève company during her husband's absences for work.[97] He read to Geneviève, not light fiction but serious republican history: Jules Michelet's *History of the French Revolution* and Alphonse de Lamartine's *The Girondins*. He also read her *Charlotte Corday* – whether he chose Lamartine's account or Michelet's version in *Women of the Revolution* he does not say – and Edmond Cottinet's drama about the Gallic hero, *Vercingetorix*, hot off the press.[98] What determined those choices and what conversations they may have inspired remain unknown, but political discussion, republican sensibility and tender affection were deeply intertwined in this father–daughter relationship.

The extended families of both Geneviève and Charles visited them at Sèvres, Eugénie and Jules Ferry among them. Charles and Hortense Floquet made day visits and stayed for a short vacation.[99] Laurent-Pichat and Rosine had already left for Aix-les-Bains, however, when Geneviève went into labour in October, though her father rushed back to Sèvres on news of the birth. Geneviève had no mother with her in childbirth, as Clémence had had Rosine. Rather, the women of Charles's family, Mmes Floquet and Ferry, supported her as she gave birth to her daughter.[100]

Eugénie Rosine Juliette Geneviève, known familiarly as Ginette, was the first grandchild for Charles's family as well as for Laurent-Pichat, and both families welcomed her warmly. Naming her Eugénie signalled her entry into her paternal family, acknowledging the family matriarch, her great-grandmother Eugénie Kestner, as well as Charles's deceased mother and his sister Mme Ferry (who had no children). The remaining names incorporated Ginette into her maternal family. The prominence given to Rosine in the litany reflected Geneviève's attachment to the aunt who had mothered her, while the name Juliette evoked Achille's wife (legally not 'Victorine' but Juliette) and their short-lived daughter.[101]

Laurent-Pichat made a short visit to Sèvres to meet his granddaughter. Back in Aix on 1 September, his first thought was for his fellow-grandfather, Camille Risler, in Thann. Their shared role provided the impetus for intensifying their friendship: 'I've just returned from Sèvres and I embrace you. I won't say more than that. Fingernails, a head of hair, seven pounds [*livres*] and already charming ... as for the mother, she is admirable.'[102] He wrote more fully to Risler a month later:

> Amédée Beaujean was struck by Ginette's resemblance to her father Charles ... We'll have lots of other impressions. I'll pass them on, if you permit ... I have loved you for a long time and since we've been drawn even closer together by tenderness and by [family] duty, I want to tell you everything, especially given that you'll be a long way away for several more weeks.[103]

As the living expression of family, Ginette embodied the attachment between her two grandfathers. In emphasising her reputed resemblance to her father, Laurent-Pichat reached out to the Risler family and reaffirmed his attachment to his friend Camille, Charles's father. Significantly, he used the language of love and tenderness to describe that friendship: such words were not spoken lightly. These were not the sentiments of a passionate youth, as in the 1840s, but of a man of mature years. For Laurent-Pichat, who thirsted for and valued intimacy, friendship remained deeply held and strongly felt.

The death of Camille Risler in June 1881 thus marked Laurent-Pichat deeply. He wrote to Mme Kestner: 'I lost in Charles's father a friend who understood me and who loved me.'[104] Risler had accepted and appreciated him as he was. In these painful circumstances, Ginette was again summoned as the living link between the grandfathers and thus between the two families:

> When I see poor, dear Ginette, who didn't know her grandfather, I think of him ... The smiles she gives me – I always divide them in two ... If I live long enough ... I will tell Ginette about her grandfather. It will be one of those moving family stories that will stay with her, that she will keep, and that she will pass on. I promise myself to fulfil this duty.[105]

In March 1882, a second daughter was born to Geneviève and Charles. Again, this child was a living link between her families. Known familiarly as Charlotte, her full name – Léonie Charlotte Camille Risler – carried the memory of her father Charles and of her two grandfathers.[106] Mme Ferry and Mme Charras were among the first to welcome the new baby.[107]

Later that year, the Ferrys and the Rislers holidayed together in Saint-Dié.[108] Then in 1883, just as Laurent-Pichat assumed the presidency of the Republican League for the Revision of the Constitution, Geneviève and her daughters travelled to Arcachon to holiday once again with Eugénie Ferry; they were joined by Charles Risler and Jules Ferry, along with Jules's brother Charles Ferry and his son Abel.[109] Polite greetings were exchanged through Geneviève's correspondence with her father, Laurent-Pichat sending the Ferrys his 'respectful greetings', the Ferrys expressing their thanks and sending their 'best wishes'.[110] But this exchange lacked the warmth and spontaneity of Ferry's instructions to his wife ahead of his arrival: 'Embrace the mayor [that is, Charles] and the mayoress [Geneviève], Ginette, Charlotte and our dear Abel [Ferry]. What a wonderful holiday [it will be] to spend 48 hours with this gathering of angels between the sea and the pines.'[111] As political relations between Ferry and Laurent-Pichat became more contentious, the children were called upon more strenuously as embodiments of family, unwittingly doing the work of sustaining family cohesion. Ferry expressed his fondness for Ginette and Charlotte in a letter to Eugénie: 'The little ones are two cherubs, one quite heavenly with her clear eyes and the beautiful smile that she bestows on me so graciously, the other delightfully boisterous which gives her a particular charm, wild and indomitable.'[112]

Ferry had apparently not shared with Geneviève his opinion of the League, those 'termites', perhaps to spare her anguish. She wrote to her father from Arcachon: 'The newspapers of the last few days have informed us that you have been named president of a new League for [constitutional] revision; but if it's an honour for you it must also keep you busy.'[113] She exhibited her characteristic desire to please, but whether she was trying to remain neutral or was ignorant of the organisation's opposition to Ferry is impossible to say.

Eugénie Ferry again served as a buffer during this tense period, as she had in 1879, and little Ginette had a further mediating role to play. Photographs of Laurent-Pichat's grandchildren taken with their aunt Eugénie provided the opportunity for him to reach out across the political divide: 'The [portrait] of Ginette beside Madame Ferry is so like her that your sister-in-law could steal your daughter and plead her case against you. They look so much like mother and daughter that a lawyer could find elements that would make you lose the case.'[114] Even if there was a strong family resemblance, Laurent-Pichat's insistence on the visible signs of their relationship allowed him to acknowledge the bond between the families in a positive fashion, ensuring that his daughter was not caught in a political snare.

From 1883, politics virtually disappeared from the father–daughter correspondence. That the subject was too fraught to be broached easily between them underlines the porous nature of the border between the intimate and the political. Laurent-Pichat's letters focused on news of the extended family. He did not even identify his many meetings as meetings of the League (which is clear in his journal), let alone talk about the League's objectives. He was deliberately vague: 'I was happy to go for a walk on leaving the meeting that I had chaired, where it was very warm.'[115]

The men of the family assumed an array of political roles in the 'Republic of republicans'. In the process, conflicting visions and priorities emerged within the family as they did within the broader republican community. Rather than being a private realm removed from politics, the intimate realm remained a highly politicised space: individuals inevitably brought political identities and sympathies into their relations with family. Just as republicans in the National Assembly had to learn, as far as possible, to live with each other's differences, families, too, had to put aside differences around the dinner table or at the holiday home for the common good.

This extended family worked hard to manage differences and prevent conflict when personal emotions and political loyalties were at odds. The practices of friendship were called on to aid that process, as Laurent-Pichat continued to cultivate his friendships with those close to Jules Ferry. That Laurent-Pichat and Geneviève now avoided politics in their letters nevertheless shows how serious political differences could be, since their relationship had been built on shared political interest as well as on deep affection. That avoidance highlights the strong family attachment that bound members together and the determination to balance the bonds of family with the interests of the Republic. The so-called intimate and political realms remained deeply intertwined and interdependent in the 'Republic of republicans'.

Notes

1. See Chastenet, *Histoire de la Troisième République*, II: *La République des républicains, 1879–1893* (Paris: Hachette Littérature, 1954).
2. Nord, *Republican Moment*.
3. LLP, Journal, 17–20, 27 Oct. 1877.
4. *Ibid.*, 29 Oct., 3, 9, 10, 22 Nov., 28, 29, 30 Dec. 1877.
5. See chapter 8.
6. LLP, Journal, 6 Jan., 7, 25–30 Sept., 1–6 Oct. 1878.
7. *Ibid.*, 14 Feb. 1881.
8. www.annuaire-mairie.fr/ancien-maire-paris-7e-arrondissement.html
9. LLP, Journal, 22 Nov., 18, 23 Dec. 1881.
10. *Ibid.*, 9 Oct. 1879; Maurice Agulhon, *Marianne au pouvoir: L'Imagerie et la symbolique républicaines de 1880 à 1914* (Paris: Flammarion, 1989), pp. 70–74; Nord, *Republican Moment*, pp. 202–5.
11. LLP, Journal, 14 July 1880. See the front cover for a depiction of this event.
12. *Ibid.*, 14, 19 July 1880.
13. On masculine camaraderie, see Taithe, 'Neighbourhood boys and men', pp. 73–5.
14. Grévy, *La République des Opportunistes*, pp. 36–42. On the significance of Voltaire to republicans, see Nord, *Republican Moment*, pp. 195–7.
15. LLP, Journal, 27, 30 May 1878; Jean-Claude Wartelle, 'La Société d'anthropologie de Paris de 1859 à 1920', *Revue d'histoire des sciences humaines*, 10 (2004), 125–71 (142). See *La République française*, 1 June 1878.
16. *Le Centenaire de Voltaire: Fête du 30 mai 1878* (Paris: Imp. Dubuisson, 1878).
17. BHVP, 14, fos 51–67: text of LLP's speech; extracts in *La République française*, 1 June 1878.
18. Sudhir Hazareesingh, 'Le Grand Orient de France sous le Second Empire et les débuts de la Troisième République', in Eric Saunier and Christine Gaudin (eds), *Franc-maçonnerie et histoire: bilan et perspectives* (Mont-Saint-Aignan: Presses universitaires de Rouen et

du Havre, 2003). For an overview, see Nord, *Republican Moment*, pp. 15–30.
19 James Smith Allen, *A Civil Society: The public space of Freemason women in France, 1744–1944* (Lincoln, NE: University of Nebraska Press, 2021).
20 'Hovelacque, Abel Alexandre', in Schweitz, *Les Parlementaires*, pp. 314–16; Wartelle, 'La Société d'anthropologie', esp. 140–46; Nord, *Republican Moment*, pp. 41–4.
21 Charles Risler and Gaston Laurent-Atthalin, *Neuf-Brisach: Souvenirs de siège et de captivité*, 2e édition (Paris: Berger-Lévrault, 1881).
22 Pierre Chevallier, *Histoire de la Franc-Maçonnerie française*, 3 vols (Paris: Fayard, 1974–5), II, pp. 538–9; III, p. 178; Grévy, *La République des Opportunistes*, pp. 146, 346, n. 101.
23 Quoted in Chevallier, *Histoire de la Franc-Maçonnerie*, II, p. 539.
24 LLP, Journal, 13 Dec. 1878.
25 *Ibid.*, 13 Feb. 1879. See Grévy, *La République des Opportunistes*, pp. 142–9.
26 Lalouette, 'Laurent-Pichat, Léon', in Mayeur and Corbin (eds), *Les Immortels du Sénat*, pp. 380–82; LLP, Journal, 13 Feb. 1879.
27 Auspitz, *The Radical Bourgeoisie*, pp. 1–7.
28 *Ibid.*, p. 145; Harrison, *The Bourgeois Citizen*, pp. 95–7, 148–50; Agulhon, *Le Cercle*, pp. 51–4.
29 Quoted in Auspitz, *The Radical Bourgeoisie*, p. 6.
30 On the petition, see *ibid.*, p. 93; LLP, Journal, 14 March 1876. LLP attended several education 'circles' and does not always specify which one.
31 For example, third arron.: LLP, Journal, 22 Aug 1873, 9 Oct. 1874, 10 Jan. 1875, 25 Dec. 1876, 3 Nov. 1880, 20 Oct. 1882; seventh arron.: 17 Nov. 1878, 21 Nov. 1880, 27 March 1881, 6 April 1883, 11 March 1884. See Auspitz, *The Radical Bourgeoisie*, pp. 125, 136–7.
32 LLP, Journal, 10 Nov. 1872; 6 Jan 1877; 21, 23 Nov., 7 Dec. 1879; 20 March, 15, 24 April 1880. On the libraries, see Nord, *Republican Moment*, pp. 210–12; Harrison, *The Bourgeois Citizen*, pp. 144–8.
33 BHVP, 6, nos 118, 119: LLP to GR, 18, 19 April 1881; LLP, Journal, 18 April 1881.
34 Nobuhito Nagaï, *Les Conseillers municipaux de Paris sous la IIIe République* (Paris: Publications de la Sorbonne, 2002), chapter 3, pars 9–21.
35 LLP, Journal, 10 Dec. 1882.
36 Charles Risler, *L'Association Générale d'Alsace-Lorraine* (Paris: Berger-Levrault, 1880), pp. 6–7; *La Revue alsacienne*, 8e année, 6e livraison (April 1885), 280.

37 Sarah H. Curtis, 'Charitable ladies: Gender, class and religion in mid-nineteenth-century Paris', *Past and Present*, 177 (2002), 121–56; Elizabeth C. Macknight, 'Faiths, fortunes and feminine duty: Charity in Parisian high society, 1880–1914', *Journal of ecclesiastical history*, 58:3 (2007), 482–506.
38 Rebecca Rogers, 'Quelles écoles professionnelles pour les jeunes filles pauvres? Débats et réalisations en Algérie et en France métropolitaine (années 1860)', *Revue d'histoire du dix-neuvième siècle*, 55:2 (2017), 109–23; 'Lemonnier, Elisa née Grimailh', in https://maitron.fr; Julie Toussaint, 'Lemonnier, Mme Elisa', in *Nouveau dictionnaire de pédagogie et d'instruction primaire publié sous la direction de Ferdinand Buisson*, available at http://www.inrp.fr/edition-electroni que/lodel/dictionnaire-ferdinand-buisson/document.php?id=3044. Accessed August 2020.
39 LLP, Journal, 26 Aug. 1871, 29 Oct. 1878, 21 Nov. 1881. On Mme Kergomard, see 'Chronique de l'enseignement primaire en France', *La Revue pédagogique*, 17 (1890), 189–92; 'Kergomard, Pauline, née Reclus', in https://maitron.fr
40 Louise Michel, 'Ouverture', *Le Télémarque*, 1:31 (2007), 7–9, available at https://doi.org/10.3917/tele.031.0007
41 LLP, Journal, 20 Feb. 1875; 13 March 1877; 24 Oct. 1878; 10 March, 8 April 1879; 24 Oct. 1881; 8 Dec. 1884.
42 Macknight, 'Faiths, fortunes and feminine duty', 483.
43 LLP, Journal, 27 March 1882.
44 LLP, Journal, 22 Nov. 1873, 5 April 1880. On the Simons, see Moses, *French Feminism in the Nineteenth Century*, pp. 173, 177, 185.
45 LLP, Journal, 1 April 1873, 16 March 1875, 12 March 1878, 20 April 1881, 25 March 1882, 26 March 1884, etc.
46 *Ibid.*, 1 April 1873; 16, 18 March 1875.
47 See the Association's history: *AGAL Paris 1871 à 1996* (Paris: Association Générale d'Alsace et de Lorraine, 1996), pp. 19–20, 46–7. I thank the president of AGAL, M. Jean-Yves Grenier, for providing me with a copy. Also Charles Risler, 'L'Association Générale d'Alsace-Lorraine', *Revue alsacienne: Littérature, histoire, sciences, poésie, beaux-arts*, Nov. 1879–Oct. 1880, 53–60 (53).
48 Susan Foley, '"The Christmas tree of the Alsatians and Lorrainers": Spectacle, emotion, and patriotism in Paris during the early Third Republic', *French Historical Studies*, 41:4 (2018), 681–710; Susan Foley, 'The Christmas tree becomes French: From foreign curiosity to philanthropic icon, 1860–1914', *French History and Civilization*, 7 (2016), 139–57.

49 Edouard Siebecker, *Poésies d'un vaincu* (Paris: Berger-Levrault, 1882), pp. 262–5; Foley, "'The Christmas tree of the Alsatians'", 684–6. The daughters of Charles and Geneviève, Ginette (Mme Claretie) and Charlotte (Mme Canet), were on the committee in 1940: *AGAL Paris 1871 à 1996*, p. 48.
50 Foley, '"The Christmas tree of the Alsatians'", 686.
51 Laurent-Pichat's journal records Geneviève and Charles both working at the event on 25 Dec. each year between 1877 and 1883.
52 LLP, Journal, 25 Dec. 1874.
53 Compare Bonnie G. Smith, *Ladies of the Leisure Class*, chapter 6.
54 Toussaint, 'Lemonnier, Mme Elisa'; Phyllis Stock-Morton, 'Secularism and women's education: The case of the *école professionnelle de jeunes filles* of Marseille', *French History*, 10:3 (1996), 355–74.
55 Foley, 'The Christmas tree becomes French'.
56 LLP, Journal, 30 Jan. 1879.
57 *Ibid.*, 4 Feb. 1879.
58 On Grévy's hostility to Gambetta, see Chastenet, *Histoire de la Troisième République*, I, pp. 254–5, 352–5. Gaillard places more weight on social class: *Jules Ferry*, pp. 342–3.
59 LLP, Journal, 13 Jan., 12 May 1880.
60 Gabriel Hanotaux, *Histoire de la France contemporaine, 1871–1900*, IV: *La République parlementaire* (Paris: Ancienne librairie Furne, [1908]), p. 447.
61 LLP, Journal, 8, 28 Feb. 1879; *Annales du Sénat et de la Chambre des Députés. Sénat, Séance du vendredi 28 février 1879*, pp. 201–220.
62 Laurent-Pichat's journal records many meetings on the amnesty question, beginning in December 1873. See chapter 7 on the 1875 bill.
63 LLP, Journal, 17 June, 3, 9 July 1880.
64 BHVP, 6, nos 97, 101: LLP to Charles Risler, 8 Aug., 12 Sept. 1879.
65 BHVP, 7, fos 48–9: LLP to Mme C. Kestner, 8 Sept. 1879; *ibid.*, fos 27–8: LLP to Camille Risler, 12 Sept. 1879.
66 BHVP, 6, nos 98–100: LLP to GR, 2, 4, 7 Sept. 1879.
67 AN 276AP/1: LLP to Scheurer-Kestner, 11 March 1881.
68 Hanotaux, *Histoire de la France contemporaine*, IV, pp. 454–7; Chastenet, *Histoire de la Troisième République*, I, pp. 359–61.
69 LLP, Journal, 7 March 1880; Chastenet, *Histoire de la Troisième République*, I, p. 368.
70 LLP, Journal, 16, 18 June 1879; BHVP, 6, nos 92–4: LLP to GR, 10, 14 July, 3 Aug. 1879.
71 LLP, Journal, 16, 17 Nov. 1878. See Auspitz, *The Radical Bourgeoisie*, pp. 67–9.

72 'Réunion de l'Association polytechnique', *Le Voltaire*, 22 July 1879, pp. 2–3.
73 'Discours de M. Jules Ferry', *La République française*, 22 July 1879.
74 Jules Ferry, *Lettres de Jules Ferry 1846–1893* (Paris: Calmann-Lévy, 1914), nos 112–20.
75 LLP, Journal, 20 July 1879.
76 BHVP, 6, unnumbered, fos 398–9: LLP to Charles Risler, 30 [July 1879].
77 *Ibid.*, no. 95: LLP to GR, 20 [July 1879]. For the deleted passage, see *ibid.*, no. 96: LLP to GR, 23 July 1879.
78 *Ibid.*, no. 95: LLP to GR, 20 [July 1879]; *ibid.*, unnumbered, fos 398–9: LLP to Charles Risler, 30 [July 1879].
79 Robert Aldrich, *Greater France: A history of French overseas expansion* (London: Macmillan, 1996), pp. 100–101.
80 Jacques-W. Binoche-Guedra, 'La Représentation parlementaire coloniale (1871–1940)', *Revue historique*, 280:2 (1988), 521–35; Jacques Binoche, *Les Parlementaires d'outre-mer*, Edilivre, undated, pp. 14–15. Available at www.furet.com/media/pdf/feuilletage/9/7/8/2/3/3/4/1/9782334150804.pdf. Accessed 20 April 2021.
81 LLP, Journal, 13, 30 Nov. 1875.
82 Elizabeth Heath, 'Creating rural citizens in Guadeloupe in the early Third Republic', *Slavery and Abolition*, 32:2 (2011), 289–307; Aldrich, *Greater France*, pp. 21–2, 212–15.
83 LLP, Journal, 26 Feb., 17 June, 30 Dec. 1876; 13 June 1877.
84 *Ibid.*, 30 Jan. 1874, 11 Dec. 1876; 12 May 1880.
85 Nelly Schmidt, *Victor Schœlcher et l'abolition de l'esclavage* (Paris: Fayard, 1994); Lawrence Jennings, *French Antislavery: The movement for the abolition of slavery in France, 1802–1848* (Cambridge: Cambridge University Press, 2000); Yun Kyoung Kwon, 'Forgotten island of the Liberator: Haiti's influences on Victor Schœlcher's abolitionism, 1833–1848', *Histoire sociale/Social history*, 53:107 (2020), 69–90.
86 LLP, Journal, 27 July 1879. See Aldrich, *Greater France*, pp. 21–2.
87 LLP, Journal, 24 April 1865.
88 'Melvil-Bloncourt, Suzanne (vicomte)', in https://maitron.fr; Bryan LaPointe, '"Moral Electricity": Melvil-Bloncourt and the trans-Atlantic struggle for abolition and equal rights', *Slavery and Abolition*, 40: 3 (2018), 543–62.
89 *Journal officiel de la République française*, Sénat, 12 May 1881; LLP, Journal, 12 May 1881.
90 Michel Mourre, 'La Gauche radicale' and 'Le Parti radical sous la IIIe République', in *Dictionnaire encyclopédique d'histoire*, pp. 2363; 4597–8; Chastenet, *Histoire de la Troisième République*, I, p. 436.

91 *Ligue républicaine pour la révision de la constitution: Instructions pratiques du bureau de la ligue pour l'organisation des groupes révisionnistes* (Paris: 1883); LLP, Journal, 15 March 1883.
92 'Manifeste de la Ligue révisionniste', *Le Radical*, 17 Jan. 1884.
93 *Ibid.*; Bertrand Joly, 'Une manifestation de l'antiparlementarisme de l'extrême-gauche: La Ligue républicaine pour la révision de la Constitution (1883–1884)', *Actes du 57e congrès de la CIHAE: Assemblées et parlements dans le monde, du Moyen-Age à nos jours*, sous la direction de Jean Garrigues et al. (Paris: Assemblée nationale, 2010), pp. 1404–30.
94 Quoted Joly, 'Une manifestation', p. 1423.
95 A. Gaulier, 'Le Mot d'ordre', *Le Rappel*, 26 Aug. 1884.
96 LLP, Journal, 30 July 1880.
97 *Ibid.*, 25 June, 21 July–25 Aug. 1880.
98 See Edmond Cottinet, *Vercingetorix: drame en 5 actes en prose* (Paris: C. Lévy, 1880).
99 LLP, Journal, 17, 18, 24 July; 9, 20 Aug. 1880.
100 AD des Hauts-de-Seine, naissances, commune de Sèvres, 1880, no. 133: Eugénie Rosine Juliette Geneviève Risler (31 Aug. 1880); LLP, Journal, 29–31 Aug. 1880; BHVP, 6, no. 108: LLP to Charles Risler, 1 Sept. 1880; *ibid.*, nos 112, 113: LLP to GR and Charles Risler, 12, 14 Sept. 1880.
101 AP mariages, V3E/M302: Louis Achille Deslandes/Juliette Asselin, 29 July 1858; AP 3e arron.: naissances, V4E 222: Juliette Deslandes, 7 March 1862; décès, V4E 230: Juliette Deslandes, 4 April 1862.
102 BHVP, 7, fo 31: LLP to Camille Risler, 1 Sept. 1880.
103 *Ibid.*, fos 33–4: 7 Oct. 1880.
104 BHVP, 7, fos 50–51: LLP to Mme Charles Kestner, 12 Aug. 1880.
105 *Ibid.*
106 AP naissances, 7e arr., V4E 3355: Léonie Charlotte Risler, 6 March 1882. Her marriage certificate gives her name as Léonie Charlotte Camille Risler (6 June 1904).
107 LLP, Journal, 4 March 1882.
108 BHVP, 7, no. 110: GR to LLP, Saint-Dié, 10 Aug. 1882.
109 LLP, Journal, 11 March 1883; BHVP, 7, no. 114: GR to LLP, Arcachon, 13 March 1883.
110 BHVP, 6, nos 146, 148: LLP to GR, 19, 25 [March 1883]; BHVP, 7, nos 115, 116: GR to LLP, Arcachon, 22, 24 March [1883].
111 Jules Ferry to Mme Ferry, 16 March 1883, in *Lettres*, no. 135.

112 *Ibid.*, late July 1883, no. 139.
113 BHVP, 6, nos 146, 148: LLP to GR, 19, 25 [March 1883]; BHVP, 7, nos 115, 116: GR to LLP, 22, 24 March 1883.
114 BHVP, 6, no. 135: LLP to GR, 21 [Aug.?] 1882.
115 BHVP, 6, nos 143, 146: LLP to GR, 13, 19 March 1883; LLP, Journal, 16, 19 March 1883.

Conclusion

On 12 June 1886, the President of the Senate opened the session with an announcement:

> I regret to announce the death of ... M. Laurent-Pichat, Life Senator (movement [among the Senators]) ... You know the life of M. Laurent-Pichat, his literary talent, his devotion to democratic ideas. Elected Deputy in 1871, Senator in 1875, he brought to political life the ardour and generosity that had always distinguished him. M. Laurent-Pichat died, aged 63, surrounded by the affection of his numerous friends and the esteem of his colleagues, whose spokesperson here I have the sad duty to be. (Lively approval and applause on the left).[1]

Even though he had been in ill health for some time, his political colleagues had clearly not seen him in any danger and Laurent-Pichat's death took them by surprise.

To his daughter, however, Laurent-Pichat had complained that his 'bag of infirmities' was filling up. 'I am attacked on every side', he wrote. 'I can't breathe and I can't stand upright.'[2] A severe attack of gout in December 1884 had impaired his mobility, even the renowned Dr Charcot providing little relief. Laurent-Pichat had required Geneviève's aid to attend the Senate. Not until mid-February 1885 could he 'walk a few steps unaided'.[3] His handwriting became increasingly illegible. Worse, the struggle to write went hand in hand with the struggle to find words: 'When I look at a letter and at my handwriting, my thoughts are far from gay ... When I can't find a word, I am furious and ashamed. One should act like a sick dog. Stay silent and wait.'[4] In June, he struggled to compose his customary verses for Clémence's birthday: 'Will you understand them? Will you read them? Are they acceptable?' He feared that he could 'no longer write and no longer think', continuing: 'My pen escapes me. My thoughts will escape me too despite myself.'[5]

Laurent-Pichat suffered emotionally from the deaths of some of those closest to him in the 1880s. In 1881, he received word from Ernest Hébert that the Princesse de Beauvau had died. His journal entry hinted at his sorrow as he wrote her name there for the first time: 'Ludmille is dead'.[6] A letter to Max Radiguet was much more explicit: 'If you had been here I would have spoken about it. I needed a word of friendship from you. I lost someone who had played a long and important role in my life and I had to endure this sorrow in silence. Never speak to me about it. I will talk about it in my own time.'[7] In 1885, Clémence's second son, 'poor little Paul', died suddenly in April, aged thirteen months, followed a fortnight later by Amédée's mother. Ill health meant that Laurent-Pichat was unable to travel to Chablis for her funeral. Nor could he attend the funerals of friends.[8]

On 22 May 1885, the death of Victor Hugo – personal friend and leading radical colleague in the Senate – accentuated these losses. Laurent-Pichat's reflections on this event showed that his mind was in perfect order. After lying in state at the Arc de Triomphe, Hugo's remains were transferred on 31 May to the Pantheon, newly invested as a republican mausoleum. The immense procession accompanying the body to its resting place took more than seven hours to reach its destination. Thousands of spectators lined the route, and twenty thousand people gathered at the Pantheon to pay tribute.[9] Laurent-Pichat had serious reservations about such pomp. He enjoyed the 'unwitting irony' of composer Charles Gounod, who declared: 'Hugo was a great man! We do well to honour him. But there is a limit! This is too much! It is excessive. What will they do for me!?'[10] The ideal republican funeral, for Laurent-Pichat, was not that of Hugo but that of Jean-Baptiste Charras: 'Swiss citizens carried him in their arms to the cemetery where he rests … there was no publicity! No drummers accompanied his cortège! Americans did not rent the windows of houses [to watch the procession].' In writing of Charras, Laurent-Pichat's mind turned again to their cherished relationship: 'That man loved me',[11] he wrote. The importance he placed on being loved by his friends had not diminished.

Laurent-Pichat's correspondence with his daughter ended a month later, on 29 June 1885, the same day that his personal journal came to an abrupt end. He may have suffered a stroke, since he became paralysed and was confined to a wheelchair.[12] Reporting Laurent-Pichat's death the following year, *La République française* noted that 'he had suffered for about a year from paralysis, which kept him from attending the Senate'.[13] However, Laurent-Pichat's votes continued to be registered in the Senate by one of his colleagues until the day before his death.

Laurent-Pichat's funeral on 14 June 1886 was a republican commemoration, though hardly on the same scale as Hugo's. Despite the Pentecost holiday, newspapers reported five or six hundred people in attendance.[14] The Senate sent a delegation, as was customary. Former Presidents of the Council of Ministers, Henri Brisson and Jules Ferry, attended – Ferry no doubt drawn by both family ties and memories of their long republican comradeship, despite their recent differences. Both the Paris municipal council and the General Council of the Seine sent delegations. So did the Polytechnic Association, of which Laurent-Pichat had been president. The *Groupe fraternel des anciens défenseurs de la patrie*, which had made him an honorary member, formed a guard of honour. Also present were Etienne Arago and Louis Ulbach – his friends since their youth – while the list of republican colleagues who gathered at Père Lachaise cemetery for this civil burial was very long.

Like the republican funerals of the 1860s, Laurent-Pichat's funeral celebrated the political virtues of the fallen warrior. So did the obituaries that flowed in the press. Such tributes are often exaggerated, but they nevertheless provide some insights into how Laurent-Pichat was regarded at the time of his death. The deceased man's devotion to the republican cause, proved by actions not just words, remained as important in 1886 as in the 1860s. Laurent-Pichat's unwavering republican conviction was thus remarked on by all.[15] Commentators recalled not only his financial support for 'most of the newspapers that marked the awakening of republican ideas' during the Second Empire, but also his wide-ranging contributions to the movement: 'His devotion to the Republic was absolute. He gave all, his pen, his time, his fortune, his freedom, in the service of democracy.'[16]

The testimonials also extolled his decency. He was remembered as an honourable man, well regarded by friends and adversaries alike: his role in settling disputes over honour, as César de Mahy remarked, was testament to his widely acknowledged integrity.[17] For another, he was a man of 'utter sincerity, utter good faith, utter generosity of spirit'; he personified 'the republican as a gracious man' (*le républicain galant homme*).[18]

The tributes to Laurent-Pichat nevertheless reflected the fault lines crossing the republican movement in the 1880s. The radicals around Camille Pelletan claimed Laurent-Pichat as one of their staunchest colleagues in the Senate; they remembered his efforts to prevent the slaughter of the Paris Commune and to achieve the amnesty for Communards. In praising his steadfast adherence to a radical republican agenda, they took the opportunity to score points against their more conservative colleagues, prone to political compromise: 'As he was in the February Revolution [of 1848], so he was under the Empire and – what is rarer – under the Republic.'[19]

By the last years of Laurent-Pichat's life, republicans faced political challenges not only from the Right, but also from the Left. In the emerging industrial economy, the problem of endemic poverty was increasingly apparent. Socialism began to make inroads among workers, particularly as economic conditions deteriorated after 1880. The first socialist was elected to the National Assembly in 1881, and socialists were beginning to win seats on municipal councils.[20] The question of where republicans stood on 'the social question' became more urgent. Were they drivers of democratic change and economic equality or defenders of the status quo? Laurent-Pichat's personal history illustrates the struggles that bourgeois republicans faced in finding workable solutions to the problems of these years.

Laurent-Pichat had a long history of generosity to the needy. Over the years, his diary reported innumerable requests for financial assistance, which were frequently granted. Specific acts of generosity were remembered at his funeral: Louis Greppo noted that Laurent-Pichat had donated more than ten thousand francs to the families of political prisoners after the Paris Commune.[21] Another colleague remembered that, following the prosecution and suspension of *Le Phare de la Loire* in 1865, Laurent-Pichat had paid the wages of the workers who had been stood down.[22]

But personal generosity was no answer to 'the social question'. There are signs that Laurent-Pichat, always on the radical wing of the republican movement, was groping his way to more meaningful solutions, though he had reached no coherent position by the time of his death. That he was a founder and administrator of the Society for the Promotion of Maternal Breastfeeding, established in 1876, suggests his recognition, at least, of the need for a more structured approach to social welfare, even if this solution remained paternalistic and piecemeal.[23] Organisations aiding needy mothers and babies were popular with many republicans in the 1880s.[24] But the notion of a universal system of social entitlement was hotly contested, and the 'solidarism' whereby republicans would offer self-help 'mutualist' solutions as an alternative to socialist ones was still in its infancy.[25] Where Laurent-Pichat would have stood on these broader questions is unknown.

There are signs, too, that Laurent-Pichat had come to see the problem of poverty as one of social injustice. M. de Lapommeraye of the Polytechnic Association, which offered technical education to workers, stated in his eulogy that Laurent-Pichat had regarded the work of the Association as (in Laurent-Pichat's words) 'a work of social reparation': it was an 'essentially democratic' undertaking, marked by a 'spirit of fraternity', through which the Association 'make[s] *reparation* to those deprived of instruction'.[26] This suggests that Laurent-Pichat saw lack of education and opportunity as an injustice to be made good, not merely an occasion for philanthropy, though again the work of the Association offered only a piecemeal solution.

M. Deschamps, Vice-President of the Paris municipal council, echoed Lapommeraye's assessment. Laurent-Pichat had declared to the Council, he reported, that the time for prevarication was over and that 'the Republic would only last if it set out generously on the path of social reform'.[27] What social reforms he envisaged we do not know. The Republic's slowness to embrace reform, however, would see it come under serious threat in the 1890s, as others promised the disinherited alternative routes to security.

If the eulogies at Laurent-Pichat's funeral pose some interesting questions about his thinking in 1886, the silences at his funeral are also significant. None of the leaders of the republican movement at that time, none of Laurent-Pichat's longstanding republican colleagues, delivered eulogies. Charles Floquet, a friend of many years standing (and Geneviève's uncle by marriage), President of the Chamber of Deputies at the time of Laurent-Pichat's death, was in attendance. So were long-familiar figures in Laurent-Pichat's life like Paul-Armand Challemel-Lacour, Alphonse Peyrat and Jules Ferry. The task of speaking as a colleague fell, however, to César de Mahy, Deputy for Réunion, who had first met Laurent-Pichat only in 1871.

Laurent-Pichat had burned some of his political bridges in the final years of his life, and in doing so he also placed himself on the wrong side of republican history. His role in the Republican League for the Revision of the Constitution in 1883 – he was one of only six Senators to join – had seen him align himself with the Radical Left and the Extreme Left. In early 1885, he was one of a small number – about twelve – who formed an Extreme Left group in the Senate (which had three hundred members). While it was common to belong to multiple republican groupings, members of the Extreme Left agreed not to be part of any other group.[28] Laurent-Pichat had some friends in this ginger group, most notably Victor Schœlcher and Alfred Naquet, but at the same time he weakened his political ties with the majority of his republican friends, who remained in the mainstream Left. Whether he thereby weakened his personal ties as well is unclear since no correspondence with friends survives after 1881.

The objectives of the Extreme Left were also unclear, since 'the members prefer[red] not to establish in advance a narrow and strict programme'.[29] Indeed, they rarely voted with one voice. But it is clear that discontent with the constitutional revision of November 1884, which abolished the lifetime seats but preserved the Senate, had motivated the formation of this group.[30] With hindsight, Scheurer-Kestner (who had voted in favour) would regret the abolition of those lifetime positions, attributing the move to the 'ultrademocratic prejudices' of the moment.[31] Laurent-Pichat retained those 'prejudices', as did others on the Extreme Left like Naquet.[32] But in the light of that painfully negotiated constitutional revision, any attempt to reopen the debate threatened a newly won peace, and perhaps even the Republic, given that the main proponents of further revision were the Bonapartists.

Similarly, in voting against credits for France's 'mission' in Indochina, requested by Ferry's successor Henri Brisson in December

1885, Laurent-Pichat and others of the Extreme Left, while a tiny minority, added a destabilising element to a fraught situation, and found themselves in the company of a host of conservatives.[33] Deschamps, of the Paris municipal council, observed at Laurent-Pichat's funeral: 'Contrary to what happens too often, as he got older Laurent-Pichat became more and more firm in his political convictions.'[34] His colleagues perhaps wondered whether his resolute adherence to radical ideas constituted admirable fidelity or curmudgeonliness.

Convention decreed that women should not attend funerals, so only the men engaged in the commemoration of Laurent-Pichat at his graveside. However, while the women's acts of mourning were undertaken out of the public eye, they had enduring public significance. Geneviève immediately began creating a scrapbook of the tributes to her father published in more than forty newspapers and periodicals across France. She copied some testimonials by hand and added to the collection over several years.[35] This provided an opportunity to grieve, offering the consolation that others remembered and appreciated her father. She included in her collection gestures of public memorialisation, such as the Paris Municipal Council's decision to rename a street in the sixteenth arrondissement in Laurent-Pichat's honour.[36] Geneviève also preserved Laurent-Pichat's extensive library as a memorial. Only after her death in 1912 would this 'superb library ... of books that were read', not just collected, be sold. The catalogue ran to 142 pages.[37]

Geneviève, Rosine and Clémence also embarked on a joint project of memorialisation that culminated in the publication in 1893 of *Heures de fêtes*, a collection of the private verse that Laurent-Pichat had composed over many years for these women and for their children. Three hundred copies were printed. There was no preface, but a short verse indicated the theme of the book, declaring that 'family songs are the best' because 'the whole heart is in them'.

The volume was a poignant celebration of family life. The earliest piece in the collection, entitled 'To my sister', dated from 1849: Rosine had saved this poem for more than thirty years. The remainder were verses written for Geneviève and Clémence in the 1860s and 1870s, and others addressed to their children. The most recent poem marked the third birthday of Laurent-Pichat's second granddaughter, Charlotte, in March 1885. The only child whose verses were not included was 'poor little Paul', whose short life would have added a note of sadness to a volume devoted to happy memories (Clémence's fifth child, Amédée, was not yet born).[38] The book celebrated both Laurent-Pichat's delight in being a family man, and the women's delight in the family life they had shared with him. Assembling the material provided occasions for reminiscence and was part of the process of mourning Laurent-Pichat. It is significant, however, that the women published this collection, placing it in the public domain. Their goal was not just to remember Laurent-Pichat themselves but also to reveal him to others, and the man they sought to reveal was not just a political figure but also a loving family man.

The women's gesture in publishing *Heures de fêtes* points to the broader significance of their memorialising efforts, which found their fullest expression in the assembling of a family archive. Through this archive, the place of Laurent-Pichat and his family in the unfolding story of French republicanism can be traced. Geneviève played a key role, collecting and ordering her father's papers. Her personal imprint remains on his letter of 29 June 1885, which bears the annotation: 'Last letter of my father. G. R.'[39] The letters that he had sent to his daughter and her letters to him (which he had carefully saved) became precious remnants of that relationship. Similarly, after Genevieve's death, her daughters Ginette and Charlotte preserved those letters between their mother and grandfather, and the letters that they themselves had exchanged with their grandfather in childhood. One of Laurent-Pichat's granddaughters, probably Ginette, has left her trace in the collection, too, annotating one document: 'Childhood of my grandfather Laurent-Pichat.'[40] Rosine also played a significant role in creating the archive, given that a large number of poems written to her by Laurent-Pichat when they were young are preserved there.[41] Clémence's copy of her uncle's verses commemorating their family holiday at Luchon in 1868 ensured that those verses, too, survived. Moreover, Geneviève's scrapbook of newspaper clippings found its afterlife in the archive, even if many of its precious contents are now more readily available online through Retronews, the digitised repository of French newspapers.

The archive commemorated the family's integrity and cohesion. Moreover, it testified to the critical role of families like this one in the creation of the Third Republic. Personal papers recorded this family's dinners and soirées, their beachside holidays with invited guests, their family visits to Sainte-Pélagie and to the tomb of Charras. By preserving this record of family activities, the archive celebrates the family as cradle and bulwark of republicanism. It reveals the creation of the Republic as a project pursued in collaboration by family members, not just the work of the men in political roles. By preserving this material, therefore, the women wrote themselves into the republican story, revealing their active participation in the work of the Republic, even as they wrote themselves out of that story by largely failing to preserve their own papers. That this book could be written is testimony to their work. Yet with the memorialising of Laurent-Pichat complete, their chronicling of family life ceased and with it our access to the social and political story of these women and their children.

Funerals always elicit reminiscences. Laurent-Pichat's did for Henri Fouquier, who wrote in his obituary: 'I often find myself regretting the good old days when the Republic was not triumphant, when the press was still persecuted and we were all such good friends and so united.'[42] By the 1880s, the 'generation of 1848' – those who had experienced the hopes of the Second Republic and then fought for the Third Republic through the long years of Empire – was slowly disappearing. Almost all those who followed Laurent-Pichat's coffin, observers noted, were 'grey or greying'.[43] Those in attendance were friends and colleagues of long standing, keen to pay their last respects to a valued and admired colleague.

Indeed, some did more than admire Laurent-Pichat: they loved him. Ulbach was devastated by the loss of the friend that he had 'loved for nearly fifty years'; de Mahy's friendship was of more recent origin, but for him, the funeral oration was the opportunity to declare 'how much we loved him, how much he deserved to be loved'.[44] It is remarkable how frequently these republican men used the word 'love' to describe their sentiments for each other. If Ulbach and de Mahy now used it in speaking of Laurent-Pichat, Laurent-Pichat had used it frequently in describing his relations with Jean-Baptiste Charras, Camille Risler and Auguste Scheurer-Kestner as well as his youthful relationships with Ulbach and Henri Chevreau. That these friendships in many cases spanned decades attests to their significance and to their solidity. Laurent-Pichat, always so quick to declare his love for his friends and so keen to know that he was loved by them, would have been gratified by such tributes.

These friendships were not, as this study has shown, relationships of political convenience designed to advance the ambitions of the moment; they reflected deep attachment and gave meaning to friends' lives. Expressions of love between friends highlight, furthermore, the importance of emotion in men's political lives as well as in their personal lives, which were closely interrelated. As Laurent-Pichat's social network illustrates, the geography of republican politics from the 1860s to the 1880s encompassed both the home and the *cercle*. The home was the incubator in which republican ideas were explored and reproduced, shared and exchanged. It was a place of personal and political succour in a hostile world.

This book has argued, therefore, that, like friendship, family bonds and family sociability remained essential to the making of the Republic, both during the Second Empire and throughout the 1870s. César de Mahy's eulogy for Laurent-Pichat testifies eloquently to that finding:

> The republican representatives, who had come from every corner of France, hardly knew each other, in the early days, which were still troubled and agitated. Laurent-Pichat was the first to open his house and bring us together in his home. So many precious friendships were formed there under the auspices of his charming family, and the warmth, the mutual confidence, the courteous relations, contributed to the formation of the Republic in those dangerous times when republicans, in a minority in the National Assembly, had such a need to get to know one another, to come together, to support and love each other. We have witnessed that and we should not forget it![45]

This study has aspired to illuminate the historical moment that de Mahy describes and to underline its critical role in the formation of the Third Republic.

The circumstances in which the Republic had been formed were disappearing by the 1880s, however, and the lives of Laurent-Pichat's grandchildren and their generation would differ dramatically from his. With the Republic constitutionally enshrined, young men no longer needed to pursue that quest, as their fathers and grandfathers had. Political talent was less significant in selecting a worthy son-in-law than it had been for earlier generations. Laurent-Pichat's granddaughter Ginette would marry a renowned lawyer, Georges Claretie; Charlotte would marry Henry Albert Canet, a tennis player who would win two bronze medals at the 1912 Olympic Games.[46] Young women's lives, too, were changing. Clémence's son André, Professor of Anatomy at the Paris Medical School, would marry the daughter of a prominent Jewish family and one of the earliest women doctors in France, the physician Dr Madeleine Sarah Lévi-Alvarès.[47] Politics no longer remained the existential heart of such families. With the republic apparently secure, families felt free to prioritise other pursuits. It remained to be seen whether republican families would mobilise again as the Republic came under renewed threat in the years ahead.

Notes

1. *Journal officiel*, 12 June 1886.
2. BHVP, 6, nos 181, 185: LLP to GR, 'Thursday' [1884 or 1885], undated [1885].
3. LLP, Journal, 24 Dec. 1884; 18 Jan.–10 Feb. 1885; BHVP, 6, no. 180: LLP to GR, 'Friday 5:30' [1884].
4. BHVP, 6, no. 183: LLP to GR, undated ['Sat. 13'].
5. *Ibid.*, no. 186: undated [1885].
6. LLP, Journal, 14, 16 Nov. 1881.
7. LLP to M. Radiguet, 20 Nov. 1881. Copy in APF: GC, notebook, unpaginated.
8. LLP, Journal, 24 Feb. 1884; 11, 19 April, 16, 18 June 1885.
9. Avner Ben-Amos, 'Les Funérailles de Victor Hugo', in *Les Lieux de mémoire*, ed. Pierre Nora, I: *La République* (Paris: Gallimard, 1984), pp. 473–522.
10. BHVP, 6, no. 184: LLP to GR, '31' [May 1885]. Emphasis original.
11. *Ibid.*
12. BHVP, MS-FS-07-0012, vol. 15: scrapbook of press reports on the death of LLP, created by his daughter Geneviève (hereafter BHVP, 15): Louis Ulbach, 'Laurent-Pichat', *Le Gil Blas*, 14 June 1886.
13. BHVP, 15: *La République française*, 14 June 1886. That Geneviève Risler included this cutting in her scrapbook suggests its accuracy.
14. *Le Phare de la Loire*, 15 June 1886; Gustave Isambert, *La République française*, 16 June 1886.

15 BHVP, 14, fo 105: 'Discours de M. Deschamps'; 'Allocution prononcée par M. Gustave Humbert'; Mirliton, 'Notes Parisiennes', *L'Evènement*, 13 June 1886.
16 BHVP, 14, fo 104: 'Discours de M. de Mahy'; *La Justice*, 13 June 1886.
17 BHVP, 14, fo 104: 'Discours de M. de Mahy'.
18 Mirliton, 'Notes Parisiennes', *L'Evènement*, 13 June 1886. For similar views, see newspaper cuttings of articles by Gustave Isambert, A. Fichot and Louis Ulbach, BHVP, 15, fos 32–3.
19 *La Justice*, 13 June 1886.
20 Chastenet, *Histoire de la Troisième République*, I, pp. 438–43.
21 Reported in *Le Phare de la Loire*, 15 June 1886.
22 BHVP, 14, fo 104: 'Discours de M. de Mahy'.
23 BHVP, 15, fo 32: 'Bulletin de la Société pour la Propagation de l'Allaitement maternel, mars 1887'.
24 Elinor A. Accampo, 'Gender, social policy and the formation of the Third Republic', in Elinor A. Accampo, Rachel G. Fuchs and Mary Lynn Stewart (eds), *Gender and the Politics of Social Reform in France, 1870–1914* (Baltimore, MD: Johns Hopkins University Press, 1995), pp. 1–27; Foley, 'The Christmas tree becomes French'.
25 See Zeldin, *France*, I, pp. 640–82; Sanford Elwitt, *The Third Republic Defended: Bourgeois reform in France, 1880–1914* (Baton Rouge, LA: Louisiana State University Press, 1986).
26 BHVP, 14, fo 103: 'Discours de M. de Lapommeraye'. Emphasis original.
27 *Ibid.*, fo 105: 'Discours de M. Deschamps'.
28 'Un Groupe radical au Sénat', *Le Petit Troyen*, 11 Feb. 1885; 'Un Groupe radical au Sénat', *Le Petit Quotidien*, 15 Feb. 1885.
29 'Un Groupe radical au Sénat', *Le Petit Quotidien*, 15 Feb. 1885.
30 See *La République française*, 8 Nov. 1884.
31 Auguste Scheurer-Kestner, *Souvenirs de jeunesse* (Paris: Charpentier, 1905), pp. 299–300.
32 *Ibid.*, p. 325.
33 *Journal officiel*, 26 Dec. 1885; *La République française*, 28 Dec. 1885.
34 BHVP, 14, fo 105: 'Discours de M. Deschamps'.
35 BHVP, 15, 88 fos.
36 *Ibid.*, fos 72–3.
37 Henri Fouquier, 'La Vie de Paris', *Le XIXe Siècle: journal républicain*, 16 June 1886. See the sale catalogue: *Bibliothèque de L. Laurent-Pichat* (Paris: Henri Leclerc, L. Giraud-Badin, 1927).
38 AD Yonne, 2E 68/30, 5 Mi 1259/5: Chablis: NMD (1887–1891), no. 29: Amédée Alexandre Léonce Hovelacque, 10 Aug. 1890.
39 BHVP, 6, no. 188: LLP to GR, 29 June 1885.

40 BHVP, 16 (2), following fo 37: 'L'Enfance de Gd-Père Laurent-Pichat'. Ginette's granddaughter, Mme Lesieur, donated the collection to the BHVP in 1987.
41 See esp. BHVP, 16 (1) and 16 (2): 'Poésies de jeunesse'.
42 Fouquier, 'La Vie de Paris'.
43 *Le Phare de la Loire*, 15 June 1886; *La République française*, 16 June 1886.
44 BHVP, 15: Ulbach, 'Laurent-Pichat'; BHVP, 14, fo 104: 'Discours de M. de Mahy'.
45 BHVP, 14, fo 104: 'Discours de M. de Mahy'.
46 AP, Mariages 7ᵉ arron., V4E 8683, no. 282: Georges Claretie/Eugénie ('Ginette') Risler, 30 April 1902; 7M 152, no. 400: Henry Albert Canet/Léonie Charlotte ('Charlotte') Risler, 4 June 1904; https://olympics.com/en/athletes/albert-henri-canet#
47 'André Hovelacque (1880–1939)', *La Presse médicale*, no. 65, 16 Aug. 1939: AP, Mariages 16e, V11E 530, 1911, no. 1101: André Hovelacque/Madeleine Sarah Lévi-Alvarès, 24 Aug. 1911.

Appendix

The social and political network of Léon Laurent-Pichat

This guide includes those individuals mentioned in the book who were part of the network of Léon Laurent-Pichat (LLP) for a sustained period. A few have been impossible to identify and have been omitted. The guide is based primarily on my own research but also draws on standard biographical sources (Robert and Coigny, Maitron, Schweitz, etc.) listed below, in the Bibliography.

Adam, Edmond (Antoine Edmond) (**1816–1877**): assistant mayor of Paris (March 1848); member of the Conseil d'état (1849); resigned following the coup d'état (1851); helped finance Adolphe Peyrat's *L'Avenir national* (1865); married Juliette Lambert (1868); ally of republican leader Léon Gambetta; briefly a member of the Government of National Defence (1870); served with LLP on the commission to publish the records of the Second Empire (1870); elected to the National Assembly as a member of Gambetta's Republican Union (1871–75); helped fund Gambetta's newspaper, *La République française* (est. 1871). Elected Life Senator (1875). Many *affaires d'honneur* including: with LLP, witness for Amédée Langlois (1873); witness for LLP (1875); LLP witness for Adam (1876).

Adam, Juliette, née Lambert (**1836–1936**): author, journalist, *salonnière*, feminist; married Edmond Adam and generally wrote under her married name; influential patron of republican politicians, especially Léon Gambetta; founded *La Nouvelle Revue* (1879); fiercely revanchist, she became alienated from Gambetta in the 1880s over France's foreign policy.

Allain-Targé, Henri (François Henri René) (**1832–1902**): married Geneviève Villemain (1857); opposition journalist (1860s); ally of

Léon Gambetta; stood unsuccessfully in legislative elections (1869, 1871); elected to the Paris municipal council (July 1871); with Gambetta, co-founded *La République française* (1871); attended the wedding of LLP's niece Clémence Beaujean (1875); elected to the National Assembly as a member of Gambetta's Republican Union (1876); Minister for Finance in Gambetta's government (1881–82); Minister for the Interior in Brisson's government (1885). Several *affaires d'honneur,* including: LLP witness for him (1875). Defeated in the 1889 elections, he retired from politics.

Anquez, Léonce (Henri-Louis-Léonce) **(1821–1889):** Professor of History at the lycée Saint-Louis (from 1858); author of several books on Protestantism in France; author of *Histoire de France* (1871); Inspector-General of Public Instruction (from 1882). Friend of the Laurent-Pichat and Beaujean families; attended the First Communions of Clémence Beaujean (1865) and Geneviève Laurent-Pichat (1868); attended Clémence Beaujean's wedding (1875).

Arago, Emmanuel (François Victor Emmanuel) **(1812–1896):** member of the Provisional Government (1848); elected to the National Asssembly (1848–51); opposition Deputy (1869); member of the Government of National Defence (1870); elected to the National Assembly (1871–76); Senator for Pyrénées-orientales (1876–96). Attended the wedding of LLP's niece Clémence Beaujean (1875). Nephew of Etienne Arago.

Arago, Etienne Vincent (1802–1892): writer of popular melodramas; aide-de-camp to Lafayette during the Revolution of 1830; participated in the revolution of February 1848; exiled (1849) until the amnesty (1859); contributed with LLP to *La Réforme littéraire* (1861–62) and *Le Phare de la Loire* (1864–65); served on the Shakespeare committee with LLP (1864); briefly mayor of Paris (1870); served with LLP on the commission to publish the records of the Second Empire (1870); with LLP, member of the Republican Circle of the Seine and the Family Circle; uncle of Emmanuel Arago. Friend of J.-B. Charras (from 1830); friend of the Kestner family, as well as of LLP.

Babaud-Laribière, Mme (??-??): widow of republican politician François-Saturnin-Léonide Babaud-Laribière (1819–1873); aunt of Abel Hovelacque; helped arrange the marriage between Hovelacque and Clémence Beaujean (1875).

Appendix 271

Barni, Jules Romain (1818–1878): Professor of Philosophy; sacked for refusing the oath of loyalty to Louis-Napoleon (1851); contributed (with LLP) to *La Revue de Paris* and *La Liberté de Penser*; exiled to Geneva, where he taught philosophy and wrote several major works; a founder of the International League for Peace and Freedom (1867); returned to France (1870); elected to the National Assembly (1872); colleague of LLP in Gambetta's Republican Union; freemason; retired from politics (1877) owing to ill health.

Barthélemy-Saint-Hilaire, Jules (1805–1895): Professor of Ancient Philosophy at the Collège de France; journalist; opposition activist (1830s); elected to the National Assembly (1848); author of the Second Republic's education policies; attended the wedding of LLP's sister Herminie (1859); opposition Deputy (1869); elected to the National Assembly (1871): joined the Centre-Left faction; Life Senator (1875); Minister for Foreign Affairs in the Ferry government (1880–81).

Beaujean, Amédée (Emile-Ambroise-Amédée) **(1821–1888)**: after several brief postings, Professor of Classics at the lycée St-Louis (1850), lycée Napoléon (1855) and lycée Louis-le-Grand (1863); published *Breviarium historiae graecae* (1860); member of the 'Society for the Encouragement of the Study of Greek in France' (from 1870); his *Petit dictionnaire universel ou Abrégé du dictionnaire français d'E. Littré, augmenté d'une partie mythologique, historique, biographique et géographique* (Paris: Hachette, 1877) won him a medal from the Society for the Promotion of Works Useful to Education (1877) and the Legion of Honour (1878); Inspector-General of Public Instruction (1879); keen amateur musician and photographer. Married LLP's sister Rosine Deslandes (1851); father of Clémence (b. 1853).

Beaujean, Clémence (1853–1933): daughter of Amédée Beaujean and Rosine Deslandes; niece of LLP; married Abel Hovelacque (1875); mother of Geneviève, Valentine, André, Paul and Amédée.

Beaujean, Mme Rosine: see Deslandes, Rosine.

Beauvau-Craon, Ludmille, née Komar, Princesse de (1820–1881): Polish countess; second wife of Second Empire Senator Prince Charles de Beauvau-Craon; two daughters, Elisabeth and Béatrix; close to the Polish expatriate elite, including Chopin; philanthropist;

active in Parisian cultural circles alongside LLP, whose family records name her as the mother of Geneviève Laurent-Pichat; friend of Mme Rosine Beaujean.

Blanc, Louis (Jean Joseph Charles Louis) **(1811–1882)**: member of the Provisional Government (1848); promoted the 'organisation of labour' through workers' co-operatives to address poverty; exiled (after June 1848); returned to France (1870); elected to the National Assembly, then the Chamber of Deputies (1871–81); campaigned for amnesty for Communards.

Broca, Paul (Pierre Paul) **(1824–1880)**: surgeon; anthropologist; founder of the Society of Anthropology (1859); studied brain structure seeking links to racial difference, a now disproved idea; identified the region of the brain controlling speech (1861); patron and colleague of Abel Hovelacque at the Paris School of Anthropology; attended Hovelacque's wedding to LLP's niece Clémence Beaujean (1875).

Carnot, Hippolyte (Lazare Hippolyte) **(1801–1888)**: opposition Deputy (1839–48); supported Revolution of February 1848; briefly Minister for Education during the Second Republic (1848); opposed the coup d'état (1851); refused the oath of loyalty to the Emperor; attended the wedding of LLP's sister Herminie (1859); active in opposition politics (1860s); elected to the National Assembly (1871); Life Senator (1875).

Challemel-Lacour, Paul-Armand (1827–1896): Professor of Philosophy; journalist; exiled following the coup d'état (1851–59); with LLP, contributed to *La Réforme littéraire* (1861–62); as Prefect of the Rhône (1870) suppressed the Lyon Commune (1871); elected to the National Assembly (1872); attended the wedding of LLP's niece Clémence Beaujean (1875); elected to the Senate (1876); close to Léon Gambetta and a leading contributor to *La République française* from its inception (1871); diplomat (1879–82); minister in the Ferry government (1883); vice-President then President of the Senate (1890s).

Charcot, Jean-Martin (1825–1893): renowned neurologist and specialist in disorders of the nervous system; consulted by LLP (1884–85); consulted by LLP's sister Herminie (1879).

Charras, Jean-Baptiste Adolphe (1810–1865): participated in the Revolution of 1830; career soldier; served in Algeria (1840s); supported the February Revolution of 1848; elected to the National Assembly (1848, 1849); proscribed following the coup d'état (1851); settled in Switzerland, where he financed *Le Confédéré*; political hero of LLP; married to Mathilde Kestner (1858); rejected the amnesty (1859); remained in Bâle until his death.

Chassin, Charles-Louis (1831–1901): lawyer who refused oath of loyalty to the Emperor; became a journalist; with LLP, contributed to *La Revue de Paris* (1858); fellow-correspondent (with LLP) of *L'Association* (Belgium) and *Le Confédéré* (Switzerland); linked to Garibaldi and the Hungarian nationalists; freethinker, anticlerical; active in the League for Peace and Freedom; was prosecuted several times for press offences; under the Third Republic, became editor-in-chief of the *Journal officiel* (the record of parliamentary proceedings).

Chauffour, Victor (Marie-Victor) (1819–1889): Professor of Law at Strasbourg; elected to the National Assembly (1848); forced out of public life by the coup d'état (1851); became businessman and writer; with LLP, contributed to *La Réforme littéraire* (1861–62); husband of Fanny Kestner (1831–1850); father of Fanny Chauffour; uncle of LLP's son-in-law Charles Risler; witness for Eugénie Risler at her marriage to Jules Ferry (1875).

Chevreau, Henri (Julien-Théophile-Henri) (1823–1903): son of Jean-Henri Chevreau and Eulalie Collas; close friend of LLP in adolescence; attended the lycée Charlemagne with LLP; with LLP, published *Les Voyageuses* (1844); became a Bonapartist; was appointed to several important posts, including imperial Senator (1865), Prefect of the Seine (1870) and Minister of the Interior (1870); fled to England (1870–77); failed in subsequent efforts to return to politics.

Chevreau, Jean-Henri (1794–1854): ran a boarding school at Saint-Mandé (attended by LLP); Bonapartist representative in the *Corps législatif* (1852–54); father of Henri.

Clemenceau, Georges Benjamin (1841–1929): medical doctor; unsuccessfully sought to marry Hortense Kestner; in America (1865–69), became an admirer of American democracy; married

American Mary Eliza Plummer (1869; divorced 1891); participated in the uprising of 4 September 1870 that proclaimed the Third Republic; mayor of the eighteenth arrondissement of Paris (1870); elected to the National Assembly (1871); joined Gambetta's Republican Union (1871); active (with LLP and others) in the 'Republican League for the Rights of Paris'; elected to the Paris municipal council (July 1871–76); president of the Paris municipal council (1875); attended the wedding of LLP's niece Clémence Beaujean (1875); Deputy for Paris (from 1876); advocated for amnesty for Communards; leader of the Extreme Left republicans (1880s); founded the influential newspaper *La Justice* (1880); vocal opponent of Jules Ferry; defeated in 1893 but returned to prominence as Prime Minister (1906–09; 1917–20). Numerous *affaires d'honneur*, including: with LLP, witness for Georges Perin (1874).

Delescluze, Charles (Louis Charles) (**1809–1871**): radical republican journalist; fought in the Revolution of 1830; led uprising against the conservative republican government (June 1848); imprisoned (March 1849); convicted again (March 1850); fled to England (until 1853); sentenced to ten years' jail, part of which he served on Devil's Island; returned to Paris after the amnesty (1859); journalist-friend of LLP (from at least 1862); editor of radical paper *Le Réveil* (1868–1871), of which LLP was financial supporter and literary editor; served several further prison sentences for press offences; prosecuted (1869) for campaigning to memorialise Alphonse Baudin, republican Deputy killed during the 1851 coup d'état (acquitted); elected mayor of the nineteenth arrondissement (1870); a leader of the Paris Commune (1871); died on the barricades.

Denfert-Rochereau, Aristide (Pierre Philippe Marie Aristide) (**1823–1878**): career soldier, named 'the lion of Belfort' after successfully defending that fort against the Prussian siege (1870); elected to the National Assembly, then Chamber of Deputies (1871, 1877); ally of Gambetta. Part of LLP's social circle (from 1872); attended the wedding of LLP's niece Clémence Beaujean (1875).

Deslandes, Herminie (1839–1883): daughter of Geneviève Leroi and Louis-Achille Deslandes; half-sister of LLP. Married Siagre-Emile Lefort, notary, brother of Henri Lefort (1859); mother of Jeanne and Elisabeth.

Deslandes, Louis-Achille (1799–1840): hatter; married Geneviève Leroi (1823); father of Clémence, Rosine, Louis-Achille and Herminie.

Deslandes, Louis-Achille (1832–1878): son of Louis-Achille Deslandes and Geneviève Leroi; half-brother of LLP. Distiller; married Juliette Deslandes – 'Victorine' – (1858); father of Georges and Juliette.

Deslandes, Rosine (1829–1915): daughter of Geneviève Leroi and Louis-Achille Deslandes; half-sister of LLP. Married Amédée Beaujean (1851); mother of Clémence; raised her motherless niece, Geneviève Laurent-Pichat. Active in the movement for secular professional education for girls; political confidante of her half-brother LLP.

Despois, Eugène André (1818–1876): Professor of Rhetoric at the lycée Louis-le-Grand; colleague of Amédée Beaujean (1849–50); resigned (1851) to avoid swearing loyalty to Emperor Napoleon III; writer and journalist; with LLP, contributed to *La Revue de Paris*, *La Réforme littéraire* (1861–62) and *L'Association* (1864); assistant librarian at the Sorbonne (from 1870).

Du Camp, Maxime (1822–1894): writer and journalist; a founder (1851) of *La Revue de Paris* of which he later became joint owner with LLP; friend of Gustave Flaubert, he encouraged *La Revue*'s serialisation of Flaubert's *Madame Bovary* (1856); LLP cited his *Chants Modernes* (1855) in his own collection of verse *Chroniques rimées* (1856); elected to the Académie française (1880).

Duprat, Pascal Pierre (1815–1885): historian and journalist; elected to the National Assembly (1848); exiled following the coup d'état (1851); edited *La Libre Recherche* (Brussels, 1855–57), to which LLP contributed; became representative of the Third Republic to Chile.

Favre, François (1819–1892): lifelong friend of LLP; sentenced to three years' jail for his revolutionary and anticlerical views (1850); took refuge in Belgium (until 1854); founded (with Louis Ulbach) *Le Monde maçonnique* (1858); with LLP, contributed to *La Revue de Paris*, *Le Phare de la Loire*, *La Réforme littéraire* and Delescluze's paper, *Le Réveil*; mayor of the seventeenth arrondissement of Paris (1870–71); resigned under the Paris Commune; with LLP, member of both the Republican Circle of the Seine and the Family Circle (1871–73); unsuccessful in the elections of July 1871; returned to journalism; librarian at the Conservatoire des Arts et Métiers (from 1880 until his death).

Ferry, Jules François Camille (1832–1893): political ally of LLP (from 1859); opposition Deputy (1869); member of the Government of National Defence (1870–71); fell out with LLP over his role in crushing the Paris Commune (1871); elected to the National Assembly, then Chamber of Deputies (1871–89); married Eugénie Risler (1875); Minister for Public Instruction and Fine Arts in the Waddington government (1879); Prime Minister (September 1880 to November 1881; February 1883 to March 1885); architect of the republican education laws and of French colonial policy.

Ferry, Mme Eugénie: see Risler, Eugénie.

Floquet, Charles Thomas (1828–1896): prosecuted several times for republican activism (1860s); married Hortense Kestner (1869); uncle of LLP's son-in-law Charles Risler; deputy mayor of Paris (1870); active with LLP in the 'Republican League for the Rights of Paris' (1871); elected to the National Assembly, then Chamber of Deputies (February 1871–81); municipal councillor for Paris (1872); President of the municipal council (1874); Vice-President of the Chamber of Deputies (1881); Prefect of the Seine (1882); President of the Chamber of Deputies (1885; 1889–93); Prime Minister (1888). Several *affaires d'honneur*, including: with LLP, as witness (1879). Defeated in the 1893 legislative elections; Senator for the Seine (1894–96).

Frébault, Charles-Félix (1825–1902): surgeon in the National Guard (1870); municipal councillor for Paris (1871–76); Deputy for the Seine (1876–1889; 1893–1898); member of Gambetta's Republican Union; sought LLP's assistance in the 1877 elections.

Gambetta, Léon (1838–1882): lawyer; came to prominence defending Charles Delescluze (1869); opposition Deputy (1869); prominent in the Government of National Defence (1870); elected to the National Assembly, then Chamber of Deputies, for various constituencies (1871–82); leader of the Republican Union

(1871–82), to which LLP belonged; active with LLP in the Family Circle; personal friend of LLP and his family. Several *affaires d'honneur*, including: with LLP, as his witness (1874). As leader of the largest republican group in the Chamber of Deputies in the 1870s, he might have become Prime Minister but was passed over until 1881. Lived in a free union with Léonie Léon.

Gautier, Théophile (Pierre Jules Théophile) **(1811–1872)**: renowned poet and travel writer; literary, art and theatre critic; admirer of Victor Hugo; director of *La Revue de Paris* (1851–56; with LLP from 1853); editor of *L'Artiste*, where he promoted 'art for art's sake' (rejected by LLP). Became librarian for Princess Mathilde Bonaparte, cousin of the Emperor.

Greppo, Louis (Jean-Louis) (1810–1888): silkworker; participated in the Lyon uprisings of 1831 and 1834; belonged to several secret societies; elected to the National Assembly (1848; 1849); exiled in Belgium from the coup d'état until the amnesty (1851–59); implicated in further plots (1860s); mayor of the fourteenth arrondissement (1870); elected to the National Assembly, then Chamber of Deputies (from 1871); ally of Gambetta; supported amnesty for Communards, organising aid for their families, to which LLP contributed regularly.

Grévy, Jules (François Judith Paul) **(1807–1891)**: lawyer; briefly imprisoned at the coup d'état (1851); opposition Deputy (1868); elected to the National Assembly (1871); president of the Chamber of Deputies (1876); President of the Republic (1879–87) – first republican to hold the post.

Grousset, Pascal (1844–1909): medical doctor and journalist; editor in chief of *La Marseillaise* (1869); elected to the Paris Commune (March 1871) where he remained a militant figure; prosecuted (June 1871); deported to New Caledonia (1872); escaped to Sydney, Australia (1874); back in France, was elected as an independent socialist, refusing to join the socialist federation (Section française de l'Internationale ouvrière, SFIO) in 1905.

Hachette, Jean-Georges (1838–1892): likely the 'Hachette' who was part of LLP's social circle; in 1864, succeeded his father, Louis, as head of the publishing empire that still bears the family name.

Hérold, Ferdinand (Louis Joseph Ferdinand) **(1828–1882)**: lawyer; prosecuted several times under the Empire for republican activities; stood unsuccessfully in the 1869 elections; member of the Government of National Defence (1870); defeated in the 1871 elections; elected to the Senate (1876); Prefect of the Seine (1879). LLP lobbied him (1881) to appoint his son-in-law Charles Risler as mayor of the seventh arrondissement.

Hovelacque, Abel (Alexandre-Abel) **(1843–1896)**: scholar, protégé of Paul Broca; Professor of Linguistic Anthropology in the Paris School of Anthropology (1876); author of numerous books and scientific papers; nephew of Second Republic Deputy and Prefect of the Charente (1870), François-Saturnin-Léonide Barbaud-Laribière. Married Clémence Beaujean, niece of LLP (1875); father of Geneviève, Valentine, André, Paul and Amédée. Elected municipal councillor for the seventh arrondissement (1878; 1881; defeated 1884); elected for the thirteenth arrondissement (1886; 1887). Active in the Anthropological Society and the Voltaire Society; freemason; with LLP and Charles Risler, founded the lodge *La Fédération maçonnique* (1882); elected Deputy for the Seine as an independent Republican Left candidate (1889–93; 1893–94); resigned due to ill health.

Hugo, Victor-Marie (1802–1885): renowned author and leader of the Romantic movement; elected to the National Assembly (1848) as a conservative; became a republican following the coup d'état (1851); remained in self-imposed exile until the fall of the Empire (1870); elected to the National Assembly (Feb. 1871; defeated July 1871); elected Life Senator (1876); allied with Louis Blanc, LLP (and others) to secure amnesty for the Communards (1880).

Kergomard Pauline, née Reclus (1838–1925): teacher and writer; as Inspector of infant schools (1879) developed a programme of instruction for those schools; first woman elected to *Conseil général de l'instruction publique* (1886); member of the proto-feminist National Council of French Women.

Kestner, Charles (1803–1870): dye manufacturer in Thann (Alsace); married Eugénie Rigau (1827); five daughters: Eugénie, Fanny, Mathilde, Céline and Hortense; elected to the National Assembly (1848); opposed the coup d'état (1851); imprisoned and exiled to Switzerland; defeated by the official candidate in elections of 1852; led opposition in Thann and Mulhouse to the plebiscite of 8 May 1870.

Kestner, Mme Eugénie: see Rigau, Eugénie.

Komar, Ludmille: see Beauvau-Craon, Ludmille, née Komar.

Lalanne, Ludovic (1815–1898): historian; managing editor of *La Correspondance littéraire* (1860–65) to which LLP contributed; friend of LLP and his family from 1864; attended the wedding of LLP's niece Clémence Beaujean (1875).

Lamartine, Alphonse Marie Louis de Prat de (1790–1869): poet, politician and historian; leading figure in the Romantic movement from the publication of his *Méditations poétiques* (1820); literary hero of LLP and his friends (1830–40s); head of the Provisional Government (Feb. 1848); elected to the National Assembly (April 1848); lost power following the June uprising; stood unsuccessfully in the presidential elections (December 1848); devoted himself to literature thereafter; contributor (with LLP) to *La Revue de Paris*.

Lapommeraye, Henri de (1839–1891): probably the 'Lapommeraye', President of the Polytechnic Association, who spoke at LLP's funeral; writer and theatre critic; renowned public speaker; appointed to the Chair of history and dramatic literature at the Conservatoire national de musique et de déclamation (1879).

Laprade, Pierre Marie Victor de (1812–1883): writer and poet; elected to the Académie française (1858); elected to the National Assembly (Feb. 1871); Centre-Right; resigned in 1873 for health reasons.

Laurent-Pichat, Geneviève (1856–1912): daughter of LLP; her mother never officially identified (family records name the Princesse de Beauvau). Raised by her father and her aunt, Mme Rosine Beaujean; married Charles Risler (1877); mother of Ginette and Charlotte.

Lefèvre, Henri (1825–1877): Elected to the National Assembly (July 1871); colleague of LLP in Gambetta's Republican Union; frequent visitor to LLP's home; attended the wedding of LLP's niece Clémence Beaujean (1875). Affaire d'honneur: witness for LLP (1873).

Lefort, Emile (Siagre-Emile) (1827–1904): notary at L'Isle-Adam, later Juge de Paix (1860s–1870s); married LLP's sister Herminie (1859); father of Jeanne and Elisabeth; brother of LLP's colleague Henri Lefort.

Lefort, Henri François (1828–1917): republican activist from his youth; proscribed briefly (1851); prosecuted several times (1850s); took shelter in Guernsey; friend of Victor Hugo; returned to Paris following the amnesty (1859); editor of Adolphe Peyrat's *L'Avenir national* (1859); secretary of *La Réforme littéraire* (1861–82); a founder (though only briefly a member) of the First International (1863); author (with Henri Tolain) of the 'Manifesto of the Sixty' promoting worker candidatures and workers' rights (1864); admirer of Pierre-Joseph Proudhon; a founder of the co-operative movement; contributor (with LLP) to *L'Association* (1864). Younger brother of Siagre-Emile Lefort, who married LLP's sister Herminie (1859); attended the First Communion of Clémence Beaujean (1865).

Lepère, Charles (Edmé Charles Philippe) **(1823–1885)**: lawyer active in opposition politics in Auxerre; elected to the National Assembly (Feb. 1871); member of Gambetta's Republican Union; with LLP, member of the *commission de permanence* (1875); attended the wedding of LLP's niece Clémence Beaujean (1875); held ministries in the governments of Jules Dufaure (1877–79) and Waddington (1879–80); forced to resign as Minister for the Interior over the anticlerical laws (1880); re-elected for Auxerre (1881); president of the Radical Left faction (1881).

Leroi, Geneviève (1806–1863): mother of LLP; used the pseudonym 'Rosine Laurent' at his birth; married Louis-Achille Deslandes (1823); as Mme Deslandes, mother of Clémence, Rosine, Louis-Achille and Herminie.

Lissagaray, Prosper-Olivier (1838–1901): republican, later socialist, journalist; an organiser of the public lectures at the rue de la Paix to which LLP contributed (1862); founded *La Marseillaise* with Henri Rochefort (1870); following a series of convictions, fled to Belgium until the declaration of the Republic (Sept. 1870); member of the Government of National Defence (1870); fought for the Paris Commune (March 1871); founded radical newspapers *L'Action* and *Le Tribun du Peuple*; escaped to Brussels and then England, where he met Karl Marx and became close to Eleanor Marx; returned to Paris (1880) where he continued his political activism. Author of a major history of the Paris Commune of 1871, based on interviews with fellow-participants.

Lissajous, Jules-Antoine (1822–1880): Professor of Physics at the lycée Saint-Louis and colleague of Léonce Anquez; his daughter, Jeanne-Antoinette, was a friend of Geneviève Laurent-Pichat.

Littré, Emile (Maximilien Paul Emile) **(1801–1881)**: renowned for his four-volume *Dictionnaire de la langue française* (commenced 1844; published 1863–73); accomplished linguist; admirer and promoter of the ideas of Auguste Comte ('positivism'). Participated in the Revolution of 1830; elected to the Académie française (1871); elected to the National Assembly (1871); Life Senator (1875); freemason; urged religious tolerance; converted to Catholicism on his death bed.

Mac-Mahon, Marshall Patrice, Duc de Magenta (1808–1893): career soldier; monarchist; commander-in-chief of French forces defeated in the Franco-Prussian War (1870–71); surrendered his army at Sedan (Sept. 1870); appointed to head the government by the conservative-dominated Assembly (May 1873); dismissed the republican government despite its majority, installing a monarchist government (May 1877); resigned following the republican electoral victory (Oct. 1877).

Mahy, François-Césaire de (1830–1906): born at Saint-Pierre, Réunion; educated in France; medical doctor and journalist; returned to Réunion (1857); representative for Réunion in the National Assembly, then Chamber of Deputies (1870–1906); member of Gambetta's Republican Union. With his family, attended the wedding of LLP's niece Clémence Beaujean (1875). Keenly interested in colonial policy; Minister for Agriculture (1882–83); Minister for the Navy and for Colonies (1883; 1887–88).

Melvil-Bloncourt, Suzanne, Vicomte (1823–1880): born in Guadeloupe; educated at the lycée Louis-le-Grand, Paris; involved in radical student politics (1840s); contributed to radical newspapers (1848); briefly imprisoned (1851); elected to represent Guadeloupe in the National Assembly (April 1871); participated in the Paris Commune, then took his seat in the National Assembly on the Extreme Left; fled to Geneva when his Communard past was revealed (1874); sentenced to death *in absentia*; returned to Paris following the amnesty for Communards (1880).

Millard, Auguste (1830–1915): LLP's family doctor and friend; with his family, belonged to LLP's social circle; attended the wedding of LLP's sister Herminie (1859) and of LLP's niece Clémence Beaujean (1875).

Miot, Jules (1809–1883): deported to Algeria following the coup d'état (1851) for attempting to lead an uprising; was pardoned and returned to France (1860); established a secret society (1861); served three years in Sainte-Pélagie (1862–65) for plotting an uprising; met LLP in prison; in England (1866–69) joined the First International; member of the Paris Commune (1871); fled to Switzerland (May 1871) and was condemned to death *in absentia*; returned to France in 1881 following amnesty of 1880.

Nadaud, Gustave (1820–1893): singer and songwriter whose political songs were banned under the Second Empire; major figure in the singing society *La Goguette de la Lice chansonnière* (est. 1831); friend of LLP and his family.

Naquet, Alfred Joseph (1834–1916): militant follower of Auguste Blanqui; sentenced to fifteen months' prison (Dec. 1867) for belonging to a secret society; prosecuted again for writings (1869); fled to Spain. Participated in the uprising that proclaimed the Third Republic (Sept. 1870); elected to the National Assembly (July 1871) where he joined the Extreme Left. Attended the wedding of LLP's niece Clémence Beaujean (1875). Best remembered as the author of the law legalising divorce (1884).

Pelletan, Camille (Charles Camille) (1846–1915): son of Eugène; radical journalist and politician; in his youth, a friend of avantgarde poets Rimbaud and Verlaine; critic of Gambetta's 'opportunism'; supporter (with LLP) of amnesty for Communards; ally of Clemenceau and editor of his newspaper, *La Justice* (est. 1880); freemason; anticlerical; elected to the Chamber of Deputies (1881–1912); opposed colonial expansion; joined the *Parti radical-socialiste* (est. 1901); Minister of the Navy (1902–05) in the government of Emile Combes.

Pelletan, Eugène (Pierre Clément Eugène) **(1813–1884)**: father of Camille Pelletan; writer and journalist; author of *La Femme au XIXe siècle* (1869). Attended the wedding of LLP's sister Herminie (1859); contributor (with LLP) to *La Réforme littéraire* (1861–62); imprisoned for press offences (1862); opposition Deputy (1863–70); member of the Government of National Defence (1870); elected to the National Assembly (1871–76); Senator for Bouches-du-Rhône (1876–84); Vice-President of the Senate (1879); Life Senator (1884).

Perin, Georges (1838–1903): lawyer and journalist; contributor (with LLP) to *Le Phare de la Loire*; ally of Gambetta, Eugène Pelletan and later Georges Clemenceau; elected to the National Assembly, then the Chamber of Deputies (from 1873); sat on the Extreme Left; fierce opponent of Jules Ferry's colonial policies. *Affaires d'honneur*: witness several times for Georges Clemenceau; LLP witness for Perin (1874); Perin witness for LLP (1875). Attended the wedding of LLP's niece Clémence Beaujean (1875).

Peyrat, Alphonse (Jean-Alphonse) **(1812–1890)**: opposition journalist from the 1830s; founder and editor of *L'Avenir national* (1865) to which LLP contributed articles and funds; prosecuted (with Quentin and Delescluze) for the 'Baudin affair' (1869); elected to the National Assembly (1871–76); sat with the Extreme Left; Senator for the Seine (1876–90).

Pichat, Etienne (? –1838): father of LLP from a liaison with Geneviève Leroi; wealthy businessman and merchant; his three marriages produced one child, Valérie (1823–30); adopted LLP (1837).

Pozzi, Samuel Jean (1846–1918): society doctor and gynecologist; author of numerous scientific papers; established the first Chair of Gynecology in Paris (1884); elected Senator (1898); did not seek re-election. Attended the marriage of LLP's niece Clémence Beaujean (1875). Friend of Marcel Proust; friend and reputed lover of Sarah Bernhardt; Dreyfusard.

Proth, Mario (1832–1891): pseudonym of Ernest Proth; writer and literary critic; friend and correspondent of LLP (from the 1860s), mentioned frequently in his journal.

Proust, Antonin (1832–1905): journalist; lifelong friend of Edouard Manet; elected to the National Assembly (1876), then the Chamber of Deputies (1877); personal secretary of Léon Gambetta; Secretary of State for Fine Arts in Gambetta's government (1881–82). Family friend as well as political ally of LLP; attended the wedding of LLP's niece Clémence Beaujean (1875).

Quentin, Charles (1826–1904): friend and colleague of LLP in the 1860s; prosecuted with Delescluze and others in the 'Baudin Affair' (1868); attended the wedding of LLP's niece Clémence Beaujean (1875); later municipal councillor; became director of *L'Assistance publique* (1880–85).

Quinet, Edgar (1803–1875): republican philosopher, writer and historian; Professor of Foreign Literature at Lyon (1839), then Paris (1842); dismissed (1846) for his vehement anticlerical lectures; participated in the Revolution of 1848; elected to the National Assembly but fled France following the coup d'état (1851). Returned to France in 1870; elected to the National Assembly (1871–75).

Radiguet, Max (Maximilien René) (1816–1899): travel writer, poet and painter; shared with LLP an interest in art; a regular presence in LLP's journal and often a dinner guest.

Ranc, Arthur (1831–1908): involved in radical politics from his youth; friend of Auguste Blanqui; prosecuted many times (1850s); fled to Switzerland, returning to France following the amnesty (1859); further prosecutions (1860s); friend of LLP from at least 1865; contributed (with LLP) to Charles Delescluze's *Le Réveil* and to Louis Ulbach's *La Cloche*; served with LLP on the commission to publish the records of the Empire (1870); elected to the National Assembly (Feb. 1871); elected to the Paris Commune (March 1871) but resigned (April); investigated (1873) for his role in the Commune; fled to Brussels; condemned to death *in absentia*. *Affaires d'honneur*: LLP witness for Ranc (1873).

Rathier, Jules (1828–1887): winegrower at Chablis (Yonne); elected to the National Assembly (Feb. 1871); defeated (Feb. 1876); re-elected (1877) with assistance from LLP and the Beaujean family; re-elected (1881); member of Gambetta's Republican Union; later elected on the radical list (Oct. 1885). The Rathier family were friends of LLP's family, attending the wedding of LLP's niece Clémence Beaujean (1875).

Rigau, Eugénie (1806–1890): wife of Charles Kestner; mother of Eugénie, Fanny, Mathilde, Céline and Hortense; grandmother of LLP's son-in-law Charles Risler. Freethinker; major sponsor of republicanism in Alsace.

Risler, Camille (1821–1881): engineer; industrialist in Thann, Alsace; widower of Eugénie Kestner (1828–1862); father of Charles and Eugénie (Mme Ferry).

Risler, Charles (1848–1923): son of Camille Risler and Eugénie Kestner; chemist in the family dye business in Thann (Alsace); sister of Eugénie (Mme Ferry); lieutenant in the Mobile Guard of Haut-Rhin during the Franco-Prussian War; taken prisoner following the siege of Neuf-Brisach (Nov. 1870); founding member of the *Association Générale d'Alsace-Lorraine* (1871); active in the movement to restore Alsace and Lorraine to France; active freemason; married LLP's daughter Geneviève (1877); assistant mayor of the seventh arrondissement of Paris (1881); mayor of the seventh arrondissement (1882–1919).

Risler, Eugénie (1850–1920): daughter of Camille Risler and Eugénie Kestner; sister of Charles; freethinker; married Jules Ferry, republican leader (1875). Close friend of Geneviève Laurent-Pichat, her sister-in-law; witness at the marriage of her niece, Charlotte Risler, to Henry Albert Canet (1904).

Scheurer-Kestner, Auguste (1833–1899): chemist and industrialist in Thann; married Céline Kestner (1856); father of Jeanne and Suzanne; met LLP when in prison for smuggling republican materials into France (April 1862); contributor (with LLP) to *La Réforme littéraire* (1861–82); elected to the National Assembly for Haut-Rhin (Feb. 1871) but his seat was abolished when Alsace was ceded to the German Empire; elected for Paris (July 1871); member of Gambetta's Republican Union; with LLP, member of both the Republican Circle of the Seine and the Family Circle; elected Life Senator (1875); prominent supporter of Alfred Dreyfus (the 'Dreyfus Affair', 1897–98). *Affaire d'honneur*: witness for LLP (1873).

Schœlcher, Victor (1804–1893): renowned and lifelong opponent of slavery, inspired by visiting America in his youth; freemason; elected

Deputy for Martinique (1848–49); drafted the decree abolishing slavery under the Second Republic (1848); exiled 1851; returned to France 1870; elected to represent Martinique in the National Assembly (1871); member of Gambetta's Republican Union; joined the 'Society for improving the condition of women' (1875); admirer of black revolutionary Toussaint-Louverture; friend of LLP (from at least 1870).

Simon, Jules François (1814–1896): Professor of Philosophy, sacked for his republican views; elected Deputy 1848; opposed the coup d'état (1851); elected opposition Deputy (1863, 1869); member of the Government of National Defence (1870); conservative republican; vehement opponent of Gambetta; minister in the Thiers government (1871–73); appointed Prime Minister by President MacMahon (1876) but after conflict with MacMahon resigned (1877): republicans gained control of the lower house in subsequent elections (Oct. 1877); played a key role in the defeat of Article 7 of Ferry's education laws; sympathetic to the incipient movement for women's rights, but argued for their protection by men and rejected their workforce participation. Attended the wedding of LLP's sister Herminie (1859); LLP's sister, Mme Rosine Beaujean, worked with Mme Simon on secular education for girls (1873–80).

Spuller, Eugène (1835–1896): lawyer, journalist and writer; editor of Gambetta's newspaper *La République française* from 1871; elected to represent Paris in the National Assembly, then the Chamber of Deputies (1876–85); elected Deputy for Côte d'Or (1885–92); Vice-President of the Chamber (1890, 1891); Senator for Côte d'Or (1892–96); Under-Secretary in Gambetta's government (1881–82); held ministries in several later governments. Political colleague and family friend of LLP; attended the wedding of LLP's niece Clémence Beaujean (1875).

Thiers, Adolphe (Marie Joseph Louis Adolphe) **(1797–1877)**: leading figure in the Orleanist monarchy (1830s–1840s); spokesperson for the moderate opposition under the Second Empire; elected to the National Assembly (Feb. 1871); played a leading role in suppressing the Paris Commune; installed as 'chief of the executive power of the French republic' (president) by the conservative-dominated Assembly; tried to rally political factions around a conservative republic; most republicans cautiously accepted him; monarchists rejected his overtures; defeated in the National Assembly (1873) and replaced by Marshall Mac-Mahon.

Tiersot, Edmond (1822–1883): medical doctor; republican activist during the Second Empire; assistant mayor of Bourg-en-Bresse (1870); elected to the National Assembly, then the Chamber of Deputies (1871–81); member of Gambetta's Republican Union.

Tirard, Pierre Emmanuel (1827–1893): mayor of the second arrondissement of Paris (1870–71); member of Gambetta's Republican Union; elected to the National Assembly, then the Chamber of Deputies (1871–83); Life Senator (1883–93); held ministries in successive republican governments from 1879; Prime Minister (1887–88, 1889–90). Attended the wedding of LLP's niece Clémence Beaujean (1875).

Tolain, Henri (1828–1897): engraver; republican activist; supporter of co-operatives and mutualism; stood for election unsuccessfully (1863); stood in the by-election of 1864, financed by LLP; with Henri Lefort, composed the 'Manifesto of the Sixty' seeking workers' rights and the election of working-class representatives; a Paris correspondent for the First International but remained an advocate of mutualism and private property; mayor of eleventh arrondissement (1870); elected to the National Assembly (1871); denounced the Paris Commune; elected Senator (1876).

Ulbach, Louis (1822–1889): lifelong friend of LLP; attended the lycée Charlemagne with LLP; writer and journalist; editor of *Le Propagateur de l'Aube* (Troyes, 1848–51) to which LLP contributed; editor with LLP of *La Revue de Paris*; contributor with LLP to *La Réforme littéraire* (1861–62); served on the Shakespeare committee with LLP (1864); founded *La Cloche* (1868–72); jailed for press offences (1868); author of numerous novels and plays; sought refuge with LLP when threatened with arrest during the Paris Commune (1871); became librarian at the Bibliothèque de l'Arsenal (1878); founded *La Revue de Famille* with Jules Simon (1888). Attended the wedding of LLP's sister Herminie (1859) and of LLP's niece Clémence Beaujean (1875).

Bibliography

I: Archival sources

1. Bibliothèque historique de la ville de Paris (BHVP)

Fonds Claretie: MS-FS-07

This is the main repository of documents pertaining to Léon Laurent-Pichat and his extended family. The volumes used for this study are:
  vol. 1 (MS-FS-07-0001): Documents relating to Charles Kestner and his wife, Eugénie Kestner.
  vol. 5 (MS-FS-07-0005): Documents relating to Neuf-Brisach and the *Association Générale d'Alsace Lorraine*, 1872–1910.
  vols 6–20 (MS-FS-07-0006–MS-FS-07-0019): Documents relating to Léon Laurent-Pichat (hereafter LLP):
    vol. 6 (MS-FS-07-0006): Letters, LLP to Geneviève Risler, née Laurent-Pichat (hereafter GR, GLP) and son-in-law, Charles Risler.
    vol. 7 (MS-FS-07-0006): Letters, LLP to members of the Risler and Kestner families; letters, LLP to his granddaughters; letters, GR, GLP to LLP.
    vols 8–9 (bound in one volume, MS-FS-07-0007): LLP, Journal, Oct. 1861– Feb. 1879.
    vol. 10 (MS-FS-07-0008): LLP, Journal, Feb. 1879–June 1885.
    (Volumes 8–10 are cited throughout as 'LLP, Journal'.)
    vol. 11 (MS-FS-07-0008): LLP, letters, notes and travel writings, 1841–1869.
    vol. 12 (MS-FS-07-0009): Clémence Hovelacque, journal, 1867 [1868].
    vol. 14 (MS-FS-07-0011): LLP, literary and political career, 1860–75.
    vol. 15 (MS-FS-07-0012): Press reports on LLP's death, 1886.
    vols 16–20 (MS-FS-07-0013–MS-FS-07-0019): LLP, literary works.
    vol. 16 (MS-FS-07-0013–MS-FS-07-0014): LLP, poetry written in his youth: vol. 16 (1) 1845–49; vol. 16 (2) 1849–51.
    vol. 17 (MS-FS-07-0015): LLP, poetry, 1836–89.

vol. 18 (1) (MS-FS-07-0016): LLP, MS of *Libres Paroles*, 1847.
vol. 18 (2) (MS-FS-07-0017): LLP: MSS of various works, 1847–50.
vol. 19 (MS-FS-07-0018): LLP, literary lectures, rue de la Paix, 1862.
vol. 20 (MS-FS-07-0019): LLP, poetry, 1862.

2. Archives privées de la famille, détenues par Mme Caroline Lesieur Flury (APF)

Family photographs; copies of notarial documents; notebook of Mme Eugénie (Ginette) Claretie (GC), née Risler (granddaughter of LLP).

3. Archives nationales (AN)

a) Pierrefitte-sur-Seine:

248AP/1: Fonds Laurent-Pichat: letters to LLP, 1861–1885, dossiers 2–7.
276AP/1: Fonds Scheurer-Kestner: LLP, letters to Scheurer-Kestner, 1862–1881.
418AP/1, 456MI: Letters of the Ferry family; letters between Jules Ferry and his wife Eugénie.
F[17]: Instruction publique: Dossier 20117: Emile Ambroise Amédée Beaujean, personnel file.

b) Paris:

Minutier central:
AN MC/ET/LXXXIV/892: Testament de M. Pichat, 5 Sept. 1832.
AN MC/ET/XXXIII/1204: Reconnaissance d'enfant naturel par Mme Deslandes, 5 Sept. 1851.
AN MC/ET/XXXIII/1205: Contrat de mariage, Amédée Beaujean / Rosine Deslandes, 26 Nov. 1851.
AN MC/ET/LXXXIV/1114: Contrat de mariage, Louis-Achille Deslandes / Juliette Asselin, 29 July 1858.
AN MC/ET/LXXXIV/1118: contrat de mariage, Siagre-Emile Lefort / Herminie Deslandes, 31 March 1859.
AN MC/ET/LXXXIV/1136: 'Reconnaissance d'enfant naturel par Mr. Laurent-Pichat', 29 June 1861.
AN MC/ET/LXXXIV/1158: Vente par M. et Mme Sicre de Fontbrune à M. Laurent-Pichat, 9 April 1864.
AN MC/ET/XVIII/1403: Contrat de mariage, Abel Hovelacque / Clémence Beaujean, 20 Jan. 1875.
AN MC/ET/LXXXIV/1237: Contrat de mariage, Charles Risler / Geneviève Laurent-Pichat, 15 June 1877.
AN MC/ET/LXXXIV/1304: Inventaire après décès, Léon Laurent-Pichat, 23 June 1886.

ANMC/ET/84/1912-04-19-HUGOT: Inventaire après décès, Geneviève Laurent-Pichat, 19 April 1912.
Base Léonore (Legion of Honour):
Charles, Prince de Beauvau: LH/158/66 (1855).
Emile Ambroise Amédée Beaujean: LH/155/34, no. 20675 (1878).

4. Archives départementales (AD)

a) Hauts-de-Seine:

E NUM PLE87: Naissances, commune de Plessis-Piquet: Beaujean, Clémence, 24 June 1853.
E NUM SEV95 (1880), no. 133: Naissances, commune de Sèvres: Eugénie Rosine Juliette Geneviève Risler, 31 Aug. 1880.

b) Val de Marne, commune de Saint-Mandé:

6M5: Census, 1817.
1NUM067 2–4: Census: 1831, 1836, 1841.
28J 947: Acte de baptême, Léon Laurent, 28 Jan. 1832.

c) Yonne:

2E 68/30, 5 Mi 1259/5: Chablis: NMD (1887–1891), no. 29 [naissance]: Amédée Alexandre Léonce Hovelacque, 10 Aug. 1890.

d) Yvelines:

5M179BIS, 9: 62/214: Naissances, Mandres-les-Rose (Val de Marne): Geneviève Elisabeth Rose Leroi, 9 April 1806.

5. Archives de Paris (AP)

Naissances:

V3E/N1322: Léon Laurent, 11 July 1823.
V3E/N1803: Clotilde Valérie Pichat, 3 Dec. 1823.
V4E 222: 3e arron., Juliette Deslandes, 7 March 1862.
V4E 3355: 7e arron., Léonie Charlotte Risler, 6 March 1882.

Mariages:

V3E/M302: 5e arron., no. 8: Rosine Deslandes / Amédée Beaujean, 27 Nov. 1851.

V3E/M302: 8ᵉ arron., no. 26: Louis-Achille Deslandes / Juliette Asselin, 29 July 1858.
V4E 3294: 7ᵉ arron., no. 50: Abel Hovelacque / Clémence Beaujean, 26 Jan. 1875.
V4E 3314: 7ᵉ arron., no. 367: Charles Risler / Marie-Geneviève Laurent-Pichat, 20 June 1877.
V4E 8683: 7ᵉ arron., no. 282: Georges Claretie / Geneviève [Ginette] Risler, 30 April 1902.
7M 152: 7ᵉ arron, no. 400: Henry Albert Canet / Charlotte Risler, 4 June 1904.
V11E 530, 16ᵉ arron., no. 1101: André Hovelacque / Madeleine Sarah Lévi-Alvarès, 24 Aug. 1911.

Décès:

V3E/D1189: Étienne Pichat, 20 April 1838.
V4E 230: 3ᵉ arron., Juliette Deslandes, 4 April 1862.
V4E 677: 6ᵉ arron., Geneviève Leroi, Veuve Deslandes, 27 Nov. 1863.

Miscellaneous:

D6J: Registre paroissial, Eglise de Sainte-Elisabeth-de-Hongrie, mariages: Geneviève Elisabeth Rose Leroi / Louis-Achille Deslandes, 29 Oct. 1823.
AP 704/73/2: Collège royal de Charlemagne. Entrées et sorties, 1838–1841.

6. Bibliothèque de l'Assemblée nationale (BAN)

MS1777: Letters, Léon Gambetta / Léonie Léon.

7. Médiathèque de Saint-Dié-des-Vosges (MSDV)

M-247, VII, C42 (50): Letters, Laurent-Pichat to Jules Ferry.

II: Printed primary sources

1. Works by Léon Laurent-Pichat (chronological order)

Les Voyageuses (with Henri Chevreau). Paris: Dauvin et Fontaine, 1844.
Libres Paroles. Paris: Comptoir des Imprimeurs-unis, 1847.
Cartes sur la table: Nouvelles. Paris: Michel Lévy frères, 1855.
Chroniques rimées. Paris: A la librairie nouvelle, 1856.
La Païenne. Paris: A la librairie nouvelle, 1857.
La Sibylle. Paris: A la librairie nouvelle, 1859.
L'Art et les artistes en France. Paris: Dubuisson et Cⁱᵉ, 1859.

Le Poète anonyme de la Pologne, Sigismond Krasinski. Paris: Dubuisson et Cie, 1861.
Notes sur le salon de 1861. Lyon: Imprimerie du *Progrès*, 1861.
Exposition des amis des arts: Notes sur le salon de 1862. Lyon: Imprimerie du *Progrès*, 1862.
Les Poètes de combat. Paris: Collection Hetzel, 1862.
Commentaires de la vie. Paris: Alphonse Lemerre, 1868.
Rapport fait au nom de la 29e commission d'intérêt local, sur le projet de loi tendant à autoriser la ville de Grenoble (Isère) à contracter un emprunt de 600,000 francs, par M. Laurent-Pichat (19 décembre 1874). Versailles: Impr. de Cerf et fils [undated].
Les Réveils: Poésies. Paris: Alphonse Lemerre, 1880.
Heures de fêtes: Album intime. Nancy: Berger-Levrault et Cie, 1893.

2. Other printed primary sources

Adam, Juliette. *Nos amitiés politiques avant l'abandon de la Revanche,* 5e édition. Paris: Alphonse Lemerre, 1908.
Allain-Targé, [Henri]. *La République sous l'Empire: Lettres, 1864–1870.* Paris: Bernard Grasset, 1939.
Arago, Etienne. *Quelques mots prononcés au cimetière de Montmartre, le 21 janvier 1862 sur la tombe de Madame Lefebvre (née Marie-Reine Rolland) par M. Etienne Arago.* Paris: Impr. de A. Augros, 1862.
Bibliothèque de L. Laurent-Pichat. Paris: Henri Leclerc, L. Giraud-Badin, 1927.
Bitard, Adolphe. *Dictionnaire général de biographie contemporaine |française et étrangère.* Paris: A. Lévy et Cie, 1887.
Blaze de Bury, Henri. 'Etudes et souvenirs: Frédéric Chopin'. *Revue des deux mondes,* 15 Oct. 1883, 849–78.
Carré, Narcisse-Epaminondas. *Premier examen sur le code civil, contenant le premier livre du code, présenté par demandes et réponses, avec des définitions, notes et explications tirées des meilleurs auteurs et commentateurs, par un avocat à la Cour royale de Paris.* Paris: N.-E. Carré, 1823.
Le Centenaire de Voltaire: Fête du 30 mai 1878. Paris: Impr. Dubuisson, 1878.
Chateaubriand, François-René de. *Œuvres complètes de Chateaubriand,* V: *Itinéraire de Paris à Jérusalem et de Jérusalem à Paris, en allant par la Grèce et revenant par l'Egypte, la Barbarie et l'Espagne.* Nouvelle édition. Liechtenstein: Nevdeln, 1828; facsimile, Kraus reprint, 1975.
'Chronique de l'enseignement primaire en France'. *La Revue pédagogique,* 17 (1890), 189–92.
Code civil des Français: Edition originale et seule officielle. Paris: Imp. de la République, An XII. 1804.
Couret, Emile. *Le Pavillon des Princes: Histoire complète de la prison politique de Sainte-Pélagie depuis sa fondation jusqu'à nos jours.* Paris: E. Flammarion, 1895.

Engelhard, Maurice. 'La Contrebande politique sur la frontière du Rhin'. *Revue alsacienne*, 1882, 116–23.

L'Enterrement d'un proscrit (25 janvier 1865), discours prononcés par MM. Chauffour-Kestner, Edgar Quinet, Etienne Arago, et Ch.-L. Chassin. 3ᵉ édition. Fribourg: Impr. de C. Marchand, 1865.

Fénelon, François Salignac de la Mothe. 'Histoire d'Alibée, Persan'. In *Fables et opuscules divers composes pour l'éducation du Duc de Bourgogne* .... Paris: Hachette, 1875, XXV, pp. 82–88.

Ferry, Jules. *Lettres de Jules Ferry 1846–1893*. Paris: Calmann-Lévy, 1914.

Flaubert, Gustave. *Madame Bovary, mœurs de province, suivie des réquisitoire, plaidoirie et jugement du procès intenté à l'auteur avec introduction, notes et variantes par Edouard Maynal.* Paris: Garnier Frères, 1957.

———. *Correspondance, II (juillet 1851–décembre 1858), édition établie, présentée et annotée par Jean Bruneau.* Paris: Gallimard, 1980.

Fouquier, Henri. 'La Vie de Paris'. *Le XIXᵉ Siècle: Journal républicain*, 16 June 1886.

Gambetta, Léon. *Lettres de Gambetta, 1868–1882, recueillies et annotées par Daniel Halévy et Emile Pillias.* Paris: Bernard Grasset, 1938.

Gastineau, Benjamin. *Histoire de la souscription populaire à la médaille Lincoln*. Paris: Librairie internationale, 1865.

Gaulier, A. 'Le Mot d'ordre'. *Le Rappel*, 26 Aug. 1884.

Gautier, Théophile. *Correspondance générale*. VI: 1854–57, ed. Claudine Lacoste-Veysseye. Geneva and Paris: Librairie Droz, 1991.

Gobron, Suzanne. *Les Mémoires de Suzel: Journal de ma vie, quelques souvenirs, annotés et illustrés par Olivier Dornès.* Paris: Le Trigramme, 2002.

La Fontaine, Jean. 'The Shepherd and the King'. In *The Complete Fables of Jean La Fontaine*. Proquest eBook central, University of Illinois Press, 2006, Book X, pp. 277–81.

Lefort, Emile. *De la Loi et les droits et devoirs qu'elle apporte: Conférence faite par M. Em. Lefort, notaire, Président de la Commission d'organisation de la Bibliothèque populaire de L'Isle-Adam, le 16 janvier 1870.* Beaumont-sur-Oise: Impr. de C. Frémont, 1870.

Ligue républicaine pour la révision de la constitution: Instructions pratiques du bureau de la ligue pour l'organisation des groups révisionnistes. Paris, 1883.

Lissagaray, [P.-O.]. *Les Huit journées de mai derrière les barricades.* Brussels: Bureau du *Petit Journal*, 1871.

———. *Histoire de la Commune de 1871* [1876]. Paris: François Maspéro, 1972.

Malon, Benoît. *La Troisième défaite du prolétariat français.* Neuchâtel: G. Guillaume fils, 1871.

Mémoire pour les héritiers Pichat, appelans, contre le Sieur Thibault, ancien notaire, tant en sa qualité de tuteur du mineur Léon Laurent, se disant légataire universel d'Etienne Pichat, qu'en son nom personnel, se

disant légataire particulier dudit Pichat. Batignolles-Monceaux: Impr. A. Desrez, undated.
Monnier, Marc. 'Paillasse'. In *Théâtre des marionnettes*. Geneva: F. Richard, 1871.
Panthéon parisien: Album des célébrités contemporaines photographiés par Et. Carjat [1864], reprint BNF Hachette Livre.
Ponsard, René. 'Les Emigrants'. *La Rive gauche*, 26 Feb. 1865.
Ponzio, J.-G. *Les Chants du peuple*, préface de L. Laurent-Pichat. Nîmes: Impr. de Clavel-Ballivet, 1864.
Le Procès des treize en premier instance. Paris: E. Dentu, 1864.
Proth, Mario. *Charles Floquet*. Paris: A. Quantin, 1883.
Quinet, Edgar. 'Discours sur la tombe de Charras, 25 janvier 1865'. In *Le Livre de l'exilé, 1851–1870: Après l'exil, manifestes et discours, 1871–1875* [1895]. Geneva: Slatkine reprints, 1989, pp. 580–83.
Ranc, Arthur. *Ranc: Souvenirs, correspondance, 1831–1908*. Paris: Edouard Cornély et Cie, 1913.
Reynaud, Charles. 'A Laurent-Pichat: Sonnet' [juillet 1850]. In Charles Reynaud, *Epitres, contes et pastorales, notice biographique par A. Fabre*. Paris: E.-J. Savigné, 1877.
Risler, Charles. *L'Association Générale d'Alsace-Lorraine*. Paris: Berger-Levrault, 1880.

———. 'L'Association Générale d'Alsace-Lorraine'. *Revue alsacienne: Littérature, histoire, sciences, poésie, beaux-arts*, Nov. 1879–Oct. 1880, 53–60.

———. *Rapport général présenté à la délégation cantonale ... sur le fonctionnement des cantines scolaires par Charles Risler, maire du VIIe arrondissement*. Paris: Typographie Georges Chamerot, 1886.

——— et Gaston Laurent-Atthalin. *Neuf-Brisach: Souvenirs de siège et de captivité*. 2e édition. Paris: Berger-Levrault, 1881.
Rotonde du Temple. M. Laurent-Pichat propriétaire. Paris: Imp. centrale des chemins de fer de Napoléon Chaix, [1863].
Saint-Ferréol, A. *Les Proscrits français en Belgique: Ou la Belgique contemporaine vue à travers l'exil*, I. Brussels: C. Muquardt, 1870.
Scheurer-Kestner, Auguste. *Souvenirs de jeunesse*. Paris: Bibliothèque Charpentier, 1905.
Siebecker, Edouard. *Poésies d'un vaincu*. Paris: Berger-Levrault, 1882.
Tolain, H. *Quelques vérités sur les élections de Paris, 31 mai 1863*. Paris: E. Dentu, 1863.
Ulbach, Louis. *Gloriana*. Paris: W. Coquebert, 1844.

———. *La Politique à l'atelier: Lettres de Jacques Souffrant, ouvrier*. Troyes: Vigreux-Jamais, 1850.

———. *Lettres à Jacques Souffrant, ouvrier*. Paris: Garnier Frères, 1851.
Vapereau, Gustave. *Dictionnaire universel des contemporains*. 3e édition. Paris: L. Hachette, 1865.
Vaudin, Jean-François. *Gazettes et gazetiers: Histoire critique et anecdotique de la presse parisienne, deuxième année*. Paris: E. Dentu: 1863.

3. Newspapers and periodicals

Annales de l'Assemblée nationale: compte rendu in extenso des séances, annexes [1871–1875], séance du 29 juillet 1875.
Annales du Sénat et de la Chambre des Députés. Sénat, Séance du vendredi 28 février 1879.
L'Assemblée nationale, 2 Aug. 1856.
L'Avenir national, 1865–73.
Le Charivari, 12 March 1856.
La Correspondance littéraire, 1861–65.
L'Evènement, 13 June 1886.
Le Figaro, 15 May 1857.
Le Flambeau républicain, 1871.
La Gironde, 29 April, 2 Dec. 1863.
La Jeunesse: Journal littéraire, 1861.
Journal des débats politiques et littéraires, 22 Nov. 1857.
Journal officiel de le République française, 1873–86.
La Justice, 13 June 1886.
Le Messager des théâtres et des arts, 14 Aug. 1853.
L'Opinion nationale, 17 Feb. 1864.
Le Petit Quotidien, 15 Feb. 1885.
Le Petit Troyen, 11 Feb. 1885.
La Petite République française, 9 Oct. 1877.
Le Peuple, 30 Nov. 1863.
Le Phare de la Loire, 1862–68, 1886.
La Presse, 16 July 1856, 5 Nov. 1864.
Le Propagateur de l'Aube, 1849–51.
Le Radical, 17 Jan. 1884.
Le Rappel, 5 April 1871.
La Réforme littéraire, 1862.
La République française, 1872–86.
Le Réveil, 1868–70.
La Revue alsacienne, April 1885.
La Revue de Paris, 1851–58.
Le Siècle, 25 May 1856.
Le Soir, 5 July 1875.
Le XIXe Siècle, 16 June 1886.

III: Secondary sources

1. Books

AGAL *Paris 1871 à 1996*. Paris: Association Générale d'Alsace et de Lorraine, 1996.

Agulhon, Maurice. *Le Cercle dans la France bourgeoise, 1810–1848*. Paris: Armand Colin, 1977.
———. *The Republic in the Village: The people of the Var from the French Revolution to the Second Republic*, trans. Janet Lloyd. Cambridge: Cambridge University Press; Paris: Editions de la maison des sciences de l'homme, 1982.
———. *Marianne au pouvoir. L'Imagerie et la symbolique républicaines de 1880 à 1914*. Paris: Flammarion, 1989.
Aldrich, Robert. *Greater France: A history of French overseas expansion*. London: Macmillan, 1996.
Allen, James Smith. *A Civil Society: The public space of Freemason women in France, 1744–1944*. Lincoln NE: University of Nebraska Press, 2021.
Audoin-Rouzeau, Stéphane. *1870: La France dans la guerre*. Paris: Armand Colin, 1989.
Auspitz, Katherine. *The Radical Bourgeoisie: The ligue de l'enseignement and the origins of the Third Republic, 1866–1885*. Cambridge: Cambridge University Press, 1972.
Barnes, Julian. *The Man in the Red Coat*. London: Jonathan Cape, 2019.
Bellanger, Claude, et al. *Histoire générale de la presse française*. II: *De 1815 à 1871*; III: *De 1871 à 1940*. Paris: Presses universitaires de France, 1969, 1972.
Ben-Amos, Avner. *Funerals, Politics and Memory in Modern France, 1789–1996*. Oxford: Oxford University Press, 2000.
Berenson, Edward. *The Trial of Madame Caillaux*. Berkeley, CA: University of California Press, 1992.
Bury, J.P.T. *Gambetta and the Making of the Third Republic*. London: Longman, 1973.
Caine, Barbara, ed. *Friendship: A history*. London: Equinox, 2008.
Chapman, Guy. *The Third Republic of France*. New York: St. Martin's Press, 1962.
Charle, Christophe. *A Social History of France in the Nineteenth Century*, trans. Miriam Kochan. Oxford: Berg, 1994.
———. *Le Siècle de la presse, 1830–1939*. Paris: Editions du Seuil, 2004.
Chastenet, Jacques. *Histoire de la Troisième République*. I: *Naissance et jeunesse*; II: *La République des républicains, 1879–1893*. Paris: Hachette Littérature, 1952.
Chevallier, Pierre. *Histoire de la Franc-Maçonnerie française*, 3 vols. Paris: Fayard, 1974–5.
Collingham, H.A.C. *The July Monarchy: A political history of France, 1830–1848*. London: Longman, 1988.
Collins, Irene O. *The Government and the Newspaper Press in France, 1814–1871*. Oxford: Oxford University Press, 1959.
Corbin, Alain. *The Lure of the Sea: The discovery of the seaside in the Western world, 1750–1840*, trans. Jocelyn Phelps. Cambridge: Polity Books, 1994.

Daumard, Adeline. *La Bourgeoisie parisienne, 1815–1848*. Paris: S.E.V.P.E.N, 1963.

———. *Les Bourgeois et la bourgeoisie en France depuis 1848*. Paris: Aubier, 1987.

Daumas, Maurice. *Le Mariage amoureux: Histoire du lien conjugal sous l'Ancien Régime*. Paris: Colin, 2004.

Dauphin, Cécile. *Prête-moi ta plume… Les manuels épistolaires au XIXe siècle*. Paris: Editions Kimé, 2000.

———, Pierrette Lebrun-Pézerat and Danièle Poublan. *Ces bonnes lettres: Une correspondance familiale au XIXe siècle*. Paris: Albin Michel, 1995.

Davidoff, Leonore. *Thicker Than Water: Siblings and their relations, 1780–1920*. Oxford: Oxford University Press, 2011.

———. *The Best Circles: Society, etiquette and the season*. London: Croom Helm, 1973.

——— and Catherine Hall. *Family Fortunes: Men and women of the English middle class, 1780–1850*. Revised edition. London: Routledge, 2002.

Davidson, Denise Z. *France After Revolution: Urban life, gender, and the new social order*. Cambridge, MA: Harvard University Press, 2007.

Davies, Helen. *Emile and Isaac Pereire: Bankers, socialists and Sephardic Jews in nineteenth century France*. Manchester: Manchester University Press, 2015.

Dessal, Marcel. *Un Révolutionnaire Jacobin Charles Delescluze, 1809–1871*. Paris: Marcel Rivière et Cie, 1952.

Dommanget, M. *Blanqui et l'opposition révolutionnaire à la fin du Second Empire*. Paris: A. Colin, 1960.

Ellis, Jack D. *The Physician-Legislators of France: Medicine and politics in the early Third Republic, 1870–1914*. New York: Cambridge University Press, 1990.

Elwitt, Sanford. *The Third Republic Defended: Bourgeois reform in France, 1880–1914*. Baton Rouge, LA: Louisiana State University Press, 1986.

Evans, David Owen. *Social Romanticism in France, 1830–1848*. New York: Octagon Books, 1969.

Foley, Susan K., and Charles Sowerwine. *A Political Romance: Léon Gambetta, Léonie Léon and the making of the French Republic, 1872–1882*. Houndmills: Palgrave Macmillan, 2012.

Ford, Caroline. *Divided Houses: Religion and gender in modern France*. Ithaca, NY: Cornell University Press, 2005.

France, Peter, ed. *The New Oxford Companion to Literature in French*. Oxford: Clarendon Press, 1989.

Freeze, ChaeRan Y. *A Jewish Woman of Distinction: The life and diaries of Zinaida Poliakova*. Waltham, MA: Brandeis University Press, 2019.

Fuchs, Rachel G. *Poor and Pregnant in Paris: Strategies for survival in the nineteenth century*. New Brunswick, NJ: Rutgers University Press, 1992.

———. *Contested Paternity: Constructing families in modern France*. Baltimore, MD: Johns Hopkins University Press, 2008.

Furet, François. *Revolutionary France, 1770–1880*. Oxford: Oxford University Press, 1992.
Gaillard, Jean-Michel. *Jules Ferry*. Paris: Fayard, 1989.
Garrioch, David. *The Formation of the Parisian Bourgeoisie, 1690–1830*. Cambridge, MA: Harvard University Press, 1996.
Gay, Peter. *The Bourgeois Experience: Victoria to Freud*. III: *The Tender Passion*. New York: Oxford University Press, 1986; V: *Pleasure Wars*. New York: Norton, 1998.
Godbeer, Richard. *The Overflowing of Friendship: Love between men and the creation of the American Republic*. Baltimore, MD: Johns Hopkins University Press, 2009.
Goodman, Dena. *Becoming a Woman in the Age of Letters*. Ithaca, NY: Cornell University Press, 2009.
Grassi, Marie-Claire. *Lire l'épistolaire*. Paris: Armand Colin, 1998.
Grévy, Jérôme. *La République des Opportunistes, 1870–1885*. Paris: Perrin, 1998.
Guyer, Christopher. *The Second French Republic, 1848–1852: A political reinterpretation*. New York: Palgrave Macmillan, 2016.
Hanotaux, Gabriel. *Histoire de la France contemporaine, 1871–1900*. IV: *La République parlementaire*. Paris: Ancienne librairie Furne, [1908].
Harrison, Carol E. *The Bourgeois Citizen in Nineteenth Century France: Gender, sociability, and the uses of emulation*. Oxford: Oxford University Press, 1999.

———. *Romantic Catholics: France's postrevolutionary generation in search of a modern faith*. Ithaca, NY: Cornell University Press, 2014.
Harvey, David. *Paris, Capital of Modernity*. New York and London: Routledge, 2003.
Hause, Steven C., with Anne R. Kenney. *Women's Suffrage and Social Politics in the French Third Republic*. Princeton, NJ: Princeton University Press, 1984.
Heuer, Jennifer Ngaire. *The Family and the Nation: Gender and citizenship in revolutionary France, 1789–1830*. Ithaca, NY: Cornell University Press, 2005.
Heywood, Colin. *Growing Up in France from the Ancien Regime to the Third Republic*. Cambridge: Cambridge University Press, 2007.
Hobsbawm, Eric. *The Age of Capital, 1848–1875* [1975]. London: The Folio Society, 2005.
Hochschild, Arlie Russell. *The Managed Heart: Commercialisation of human feeling*. Revised edition. Berkeley, CA: University of California Press, 2012.
Horowitz, Sarah. *Friendship and Politics in Post-Revolutionary France*. University Park, PA: Pennsylvania State University Press, 2018.
Houbre, Gabrielle. *La Discipline de l'amour: l'Education des filles et des garçons à l'âge du romantisme*. Paris: Plon, 1997.
Howard, Michael. *The Franco-Prussian War*. London: Routledge, 2021.

Jennings, Lawrence. *French Antislavery: The movement for the abolition of slavery in France, 1802–1848*. Cambridge: Cambridge University Press, 2000.
Johnson, Christopher H. *Becoming Bourgeois: Love, kinship and power in provincial France, 1670–1880*. Ithaca, NY: Cornell University Press, 2015.
Johnson, Martin Phillip. *The Paradise of Association: Political culture and popular organizations in the Paris Commune of 1871*. Ann Arbor, MI: University of Michigan Press, 1996.
Klejman, Laurence, and Florence Rochefort. *L'Egalité en marche: Le féminisme sous la Troisième République*. Paris: Des femmes/Antoinette Fouque, 1989.
Knibiehler, Yvonne. *Les Pères aussi ont une histoire*. Paris: Hachette, 1987.
LaCapra, Dominick. *Madame Bovary on Trial*. New York: Cornell University Press, 1986.
Lejeune, Philippe. *On Autobiography*, ed. Paul John Eakin, trans. Katherine Leary. Minneapolis, MN: University of Minnesota Press, 1989.
Lévy, Marie-Françoise. *De mères en filles: L'Education des françaises, 1850–1880*. Paris: Calmann-Lévy, 1984.
Lewis, Philippa. *Intimacy and Distance: Conflicting cultures in nineteenth-century France*. NED-New edition. Modern Humanities Research Association, 2017. DOI: 10.2307/j.ctv16kkxgs.
Loiselle, Kenneth. *Brotherly Love: Freemasonry and male friendship in Enlightenment France*. Ithaca, NY: Cornell University Press, 2014.
Linton, Marisa. *Choosing Terror: Virtue, friendship and authenticity in the French Revolution*. Oxford: Oxford University Press, 2013.
Macknight, Elizabeth C. *Aristocratic Families in Republican France, 1870–1940*. Manchester: Manchester University Press, 2012.
Mansker, Andrea. *Sex, Honor and Citizenship in Early Third Republic France*. Houndmills: Palgrave Macmillan, 2011.
Marthe: A Woman and Her Family: A nineteenth-century correspondence. Harmondsworth: Viking, 1985.
Martin-Fugier, Anne. *Les Salons de la Troisième République: Art, littérature, politique*. Paris: Perrin, 2003.
———. *Les Romantiques, 1820–1848*. Paris: Hachette Littérature, 1998.
Mayeur, Françoise. *Histoire de l'enseignement et de l'éducation*. III: *1789–1930*. Paris: Tempus, 1981.
Mayeur, Jean-Marie, and Alain Corbin, eds. *Les Immortels du Sénat, 1875–1918: Les Cent-seize inamovibles de la Troisième République*. Paris: Publications de la Sorbonne, 1995.
McCall, Laura, and Donald Yacavone, eds. *A Shared Experience: Men, women, and the history of gender*. New York: New York University Press, 1998.
McPhee, Peter. *The Politics of Rural Life: Political mobilisation in the countryside, 1845–1852*. Oxford: Clarendon Press, 1992.

Merriman, John. *Massacre: The life and death of the Paris Commune*. New York: Basic Books, 2014.
Mollier, Jean-Yves. *Louis Hachette (1800–1864): Le Fondateur d'un Empire*. Paris: Fayard, 1999.
—— and Jocelyne George. *La Plus Longue des Républiques, 1870–1940*. Paris: Fayard, 1994.
Moses, Claire Goldberg. *French Feminism in the Nineteenth Century*. Albany, NY: State University of New York Press, 1984.
Mourre, Michel. *Dictionnaire encyclopédique d'histoire*. Nouvelle édition. Paris: Bordas, 1996.
Nagaï, Nobuhito. *Les Conseillers municipaux de Paris sous la IIIe République*. Paris: Publications de la Sorbonne, 2002.
Nora, Pierre, ed. *Les Lieux de mémoire*, 3 vols. Paris: Gallimard, 1984–1986.
Nord, Philip. *The Republican Moment: Struggles for democracy in nineteenth century France*. Cambridge, MA: Harvard University Press, 1995.
Nye, Robert A. *Masculinity and Male Codes of Honor in Modern France*. New York: Oxford University Press, 1993.
Olmsted, William. *The Censorship Effect: Baudelaire, Flaubert, and the formation of French Modernism*. Oxford: Oxford University Press, 2016.
Pellissier, Catherine. *La Vie privée des notables Lyonnais au XIXe siècle*. Lyon: Editions lyonnaises d'art et d'histoire, 1996.
Perrot, Martyne. *Le Cadeau de Noël: Histoire d'une invention*. Paris: Autrement, 2013.
Perrot, Michelle, ed. *A History of Private Life. IV: From the fires of revolution to the Great War*, trans. Arthur Goldhammer. Cambridge, MA: Harvard University Press, 1990.
Pilbeam, Pamela. *Republicanism in Nineteenth Century France, 1814–1871*. Houndmills: Macmillan Press, 1995.
Price, Roger. *The French Second Empire: An anatomy of political power*. Cambridge: Cambridge University Press, 2001.
Rauch, André, *Les Vacances en France de 1830 à nos jours*. Paris: Hachette, 1996.
Reddy, William M. *The Invisible Code: Honor and sentiment in post-revolutionary France*. Berkeley, CA: University of California Press, 1997.
——. *The Navigation of Feeling: A framework for the history of emotions*. Cambridge: Cambridge University Press, 2001.
Robert, Adolphe, Edgar Bourloton and Gaston Cougny, eds. *Dictionnaire des parlementaires français depuis le 1er mai 1789 jusqu'au 1er mai 1889*. Paris: Bourloton, 1889–1891.
Rogers, Rebecca. *From the Salon to the Schoolroom: Educating bourgeois girls in nineteenth century France*. University Park, PA: Pennsylvania State University Press, 2005.
Rougerie, Jacques. *La Commune de 1871*. 2e édition corrigée. Paris: Presses universitaires de France, 1992.
Rouillard, Dominique. *Le Site balnéaire*. Liège: Pierre Mardaga, 1984.

Ruberg, Willemijn. *Conventional Correspondence: Epistolary culture of the Dutch elite, 1770–1850.* Boston, MA: Brill, 2011.

Sancton, Tom. *Sweet Land of Liberty: America in the mind of the French Left, 1848–1871.* Baton Rouge, LA: Louisiana State University Press, 2020.

Schafer, David A. *The Paris Commune.* Houndmills: Palgrave Macmillan, 2005.

Schmidt, Nelly. *Victor Schœlcher et l'abolition de l'esclavage.* Paris: Fayard, 1994.

Schweitz, Arlette. *Les Parlementaires de la Seine sous la Troisième République.* II: *Dictionnaire biographique.* Paris: Publications de la Sorbonne, 2001.

Smith, Bonnie G. *Ladies of the Leisure Class: The bourgeoises of Northern France in the nineteenth century.* Princeton, NJ: Princeton University Press, 1981.

Smith, Mark M. *The Smell of Battle, the Taste of Siege: A sensory history of the Civil War.* Oxford: Oxford University Press, 2014.

Smith, Sidonie and Julia Watson. *Reading Autobiography: A guide to interpreting life narratives.* 2nd edition. Minneapolis, MN: University of Minnesota Press, 2010.

Sohn, Anne-Marie. *'Sois un homme!' La construction de la masculinité au XIXe siècle.* Paris: Seuil, 2009.

Sowerwine, Charles. *France Since 1870: Culture, politics and society.* 3rd edition. Houndmills: Palgrave Macmillan, 2018.

Spang, Rebecca L. *The Invention of the Restaurant: Paris and modern gastronomic culture.* Cambridge, MA: Harvard University Press, 2000.

Spitzer, Alan B. *The French Generation of 1820.* Princeton, NJ: Princeton University Press, 1987.

Steinitz, Rebecca. *Time, Space and Gender in the Nineteenth Century British Diary.* New York: Palgrave Macmillan, 2011.

Stone, Judith. *Sons of the Revolution: Radical democrats in France, 1862–1914.* Baton Rouge, LA: Louisiana State University Press, 1996.

Surkis, Judith. *Sexing the Citizen: Morality and masculinity in France, 1870–1920.* Ithaca, NY: Cornell University Press, 2006.

Taithe, Bertrand. *Defeated Flesh: Welfare, warfare and the making of modern France.* Manchester: Manchester University Press, 1999.

Tchernoff, Iouda. *Le Parti républicain sous le Second Empire, documents et souvenirs.* Paris: A. Pedone, 1906.

Tombs, Robert. *The Paris Commune 1871.* London: Longman, 1999.

Tosh, John. *A Man's Place: Masculinity and the middle-class home in Victorian England.* New Haven, CT: Yale University Press, 1999.

Verjus, Anne. *Le Cens de la famille: Les Femmes et le vote, 1789–1848.* Paris: Belin, 2002.

―――― and Denise Davidson. *Le Roman conjugal: Chroniques de la vie familiale à l'époque de la Révolution et de l'Empire.* Paris: Champ Vallon, 2011.

Vincent-Buffault, Anne. *L'Exercice de l'amitié: Pour une histoire des pratiques amicales aux XVIIIe et XIXe siècles*. Paris: Seuil, 1995.
Wawro, Geoffrey. *The Franco-Prussian War: The German conquest of France, 1870–1871*. Cambridge: Cambridge University Press, 2003.
Weill, Georges. *Histoire du parti républicain en France, 1814–1870*. Paris: Félix Alcan, 1928.
Winock, Michel. *Clemenceau*. Paris: Perrin, 2007.
Yon, Jean-Claude. *Histoire culturelle de la France au XIXe siècle*. Nouvelle édition revue et augmentée. Paris: Armand Colin, 2021.
Zeldin, Theodore. *France 1848–1945*. I: *Ambition, love and politics*; II: *Intellect, taste and anxiety*. Oxford: Clarendon Press, 1973, 1977.

2. Articles and chapters

Accampo, Elinor A. 'Gender, social policy and the formation of the Third Republic'. In Elinor A. Accampo, Rachel G. Fuchs and Mary Lynn Stewart, eds. *Gender and the Politics of Social Reform in France, 1870–1914*. Baltimore, MD: Johns Hopkins University Press, 1995, pp. 1–27.
'AHR conversation: The historical study of emotions'. *American Historical Review*, 117:5 (2012), 1487–1531.
Allen, James Smith. 'Navigating the social sciences: A framework for the history of emotions'. *History and Theory*, 42 (2003), 82–93.
'André Hovelacque (1880–1939)'. *La Presse médicale*, 65, 16 Aug. 1939.
Aprile, Sylvie. 'La République au salon: Vie et mort d'une forme de sociabilité politique, 1865–1885'. *Revue d'histoire moderne et contemporaine*, 38 (1991), 473–87.
―――. 'Bourgeoise et républicaine, deux termes inconciliables?'. In Alain Corbin, Jacqueline Lalouette and Michèle Riot-Sarcey, eds. *Femmes dans la cité, 1815–1871*. Paris: Créaphis, 1997, pp. 211–23.
Arnold, James. '"*Il fut bon père*": The *Institut de France*, funeral eulogies and the formation of bourgeois identity in early nineteenth century France'. *French History*, 29:2 (2015), 204–24.
Bellanger, Claude. 'Journalistes républicains sous le Second Empire avec des documents inédits'. *Etudes de presse*, nouvelle série, 6:9 (1954), 3–11.
Ben-Amos, Avner. 'Les Funérailles de Victor Hugo'. In Pierre Nora, ed. *Les Lieux de mémoire*. I: *La République*. Paris: Gallimard, 1984, pp. 473–522.
Binoche-Guedra, Jacques-W. 'La Représentation parlementaire coloniale (1871–1940)'. *Revue historique*, 280:2 (1988), 521–35.
Blauvelt, Martha Tomhave. 'The work of the heart: Emotion in the 1805–35 diary of Sarah Connell Ayer'. *Journal of Social History*, 35:3 (2002), 577–92.
Bossis, Mireille. 'Methodological journeys through correspondences'. In 'Men / women of letters', special issue, ed. Charles A. Porter, *Yale French Studies*, 71 (1986), 63–75.

Brodie, Marc, and Barbara Caine. 'Class, sex and friendship: The long nineteenth century'. In Barbara Caine, ed. *Friendship: A history*. London: Equinox, 2008, pp. 223–77.
Broomhall, Susan. 'Emotions in the household'. In Susan Broomhall, ed. *Emotions in the Household 1200–1900*. Houndmills: Palgrave Macmillan, 2008, pp. 1–37.
Cabantous, Alain. 'La Fin des patriarches'. In Jean Delumeau and Daniel Roche, eds. *Histoire des pères et de la paternité*. Paris: Larousse, 2000, pp. 333–58.
Chalus, Elaine. 'Elite women, social politics and the political world of late eighteenth-century England'. *The Historical Journal*, 43:3 (2000), 669–97.
Chamonard, Patrick. 'Un recrutement politique exceptionnel: l'élection des soixante-quinze premiers sénateurs inamovibles (9–21 déc. 1875)'. In Alain Faure, Alain Plessis and Jean-Claude Farcy, eds. *La Terre et la cité: Mélanges offerts à Phillipe Vigny*. Paris: Créaphis, 1994, pp. 283–309.
Chevalley, Sylvie. 'Rachel et la Marseillaise'. *1848: Révolutions et mutations au XIXe siècle*, 4 (1988), 109–11.
Counter, Andrew J., and Nicholas White. 'Introduction: The soul's sentiment: Friendship in nineteenth century France', *Romantic Review*, 110: 1–4 (2019), 1–13.
Curtis, Sarah A., and Stephen L. Harp, eds. 'Introduction'. In 'Archives in French history', special issue. *French Historical Studies*, 40:2 (2017), 177–87.
Curtis, Sarah H. 'Charitable ladies: Gender, class and religion in mid-nineteenth-century Paris'. *Past and Present*, 177 (2002), 121–56.
Daumard, Adeline. 'Affaire, amour, affection: Le Mariage dans la société bourgeoise au XIXe siècle'. *Romantisme*, 68 (1990): 33–47.
Dauphin, Cécile. 'Pour une histoire de la correspondance familiale'. *Romantisme*, 90 (1995): 89–99.
Davidson, Denise. '"Happy" marriages in early nineteenth-century France'. *Journal of Family History*, 37:1 (2012), 23–35.
Diaz, Brigitte, and José-Luis Diaz. 'Le Siècle de l'intime'. *Itinéraires: Littérature, textes, cultures*, 4 (2009), 117–46.
Emerson, Jason. 'A medal for Mrs Lincoln'. *Register of the Kentucky Historical Society*, 109:2 (2011), 187–205.
Eros, John. 'The Positivist generation of French republicanism'. *Sociological Review*, 3 (1955): 255–73.
Eustace, Nicole. 'Emotion and political change'. In Susan J. Matt and Peter N. Stearns, eds. *Doing Emotions History*. Urbana, IL: University of Illinois Press, 2014.
Faron, Olivier. 'Father–child relations in France: Changes in paternal authority in the nineteenth and twentieth centuries'. *History of the Family*, 6 (2001), 365–75.

Finn, Margot. 'The female world of love and empire: Women, family and East India Company politics at the end of the eighteenth century'. *Gender and History*, 31:1 (2019), 7–24.

Foley, Susan. ' "My God! Why was I born?" Illegitimacy, emotion, and family in nineteenth-century France'. *Journal of Family History*, 43:4 (2018), 357–73.

——. ' "The Christmas tree of the Alsatians and Lorrainers": Spectacle, emotion, and patriotism in Paris during the early Third Republic'. *French Historical Studies*, 41:4 (2018), 681–710.

——. 'The Christmas tree becomes French: From foreign curiosity to philanthropic icon, 1860–1914'. *French History and Civilization*, 7 (2016), 139–57.

——. 'Becoming a woman: Self-fashioning and emotion in a nineteenth-century family correspondence'. *Women's History Review*, 24:2 (2015), 215–33.

——. 'The Republican family and republican politics: Léon Laurent-Pichat and his kin (1861–1883)'. *French History and Civilisation*, 6 (2014), 159–71.

——. ' "A great and noble painting": Léon Gambetta and the visual arts in the French Third Republic'. *French History and Civilisation*, 4 (2011), 106–17.

——. ' "Your letter is divine, irresistible, infernally seductive": Léon Gambetta, Léonie Léon and nineteenth-century epistolary culture'. *French Historical Studies*, 30:2 (2007), 237–67.

Fox, Robert. 'Les Conférences mondaines sous le Second Empire', *Romantisme*, 65 (1980), 49–57.

Franklin, Caroline. 'Introduction: The material culture of eighteenth-century women's writing'. *Women's Writing*, 21:3 (2014), 285–9.

Frayssé, Olivier, and Laurence Grégoire. 'The French Masonic tributes to Abraham Lincoln'. *American Studies Journal*, 60 (2016), online version, 27 Sept. 2019. DOI: 10. 18422/60-10.

Gaillard, Jeanne. 'Documents: Les papiers de la Ligue républicaine des Droits de Paris'. *Le Mouvement social*, 56 (1966), 65–87.

Gammerl, Benno. 'Emotional styles – Concepts and challenges'. *Rethinking History*, 16:2 (2013), 161–75.

Gauthier, Marie-Véronique. 'Sociétés chantantes et grivoiserie au XIXe siècle'. *Romantisme*, 68 (1990), 75–86.

Giachetti, Claudine. 'Figures du père dans les romans de la Comtesse de Ségur'. *Nineteenth Century French Studies*, 38:1–2 (2009–10), 24–38.

Grange, Cyril. 'Les réseaux matrimoniaux intra-confessionnels de la haute bourgeoisie juive à Paris à la fin du XIXe siècle'. *Annales de démographie historique*, 109 (2005), 131–56.

Grévy, Jérôme. 'Les cafés républicains de Paris au début de la Troisième République. Etude de sociabilité politique'. *Revue d'histoire moderne et contemporaine*, 50:2 (2003), 52–72.

Guillet, François. 'Le duel et la défense de l'honneur viril'. In Alain Corbin, ed. *Histoire de la Virilité. II: Le Triomphe de la virilité: le XIXe siècle*. Paris: Seuil, 2011, pp. 83–124.
Havelange, Isabelle, Françoise Huguet and Bernadette Lebedeff-Choppin. 'Anquez, Henri-Louis-Léonce'. In *Les Inspecteurs généraux de l'instruction publique. Dictionnaire biographique, 1802–1914*. Paris: Institut national de recherche pédagogique, 1986, pp. 130–31.
Haynes, Christine. 'The politics of publishing in the Second Empire: The trial of *Madame Bovary* revisited'. *French Politics, Culture and Society*, 23:2 (2005), 1–27.
Hazareesingh, Sudhir. 'Le Grand Orient de France sous le Second Empire et les débuts de la Troisième République'. In Eric Saunier and Christine Gaudin, eds. *Franc-maçonnerie et histoire: Bilan et perspectives*. Mont-Saint-Aignan: Presses universitaires de Rouen et du Havre, 2003, generated 22 March 2021.
Heath, Elizabeth. 'Creating rural citizens in Guadeloupe in the early Third Republic'. *Slavery and Abolition*, 32:2 (2011), 289–307.
Hoffmann, Stefan-Ludwig. 'Civility, male friendship and Masonic sociability in nineteenth century Germany'. *Gender and History*, 13:2 (2001), 224–48.
Horowitz, Sarah. 'The bonds of concord and the guardians of trust: Women, emotion, and political life, 1815–1848'. *French Historical Studies*, 35:3 (2012), 577–603.
Houbre, Gabrielle. 'Amours fraternelles, amours romantiques'. *Adolescence*, 11:2 (1993), 295–314.
Houre, John. 'Naturalism' and 'Realism'. In Hugh Brigstocke, ed. *The Oxford Companion to Western Art*. Oxford: Oxford University Press, 2001.
Ireson, J.C. 'Poetry'. In D.G. Charlton, ed. *The French Romantics*. Cambridge: Cambridge University Press, 1984, I, pp. 113–62.
Johnson, Christopher H. 'Siblinghood and the emotional dimensions of the new kinship system, 1800–1850'. In Christopher H. Johnson and David Warren Sabean, eds. *Sibling Relations and the Transformation of European Kinship, 1300–1900*. New York: Berghahn, 2011, pp. 189–220.
Joly, Bertrand. 'Une manifestation de l'antiparlementarisme de l'extrême-gauche: La Ligue républicaine pour la révision de la Constitution (1883–1884)', *Actes du 57e congrès de la CIHAE: Assemblées et parlements dans le monde, du Moyen-Age à nos jours*, sous la direction de Jean Garrigues et al. Paris: Assemblée nationale, 2010, pp. 1404–30.
Kwon, Yun Kyoung. 'Forgotten island of the Liberator: Haiti's influences on Victor Schœlcher's abolitionism, 1833–1848'. *Histoire sociale/Social history*, 53:107 (2020), 69–90.
Lalouette, Jacqueline. 'Laurent-Pichat, Léon'. In Jean-Marie Mayeur and Alain Corbin, eds. *Les Immortels du Sénat 1875–1918: Les Cent-seize*

inamovibles de la Troisième République. Paris: Publications de la Sorbonne, 1995, pp. 380–82.

———. 'Littré, Maximilien Paul Emile'. In Jean-Marie Mayeur and Alain Corbin, eds. *Les Immortels du Sénat 1875–1918: Les Cent-seize inamovibles de la Troisième République*. Paris: Publications de la Sorbonne, 1995, pp. 399–402.

LaPointe, Bryan. ' "Moral electricity": Melvil-Bloncourt and the trans-Atlantic struggle for abolition and equal rights'. *Slavery and Abolition*, 40:3 (2018), 543–62.

Laroche-Gisserot, Florence. 'Pratiques de la dot en France au XIXe siècle'. *Annales ESC*, 6 (1988), 1433–52.

Lichtenstein, Alex, ed. 'AHR conversation: Every generation writes its own history of generations'. *American Historical Review*, 123:5 (2018), 1505–46.

Linton, Marisa. 'Fatal friendships: The politics of Jacobin friendship'. *French Historical Studies*, 31:1 (2008), 51–76.

Lucey, Michael. '*Ami ou protégé*? Balzac, Proust, and the variability of friendship'. *Romantic Review*, 110:1–4 (2019), 187–202.

Macías-González, Victor Manuel. 'Masculine friendships, sentiment, and homoerotics in nineteenth-century Mexico: The correspondence of José María Calderón y Tapia, 1820s –1850s'. *Journal of the History of Sexuality*, 16:3 (2007), 416–35.

Macknight, Elizabeth C. 'Faiths, fortunes and feminine duty: Charity in Parisian high society, 1880–1914'. *Journal of Ecclesiastical History*, 58:3 (2007), 482–506.

Mansker, Andrea. ' "Mademoiselle Arria Ly wants blood!" The debate over female honor in Belle Epoque France'. *French Historical Studies*, 29:4 (2006), 621–47.

McCormack, Matthew. 'Introduction'. In Matthew McCormack, ed. *Public Men: Masculinity and politics in modern Britain*. Houndmills: Palgrave Macmillan, 2007, pp. 1–12.

———. 'Men, "the public" and political history'. In Matthew McCormack, ed. *Public Men: Masculinity and politics in modern Britain*. Houndmills: Palgrave Macmillan, 2007, pp.13–32.

Nord, Philip G. 'The Party of conciliation and the Paris Commune'. *French Historical Studies*, 15:1 (1987), 1–35.

Perrier, Sylvie. 'The blended family in ancien régime France: A dynamic family form'. *The History of the Family*, 3:4 (1998), 459–71.

Rauch, André. 'Les Vacances et la nature révisitée, 1830–1939'. In Alain Corbin, ed. *L'Avènement des loisirs, 1850–1960*. Paris: Aubier, 1995, pp. 83–117.

Régnier, Marie-Clémence. 'Shakespeare's 1864 jubilee in France: A crown for two writers, William Shakespeare and Victor Hugo'. In Christa Jansohn and Dieter Mehl, eds. *Shakespeare Jubilees: 1769–2014*. Münster: LIT Verlag, 2015, pp. 111–27.

Rogers, Rebecca. 'Quelles écoles professionnelles pour les jeunes filles pauvres? Débats et réalisations en Algérie et en France métropolitaine (années 1860)'. *Revue d'histoire du dix-neuvième siècle*, 55:2 (2017), 109–23.

Sabean, David Warren. 'Kinship and issues of the self in Europe around 1800'. In Christopher H. Johnson and David Warren Sabean, eds. *Sibling Relations and the Transformation of European Kinship, 1300–1900*. New York: Berghahn, 2011, pp. 221–38.

Saxer, Daniela. 'Forum: History of emotions'. *German History*, 28:1 (2010), 67–80.

Scheer, Monique. 'Are emotions a kind of practice (and is that what makes them have a history)? A Bourdieuian approach to understanding emotion'. *History and Theory*, 51 (2012), 193–220.

Sloboda, Stacey. 'Between the mind and the hand: Gender, art and skill in eighteenth century copybooks'. *Women's Writing*, 21:3 (2014), 337–56.

Smith-Rosenberg, Carol. 'The female world of love and ritual'. *Signs: Journal of women in culture and society*, 1:1 (1975), 1–30.

Sowerwine, Charles. 'Democratising oratory: Léon Gambetta and the construction of male democracy in France, 1868–1882'. In Véronique Duché, ed. *Franco-Australian Connections: Essays in honour of Professor Colin Nettelbeck*. Paris: Classiques Garnier, forthcoming 2023.

Stock-Morton, Phyllis. 'Secularism and women's education: The case of the école professionnelle de jeunes filles of Marseille'. *French History*, 10:3 (1996), 355–74.

Stoler, Ann Laura. 'Intimidations of Empire: Predicaments of the tactile and the unseen'. In Ann Laura Stoler, ed. *Haunted by Empire: Geographies of intimacy in North American history*. Durham, NC: Duke University Press, 2006, pp. 1–22.

Taithe, Bertrand. 'Neighbourhood boys and men: The changing spaces of masculine identity in France, 1848–1871'. In Christopher Forth and Bertrand Taithe, eds. *French Masculinities: History, culture and politics*. Houndmills: Palgrave Macmillan, 2007, pp. 67–84.

Van den Dungen, Pierre. 'Influences et présence françaises dans la presse belge, 1830–1870'. In Marie-Eve Thérenty and Allain Vaillant, eds. *Presse, nations et mondialisation au XIXe siècle*. Paris: Nouveau Monde éditions, 2010.

Vorenberg, Michael. '*Liberté, égalité*, and Lincoln: French readings of an American president'. In Richard Cartwright and Jay Sexton, eds. *The Global Lincoln*. Oxford: Oxford University Press, 2011.

Walton, Whitney. 'Republican women and republican families in the personal narratives of George Sand, Marie d'Agoult and Hortense Allart'. In Jo Burr Margadant, ed. *The New Biography: Performing femininity in nineteenth century France*. Berkeley, CA: University of California Press, 2006.

Wartelle, Jean-Claude. 'La Société d'anthropologie de Paris de 1859 à 1920'. *Revue d'histoire des sciences humaines*, 10 (2004), 125–71.
Wilson, Ara. 'The Infrastructure of intimacy'. *Signs: Journal of women in culture and society*, 41:2 (2016), 247–80.
White, Claire. '*Patrie, peuple, amitié*: Sand and Michelet on the politics of friendship'. *Romantic Review*, 110:1–4 (2019), 149–67.
Yacavone, Donald. '"Surpassing the love of women": Victorian manhood and the language of fraternal love'. In Laura McCall and Donald Yacavone, eds. *A Shared Experience: Men, women, and the history of gender*. New York: New York University Press, 1998, pp. 195–221.

3. Theses

Aprile, Sylvie, 'Auguste Scheurer-Kestner et son entourage, étude biographique et analyse politique d'une aristocratie républicaine', Thèse de doctorat, Université de Paris I Panthéon-Sorbonne, 1994.
Batranu, Raluca, 'L'écrivain et la société: Le discours social dans la littérature française, du XVIIIe siècle à aujourd'hui', Thèse de doctorat, Communauté Université Grenoble Alpes, 2017.
Rosset, Caroline, 'Le Sourire de René: Comique, humour et ironie dans les récits de voyage de Chateaubriand', Thèse de docteur ès lettres, Université de Neuchâtel, 2012.

4. Internet sources

Basch, Sophie. 'François-René de Chateaubriand (1768–1848)'. 'Bibliotheque d'Orient', Bibliothèque nationale de France, https://heritage.bnf.fr>francois–rene–de–chateaubriand. Accessed 1 July 2021.
Binoche, Jacques, *Les Parlementaires d'outre-mer*, Edilivre, undated. Available at www.furet.com/media/pdf/feuilletage/9/7/8/2/3/3/4/1/9782334150804.pdf. Accessed 20 April 2021.
'Canet, Albert'. https://olympics.com/en/athletes/albert-henri-canet#. Accessed November 2021.
'Carreau du Temple'. www.carreaudutemple.eu/historique. Accessed November 2021.
'Deslandes, Louis-Achille'. https://gw.geneanet.org/bourelly?lang=en&n=deslandes&oc=0&p=louis+achille
Forster, Laura C. 'Radical Friendship'. www.historyworkshop.org.uk/radical-friendship/. Accessed 14 Sept. 2020.
'Freiligrath, Ferdinand'. www.britannica.com/biography/Ferdinand-Freiligrath. Accessed November 2021.
'Laurent-Pichat, Léon'. http://www.senat.fr/senateur-3eme-republique/laurent_pichat_leon1497r3.html. Accessed November 2021.
Maitron, Jean, ed. *Dictionnaire biographique du mouvement ouvrier français*, http://maitron.fr

'Meissner, Alfred von'. In Henry Garland and Mary Garland, eds. *The Oxford Companion of German Literature*, 3rd edn online 2005: www.oxfordreference.com.

Michel, Louise, 'Ouverture'. *Le Télémarque*, 1:31 (2007), 7–9. https://doi.org/10.3917/tele.031.0007.

'Risler, Charles'. www.annuaire-mairie.fr/ancien-maire-paris-7e-arrondissement.html. Accessed November 2021.

Robert, Adolphe, Edgar Bourloton and Gaston Cougny, eds. *Dictionnaire des parlementaires français depuis le 1er mai 1789 jusqu'au 1er mai 1889*. Paris: 1889–1891. Available at https://numelyo.bm-lyon.fr/f_view/BML:BML_00GOO0100137001103448309. Accessed May 2022.

Toussaint, Julie. 'Lemonnier, Mme Elisa'. In *Nouveau dictionnaire de pédagogie et d'instruction primaire publié sous la direction de Ferdinand Buisson*, www.inrp.fr/edition-electronique/lodel/dictionnaire-ferdinand-buisson/document.php?id=3044. Accessed August 2020.

Index

Académie française 205
Achille *see* Deslandes, Achille
Adam, Edmond
   friendships 151, 174, 175, 179
   political activities 154, 155, 180, 189
   on republican family 92, 93
Adam, Mme Juliette 93, 97, 121, 179, 188
adoption 25, 26, 93
affaires d'honneur see honour; duels
affection
   between friends 7, 44, 58, 120–1, 147, 183–4
   in letters 9–10, 121, 183, 205, 211, 238, 256
   maternal 22, 28
   paternal 23, 25, 27–8, 96–7, 99, 109, 126
   see also family, affectionate
Allain-Targé, Henri 130, 186, 203, 210
Alsace 155, 216–17, 231
   see also Association Générale d'Alsace-Lorraine
Amédée *see* Beaujean, Amédée
amnesty
   Communards 164, 190–1, 237, 259

Second Empire 55, 131
Anquez, Léonce 126–7, 152, 186, 205
anticlericalism 8, 184, 209–10, 215, 226, 229–30, 240
   republican press and 72, 79, 81, 82
Arago, Emmanuel 119, 140n.2, 211
Arago, Etienne
   friendships 121–2, 140n.2, 148, 152, 165, 205, 258
   family context 126, 127, 204
   journalist and writer 80, 82
   mayor of Paris 153, 155
   political activities 128, 130, 149, 153–4, 174, 210
   republican eulogies by 131–3
Arnaud de l'Ariège, Frédéric 135, 205
'art for art's sake' 65, 73
Asselin, Juliette ('Victorine', Mme Deslandes) 199, 233, 245
Assembly *see* National Assembly
L'Association 78
Association Générale d'Alsace-Lorraine 232, 234–5
Audiffret-Pasquier, Edmé-Armand-Gaston, Duc d' 177

autobiographical narratives 17, 19–21, 23, 27–8, 30, 33
L'Avenir national 79, 149

Babaud-Laribière, Mme 203–4
bachelors 93, 97, 188, 207
  family links 3, 7, 94, 99, 127
Barni, Jules 80–1, 236
Barthélemy-Saint-Hilaire, Jules 201
Bastille Day 229
Baudin, Alphonse 149, 174
Bazaine, General Achille 154, 184
Beaujean, Amédée, brother-in-law of L. Laurent-Pichat
  family roles 94, 101–2, 108–10, 136, 150, 157
  marriage to Rosine Deslandes 57, 199–201
  professional life 96, 200, 202
  republican sympathies 119–21, 140n.2, 173, 186, 227–9, 236, 239
Beaujean, Clémence (Mme Hovelacque), niece of L. Laurent-Pichat
  family life 109–12, 139, 147, 150, 152, 161
  marriage to Abel Hovelacque 203–5, 208–9, 211, 219
  republican activities 215, 232–3, 262
  republican upbringing 107–9, 112, 119–20, 136, 147, 186–7
  see also education, girls'
Beauvau-Craon, Charles-Just, Prince de 94, 96
Beauvau-Craon, Ludmille, Princesse de
  see Komar, Ludmille, Princesse de Beauvau-Craon
Belleville Programme 190, 244

Blanc, Louis 49, 187, 236, 237
Blanqui, Auguste 137–8
Bonaparte, Louis-Napoleon
  see Napoleon III, Emperor
Bonapartist(s) 171, 175, 190, 215, 216, 261
  Chevreau family as 40, 43, 57
  duels with republicans 179, 180, 181
Brisson, Henri 258, 261–2
Broca, Dr Paul 6, 203, 205
by-elections 128–9, 166, 228
  see also elections
Byron, George Gordon, Lord 41, 74

Canet, Henry Albert 266
Carnot, Hippolyte 201
Cassagnac, Paul de 181–2, 188
Catholic Church 71, 72, 132, 180, 209, 214
  see also Quanta Cura (papal encyclical)
censorship laws *see* newspaper press
Centre-Left 190–91
cercle see republican *cercle*
Challemel-Lacour, Paul-Armand 80, 93, 261
Charcot, Dr Jean-Martin 256
Charlotte *see* Risler, Charlotte (Mme Canet)
Charras, Jean-Baptiste 78, 257
  death and funeral 131–3
  History of the Campaign of 1815 148
  republican hero 136, 148, 184, 214, 264
Charras, Mme *see* Kestner, Mathilde (Mme Charras)
Chassin, Charles-Louis 78, 140n.2

Chateaubriand, François-
    René de 42
Chaudey, Gustave 135, 163
Chauffour, Victor 80, 132–3, 136,
    213, 223n.53
Chauffour-Kestner, Victor *see*
    Chauffour, Victor
Chevreau, Henri
    breakdown of youthful
        friendships 57–9
    political career 40, 57–9, 219
    youthful friendships 27, 41–4,
        93, 183, 264
Chevreau, Jean-Henri 27,
    41, 57, 59
children
    care of 28–9
    deaths of 104, 246,
        257, 263
    extramarital 3, 18, 23, 24, 93
    legitimation of 32–3, 97
    republican upbringing 92,
        112, 186–7
    role in uniting families
        244, 245–8
    see also family; education, girls'
civil burial *see* funerals
Civil Code 4, 17, 18, 23–5, 33
Claretie, Georges 266
Clémence, niece of L. Laurent-
    Pichat *see* Beaujean,
    Clémence (Mme
    Hovelacque)
Clémence, sister of L. Laurent-
    Pichat *see* Deslandes,
    Clémence
Clemenceau, Georges 155–6, 180,
    186, 208, 242
Cloche, La 159
Cointet, Mme, nurse of L. Laurent-
    Pichat 21–7 *passim*,
    43, 59

Collas, Eulalie (Mme
    Chevreau) 27, 59
commission de permanence
    see parliamentary commissions
Communards 159, 161–4, 173,
    234, 242
    see also amnesty, Communards
Confédéré de Fribourg, Le 78
conservative(s) 177, 190, 214, 241
    see also Bonapartist(s), Extreme
        Right, monarchist(s),
        Orleanist(s)
constitution (1875) 171, 176, 189
    see also Life Senator(s);
        Republican League for the
        Revision of the Constitution
constitutional crisis (1877)
    198–9, 213–214
constitutional revision *see*
    Republican League
    for the Revision of the
    Constitution
Coopération, La 138
Correspondance littéraire,
    La 79–80
correspondence *see* letters
council of hospices 154, 159
coup d'état (December 1851) 2,
    34, 40, 56
    impact on press 66, 69, 127
    repression of republicans 55–6,
        78, 127–8, 136, 174, 214
Courrier du Dimanche, Le 79, 130
Crémieux, Alphonse 230
Critique française, La 79

Decazes, Elie, Duc 179, 184
Delacroix, Eugène 99, 162
Delescluze, Charles
    Baudin affair 149
    friendships 120, 128, 140n.2,
        150, 152, 156

family context 148
From Paris to Cayenne 146
Paris Commune 146–7, 159–64
Denfert-Rochereau, Colonel Aristide 186
desire 45, 46, 58
Deslandes, Achille, brother of L. Laurent-Pichat 30, 32, 92, 152, 199–200
Deslandes, Clémence, sister of L. Laurent-Pichat 29, 30, 45
Deslandes, Herminie (Mme E. Lefort), sister of L. Laurent-Pichat 78, 92, 108, 150
  childhood and youth 30, 45, 90
  marriage to Emile Lefort 200–1, 202
Deslandes, Mme L.–A. *see* Leroi, Geneviève (Mme L.–A. Deslandes)
Deslandes, Louis-Achille, husband of Geneviève Leroi 24
Deslandes, Rosine (Mme Beaujean), sister of L. Laurent-Pichat
  family roles 90–101 *passim*, 150, 184, 186, 203, 210
  friendship with L. Laurent-Pichat 4, 5, 19–22 *passim*, 30, 94, 262–3
  marriage to Amédée Beaujean 56–7, 199–202
  political commitment 119–20, 124, 136, 176, 182, 186–9, 232–3
  role in educating Clémence and Geneviève 105–8
  role in raising Geneviève Laurent-Pichat 208, 212–13, 245
  youth 19–22, 28

see also siblings
Despois, Eugène 78, 80, 140n.2
diaries *see* journals
Dix-Neuvième Siècle 188
Du Camp, Maxime 69, 70
duels
  between politicians 177–9, 184
  between politicians and journalists 179, 179–81
  témoins (witnesses) 178–80, 183, 184
Duprat, Pascal 78

education
  girls' 104–12
    Duruy courses 108
    intellectual 108, 112
    religious 107–8
    secular 107–8, 112, 190, 236
    self-discipline 105–6, 109
    self-improvement 100, 106, 109
  republican 232–5
  'Ferry laws' 238–40
  women's roles in 232–3
education league (*ligue de l'enseignement*) 232
elections, legislative
  (1863) 128
  (1869) 149–50
  (Feb. 1871) 157
  (1876) 189–91
  (1877) 214, 216, 219, 227, 228
    family role 214–15, 217–19
  see also by-elections
elections, municipal 218, 219, 228
  see also Paris Commune, elections for
elections, Senate
  (1876) 190, 191

emotion
    in family 9, 17, 20–1, 27–9, 33, 110–13 *passim*, 219, 247, 262–3
    in friendship 5, 7, 43–5, 59, 121–5, 183–5, 238
    in politics 5, 9–11, 119, 132, 136, 155–6, 160, 214, 219, 248–9
    see also grief
'emotion work' 21
'emotive fraternalism' 7, 185, 192
Emperor Napoleon III *see* Napoleon III, Emperor
Extreme Left 174, 242, 261–2
Extreme Right 190

family
    affectionate 17–21 *passim*, 27, 29, 32–4, 92, 101, 262–3
    bourgeois 3, 17, 23, 34, 47, 92, 101–4 *passim*, 109, 112, 219–20
    conflict 25–6, 32
    inheritance issues 24–6, 31, 33, 93
    patriarchal 4, 17, 25
    political solidarity in 119–20, 228–31, 233–5, 237–40 *passim*, 244, 245–9 *passim*
    republican 4–5, 9, 34, 90, 92, 107–8, 136, 186, 198, 226–227, 263–5
    rituals 101–3, 109–12
    see also children; Civil Code; letters; marriage; siblings; sisters
Favre, François
    friendships 79, 122–5 *passim*, 140n.2, 149, 173
    political actions 128, 149, 153, 174, 191

Favre, Jules 138, 154
February Revolution *see* Revolution of February (1848)
Ferry, Charles 29, 203, 240, 247
Ferry, Eugénie *see* Risler, Eugénie (Mme J. Ferry)
Ferry, Jules
    colonial policies 241, 242
    education policies ('Ferry laws') 238–40
    family life 29, 93, 247
    family politics 236–41 *passim*, 244–8 *passim*
    Government of National Defence 154–6, 236
    marriage to Eugénie Risler 209, 210, 236
    Minister for Public Instruction and Fine Arts 236–41 *passim*
    Paris Commune 164, 165
    President of the Council of Ministers 236
    see also Republican League for the Revision of the Constitution
Figaro, Le 159, 179, 181, 218
First Communion 107, 127, 210
Flaubert, Gustave
    Madame Bovary 65, 70–1, 73
Floquet, Charles 147, 152, 179, 208, 239
    political activities 160, 165, 219, 261
Floquet, Mme *see* Kestner, Hortense (Mme Floquet)
Franco-Prussian War 150–2, 155–6, 184, 186
    see also Alsace; Government of National Defence (1870–71)
Frébault, Charles-Félix 216, 219, 228
freemasonry 6, 121, 210, 226, 229–30

Index

friendship
  adolescent 40, 43–6, 56–9
  family 34, 96, 120, 123–5, 140,
    184–6, 192, 205, 236
  female 8, 185–6, 233
  male 6–7, 120–2, 126–7,
    183–5, 227, 238, 247,
    264–5
  duels 117–19, 181, 182–3
  grief 131–3, 257
  passionate 43–6
  political action and 6, 8–9,
    119–22, 127–31 *passim*,
    140, 172–3, 227, 233, 248–9
  see also emotion; family;
    journalism; named
    individuals; siblings
funerals 131–3, 257, 258, 262
  see also grief

Gallican movement 209–10
Gambetta, Léon 9–10, 93, 174–5,
    188–9, 210, 236, 242
  duels 179, 180
  elections (1871) 166
  friendships 149, 174–5, 179,
    208, 245
  government (1881) 233
  leader of Republican Union
    174–5, 190, 214
  negotiating constitution (1875)
    189, 244
  political hostility to 177,
    181–2, 236
  see also Belleville Programme
Gautier, Théophile 51, 69, 277
General Committee of the rue
    Turbigo (electoral
    committee) 166
General Council of the Seine 258
'generation of 1848' 40, 264
Ginette *see* Risler, Eugénie
    ('Ginette', Mme Claretie)

Government of National Defence
    (1870–71) 151,
    153–5, 236
Grégori, Louis 180, 181
Greppo, Louis 128, 259
Grévy, Jules 203, 218, 236–8
grief 132, 147, 247, 264–5
Grousset, Pascal 164

Hachette, Jean-Georges 6, 99, 102
Haentjens, Alfred 179, 180
Hébert, Ernest 94, 233, 257
Herminie *see* Deslandes, Herminie
    (Mme E. Lefort)
Hérold, Ferdinand 81, 203, 228
home (concept)
  bourgeois 97, 98–9, 101,
    105–6
  idealised 21, 94, 98
  republican 4, 9, 97–9, 113, 124,
    182, 186, 227, 265
  summer retreat 100–2, 112
honour
  family 24, 25
  male 75, 130, 132, 172, 192,
    214, 259
  see also duels
Hospice Dubois 139
Hovelacque, Abel
  marriage to Clémence Beaujean
    203–5, 208–10
  municipal councillor 227–9
  political activities 210, 219,
    230, 244
Hovelacque, André 266
Hovelacque, Edouard 203,
    218
Hovelacque, Emile 203
Hugo, Victor
  amnesty activist 191, 237
  Hernani 103
  Les Misérables 54, 80
  Napoleon the Small 77

Hugo, Victor (*Continued*)
  republicanism 130, 131, 257
  Romantic writer 6, 41,
    54, 67, 73

illegitimate children *see* children,
  extramarital
L'Indépendance belge 78
Institut français 205
intimate sources 10–11, 198,
    205, 220
  emotion in 10, 21, 30, 43–4,
    106, 110
  role in relationships 10, 21,
    42–6 *passim*, 121–5, 186–7
  see also letters; poetry, intimate

Jeunesse: Journal littéraire, La 120
journalism
  friendship networks 69–70,
    77–80, 120–1
  republican 65–72, 77–83,
    137–9, 175
  see also newspaper press
Journal officiel de la République
  française 180
journals 10–11
Juliette *see* Asselin, Juliette
  ('Victorine', Mme
  Deslandes)
June Days (1848) 2, 40, 49, 53–4

Kergomard, Pauline 232
Kestner, Céline (Mme
    Scheurer-Kestner)
  family ties 124, 131, 139, 238
  republicanism 136–7, 147, 186,
    209, 233
Kestner, Charles 136, 184, 205
Kestner, Mme Charles *see* Rigau,
  Eugénie (Mme C. Kestner)
Kestner, Hortense (Mme Floquet)
  family ties 139, 179, 213,
    239, 245
  republicanism 147, 187, 201–2,
    208, 233
Kestner, Mathilde (Mme Charras)
    131, 139, 186, 207–9,
    213, 239
Khnopff, Léonie (Mme Emile
  Hovelacque) 203
Komar, Ludmille, Princesse de
  Beauvau-Craon
  mother of Geneviève Laurent-
    Pichat 93, 94, 96, 209–10
  death 257

La Forge, Anatole de 219
Lalanne, Ludovic 79, 152, 153
Lamartine, Alphonse de 41, 43, 69,
    73, 245
  republicanism 49, 52, 54, 55
Lapommeraye, Henri de 260
Laprade, Pierre 81
Laurens, Jules 106, 233
Laurent, Rosine (pseud.) *see* Leroi,
  Geneviève (Mme L.-A.
  Deslandes)
Laurent-Pichat, Geneviève (Mme
  Risler) 1, 2, 93
  birth and infancy 94–7
  childhood 99, 104–7
  children of 245–7
  creating family archive 262–3
  friendship with Eugénie Risler
    (Mme J. Ferry) 207, 236,
    240, 247
  marriage to Charles Risler 198
  affection in 205, 207,
    211–12, 217–19
  civil vs religious 209–10
  illegitimacy and 207–9,
    213, 220
  republican alliance 203, 205

miscarriage 217–19
republicanism 187, 217–19, 232–4, 239, 248
republican upbringing 107–9, 112, 119–20, 136, 147, 186–7
see also children; education, girls'
'Laurent-Pichat programme' 190–1
League of the Republican Union for the Rights of Paris 160
Lefèvre, Henri 174–5, 180, 188
Lefort, Elisabeth 108
Lefort, Emile 200–2
Lefort, Henri 280
  family ties 78, 102
  political activities 78, 80, 121, 148, 165, 201
  and radical workers 128–9
Lefort, Jeanne 108, 210
Lemonnier, Elisa 232, 236
Léon, Léonie 187, 188
Lepère, Charles 176
Leroi, Geneviève (Mme L.-A. Deslandes), mother of L. Laurent-Pichat 22–4, 31
  death 97
  marriage to Louis-Achille Deslandes 24
  reunion with adult Laurent-Pichat 30–3, 92, 96–7
  unwed mother 18–19, 22–3, 26, 31–2
letters
  family affection in 10, 109–10, 186–7, 212–13, 237–8, 241, 263
  family politics in 124, 186–7, 237–8, 240
  friendship in 10, 43, 121–5, 184–5, 238

in marriages of affection 205, 207, 211, 213
  see also education, girls'; intimate sources
Lévi-Alvarès, Madeleine Sarah 266
liberty
  America as model of 33
  the arts and 73–4
  basis of republicanism 72, 73–4
  political ideal 43, 51, 66, 121, 139, 148, 230
  versus autocracy 72, 81–2, 148
  see also newspaper press
'liberty, equality and fraternity' 129, 228
Libre pensée, La 138
Libre recherche, La 77, 78
Life Senator(s) 171, 189–90, 202, 214, 244, 256
ligue de l'enseignement see education league
L'Illustration 66
Lincoln, Abraham 50, 130–1, 241
Lissagaray, Prosper-Olivier 129
Lissajous, Jules-Antoine 176
literature
  moral role 74–7
  political role 72–7
  workers as subjects 74
  see also poetry; Romanticism
Littré, Emile 6, 200, 202
Louis-Napoléon, Prince Imperial 172
Loyson, Hyacinth 210–11

Mac-Mahon, Marshall Patrice, Duc de Magenta 150, 171, 188, 191, 197, 214
Mahy, César de 241, 259, 261, 264–5
Marianne, image of the Republic 228

marriage
  affectionate 205, 207, 211–13, 219
  bourgeois 93, 122–3, 198–201, 204, 213, 215
  choice and 4, 207
  civil vs religious 96, 209–10
  destiny of women 112
  republican 199, 201–10, 213–14, 219, 236
  see also Civil Code
Marseillaise, La 51–2, 151, 227
masonic lodges see freemasonry
Melvil-Bloncourt, Count Suzanne de 242
Michel, Louise 233
Michelet, Jules 4, 6, 92, 245
Millard, Auguste 201
Millard, Mme 233
Millet, Aimé 174
Miot, Jules 128, 137
Moilin, Tony 158
monarchist(s) 81
  Second Republic 66
  Third Republic 157, 166, 172, 184
  see also Mac-Mahon, Marshall Patrice, Duc de Magenta
Monnier, Marc, *Paillasse* 82
Morice brothers (Léopold and François-Charles) 228
mothers, unwed 18–19, 24

Nadaud, Gustave 126–7, 141n.40
Napoleon III, Emperor 2, 55–8, 77, 81, 131, 150
  see also Second Empire (1852–1870)
Naquet, Alfred 139, 261
National Assembly (Third Republic)
  colonial representation 241

constitution (1875) 189
dissolution (1877) 197, 214
functioning 176–7
republican control 227, 236
National Guard 152, 154–8 *passim*, 161
newspaper press
  censorship laws 65–6, 71, 77, 80, 138
  foreign 77–8
  prosecution of 65, 70–2, 82–3, 137–9, 148, 264
  struggle for press freedom 65, 190
  see also journalism

Orleanist(s) 190

Parent, Nicolas 181
Paris Commune (1871) 147, 154, 157–65, 174, 259
  condemnations of 163–4, 165, 191
  elections for 159
  friendships and 147, 157, 159, 164–5, 236
  repression of 158, 160–2
  see also Delescluze, Charles; Government of National Defence
Paris municipal council 203, 228, 229, 258, 260, 262
parliamentary commissions 175–7, 190, 192
Pelletan, Camille 259
Pelletan, Eugène
  friendships 80, 123, 135, 136, 201
  journalism 75, 92, 121, 130
  republican theorist 4, 90, 92, 123, 133
Pensée nouvelle, La 138

Perin, Georges 180, 181
Petite République française, La 216
pétroleuses, les (female arsonists) 163
Peyrat, Alphonse 79, 149, 261
Phare de la Loire, Le 81–3, 138–9, 259
Picard, Ernest 187
Pichat, Etienne 19, 22–7, 33
poetry
 intimate 30–1, 41–8 *passim*, 101, 110–12, 152, 262
 political 42–3, 49–58 *passim*, 75
 see also literature, political roles
Politique nouvelle, La 66
Polytechnic Association 239–40, 258, 260
positivism 73, 202, 210, 230
Pozzi, Samuel 6, 204
progress 73, 74
Propagateur de l'Aube, Le 56, 67–9, 77
Proth, Mario 160
Proust, Antonin 180, 233
public lectures (rue de la Paix) 129–30

Quanta Cura (papal encyclical) 81–2
Quentin, Charles 140n.2, 149
Quinet, Edgar 81

'Rachel' (Elisa Félix) 51–2
racism 50
Radical Left 242–4, 261
Radiguet, Max 257
Ranc, Arthur 120, 140n.2, 153–4, 179, 181–2, 188
Rappel, Le 159, 160, 244
Rathier, Jules 173, 174, 186, 188, 214–16, 218

Rathier, Marguerite 186, 215, 234
Rathier, Mme 233
Réforme littéraire, La 73, 78, 79, 80–1, 121
Renaud, Michel 180
republican *cercle* 7, 121, 173–4, 265
Republican League for the Revision of the Constitution 244, 247, 261
Republican Left
 Second Empire 149
 Third Republic 237
republicans
 bourgeois 49–50, 68, 165
 conservative wing
  Government of National Defence 153, 159, 165
  Second Empire 149
  Third Republic 172, 191, 238, 242–4, 259
 divisions among
  during Franco-Prussian War 153–7
  during Paris Commune 154–65
 gender and 112, 133, 181, 218–19, 231, 235, 262
 masculine culture among 7, 127, 177, 225–7, 230–1
 prosecution and repression of 55, 82–3, 127–8, 130, 136–7, 138, 176
 radical wing
  Second Empire 128, 147, 149
  Third Republic (1872–76) 166, 189, 190–1
  Third Republic (1877–86) 229, 230, 231, 237, 257–62 *passim*
 religious practice of 8, 107, 209–10

republicans (*Continued*)
   revolutionary 147, 159,
      163, 174
   student radicals 81, 137–8
   views on
      Abraham Lincoln 130, 131
      colonialism 131,
         241–2, 261–2
      democracy 73, 137–8, 189,
         191–2, 244
      French Revolution 202, 229,
         230, 239, 241, 244, 245
      popular radicalism 52, 66,
         68–9, 75, 128–9
      slavery 50, 59, 130–1, 242
      women as 4, 8–9, 113, 186–9,
         201, 225–6, 231–5, 262–4
   see also anticlericalism; Centre-
      Left; education, girls';
      elections; Extreme Left;
      family; friendship; Radical
      Left; Republican Left;
      Republican Union
Republican Union 174–7, 186,
      190–2, 214, 236–7, 241–2
République française, La 175, 188,
      190, 258
Réveil, Le 120, 148–9, 150, 165
Revolution of February (1848) 49,
      51–4, 66, 68, 81, 137,
      149, 259
Revue de Paris, La 65, 69–72, 77,
      80, 120
Revue encyclopédique, La 138
Rigau, Eugénie (Mme C. Kestner)
   136, 156, 184,
   186–7, 245–6
   republicanism 234, 236,
      237, 239
   role in marriage of Charles
      Risler and Geneviève
      Laurent-Pichat 205,
      207–8, 211

Rigault, Raoul 163, 165
Risler, Camille 58–9, 139, 156,
   207, 211, 213, 237,
   246–7, 264
Risler, Charles 29, 139, 240
   in Franco-Prussian war 230
   freemason 230
   marriage to Geneviève Laurent-
      Pichat 205, 207, 209–10
   mayor of seventh
      arrondissement 227–8
   political activities 230, 235, 239
   support for Alsace 230,
      232, 234
Risler, Charlotte (Mme Canet) 247,
   252n.49, 262–3, 266
Risler, Eugénie ('Ginette', Mme
   Claretie) 94, 245–8,
   263, 266
Risler, Eugénie (Mme J. Ferry) 29,
   106, 235, 285
   friendship with Geneviève
      Laurent-Pichat 207,
      236, 245–7
   marriage to Jules Ferry 208,
      210, 236
Romanticism 40–2, 44, 47, 59, 68,
   73, 165, 185
Rosine *see* Deslandes, Rosine
   (Mme Beaujean)
Rotonde du Temple, La 22, 24, 27,
   98, 204
royalist(s) *see* monarchist(s)

Sainte-Pélagie (prison) 83,
   119, 139
   republican sociability in 123,
      135, 136–8, 186
   see also Hospice Dubois
Salon (art exhibition) 74, 106,
   107, 148
salons, republican 120–1,
   129, 210

Index

Scheurer, Jeanne (Mme Pellet) 106, 147, 186
Scheurer, Mme *see* Kestner, Céline (Mme Scheurer-Kestner)
Scheurer-Kestner, Auguste
   family relationships 124–6, 135, 139, 147, 185–6, 189
   friendships 80, 121, 123–6, 165, 174, 179, 183–5
   affection 183, 185, 238, 264
   role of letters 123–5, 185
   republicanism 163–4, 165–6, 174, 189–90, 261
   in Sainte-Pélagie prison 135–7
Scheurer-Kestner, Mme *see* Kestner, Céline (Mme Scheurer-Kestner)
Schœlcher, Victor 50, 152, 242, 261
Second Empire (1852–70) 58–9, 108, 150, 265
Second Republic (1848–51) 2, 3, 34, 40, 51–3, 66, 131, 137, 201
Senate 197–8, 229, 239, 242, 244, 258, 261
   see also Life Senator(s)
separation of Church and State 82, 190
servants 102, 103–4, 152
Shakespeare tercentenary 130
siblings 29–30
   adolescence 45–7, 57
   adulthood 99, 102, 136
Siècle, Le 166, 188
siege of Paris (1870–71) 151–5
Simon, Jules 154, 164, 201, 233
Simon, Mme Louise 233
sisters 30–3, 45
'site of memory' 101
'social question' 49, 50, 259, 260
society for vocational education for women (*Société pour l'enseignement professionel des femmes*) 232–3
Spuller, Eugène 93, 186

Tablettes de Pierrot, Les 79
Thiers, Adolphe 154, 166, 171, 174, 187–8
Third Republic 178, 201, 205, 231, 241, 259
   formation 5, 6, 90, 152–3, 189, 264
   triumph (1880) 229–30
Thoré, Théophile 70
Tiersot, Edmond 235
Tirard, Pierre 235
Tolain, Henri 129
Toussaint, Julie 232
Toussaint-Louverture, François Dominique 242
Travail, Le 81

Ulbach, Louis
   friendships 40–3, 152, 258, 264
   family context 125–6, 173, 201, 204
   journalist and writer 41–2, 56, 67–9, 80
   at *La Revue de Paris* 70–1
   Paris Commune 159–60, 162, 165
   political activities 56, 59, 129–30, 210
Urbain, Raoul 158, 159

vacations 53, 100–1, 108–9, 111, 186, 207, 245, 247
Victorine *see* Asselin, Juliette ('Victorine', Mme Deslandes)
Voltaire Society 210, 229–30

Waddington, William 235–6
Wurtz, Charles-Adolphe 228

EU authorised representative for GPSR:
Easy Access System Europe, Mustamäe tee 50,
10621 Tallinn, Estonia
gpsr.requests@easproject.com

www.ingramcontent.com/pod-product-compliance
Lightning Source LLC
Chambersburg PA
CBHW051558230426
43668CB00013B/1901